D1154487

THE CRANE'S WALK

THE CRANE'S WALK

Plato, Pluralism, and the Inconstancy of Truth

Jeremy Barris

Fordham University Press

New York   2009

Library of Congress Cataloging-in-Publication Data

Barris, Jeremy.
    The crane's walk: Plato, pluralism, and the inconsistency of truth / Jeremy Barris.
        p.   cm.
    Includes bibliographical references and index.
    ISBN 978-0-8232-2913-0 (cloth : alk. paper)
    1. Truth.   2. Certainty.   3. Pluralism.   4. Plato.   I. Title.
BD171.B26   2008
121—dc22

                                        2008037467

Printed in the United States of America
11 10 09   5 4 3 2 1
First edition

To my mother, Isabel Barris, and my late father, David Barris, who taught me to see and hold to the important things, and whose lessons and qualities continue to deepen and grow in me.

To Roy Blumenthal, Stephen de Wijze, and James Mills, for more than words can say.

Contents

PART II: TRUTH AND LOVE

Preface

This is a book about establishing truth by a type of risk-taking, and the relation of that process to the nature of truth, to being one's self, and to living responsibly in a pluralistic society. I say "establishing truth" and not "knowledge," since I discuss truth not only as a property of knowledge but also as the structure of reality.

As one central theme, I try to show that we can conceive and live with a pluralism of standpoints with conflicting standards for truth, while the truth of each is at the same time entirely unaffected by the truth of the others. That is, I shall try to show that one kind of contradiction is perfectly in order: that we can, and must, conceive the same truth as in some contexts simply absolute and in others relative. I discuss the relations and transitions between these contexts in detail.

I try to show that Plato's dialogues express the views I present here. I first develop an account of the nature of truth through which to interpret his work, with only provisional reference to his dialogues. Once that is done, I investigate the dialogues in a continuous way. I believe that the framework I develop is necessary to understanding Plato, but I hope that it is also true and worthwhile in its own right, irrespective of whether it is accurate as an interpretation of his work.

Truth, as I understand it here and as I argue Plato also understood it, is often in conflict with itself. As a result, it often requires one to straddle incompatible sides of the fence and even wholly different types of terrain on each side of the fence: hence, I argue, the importance of Plato's sense of humor, and of the crane's walk in my title. When a crane walks, it moves simultaneously and apparently independently in two dimensions, vertical and horizontal. A crane can also stand equally well on one leg (or "ground") or two.

This book, then, explores the nature and importance for truth and for our lives of what might be called a delicately poised ungainliness, or a perfect, ungainly poised elegance.[1]

Acknowledgments

I would like to thank Greg Galford and Andrea Walter for many years of loving and open-eyed encouragement.

This book is presented with financial assistance from the West Virginia Humanities Council, a state program of the National Endowment for the Humanities.

THE CRANE'S WALK

INTRODUCTION

Understandings of Plato and a Feature of Truth-Seeking Thought

To try to understand the nature of truth might seem a very arrogant undertaking—and in an important sense, it is. But while not all of us try to understand the nature of truth, we all live as though we have already succeeded in understanding it. We all have ideas of how truth works, and we all act on those ideas, often in active opposition to conflicting ideas of truth. It is perhaps less arrogant, then, and less irresponsible to try to understand the nature of truth and so open our understanding to criticism and correction by ourselves and others—rather than to act firmly on the basis of an understanding we also claim no one should even try to gain. As Plato's dialogues show, he himself was very much aware of these alternatives.

Plato carefully explored the nature of what he saw as truth and its importance for life. I try to show that whatever we may think of the particular truths he saw, nevertheless just his concern for truth, and the careful *way* that he showed to explore the nature of truth and its importance for life, carry over helpfully to the exploration of our own ideas of truth and its importance. And, as I argue in this book, the exploration of the nature of truth is itself part of the nature of truth. To try to understand Plato's specific exploration of truth is therefore also already to try to understand the nature of truth and its importance for life. This book, then, even in the respects in which it deals specifically with Plato, is most importantly about the nature of truth, including the dimension of it that is the truth of individual and social life.

As one central theme, I try to show that there is a certain contradiction in the nature of truth, and that this is perfectly in order: that we can conceive and live in the context of a plurality of standpoints, each with different standards for truth, while the truth of each is also entirely unaffected by the truth of the others. That is, I try to show that we can, and must, conceive the same truth as simply absolute in some contexts and relative in others. I discuss the relations and transitions between these contexts in detail. As another central theme, I try to show that precisely this coordination of mutually exclusive conceptions of truth allows us to establish truth without the traditional problems of circularity or infinite regress. And in the course of discussing these themes, I try to show that this contradiction in the nature of truth requires us to reunderstand not only the nature of truth but also, as a result, the nature of consistency, and so also of thought.

While I try to show that Plato's dialogues express the views I discuss here, I do so by first presenting, in Part I, a detailed framework that is only provisionally an account of the dialogues, although it is fully developed in itself. I turn to discuss the dialogues in a continuous way only in Part II. As I say in the Preface, while I believe that this framework is necessary to understanding Plato, I hope it will justify itself as having value in its own right, irrespective of whether it is accurate as an interpretation of his work. I aim, then, to present a way of thinking that, I argue, solves some contemporary problems, a way of thinking that I also believe Plato already presented.

With that in mind, in this Introduction I present a short history of how Plato has been understood in order to locate my understanding in relation to it.

Plato is often ironic, saying or doing one thing in order to say or do another very different and often directly opposed thing. His irony is usually understood to occur in the context of a nonironic doctrine about, or understanding of, or attitude toward the world and the place of people in it. A more subtle variant of this interpretation is that his nonironic doctrine, understanding, or attitude is presented *by means of* his ironies. In this second view his teaching is never stated in a way that is not at first misleading. His reason for doing this, it is argued, is that he wants to require his readers to engage in the activity of thinking their own way to the answers.[1] This is what makes him a great teacher. The result of reaching the correct conclusions on the basis of the hints Plato gives is that one comes to see what makes the conclusions necessarily true. One then believes them not because one has carelessly allowed oneself to follow Plato or for some ulterior motive, but because they are true. Another result is that one is given what is indispensable to understanding the conclusions. One is given the experience of the risk of thinking and the results of that risk, this combination making up the experience of pathbreaking in good thinking. These experiences are part of what Plato's conclusions are about, and his ironic presentation helps one to gain from these experiences preparatory knowledge that his conclusions require and incorporate.

There is a lot to support this second interpretation. With the exception of Plato's few possibly authentic letters, he wrote only dialogues.[2] Nowhere in these does he speak in his own name and nowhere does he indicate that any of the characters speak in his name and so present his teaching. The doctrines presented in the dialogues are always given in the context of being addressed to very specific audiences at very specific points of a discussion. It seems likely that the content of these presentations is thoroughly adapted to the concerns and limitations of his audience as well as to making the very limited point at issue at the time.[3]

While we are justified in taking seriously any statement made in the dialogues as matter for thought, then, we are not justified in immediately drawing on a statement made in one of the dialogues to give us the truth of Plato's own position.

Near the end of the *Phaedrus*, Socrates is made to say the following about writers:

> If any of them had knowledge of the truth when he wrote, and can defend what he has written by submitting to an interrogation on the subject, and make it evident as soon as he speaks how comparatively inferior are his writings, such a one should take his title not from what he has written but from what has been the object of his serious pursuit.[4]

Plato gives us reason to think (perhaps I should emphasize that *he* does not unequivocally *say* it, but through a character in his dialogue gives us reason to think), then, that there is a distance between what the philosopher produces in writing and the activity of philosophy itself, so much so that a different name is required for each activity.

Where Plato does perhaps speak in his own voice, in the *Seventh Letter,* he states quite categorically that:

> One statement at any rate I can make in regard to all who have written or who may write with a claim to knowledge of the subjects to which I devote myself. . . . Such writers can in my opinion have no real acquaintance with the subject. I certainly have composed no work in regard to it, nor shall I ever do so in future, for there is no way of putting it in words like other studies.

Acquaintance with these subjects, Plato writes, "must come rather after a long period of attendance on instruction in the subject itself and of close companionship, when, suddenly, like a blaze kindled by a leaping spark, it is generated in the soul and at once becomes self-sustaining." And he adds that:

> I do not . . . think the attempt to tell mankind of these matters a good thing, except in the case of some few who are capable of discovering the truth for themselves with a little guidance. In the case of the rest to do so would excite in some an unjustified contempt in a thoroughly offensive fashion, in others certain lofty and vain hopes, as if they had acquired some awesome lore.

Plato pointedly notes in this passage, "I do know . . . that some others have written on these same subjects, but who they are they know not themselves."[5]

It does seem likely, then, that Plato's doctrine is not simply to be found in his writing, but that an intensive effort of interpretation is required to establish just what this doctrine is.

This view of Plato can be taken a step further. There is a lot to support the view not only that Plato is not merely presenting a nonironic doctrine in ironic fashion, but that the context in which his ironies appear is itself ironic, appearing to be one thing in order to be another very different and sometimes directly opposed thing. That is, for one possibility, the dialogues may perhaps not be what we would think of as philosophy at all. For example, Plato wrote at the end of an age of great tragic and comic poets or playwrights. Epic and both serious and satirical lyric poetry were highly esteemed. Plato may well have been a very subtle and ingeniously synthetic participator in this literary and social cutting edge of his time.[6] And it is very possible that this would have made him more estimable and more socially responsible than a philosopher in the eyes of the generality of his contemporaries. Plato, with his contemporaries, may well have considered such participation a more worthy ambition.

It is even possible, then, not only that Plato was a literary artist rather than a philosopher, but that he was not even always a highly serious artist. He may have included many things in his dialogues exclusively to be frivolous entertainment.[7]

The dialogues lend themselves to a reading of Plato as a literary figure. They abound with references to and citations of the poets and playwrights and leading lights of the contemporary known world. They are full of invention: of dramatic and narrative structure and situation, of stories, of characters, of events. And if the ironies that are clearly presented within the dialogues are given their full due, it is arguably impossible to tell not only what point is being made by the dialogue but even whether any point is being made at all.[8]

The stories told by the ancient biographers and commentators tell against this last interpretation of Plato,[9] but it is worth bearing in mind as a possibility, especially because there may be an important view of philosophy to be found in it. One way this could go is to an extreme version of the view outlined above: that Plato wrote to teach rather than to expound. He could have been requiring his readers to think for themselves about the value of thinking itself, about whether thinking itself has *any* value *at all*. As Drew Hyland points out, philosophical self-knowledge involves "a questioning stance. But as such, if it is not to be a dogmatic questioning stance, and thus self-defeating, it must be capable of questioning itself, open to the possibility of questioning the very reasonableness of questioning."[10]

In fact, this need not be to the exclusion of presenting a *nonironic* doctrine ironically. It *could* exclude a nonironic doctrine. But it could also be an undertaking required to go *together with* the doctrine or understanding, giving a perspective without which the doctrine or attitude could not be properly understood.

Conversely, this view of Plato as a teacher need not exclude Plato as thoroughly an artist if Plato is taken to *show* or exhibit his doctrine as much as to *say* it. Or, more important, if he is taken to make his point through the reader's reactions as well as through what he wrote down. (I am assuming it is what we think of as art that produces this kind of effect. But it remains an important possibility independent of the issue of whether Plato is an artist or not, even if he is taken to achieve this type of effect through other means.) If Plato was doing this, then the philosophy that is not to be found in any written work might well be found in the interaction of the reader's responses with the writing. The dialogues would then be half written and half occurring between the reader and the text. And what is found in the text would be correctly read only when its references to the reader are also taken into account. Plato's characters after all, including Socrates, typically offer misleading responses that we often find out are misleading only when they do.

I have now mentioned four understandings of Plato:[11] first, as presenting a doctrine, understanding, or attitude in a way ornamented with ironic and entertaining interchanges and situations; second, as presenting a doctrine *through* these ironies, and doing it this way for important reasons; third, as not setting out to present a doctrine or philosophical understanding or attitude at all; and finally, as presenting a doctrine that in some way *is* these ironies and entertainments. In this last understanding, the reasons for presenting the doctrine through ironies are simply the same as the reasons for the truth of the doctrine itself. Thinking itself is put into question and hence given a chance to be justified. Accordingly, the mixture of frivolous irony and serious thought that one sees on the surface of the dialogues is what one finds, much more fully and deeply, at the bottom.

A long tradition that stems from the first understanding is that Plato worked out what came to be called the theory of Ideas, or Platonic forms.[12] These are eternal, unchanging self-same beings, not accessible to the bodily senses but only to the pure intelligence. They are what truly is. The world known through the bodily senses has at best only a secondary reality, a secondary being, because it is self-contradictory: it does not make sense. Sensible things are truly said to be contradictory. For example, when they are related to other things, they are larger than one thing and, while staying the same, smaller than another. They arise and decay, changing from being one thing to being another, incompatible thing. Further, what makes sensible things and events what they are does not seem to be located in those things. A table has a color and position, for example, but what makes it a table has nothing to do with those details. It would still be a table with any other color and position. And this special thing that makes it a table is shared with all other tables. Again, the details of color, position, and varieties of shape have nothing to do with what makes them tables. They are all exactly the same, considered just as being tables. Since all this special thing is, is what makes them tables, it is exactly the same in all tables. In fact it is one and the same thing, what makes all tables tables, while they are many. It is not, then, located simply in any of the tables. And since it is what *makes* them tables, it is more real than they are. This thing is the idea of the table.

These are perhaps trivial ways of playing with words: "what makes a table a table must be more real than the table." But these ways of playing with words are themselves real. And this is just the philosophical issue: What is involved in our decisions as to which parts of reality are seriously real and which are not? My suggestion, ultimately, is that Plato does not simply counterpose an alternative decision to the everyday one, but thinks about this decision itself. But I will get to that. In the meantime, as the Stranger in the *Sophist* says:

> Possibly . . . our minds are in the same state of confusion about reality. We profess to be quite at our ease about the real and to understand the word when it is spoken, though we may not understand the unreal, when perhaps we are equally in the dark about both.[13]

From the point of view of the theory of Ideas, then, sensible things are self-contradictory. But in being self-contradictory, they give us clues as to what and how the world must really be when understood so that it makes sense. This reality of the world, or the properly real world, is the world of Ideas. They are the true being of sensible things, which are only imperfect copies of them. Sensible things only truly have being, only truly are, by "participating" in these Ideas or forms. The problem arises here, for this theory, of explaining how the transient sensible things "participate" in the eternal Ideas, given that these are two so very different kinds of things.

In the *Republic*, Plato tells us, according to this traditional interpretation, that these Ideas in turn get their being from the highest Idea, the Idea of the Good. In the *Sophist*, he gives us indications as to how the Ideas themselves go together with or relate to each other—participate in each other—without being self-contradictory. In the *Timaeus* and the *Philebus*, he suggests how they connect with the sensible world, including human bodily experience. And in the *Parmenides*, so the tradition goes, Plato offers a devastating criticism of his own theory of Ideas, displaying the courage and integrity of the finest of philosophers.

This tradition has found some very prestigious sympathy. It was, for example, taken as a precursor by many Christian thinkers.[14] It has also found some very influential critics, who did not necessarily favor an alternative reading of Plato. Aristotle devoted much of his *Metaphysics* to showing that the theory of Ideas is both nonsensically false and redundant. It nonsensically creates a second copy of the same world that is nonetheless radically different from it in nature. Aristotle in fact comments at one point that "the forms . . . are meaningless sound."[15] And the independently existing Ideas do not explain anything, since the natures of the separate things they supposedly express, and *are*, have to be already *in* the things if there are to be any things, with any natures at all, to explain. This theory therefore indicates an inadequate starting point in Plato's thinking, or at least in the similar thinking of Plato's students in the Academy.[16]

Although Aristotle was himself Plato's student in the Academy and so had Plato's teaching at firsthand, one might already wonder at this point about at least two things in Aristotle's criticism. First, there is almost no deliberate irony in Aristotle (or at least in his surviving works). One might wonder if he missed the point of Plato's irony—or if, understanding the complexities of Plato's mode of presenting his thought, Aristotle was content knowingly to misrepresent him. Plato's method may be appropriate to dealing only with some kinds of concern and consequently may obscure and even hide other kinds of concern altogether. A sophisticated and inadequate theory, however, is enormously helpful in that it provides a detailed backdrop against which to present a contrasting theory. Aristotle's aim may not have been to refute Plato but to reveal and clarify certain concerns with the help of the theory of Ideas, while remaining fully aware that this theory was developed for wholly unrelated purposes.

Second, Aristotle's *Metaphysics* is devoted to the question of what being is, which he saw as the most important philosophical question.[17] What later came to be called "Metaphysics" by the editors of Aristotle's work was for Aristotle "first philosophy."[18] But Plato devoted no work to what Aristotle saw as first philosophy. Plato asked about being itself only in connection with other "first" Ideas. And in the *Republic*, he has Socrates identify the "greatest thing to learn"[19] as the Good, which Socrates describes there as "beyond being,"[20] using the same word for "being" ("ousia") that Aristotle uses for the primary kind of being which is the subject of his first philosophy. One might wonder, again, if Aristotle was not really concerned with something very different from Plato's primary concerns. If so, his refutation of the theory of Ideas again would not be a refutation of Plato's thinking but a way to clarify and explore things that had little or nothing to do with Plato's thought by setting them off against a convenient and familiar model given as an incidental by-product by Plato's methods.

The theory of Ideas could have been one among a number of elaborated metaphors via which Plato thought, and not necessarily an especially important one, while for *Aristotle* it was important because the *limitations* of this particular metaphor were peculiarly and positively suited to showing the validity of ways of thinking that were less limited for addressing *his* unrelated concerns in rigorous detail.

In keeping with my comments about Plato's possible use of irony, it is arguable that there are strong similarities in the ways in which Plato and Aristotle used the theory of Ideas, each using it to say something else for his very different ends. If so, Plato was much more subtle about it. I shall argue that this subtlety runs to the root and core of his philosophy.

Another, less prominent tradition, also beginning in the ancient world and gathering strength since the early nineteenth century, moves toward one or another or a combination of the other three understandings of Plato that I sketched above.[21] For some strands of this tradition, it is not true that Plato developed a "theory of Ideas" at all. If one pays careful attention to the details of what Plato writes in the dialogues and the details of the settings and contexts he elaborately presents to us, one can see that he never means what he says about an otherworldly "heaven of Ideas." This is an elaborate ironic metaphor for something very different, and this something else is elaborated for us in the many passages and details otherwise overlooked as merely ornamental and entertaining. The significance of irony and metaphor itself is presented as central in Plato's dialogues. The use of irony and of metaphor or image is a way of acknowledging the limitations of human knowledge and of living in accordance with it. The Good itself is not the highest of the Ideas; in fact is not an Idea at all. It is more like the basic fact that things always have more to reveal of themselves and that this always-being-more is involved in how they fit together in making up a world in which we live meaningfully and well.[22] Reading the dialogues quite literally—and this, ironically, means reading the metaphors as metaphors and the ironies as ironies—one finds a very subtle and consistent thinking that involves none of the problems long identified in the "theory of Ideas." The criticism of this theory in the *Parmenides* is, then, in simple harmony with the rest of the dialogues, saying explicitly what they say implicitly.

I shall follow neither of these two traditions of interpretation—or rather, I shall follow both of them. I shall argue both that Plato had a nonironic and central theory of Ideas *and* that he was ironic about it. I shall argue that he both held to the theory of Ideas *and* did so *because* it is wrong in the specific ways in which it is wrong. In fact, I shall argue for the suggestion I offered as an addition to the third view above, that Plato questioned the value of thinking (and so sense-making) *itself* and did so as part of the right way *to pursue thinking*, to have a rigorous understanding or theory. I shall emphasize, then, that he anticipated Aristotle's criticisms, notably in the *Charmides* and the *Theaetetus*, for example, and not only in the *Parmenides*. And I shall argue that subtly nuanced as Aristotle's thinking is, Plato possessed sufficiently greater subtlety to be able to appreciate what many postmodern philosophers, such as Derrida, have also come to accept: the importance for truth of simple nonsense and redundancy rightly positioned with respect to sense and substance, that is, the worth of theoretical clumsiness rightly maintained and poised.

These are highly contentious claims. But I do not think they are especially unlikely. I shall try to show that the evidence for them leaps out at one all over the dialogues.

I believe that this paradoxical stance allows us to engage profoundly with a number of problems of contemporary life, as I believe it engaged with the problems of Plato's age and society. How it does so will have to emerge as the discussion proceeds. But one thing can already be emphasized: if Plato does balance sense and nonsense in this way, then he does not prejudge the validity of sense or careful thought themselves. This automatically means that his paradoxical stance positions us for a very deep exploration into the foundations of sense and thought themselves. And such an exploration must presumably have profound implications for everything that is built on those foundations.

If, as I shall argue, this stance is justified by the nature of truth, then it is not just Plato's particular choice, but it expresses the nature of thought itself when it tries to establish truth. That is, it describes the way we all already think when we are concerned with truth.

By way of a culturally closer model for what I am getting at by this idea of a poised positioning with respect to sense and nonsense, substance and redundancy, I should like to look at the ironic opening sentence of Jane Austen's *Pride and Prejudice*. "It is a truth universally acknowledged, that a single man in possession of a good fortune, must be in want of a wife."[23] This is both false and redundant. It is false, because it is neither a truth nor universally acknowledged. And it is redundant, because if it is universally acknowledged, it adds nothing by being stated here. But in a sense, as I shall argue below, it is also true and in need of being pointed out.

Part of what makes this quote helpful for my purposes is that its combination of being both false/redundant and true/contributing expresses the reality of a certain kind of consciousness, one insensible to the possibility of fundamentally differing consciousnesses with fundamentally differing views. It is for this consciousness that "it is a truth universally acknowledged." This kind of consciousness vividly illustrates the coordination of sense and nonsense, and of truth and falsehood, that, I argue, belongs to all consciousness, and in fact to sense and reality themselves. Further, as I try to show in the course of this book, Plato deals centrally with this kind of consciousness. It is a social and political expression of what Socrates describes as the most abhorrent falsehood, a falsehood people hold "in the most vital part of themselves and about their most vital concerns," and of which they are "blindly ignorant":[24] in other words, as (I think) he often expresses it, this is an ignorance both of one's self and, more or less equivalently, of one's own ignorance. Part of the value of Plato's exploring this kind of consciousness is that it eliminates what defines philosophy: the ability to question one's own views, or even to be aware of them in distinction from others. By taking up the view of this kind of consciousness, I believe, Plato avoids prejudging the value and status of philosophy, of deep and careful thought, itself. Consequently he can explore its nature, foundations, and whatever value it may have all the more thoroughly.

Finally, that there are consciousnesses insensible to the possibility of fundamentally different consciousness is a social and political fact as well as a psychological and metaphysical one. This model will therefore also help us to see the social and political relevance of the coordination of sense and nonsense that it illustrates.

I turn now to developing the model.

Clearly, the reality of a differing consciousness can become evident only in separating one's view from that of the world as it appears to a consciousness that is primarily insensible of others. This separation opens up an awareness of appearances or realities with which primarily other-insensible appearances or realities can be contrasted and so noticed. It also opens up an awareness of other-insensible consciousness and appearances as themselves being part of reality. Now, if other-insensible consciousness remains all there is for itself, all that appears to it, there is nothing for it to be contrasted with and so no way for *it* itself to appear even to *itself*, as a reality or otherwise. The view that allows to other-insensible consciousness an awareness of other kinds of awareness also allows a first perception of it itself as a conceivable reality in its own right. This means that what I have called "other-insensible" consciousness is really also insensible of *itself* as something distinguishable in fundamental characteristics from other consciousnesses. It is insensible of consciousness itself as fundamentally diverse, of its own nature as potentially fundamentally other to another consciousness or in some respect to itself.

A description of the reality of other-insensible consciousness, then, requires a viewpoint different from that of other-insensible consciousness, since this consciousness does not exist for itself as distinguished from other kinds of consciousness. If there is *anything* to be said about other-insensible consciousness, in its defense or otherwise, and even as to its existence, a viewpoint different from its own is needed. And a description of the reality of other-insensible consciousness also requires this viewpoint to be combined with that of other-insensible consciousness itself, since the other-insensible viewpoint is precisely the reality that is being described. But other-insensible consciousness is defined by its excluding other viewpoints. These requirements for describing other-insensible consciousness are therefore both incompatible and necessary. Hence the incompatible assertions about the first sentence of *Pride and Prejudice* made above.

Such a consciousness, it is important to note, can be described not only as insensible of fundamental differences in consciousness but also, incompatibly, as having a different idea of what difference in consciousness itself *can be* from the idea of it had by other-sensible consciousness. (These descriptions are incompatible because if one is unaware of the possibility of difference, one cannot think of that possibility in one way rather than another.) What it is to be different at all, with respect to consciousnesses, and consequently what it is to be self and what it is to be other, can be said to be differently understood and lived by this consciousness. Here is another useful example from Jane Austen's *Emma*:

> [H]e was now obliged to part with Miss Taylor too; and from his habits of gentle selfishness and of being never able to suppose that other people could feel differently from himself, he was very much disposed to think Miss Taylor had done as sad a thing for herself as for them, and would have been a great deal happier if she had spent all the rest of her life at Hartfield. . . .
>
> "Poor Miss Taylor!—I wish she were here again. What a pity it is that Mr. Weston ever thought of her!"
>
> "I cannot agree with you, papa . . . you would not have had Miss Taylor live with us for ever . . . when she might have a house of her own?"
>
> "A house of her own!—but where is the advantage of a house of her own? This is three times as large."[25]

What would Miss Taylor want with a house of her own? Emma's father simply cannot see from such a viewpoint. Similar inabilities to see have characterized large groups in modern Western history. What would a black man want with an education, a woman with a vote or a career, a woman with a wife? And the typical early response to such a person's demonstrating that s/he really does want these things is that by doing so, s/he then disqualifies herself absolutely: s/he is unnatural, no longer falls within her own species, is not after all really, for example, a woman, no longer represents even herself (having abandoned his/her own nature).[26]

What it is possible for difference in consciousness to be *is* different here, even though within the limits of an other-insensible consciousness, since that consciousness is itself part of reality. And the present use of the word "difference," in describing differences in what it is to be different, in fact shares the same peculiarity of sense/nonsense that I am arguing of the sentence from *Pride and Prejudice*. This follows from the fact that an accurate description of such a consciousness requires both its own view and aspects of views it wholly excludes. Putting this in more detail, the other-insensible consciousness by definition has no sense of fundamental difference. But it can only be described at all, can only be said to be or have or not be or have anything, by a contrasting view. For such a contrasting view, other-insensible consciousness does have a different view of difference. Less misleadingly put, other-insensible consciousness *is* then partly a different view of difference, since it *is* nothing but a view and the elements of the view, and so it does *have* a different view of difference. For the contrasting view, then, other-insensibility has a different construal of difference, and that contrasting view (and hence what has sense for that view) is part of what is required for the other-insensible view to be described at all. So, once it can be described as having no construal of difference at all, it can also be described as having a construal of difference differing from others. Just as in the structure of Austen's ironic sentence from *Pride and Prejudice*, both of these incompatible ways of phrasing the nature of insensibility-to-self are sometimes simultaneously necessary.

In general, beyond other-insensible consciousness, each phrasing of anything puts blinkers on one's thinking and perceiving it (including what I am about to say), and some things that have to be thought and seen require a perception of the blinkers themselves: hence at least a second, incompatible perception. This is not possible for physical vision, but there is no reason that understanding should have to work by the same logic as sensation. Here is at least one reason for the distinction in Plato's dialogues between the sensible and the intelligible.

Given that Plato makes his points with reference to his readers' own responses and mistakes and not only his characters', he offers evidence that all of us who can learn these points are conscious both other-sensibly and other-insensibly: otherwise we would not make the same mistakes as the characters do when we read his works. It follows that the difference between the two kinds of consciousness is not that other-sensible consciousness is a simple opposite of other-insensibility, but rather that it is conscious of its own possible other-insensibility and is willing and able to learn fresh other-sensibility.

One way of expressing the point of this book is that it sketches what is involved in a way of speaking, thinking, and living that takes into account the possibility of the different validities of incompatible phrasings and, further, the actuality of the specific validities of incompatible phrasings, where more than one is relevant. Or—since, as I shall argue, we need to think of this not only in terms of conscious awareness and linguistic meaning but also in terms of "the sense of the world" or the structure of reality—where more than one position or framework or paradigm of the world is in the situation or in question.

In fact, we can already sketch a bridge from our model of characteristics of consciousness to the structures of sense, truth, and reality themselves along the lines I have started to develop. When a view includes an idea that something is true, that idea is part of what the view *is*. That is, the truth or reality of the view includes this idea, and this idea is therefore part of the truth *about* the view. Now this remains true whether or not the idea that the something is true is itself in fact true. That is, we can certainly say that the other-insensible consciousness is simply wrong, that its view is simply false; but that judgment in no way affects that its wrong view is part of the truth. It is the truth about a *view* that we are dealing with, not the truth about an object without inwardness for which the external truth is the only truth. The mistaken construal is a real part of the view and of the situation that includes that view, and the truth of that situation must therefore include the view through the mistake.[27] As Thomas Nagel expresses the genuine reality that belongs to subjectivity, "appearance and perspective are essential parts of what there is"; and "the subjectivity of consciousness is an irreducible feature of reality—without which we couldn't do physics or anything else— and it must occupy as fundamental a place in any credible world view as matter, energy, space, time, and numbers."[28]

It is not usually puzzling or interesting that mistakes are a real part of the view that makes them, that it is true that mistakes exist. This is something we all acknowledge and work with in the ordinary course of things. But in the case of an other-insensible consciousness, it does become puzzling and interesting, because this kind of consciousness excludes all real difference from itself, so that part of the mistake whose existence we must accept is that the mistake has no alternatives by contrast with which it can be considered a mistake at all. As a result, the truth of its mistakes can be described only through the kind of coordination of mutually exclusive views or positions I have discussed.

From the exclusive viewpoint of other-insensible consciousness, then, Austen's opening sentence in *Pride and Prejudice* is not false, only redundant. From the viewpoint that allows this consciousness to appear as a reality in its own right at all, the sentence is not redundant, only false. And both viewpoints are parts of reality as seen by the second view. Neither view can simply be dismissed in considering reality by the second view, until such time as the world becomes perfect by the exclusive standards of one of the views.

And then reality will have changed, so that we are still left with the reality of both views in thinking about the reality before the change.

As a result, the second view needs the irony to say the truth, or to say truly. It needs the clumsy wrong statement rightly maintained and poised with respect to sense and substance. It needs this to say the truth of a contradictory reality without itself simply being part of the contradictions, simply being wrong or nonsensical. (I say "without *simply* being wrong or contradictory," since the contrast is not between being wrong or contradictory and being right or coherent but, as with other-insensibility, between being *simply* contradictory or wrong and being right in a certain kind of coordination with being contradictory or wrong.)[29] And the second view needs to be able to say or think the truth in order to ensure as much as it can that it takes its measure from and is measured by the good for all, rather than unnecessarily risking that its measure is the blindness of insensibility or a partial, self-serving prejudice.[30] It needs to be able to say or think the truth in order that its actions, and its actions of saying or thinking themselves, be true. In order, that is, to be able to act responsibly, as much as possible in accordance with the reality of the situation.

It is true that the truth can be said in separate statements, so that one paradoxical or ironic statement is not produced. But the irony is not simply in the language; it is in the situation. The falsehood, or behavior and thought out of accordance with truth, is in the situation, and the relation to each other of the separate statements about it, properly or truly thought about, will involve that irony. If it does not, the truth of the situation has not been captured.

This is all another way of saying that metaphor is sometimes primary with respect to and constitutive of truth.[31] Irony, as a way of saying one thing by saying another, incompatible thing, is a kind of extended metaphor. Clearly Plato's dialogues are extended metaphors for issues extending beyond their particular situations and characters. If they are to be thoroughly thought about, their metaphoric character itself must be taken into account. And the very evident use of irony in Plato's works, especially irony that frames the work by opening and closing it, indicates that he was at least perfectly capable of taking this metaphoricity into account himself. That is, it is likely that this idea of the occasionally metaphorical foundation of truth is not merely a basis to read his works against or to enhance his intentions but is very likely a basis necessary to reading his intentions at all.

It is worth considering, for example, that the literary dimensions of Plato's work include not only the comic and tragic aspects of drama—the dialogues are, after all, dialogues—but also an aspect of epic poetry. The dialogues are often framed in a narrative told long after the events of the dialogue, and perhaps it is not too much of a stretch to think of the extended metaphors that they are as extended or epic similes. Part of the issue here is that Plato may have engaged himself not simply in the literary forms that preceded him but in the insights or wisdom that those forms embodied.[32] The widely discussed rift between philosophy and the poetic tradition—ancient comedy and tragedy (and not only epic) were poetic—may not be a genuine rift at all, or may be one that Plato attempted to overcome.

I argue, then, that Aristotle and the long tradition are right in ascribing to Plato a theory of Ideas, but that Aristotle was wrong simply to refute it, while the long tradition is wrong not to submit it to Plato's refutational irony. And I argue that the tradition of this century is right to deny a theory of Ideas to Plato, but wrong not to submit that denial itself to Plato's refutational irony.

This kind of interpretation may seem far too clever to be realistic. It may seem to imply that Plato's work could reach very few readers and that even then a reliable interpretation would be very hard to reach. In fact, the "Plato as fundamental teacher" view answers this difficulty. If the readers are taught to think more carefully, then it makes no difference whether they uncover Plato's view. They have already benefited in important and self-increasing ways. G. C. Field offers, however, the following highly sensible suggestion:

> [W]e suppose . . . that from first to last Plato's main object in writing, as in all his other activities, was to do something to meet the needs of his own time. He wrote primarily to help people to think rightly. That means that any views definitely advocated in a dialogue and any views towards which the arguments of a dialogue inevitably led were views that Plato regarded as certainly or probably true. If a dialogue did not come to any positive conclusion, but opened up certain questions or suggested certain lines of thought, it means that Plato regarded work on these lines as likely to be fruitful. . . . in this sense the dialogues express Plato's own views throughout. And that is their chief object.[33]

My suggestion is that Plato does what Field supposes *and* something more complex. I shall discuss at various points how nonironic readings of the dialogues result in views that *approximate, in the results of acting on them,* the view that a self-critical ironic reading presents as *descriptive statements*. In accordance with another tradition of Plato interpretation, then, I suggest an "esoteric" and "exoteric" level of the dialogues. But I shall argue that these levels are in an important sense the same.

There is a wonderful subtlety in Plato, and a beautiful delicate ungainliness, and they stand together. I shall argue that this is the point of leverage of Plato's thinking and work and perhaps his life: of his doctrine, understanding, or attitude.

And again, if these qualities are justified by the nature of truth, they are qualities not just of Plato's thought but of truth-seeking thought in general, that he succeeded in making visible.

As I have suggested, in a sense it makes no difference whether one succeeds in finding or even tries to find out what, for instance, Plato thought he was doing in the dialogues or whether they end up having provoked in one a different understanding that coincidentally happens to fit them. What is important is that the understanding one develops puts one in the direction of some truth ("some" in the senses of both "some of" and "some or other"). This is my primary aim. As Plato has Socrates say in the *Charmides*, even where an attempt at refutation is concerned, and not merely the presentation of a different view:

> "How can you believe," I exclaimed, "that if I'm trying my hardest to refute you, I'm doing it for any other reason than that for which I'd investigate what I say myself! You see, my great fear is that I may some time not notice that I'm thinking I know something when in fact I don't. And this, I tell you, is what I'm doing now: looking at the argument mostly for my own sake, but perhaps for the sake of my friends as well. Or don't you think that it is a common good for almost all men that each thing that exists should be revealed as it really is?"

Socrates adds, "Never mind whether it's Critias or Socrates who is the one refuted. Just concentrate on the argument itself, and consider what on earth will become of it if it is examined." And Plato has Critias not simply take *this* truth for granted either: "I'll do that," he responds, "because I think that what you're saying is quite reasonable."[34]

As Aristotle famously said in arguing against the Ideas that "have been introduced by friends of our own. . . . [W]hile both are dear, piety requires us to honour truth above our friends."[35] Of course it remains a question whether it is in fact possible for someone to pursue the truth in this open-ended way. Finding the truth about this itself depends on taking the possibility seriously before dismissing or accepting it. I try to show how Plato considers it and what conclusion he comes to.

What Plato thought he was doing of course remains important and interesting in other senses, and I try to orient myself toward that truth as well.

Plato's work is often divided into early, middle, and late periods, and the views the dialogues present are understood as different in each of them. Typically, the "earlier" and shorter dialogues are understood to represent Socrates' views, while the later dialogues increasingly present Plato's own, developing views. I shall not respect this view of the dialogues, but I shall treat them as all expressing the same basic standpoint, perhaps more or less fully developed.

The justification for the idea of fundamentally different periods rests either on interpretations of the evidence given by the content of the dialogues or on stylometric evidence.[36] The evidence given by the content is highly controversial.[37] I shall not repeat the main arguments here against the "periods" view, since they have been very thoroughly covered by others.[38] Apart from these arguments, my own interpretation of the dialogues' content suggests that they all express the same basic standpoint. Since the "periods" view rests exactly on this type of interpretation, it depends on the kind of work presented here and not the other way round. My own reading of the dialogues consequently offers reasons to reject the "periods" view.

With respect to stylometric evidence, on the other hand, current scholarship shows it to be highly inconclusive. In fact, as Debra Nails notes, "there is unanimity about almost nothing across the various methods of ordering the dialogues."[39]

I shall therefore take it as legitimate to explore the possibility that the chronology of the dialogues is unimportant with respect to the basic views they express.

The book is divided into two parts. In Part I, I present the account of truth or framework that I believe Plato's work expresses. I do so in a way that, while it is fully developed in itself, is provisional with respect to his dialogues. This presentation tries to describe, justify, connect, and show the importance of a number of assumptions that I argue Plato works with and subtly validates.

Part II has five chapters. In the first I give an overview of my interpretation of Plato; in the next three I try to test and present this interpretation in finer detail by looking at the whole of a short dialogue and at details of the overall structure of several long dialogues. In the brief conclusion I make some very general remarks about the significance of Plato's framework.

PART I

Ideas of Truth and Knowledge

The scrutiny of the grammar of a word weakens the position of certain fixed standards of our expression which had prevented us from seeing facts with unbiased eyes. Our investigation tried to remove this bias, which forces us to think that the facts *must* conform to certain pictures embedded in our language.

—Wittgenstein, *The Blue and Brown Books*, 43

Is it a contradiction if I say: "This is beautiful and this is not beautiful" (pointing at different objects)? And ought one to say that it isn't a contradiction, because the two words "This" mean different things? No; the two "This's" have the *same* meaning. "Today" has the same meaning today as it had yesterday, "here" the same meaning here and there. . . .

"This is beautiful and this is not beautiful" *is* a contradiction, but it has a use.

—Wittgenstein, *Remarks on the Philosophy of Psychology*, 1:9e

INTRODUCTORY

Internal and External Connections

A very good way to read Plato is, perhaps, the way Jacob Klein stunningly exemplifies.[1] He reads each dialogue as it is presented to us by Plato, and pauses at each ambiguity to identify the different and often incompatible ways of understanding statements and interchanges, until the specific way divergent possible meanings accumulate begins itself to indicate how one should understand the dialogue as a whole.

This is not the approach I take here. I begin with an idea of what Plato's standpoint is and try to show that this idea fits. This is more like the approach in Hans-Georg Gadamer's exploration of Plato's *Philebus*, in the first half of which, he writes, "The task was . . . to make the horizon of Plato's philosophizing stand out," in the service of "the interpretation of the *Philebus* which I undertake in the second."[2] It is an important part of my discussion that I do not leave it there. Apart from the need to justify my approach, the idea of an "approach" at all is rightly questionable to many philosophers, since it suggests that we can arbitrarily pick and choose where we start and how we come to understand things. In fact what I want to say by using the idea of approach, and what I argue Plato similarly wanted to say, cannot be understood without first appreciating why these philosophers are right to reject the idea of an "approach." I therefore discuss at various points the significance of the present approach in the light of the idea of "approach" itself.[3]

One possible preliminary justification for this alternative way of reading—which is in fact a more traditional, "doctrinaire" approach—is that truth, including the truth about Plato's dialogues, might be such that one can think from the same place as Plato did, from the independent source of truth, rather than trying to get access to it exclusively from his writings or from a tradition of thought and writings.[4] As Plato has Socrates say in the *Phaedrus*, "it shows great folly . . . to suppose that one can transmit or acquire clear and certain knowledge of an art through the medium of writing, or that written words can do more than remind the reader of what he already knows on any given subject."[5] If Plato's writing of the dialogues is to have any sense, then, it presupposes—and in this dialogue explicitly suggests—that one can find the same truth without those dialogues. (It is true that this explicit statement is only made by a character, and only one character, in a single dialogue. But as I indicate early in the introduction to the book as a whole [see note 3 there], Plato was aware of the need to take cogent positions into account whatever their source, so there is some basis for taking this statement seriously.)

In fact, since Plato's dialogues have a great deal to do with the search for truth, there is in any event a large overlap between the orientation toward truth in general, without reliance on Plato's dialogues, and the orientation toward the truth about the dialogues themselves. This is captured in the ambiguity of the genitive in the phrase, "the truth of Plato's dialogues."

Plato presents Socrates as having relied on a guiding *daimonion* or divine spirit.[6] Perhaps this guiding voice emerged from such a general source of truth. (As always where there is a conflict concerning what is said to be real, the choice of language or articulation is very important. If one says, "what Socrates regarded as a *daimonion*," one suggests that it might not really have been that. One is already biased toward a certain strongly particular interpretation of the reality one represents here. If, on the other hand, one says, "the *daimonion* emerged," one suggests that it was definitely a *daimonion*. One is already biased toward another strongly particular interpretation of the reality in question. This is just the difficulty of important articulation that I argue Plato resolved, and with far-reaching consequences for other kinds of problems.)

It is also perhaps this source that Wittgensteinian philosophers invoke when they use (or used to use) the otherwise redundant phrase: "I want to say." In this way they meaningfully acknowledge—whether conscious of the motive that originated the phrase or out of customary habit—that the source of their thought is at the time unknown to them. And the decision to make this fact explicit in turn indicates that it is important to bear in mind, for a time, the unknown and unthought nature of this source: that this source *ought* to remain vague, unthought and unknown, for that time. It treats the very reality and nature of the source as indeterminate at the time, so that not knowing and not thinking it *is* the true knowledge and thinking of it. It is a meaningful phrase because it functions by referring to something indeterminate, the unknown source, in a way that actively maintains exactly that indeterminacy while some other issue than the nature of that source is being investigated.

Many contemporary philosophers, on the other hand, hold that texts, or other things understood in the way texts must be understood, are the last court of appeal for our access to the truth. Unless a reliable *daimonion* has assured one of this—and of course the question is: How does one know that the *daimonion* is reliable? (a question of which Plato's Socrates was by no means unaware)[7]—it is a risk to take it as truth. Here I also take the other risk: that it is not so. I shall discuss the balancing of such risks and its significance.

Another possible preliminary justification is that my approach fits the structure of Platonic dialogue. It lets my own view stand out strongly, so that if there turns out to be a contrast between two views, mine and Plato's, this contrast can be identified more clearly and easily in a dialogue between the two. And if there does turn out to be a contrast, it can help, just by being the specific contrast it is, to establish exactly what the truth is in either view: what either view independently truly shows and is. Since, in addition, both views are aiming at truth rather than simply the truth of Plato's dialogues, this would seem to accord better with Plato's aims than the exclusive subordination of the interpreter's assumptions to the uncovering of Plato's.

Perhaps, even, the truth of Plato's dialogues is not to be found in them at all, but *only* in a dialogue between his text and another view external to it. Given that he insists again and again on showing us truth in the process of being negotiated (I use "negotiated" in both the senses of "bargaining" and "carefully making one's way through obstacles") in dialogue and on explaining the virtue of this procedure, Plato seems to have thought just that.

In Part I, I present the framework or account of truth that I believe Plato's work expresses, in a way that is fully developed in itself but is only provisional with respect to his dialogues. I develop and discuss this framework with respect to themes that run through the dialogues in general as well as with respect to contemporary issues. In Part II I present the more fully developed discussion of Plato's own work, reading several of his dialogues, each as a whole and in detail, through the account developed in Part I, in this way both illustrating and testing that framework.

To present the framework in Part I, I elaborate a number of ideas that I believe are basic to Plato's philosophy, but I do not present them in a way that is simply systematically connected. That is, while I do develop a continuous line of argument through the sequence of these basic ideas, each of them also leads independently in a variety of unrelated and equally fundamental directions, and the many possible ways of connecting them are not

sorted out and organized. Many of these connections may be entirely mutually irrelevant, and many others may conflict with and contradict each other.
These possibilities are not identified and ordered here so as to account for
the conflicts and guard against being misled by the irrelevancies. Part of the
point of the book is to show both that this kind of lack of organized connection or even any significant connection—a kind of mutual irrelevance or
being-external-to—is one of Plato's themes and also that, independently of
Plato, it is sometimes satisfactory—and in fact required—from the viewpoint of the most rigorous connection and organization of ideas.[8]

Differently put, the principles of a rigorous viewpoint properly thought
through should emerge as justifying certain kinds of absence of rigor, and as
themselves being justified only with reference to such "unrigorousnesses."
Central to my theme and method, then, is a loose and also rigorously connected relation of looseness and rigorous connection themselves.

I believe that Plato presupposes and subtly justifies the ideas I discuss and
also this kind of connection, but without explicit elaboration. As I present
them, I shall try to give evidence that he does in fact have them in mind.
But as should become clear, even if they are not Plato's, they are centrally
relevant to the issues he does present, so that *we* need to get clear on them
in order to know how to regard what he presents. And again, in any event,
whether or not they are Plato's, they should also, if they are well thought
out, be worthwhile in their own right.

In fact, I suggest that the unity of the whole body of Plato's dialogues is
just this coordination of loose and rigorous connection. If this is true, each
dialogue is autonomous, needing to be read entirely in its own terms, and
each dialogue is *also* relevant to each of the others. Further, as I argue of
these kinds of connection, the dialogues are often mutually relevant only
because of or *as a result of* their mutual irrelevance. In the *Statesman*, Plato
has the Stranger offer a suggestion that illuminates this senseless-sounding
statement: "the method of example . . . operates, does it not, when a factor
identical with a factor in a less-known object is rightly believed to exist in
some other better-known object *in quite another sphere of life?*"[9] An example
can help understanding precisely because it operates by drawing on "quite
another sphere." It is helpful or its relevance can be drawn on only because
it makes use of irrelevance, of an important detachment or distance from
the subject at issue.

In much of my discussion of these loose and rigorous connections, I rely
on the terms "external" and "internal." By internal (or logical, or conceptual, or organic) connections or relations between two things or kinds of

things, I mean that part of what makes one of the things what it is is part of what makes the other thing what it is. These relations are also typically called "essential" relations. But since part of what is in question in the present discussion is what it truly *is* to *be* something, that is, what an essence is, I shall try to avoid this term in the initial stages of the discussion. The meaning of the other terms will also have to be revised; but one has to work with something.

By external (or nonlogical, or irrelevant, or additive, or artificial) connections or relations, I mean relations that require no further thought to be fully grasped than just noticing them. Unlike internal relations, there is no support for the relation in the natures of the things being related. There is nothing more that *belongs* to an external relation than just what one grasps at the time, nothing more that can be discovered from it about the things it relates. The connection does not stem from the nature of either related thing, cannot be figured out from what it is, but is to be found by looking at circumstances that just happen to be associated with it at the time.

I suggest, then, that Plato explores the significance of external, trivial connections as a dimension of systematic logical rigor. That is, he explores the importance of simple and trivial occurrences such as the meaningful presentation of examples (among many other kinds of trivia) without explicit thought about them. In a different (but, I hope to show, relevant) context, that of the theory of Ideas, Plato suggests at least that "trivia" are worth thinking about:

> Are you also puzzled, Socrates, about cases that might be thought absurd, such as hair or mud or dirt or any other trivial and undignified objects? . . .
>
> Not at all, said Socrates. . . . it would surely be too absurd to suppose that they have a form. . . .
>
> That, replied Parmenides, is because you are still young, Socrates, and philosophy has not yet taken hold of you so firmly as I believe it will someday. You will not despise any of these objects then.[10]

IDEA 1

Artificiality and Nature
(Sometimes Being Is Something Else)

For the presentation of this and the first few basic ideas, I must ask the reader's indulgence. Aside from the already provisional nature of Part I with respect to Plato's work, the initial discussion of the first few ideas must necessarily be incomplete. The framework I am presenting coordinates several partly independent lines of thought, and these all need to be presented before they can be coordinated. But there also are ways in which they are dependent on each other, and these can be addressed only after some of them have already been presented. While the initial discussion of these first ideas will, I hope, nonetheless justify them quite rigorously, they will be more fully supported in the context of the later ideas.

The first idea I want to elaborate as basic to Plato is that certain kinds of artificiality or unnaturalness are sometimes also the most natural or spontaneous kinds of thing, in the very senses in which they are artificial and unnatural.[1] As will become clear, the "sometimes" qualification is as important a part of this idea as the relation between nature and artificiality. At first glance, this idea might not seem to have any bearing on Plato at all. But his works, for a start, in dealing with the truth and nature of things, teem with fictions and the artifices of wit and of provocative details of construction. I try to show that these details of his works are significant, not only as devices that direct us beyond themselves toward the truth, but because their artificiality and triviality are dimensions of truth itself in their own right. I argue that one misses the fundamentals by seeing only the depth of these details and not also their comic and human pure irrelevance.

But as I mentioned in the introductory section, it should become clear with this idea, as with the rest of the basic ideas, that even if it is not Plato's, it is still centrally relevant to issues he does deal with, so that *we* would still need to get clear on it to know how to regard what he presents. In any event, I explore the idea itself first before relating it more fully to Plato.

1.1. CHANGE OF NATURE

For example, let us say someone wants not to be prejudiced against women, homosexual men and lesbians, and/or other races, but finds that s/he *is* prejudiced. To behave artificially in a nonprejudiced fashion is then purely artificial, dishonest, at odds with the person's nature. It is arguable (let me reassure the liberal reader that I shall also argue the reverse shortly) that this, like any departure from truth, is at least in the long run destructive of the very purposes it is intended to fulfill. The person will inevitably be incapable of living up to a pattern of life to which s/he is unsuited, and will resent those for whose sake s/he is distorting her/himself. In addition, s/he will deprive him/herself of genuine, satisfying human company by remaining concealed behind a false mask. Apart from the inevitable outcome of increased and less governable antagonism toward the groups in question, the person's own happiness is very likely to be seriously hampered by loneliness and destructive feelings. Since the general principle supporting not being prejudiced is one of being fair to people, this person will in this way betray the value of not being prejudiced, by being unfair to her/himself.[2] S/he will cause him/herself great unhappiness for something s/he cannot help: being who s/he is. It seems that the reasonable thing to do is to accept one's limitations and live honestly in accordance with them; that is, with one's nature.

There is a nobility to this stance, if one retains one's moral awareness and can recognize that what one has accepted are shortcomings. One measure of this awareness is that one can then appreciate and support the lesser failings of others. This is not, perhaps, opposed to the idea (Nietzsche's, for example, or Buddhists') that everything has its place and is to be loved as it is. Everything here has its place as what it is, and moral shortcomings have their place as moral shortcomings. To see them otherwise is not to love them as they are but really perhaps to dismiss and repudiate them for not being something other than themselves.

I suggest, however, returning to the example of the prejudiced person, that consistently behaving at odds with oneself does not happen without a desire to do so. And the desire to be other than one is is itself part of what one is: it is therefore natural and spontaneous. In other words, the purely artificial behavior is a true expression of something natural.

The difficulty is to decide which is the more natural nature: who one is, or the desire of that "who" to be someone other than who one is.[3]

This conflict pervades Plato's writings but it is usually interpreted differently there from the way I have presented it. In reading Plato there is a temptation to see the Socrates character as trying to make for change in his interlocutors and to see it as unfortunate if they cannot change. But there is also a temptation to see the reason why change is called for and why an inability to change is unfortunate as being that these interlocutors are in fact already untrue to who they truly are and therefore need to correct the false "change" or difference. There is, then, a change that is seen to be necessary and a staying the same (in relation to truth) that is seen to be necessary. This requirement both to do something different and to stay the same presents the kind of question I have outlined above. But these reader's temptations also presuppose an already-made decision as to what the person's real nature is, and so really bypass that question. I suggest that they therefore miss what is really at issue in this dimension of Plato's work.

This is not only a question about how one knows which is the "same" (true) and which the "changed" (false). It is also and more fundamentally a question about what "sameness" itself *means* here, about what would be involved in *being* the "same" in the first place. Let us assume for the moment that real change in the nature of something can make sense. If the truth of the person includes the need to change, if the person is truly not being herself, then being the "same" as oneself at that point includes being the same as what one is *not* yet. Being the "same" as oneself here involves a change, and so involves either not yet being the same or being made not the same. And until the process of change is complete, there remain conflicting ways that the person "is," that the person is the "same" as herself.[4]

(It should be evident at this point that we need to get clear on this issue, whether Plato deals with it himself or not. It is directly relevant to deciding how we should treat the kind of concern that his dialogues centrally presuppose.)[5]

Now, it could be objected that it simply does not make sense at all to speak of a nature differing from itself, so that this entire way of discussing it is entirely incoherent.[6] We would therefore need an entirely different way of construing the issue of change in which, for example, what is in the person that is not the same as the person's nature is understood as simply unreal, simply false, without reality in any sense in which that nature is real. I think this objection is valid, but that it is only part of the story, since in fact it presupposes the construal that it supposedly warrants, or is another way of expressing it (an equivalent to it), rather than being a reason to adopt it. There is no reason to consider the idea of a nature differing from itself as *entirely* incoherent (rather than, say, paradoxical) unless one already thinks of what is in the person that is not the same as the person's nature as unreal. That construal is therefore so far baseless, arbitrary.

In fact, and in any event, what I ultimately want to get at is really the nature of the balance between two such mutually exclusive views. Consequently I return to this objection and alternative construal after elaborating the "change of nature is conceivable" view a little more. At that point I also discuss the balancing of the two views, and in the following idea develop that discussion further.

Returning to real change in a person's nature, then: in addition to the person's being the "same" in conflicting ways, deciding what is the "same" depends on considering whether the "artificial" change or difference is in fact the truth about the person and therefore itself the real "same." Consequently, until the change is complete, the question remains as to which of the "artificial" and the "same" is which. That indecision is itself part of the truth about the person (it is, for example, the kind of thing one might express in being honest about oneself). Being the "same" as oneself at that point must therefore also include being the same as "being undecided as to whether or not one needs to change," that is, being undecided as to which is the self one is the "same" as. Differently put, for a changing self or a self capable of change, the process or capability of change—that is, becoming different or the capability of becoming different—are themselves part of what that self is the "same" as. It follows that, as long as the process is under way, change or difference is as much part of sameness as not, and falsehood is as much part of truth as not.[7] The phrase "becoming who one is" captures the paradox.

Now, if there is something to the view that we are always capable of being mistaken about ourselves, it is *always* possible that this process of changing toward truth is necessary. It follows that in this context, difference and falsehood are *always* possibly parts, can always return as parts, respectively, of sameness and truth. While this is so far true only for subjective dimensions of reality, these are nonetheless dimensions of reality, and so of truth as such, as I argued briefly in the introduction and argue further below. In exactly what sense difference and falsehood are parts of sameness and truth, it is part of my aim to try to establish.

To return to the prejudiced person. We no longer know whether it is the artificial behavior that is rightly called artificial or whether the prejudiced behavior so far typical of the person is not, rather, what is artificial. I suggest that what has so far been called the artificial behavior *is itself the means of deciding* which is the person's more natural nature, or, as another possibility, whether both are natural to the person.

In general, a consistent pattern of behavior must be motivated; that is, it follows on a desire. Accordingly, if someone repeatedly fails to carry out a desire when given the opportunity to do so under widely differing conditions, one knows that s/he desires it less than s/he does not desire it. Just so in this case. If the person behaves artificially in a nonprejudiced way and increasingly finds the negative results detailed above, then her/his established nature is maintained (whether by a commitment of desire or as a fact about the person given before desire) to a degree that overrides his/her desired nature. That is, her/his established nature is more who s/he is than his/her desired nature. And if the negative results do not occur or do not overridingly occur, but the person finds him/herself gradually becoming more comfortable and more easily helpful (for example), then the established nature has been giving way (whether as a change of commitment of desire or as a change of false "fact" about the person given before desire) to the desired nature. And it can only do that if it was not as much or was already potentially not as much who the person was in the first place.

Among other variations here, there can of course be gradations of the degree of contrast between these two clearly different outcomes, and there can be undecidable cases in which the outcomes are equally balanced in both directions.

The desire to be other than who one is, then, which is the root cause of consistent artificiality at odds with oneself, can also be the foundation of simple naturalness, the means of establishing, in knowledge and in action or fact, what one's nature is.

1.2. THE INCONSTANCY OR "SOMETIMES ALWAYS" CHARACTER OF TRUTH

It could even be argued that someone who has not been artificial in this way cannot know who s/he is. But I suggest at this point that it is possible that human nature is only sometimes and/or in some respects not a simple unity at bottom. And here we come to the objection and conflicting construal I mention above, that change of nature is simply not conceivable. First, it is possible that the idea I have so far presupposed—that real change in a person's nature makes sense at all, even as something to consider—is simply wrong. In which case there is no conflict between one's "natures."

What someone is, after all, is simply what that person is, and contemplating change in the person is really contemplating her/him as being someone s/he is not, as being someone else—which, of course, s/he is not.

Now, the issue here is not that one can see human nature in one way or in the other, that one view may be wrong and the other right. These alternatives, of course, do not lead to the kind of paradoxes I have discussed. The issue is that seeing human nature in these ways requires us to adopt alternative views in which *the terms of comparison between the views,* like "sameness" above, *shift their meanings,* so that these views *exclude the possibility of each other.* If one's nature requires one to change (so as to become what one *is*), the meaning of nature (of "is") shifts: one "is" what one "is not" yet, one's "nature" is something other than itself. As a result, when one is engaged in considering the truth of either of these views (that change is possible for a nature, and that change is not possible for a nature), that is, when one is operating with either view's own meanings to examine the issue, *there is simply no meaningful alternative view* to contrast it with in respect of those meanings. (Given a set of meanings, again, what "is" simply "is," after all. And this applies to *either* sense of "nature," of "is," the one that intrinsically does not change or that one that intrinsically does.)

Where the terms of comparison themselves shift between the alternative views like this, there is no balanced comparison of the alternative views but only the comparison as *already* understood in the exclusive terms of one view or of the other. As a result, because the terms of comparison themselves have different meanings in each view, each view in the very act of comparison excludes the possibility of the other as having any relevant meaning of its *own,* ultimately different from the comparing view's, at all. In this situation, the particular view one is considering is the *only* meaningful and therefore possible view *there can be.* But this applies to *both* views. Here there is *more than one* view that is the *only meaningful and therefore the only possible* view.

Consequently, if one could be said to balance these alternative views at all, then it would not be the case that one view may simply be right and the other wrong, but that human nature itself is sometimes simply and exclusively and in general (always) one thing, and sometimes simply and exclusively and in general (always) another, incompatible thing.

But we *must* be able to talk about balancing both views because, as the argument above about the meaning of "sameness" in the changing person shows, each view *itself* implies or presupposes the possibility of the other (while it *also* wholly excludes it) when one contemplates change (that is, let me stress, only sometimes), and at least one of these views *does* contemplate change. Further, one can always legitimately ask whether the view that denies the sense of change is right, and so also in another way contemplate change within its framework or, rather, on the borders of its framework. (In fact, here the framework is incompatible with *itself*, for all the reasons I discussed above in the comparison of different frameworks. But this does not necessarily invalidate it: for these same reasons, "sometimes" logic, with the sense it sometimes gives to incompatibilities, applies here too.) In other words—and this is a topic to which I return below—since from within the purview of each view there are simply no alternative meaningful views and since we can nonetheless balance them against each other, we can conceive two or more incompatible views *both* of which are *absolutely* right.[8] What is more, since each view sometimes implies or presupposes the possibility of the other, if either view is right, then sometimes both incompatible views *are* absolutely right. All this is a result of talking about a "nature": what something *is*. If a conflict can be conceived or contemplated in the *nature* of something, in what it is, then that conflict is a conflict in the nature of reality itself.

One can also phrase this "sometimes" logic as: sometimes, but *only sometimes,* this dimension of reality is *always exclusively* like this;[9] or in this respect, but *only* in this respect, this dimension of reality is like this in *all* respects; or sometimes the very same thing is a different thing.

Second, this entire argument so far remains an argument, partly artificial, not simply a given piece of nature. And part of the force of the argument itself has been that the meanings of the terms on which its own sense depends, terms like "same" and "different," shift in unclear ways with unclear consequences. Consequently it will always be possible to reconsider this kind of view, and perhaps to find circumstances in which alternative views genuinely hold more weight, even while it continues to be genuinely convincing in other circumstances. It is possible, then, that not everyone has the fortune and/or misfortune to happen on such a sometime or respect in which one is not at bottom a simple unity.

This "*sometimes* not a simple unity, *sometimes* not *a* simple nature," if true, is profoundly important. It requires that we—legitimately—*shift* our criteria and the meanings of the terms on whose basis we make the *same* evaluation. For example, with respect to social and political attitudes, it requires that we sometimes, perhaps frequently, not condemn prejudiced people, including ourselves, for what they cannot help, but rather admire and encourage their nobility in undertaking the hardship of accepting their simply given, natural limitations in order to be as little destructive as possible. And it also requires the alternative, based on a conflicting idea of what naturalness *can mean,* that we perhaps recognize and appreciate the true natural givenness of people who genuinely change. They have as little choice, for example—or as much—as the others. Again, each sense of naturalness here excludes the other: that to which one ought to remain true and simply cannot change from because it is simply who one is; and that to which one ought to change in order to be really true to oneself, perhaps even together with the period of undecidedness between natures that can also be part of such a nature. And both senses of naturalness construe the *"same"* thing—they are both senses of the same thing (while also, incompatibly, being mutually exclusive)—because, again, as the argument above about the meaning of "sameness" in the changing person shows, at times of change or contemplation of change, each sense *itself implies or presupposes* the possibility of the other.[10]

"Sometimes" logic also requires that we keep open the possibilities of both kinds of naturalness and both kinds of artificiality, until the person, be it ourselves or someone else, finds in him/herself which is which.

Also, because of this "sometimes" logic, this result of undecidedness as to which conflicting meaning to attach to one's truth in order even to go about making a decision, there are points at which one has to suspend evaluation of one's own feeling and/or conduct precisely for the sake of that evaluation of feeling and conduct. One needs to avoid subjecting the decision to categories of evaluation that—since they simply exclusively describe one thing as one thing or the other as the other without also offering the possibility of suspending themselves—are themselves part of what the indecision is about. But this suspension of evaluation itself aims at a moral self-evaluation. And the undecidedness is part of the truth of what one is at such times. Carrying out the undecidedness, suspending the evaluation, is therefore itself something one can perhaps evaluate as morally prideworthy about oneself. Sometimes, then, just this suspension of evaluation of conduct and/or feeling itself can be the thing to value, to take pride in, or to be ashamed of not doing.

Evaluation here shifts to the metalevel, the level that thinks *about* the level of what is being evaluated. One can be legitimately proud of allowing oneself to be uncertain as to whether to be proud or ashamed, or as to what to be proud of. That is, one can be proud of one's ignorance about oneself. And one can be passionate or spontaneous in the suspension of indulging one's passion or in ignoring one's spontaneous feelings, in being dispassionate. One might do so, for example, in the interests of allowing the genuineness or appropriateness of the feeling to be established: this is itself a carrying out of the aims of the feeling or spontaneity.[11] This kind of dispassion is also necessary, for example, to make room to establish the legitimate claims of conflicting passions, either in oneself or between conflicting parties. Again, this is a dispassion that is itself a carrying out of the claims and aims of passion.

The need to keep open the possible validity of both sets of incompatible possibilities and evaluations as to which is the natural self and which is the artificial self, at least during the process of change or of deciding whether change is necessary, requires a kind of thinking in which the very categories of sameness and difference, nature (essence) and artifice are thought differently. There are two striking dimensions to this different thinking. First, these categories, defined as they are by mutual exclusion, must sometimes be thought together, as being in a sense the same thing, as I argued above. This last sentence itself makes no sense without that different thinking. Second, they must only *sometimes* be thought that way, as I suggested here and as I argue in the following ideas in this part. When the process of change or of decision about change comes to an end or when it has not yet begun, there is no reason to question those categories, and every reason to apply them in their customary meanings.

It follows that this different thinking must allow these mutually exclusive categories to be thought together, *and* to be thought simply separately, *and* to be thought as *both* of these—for example, when accounting for the shift from the process to a point after its end, or when accounting for *this kind of thinking itself,* whose very substance consists in considering the possibility *and* impossibility of mutually exclusive categories.

Maurice Merleau-Ponty writes, "the accusation of contradiction is not decisive, *if the acknowledged contradiction appears as the very condition of consciousness. It is in this sense that Plato and Kant, to mention only them, accepted the contradiction of which Zeno and Hume wanted no part.*"[12] He continues, however, "there is a vain form of contradiction which consists in affirming two theses which exclude one another at the same time and under the same aspect." As I argue below, the contradiction at the basis of thinking involves just this kind of mutual exclusion, but in a way that requires rethinking the idea of exclusion itself. That is, this kind of contradiction establishes the meanings of the basic categories of thinking, including the categories of "the same time" and "the same aspect," so that it cannot simply be said to be governed by those categories. On the other hand, it is itself *also* part of what the thinking it establishes thinks about, so that it *is also* subject to those categories. Consequently I argue that it is right, but only *sometimes* right, to speak of it as this kind of contradiction.

In Plato's *Sophist*, the Stranger is made to say about some of the basic aspects of reality (among the aspects he discusses are being itself, sameness itself, difference itself) that "one of these alternatives must be true—either all will blend, or none, or some will and some will not."[13] Now these are basic aspects of reality as such, of *everything* we might mean by reality. Consequently, when one considers alternative ways of their relating to each other, one is considering the whole of reality, reality in general, in alternative ways. It is not that one is occupying a certain viewpoint and considering alternatives each accessible from it, but that each different alternative transforms the reality of one's viewpoint itself, which is part of reality-as-a-whole. It follows, then, that these alternative relations of the basic aspects of reality are incompatible even in the sense that they cannot be simultaneously thought, since each differently constitutes the very viewpoint that thinks them.[14]

Plato himself draws explicit attention to this kind of effect of the subject matter on the viewpoint that considers it and in fact devotes most of the *Sophist* to resolving an aspect of it. He argues that:

> the nonexistent reduces even one who is refuting its claims to such straits that, as soon as he sets about doing so, he is forced to contradict himself. . . . I was speaking of its *being* a thing not to be uttered. . . . Well, then, in trying to apply that term "being" to it, was I not contradicting what I said before?[15]

The problem generalizes to the entire viewpoint that considers it, since all images or likenesses, including the words with which we think and discuss, "are not" (are "nonexistent" as) the truth they represent.[16] As a result all words, and so anything that might be said about the truth, get caught up in the constraints of this subject matter. As the Stranger says in a different connection later in the dialogue, "to rob us of discourse would be to rob us of philosophy":[17] more generally, a subject matter that affects the structure of discourse affects the viewpoint that allows us access to the truth about the subject matter.

But the thinking about reality that allows the Stranger's statement about the alternatives to be made, justified, or criticized must itself allow all of these alternatives to be considered. And it must allow all of them as they are: that is, all of them in their mutually exclusive incompatibility. Whatever Plato's conclusions about reality might then be, what he does in coming to those conclusions in the first place—in *approaching* those conclusions—must exhibit a "sometimes" thinking of the kind I have described above. It must hold them together, and it cannot hold them together, and both of these alternatives are necessary, and both necessarily remain questionable.[18] And this is no longer only a matter of subjective reality but of reality in general.

This is much like the description often given of ancient Greek tragedy, the tragedy whose insights formed part of Plato's environment: a conflict between two necessities where neither of them can be denied and yet a choice must be made as to which of them to deny. But while Plato, I believe, learned from this kind of insight, it is only part of what he has to offer. Here we are dealing with a "sometimes" logic, and sometimes reality is truly described without any reference to such a conflict—or even to such a "sometimes" logic.

IDEA 2

Knowledge as Intervention: Difficulties and Solutions

The second idea I want to discuss as basic to Plato involves the relation between two properties or dimensions of knowledge. First, there is knowledge as true description, or an equivalent to true description, of what it is knowledge of. Second, there is knowledge as something that intervenes in what it describes, something that has reality in its own right and therefore has effects on, changes, what it is knowledge of.

By way of anticipation, let me note that Plato deals extensively with the effects of people's supposed or actual knowledge on themselves and other people. It will become clear that an important aspect of these effects is the relation between the one kind of knowledge and the other. This contrast also appears in a variety of forms in discussions of Plato, although without exploration of the deep difficulties it presents that I want to pursue here. One way it appears is in the idea that Socrates' refutations of his interlocutors' beliefs are aimed at moral change and not only or even primarily intellectual change. Terence Irwin, for example, suggests that for Socrates in the *Apology*, "engaging in the *elenchos* [refutation] is a means to moral reform."[1] This is a change in the *person* that is brought about by examination of claims to knowledge in the form of true description. Another way this contrast emerges is in the idea that knowledge is partly a kind of activity rather than just a collection (or system) of descriptive judgments, a state. Hugh Benson, for example, argues that for Plato's Socrates, knowledge involves a "*dunamis*," an activity of grasping, without which "the cognitive states one has . . . are not knowledge states, and with it, whatever cognitive states one has, are."[2]

The difficulty I want to explore is that the interventive property interferes with the descriptive one.[3] If knowledge changes what it is knowledge of by describing it, then the description is no longer true.

In these terms, the discussion in Idea 1 of the true natures of people and things attempts a descriptive truth of truth itself, while here I attempt to explore the significance of the interventive dimension of knowledge for truth itself.

This relation between different senses or characteristics of knowledge is immediately evident in purely human contexts and interactions. For example, if someone recognizes that s/he is primarily a selfish person, this recognition itself can provoke her/him to change. The fact of true description itself, then, changes the truth and makes the statement descriptively false. Similarly, if we truly describe someone as a primarily selfish person and we say it *to* her/him, this can provoke her/him to change. Further, even if we do not state it to the person, the knowledge itself involves our behaving toward the other person in accordance with that knowledge, and that can result in their changing.

In fact, this recognition, this descriptive truth had by the person about her/himself, *is* already a change that makes the description at least partly false. If the person can see him/herself as selfish—or dishonest, which is a clearer example here—then s/he has partially transcended that selfishness or dishonesty. She is honest in seeing her/himself truthfully as dishonest. And s/he is unselfish because by seeing him/herself from the perspectives of others, s/he is taking the concerns of others seriously, at least to the extent of being able to understand their viewpoints even while these do not serve her interests.

A possible objection to what I have said about this example is that if the person changes, then the original statement did not give the truth about the person's essence, about what s/he primarily was. Either the original statement was false, and the change in the person simply shows that, or the change was superficial, secondary, artificial, or inessential and did not affect the person as such.

This objection raises some issues it will be helpful to pursue before exploring alternative kinds of case. Recourse to the idea of an "essence" is an attempt to show at the deepest level that there is a truth of whatever has the essence, that something genuinely, truly is what it is. Consequently my comments about knowledge and its effects on truth have direct bearing on this idea of essence itself. And it is already evident that the idea of essence has direct bearing on what can be said about knowledge and its effects on truth. I therefore briefly explore the relation between knowledge (as true description) and the idea of essence before returning to the relation between the descriptive and effective characteristics of knowledge.

2.1. KNOWLEDGE AND ESSENCE

The objection stated above assumes that an essence cannot become transformed or give way to another essence. What it is to be an essence is precisely to be one thing and not another, and it makes no sense to speak of an essence becoming another essence. One tradition that works on this assumption is the one that has allowed Plato's theory of Ideas to be understood as his primary doctrine. It may be a true assumption. If it is, then, as Aristotle points out, there is no essential change, no real history or growth.[4] Any possible change is already written into the essence of the changing thing and does not involve the thing's becoming something different in any respect that has to do with its essence. The thing's secondary properties change; it itself does not.

If the opposite assumption is true and essences can change, then, as Aristotle points out[5] and Plato has Socrates argue,[6] there is no essence of anything to be truly described. What the thing is would not be definitely opposed to its being anything else. There could be no true statement about it, therefore, that would be anything like a description, since it could not exclude any number of conflicting statements. We might say as an equivalent today that truth is our conventional fixing of distinctions and categories on a chaotic world. Many of the ancient Sophists, whom Plato opposed, said just this. But these conventional ways of fixing distinctions are subject to the same difficulty, since they function only if we take them to mean something, and what they might mean falls under the same alternatives for essence outlined above.

It seems, then, that one has no choice but to assume an essence that cannot change, and my example is faulty.

Now, both of these alternatives take an essence to be what something *necessarily* is, what it *has* to be, as opposed to what it happens to have turned out to be. This second sense of essence, in contrast, both allows true description, since the thing is definitely a certain thing and not others, and it allows us to think essential change, since there is no reason why the thing cannot become something else under the right conditions.[7] This second sense of essence, however, allows us to conceive a change of essence and so returns us to the difficulty that the interventive property of knowledge can interfere with its descriptive property.

But even without that difficulty, something is lost by the second sense of essence. It rules out in advance the possibility of thinking, for example, the senses in which a wrong or right change might have been made, or in which something might be *naturally* and *permanently* best one way rather than another.[8] Certainly, one can question whether there is ever such a nature or such a nonarbitrary change. But one does not question it by ruling out the possibility of considering it at all in the first place.

The problem of thinking about essence is worse than being faced with alternative accounts of it, however. (My aim is, in fact, to show that if one looks at the problem at its worst, the radical nature of the problem itself offers a solution.) The problem is worse because one cannot even start to decide between accounts, even if one of them appears entirely satisfactory. One cannot meaningfully argue which of these or any ideas of essence is the right one. One's argument has to presuppose at least what is meant by truth: but truth also has an essence (or not), and so we would presuppose one of these ideas of essence (or no essence) even before we could start to consider the matter. In other words, we cannot come to a decision about this question without already having decided. We cannot escape the necessity of maintaining an indecision as to which idea is valid.

But on the other hand, we are therefore entitled to consider either alternative in the present case, since neither can be ruled out in advance.

Now, of course, in order to think at all, we need to begin with *some* presupposition. I suggest, however, that this very process of maintaining an indecision about essence, *together with* the following of a particular presupposition about it, has the following peculiarity. It allows us to investigate the world in such a way that whatever presupposition we follow, although decided on in advance, does not prevent itself in advance from being invalidated. That is, it allows the search for knowledge not to be circularly trapped in its starting assumptions and frame of reference. For the indecision about essence is, differently expressed, an indecision about what the very thing *is* that one is deciding about. That is, it is an indecision about the very categories on the basis of which one might make the decision at all, or might even think that there is a decision to make, or even that there is definitely something to make a decision about. It keeps open the possibility that one might need to think in ways that are excluded by the meanings of one's current assumptions and frame of reference. So this indecision in fact allows one not to be *simply* precommitted to the categories of one's presupposition even while one's thinking is also governed by them.

Given that the "nature" of something and its "essence" both refer to "what it truly is," I argued this possibility in Idea 1 in discussing the balancing of mutually exclusive construals of the nature of something. One dimension of what I want to explore in this book can be expressed as that and how this kind of indecision about essence, what I call fundamental indecision, together with a decision (or alternatively with a presupposition one did not "decide" on but that one rather found oneself following), works in establishing both truth and knowledge.

Such an indecision together with a decision is, I think, a fair description of philosophical thinking. The necessity of this combination explains why one is justified in speaking of an "approach" in serious thinking. As I mentioned at the start of this Part, the term "approach" suggests we can arbitrarily pick and choose how to go about thinking. It follows from the necessity of both fundamental indecision and a particular decision that in fact we *must* arbitrarily pick and choose, or arbitrarily find ourselves following, our initial assumption in this way.

In the process, as I discuss in Idea 4, we discover truth not only about the subject matter of our inquiry but also about ourselves, as our reasons for choosing or following the assumption emerge after the fact of choosing or following. And as I also discuss there, truth about ourselves is not simply unconnected to truth about the subject matter of our inquiry.[9]

The necessity of this combination also explains why the balancing of risks that I mentioned in the introductory section to this Part is fundamental to serious thought. One has to explore all the relevant possible assumptions and balance or weigh them against each other. But they are all explored in the context of the fundamental indecision: which means that they are all initially risks and remain risks until they have been weighed against the alternative assumptions, each explored in its own right in the context of this indecision.[10]

There is a sense in which, as I argue of Plato's theory of Ideas, the presupposition and the reasoning based on it, taken as a risk in the context of this kind of indecision, are a fiction that gives access to truth, and are indispensable for that purpose.[11] But being indispensable in finding truth, it is not *only* a fiction but has something to do with truth itself.[12] Truth here shows an internal connection to falsehood, and not only (as in the discussion in Idea 1) the other way round.[13] As Plato frequently has Socrates insist, one cannot come to know without first exploring assumptions that are brought to light only by being invalidated. For example, "Do you suppose . . . he would have attempted to look for, or learn, what he thought he knew, though he did not, before he was thrown into perplexity, became aware of his ignorance, and felt a desire to know?"[14]

The example of telling someone a truth about her/himself with which I began this Idea, then, has bearing on the fundamentals of knowledge if only because it itself requires to be treated with the indecision that I argue is pertinent to establishing essences or natures. Giving it the benefit of this kind of indecision, however, I return to its own content. Knowledge that is a true description can be an intervention that changes what it is knowledge of, and thereby invalidates itself as descriptive knowledge in such cases. The relation between these two kinds of knowledge is also involved in knowledge of the inanimate world in ways I discuss below.[15]

2.2. KNOWLEDGE AS INTERVENTION AND DESCRIPTION

To move to a less immediately concrete level, the most fundamental problem here is that statements about the world in general (for example, "everything is composed of atoms and space, or of energy") and about human beings in general (for example, "everything can be explained in terms of sex and aggression, or pleasure and pain, or reward and punishment, or social structure") are also statements about knowledge itself, since knowledge is included in the world in general and in the human constitution. And descriptive statements about the nature of knowledge immediately affect what they are statements about. This is so for two reasons. First, the act of stating or knowing adds something—itself—to the world that was not there when the description was made or thought and that is part of the "everything" that is being described. The act of stating and knowing must therefore be included in the description. But then the more inclusive statement that contains it is a new act of stating or knowing that must now be included. And so on.

Second, descriptive statements or thoughts, being items of knowledge themselves, immediately have their status affected by descriptions of the nature of knowledge. If, for example, one says, "all knowledge is really social convention,"[16] that applies to this statement itself, which thereby loses its claim to truth over other "conventions" that contradict it. Analogously, Plato has Socrates argue with respect to Protagoras's "man is the measure of all things" that "if the majority of men do not agree with him, . . . Protagoras admits, I presume, that the contrary opinion about his own opinion (namely that it is false) must be true, seeing he agrees that all men judge what is."[17] The statement invalidates itself as true and thereby grants possible validity to "conventions" that claim they are not conventions but true. The statement or knowledge is included in what it is talking about and consequently alters itself as soon as it exists.

There are, then, all sorts of truth statements that we simply cannot make or know, because of the mutual interference of the descriptive and interventive properties of truth, even though what these statements claim might be very important.[18]

In the case of knowledge about knowledge itself, the knowledge does not merely *subsequently* change what it is knowledge of and make itself false. This is a separate problem, important when we do not want to impose ourselves on a situation while still wanting our perceptions to be registered and understood in it. Knowledge about knowledge, rather, is self-altering from the start—*does not make sense from the start*.[19]

We need to have knowledge about knowledge in order to have knowledge about things in general and things as a whole. If we do not have knowledge about knowledge, it seems that we cannot have knowledge about anything, since we would not know what was valid knowledge and what was really a mistake. We certainly could not have knowledge about things as a whole, which include knowledge. And if we do not have knowledge about things as a whole, it is arguable that we have no proper context for knowledge of the parts of that whole and therefore no such partial knowledge either. This problem, then, is not merely academic.

I want to suggest, however, that, if we think through the interventive property of knowledge properly, we find a way of articulating knowledge that is description in a way that does not invalidate itself. Considering this very abstractly for the moment, if we take seriously the interventive dimension of knowledge, we can note that it also intervenes in *itself*, including its interventive dimension. That is, knowledge alters its interventive status also, and so it becomes undecidable whether its interventive property involves an interference with its descriptive property, or is so self-intervening as to cancel itself altogether and leave its descriptive property intact.[20] Knowledge becomes literally meaningless since it is undecidable in this way. And this returns us to the kind of fundamental indecision discussed above and in Idea 1. This kind of indecision, then, allows us to start over with the exploration of descriptive decisions. These descriptions need not take into account a possible interference with what they describe, because at that point the interventive property has already made even its own interference with meaning meaningless.

If we do not acknowledge the interventive aspect of description or descriptive thought, we will be perpetually claiming to know what we cannot know—precisely what Plato's Socrates tries to avoid. On the other hand, I suggest, if we grant the *unqualified* validity of the interventive property, the problem or paradox turns against and solves itself.[21] This is what I meant in my parenthetical suggestion above that the radical worst of the problem is also its solution. When rigorous thought is most rigorous, when it becomes most fully responsible and looks properly to its justification by taking itself into account and not only parts of the world other than itself, it becomes self-interfering, paradoxical, undecidable, meaningless. And precisely because it does so with radical consistency, I argue below, its very meaninglessness itself becomes meaningless.[22] In this way, rigorous thought allows an inquiry into and establishment of truth that is properly justified, because it neither leaves itself partly unquestioned nor simply rejects itself in advance.

So Plato, as I argue below, *always* shows Socrates and others making mistakes, not simply to make the truth clearer by contrast when it is found but because truth can be established only by interfering with the process of establishing truth itself, that is by making mistakes. Most generally, the very search for truth as a whole, and therefore also in its parts, which depend on that whole for their meaning, is literally meaningless, most fully mistaken, as I argued above. And it works meaningfully by accepting and engaging in that mistake, that meaninglessness. Heading off at tangents from the line of thinking toward a truth, periodically missing the point one aims to make, even going in the opposite direction, *is* part of that direct line. Socrates avoids the mistake of claiming to know what he does not know by making it, recognizing it, and working with it. He is not in a position to know that he is not making a mistake unless the process of checking is allowed, and allowing that process means pursuing the line of thought that may be mistaken.

This is why I can argue in support of one tradition that Plato's theory of Ideas is a mistake of which he was aware—and so is not a theory he held—and at the same time argue in support of another tradition that the theory of Ideas captures fundamental truth—and so *is* Plato's theory. In fact, on my argument the two traditions are not simply opposed, but each is *also* only fully justified by the other.

Continuing, then: as I argued above, if this fiction or artificiality which (as I suggested above) is careful thought does not question itself, it can get in its own way in establishing truth. Differently expressed, a truth can come into conflict with the conditions that make that truth what it is by changing those conditions. And, I propose, thinking can succeed in getting itself out of its own way by questioning itself, because questioning, being thinking, also has an interventive character. It is effective in making thinking meaningless.

As I argue further in this Part, the naïve initial impression that rigorous thought is a nonsensical artificiality—an inessential and unnecessary addition to the world—is a true impression. But it underrates at least some kinds of nonsensical artificiality, and leaves itself without the resources to notice or deal with other kinds of nonsensical artificiality that, as I discuss below, it itself already inevitably perpetrates. This underrating is a mistake that fiction writers do not make, at least in connection with their own genre. I believe that Plato did not make this mistake in connection with his genre either.

2.3. KNOWLEDGE AS INTERVENTION
AND THE ROLE OF THE CONDITIONS OF TRUTH

I turn now to some concrete and in fact fairly simple examples of how the descriptive property of truth can be maintained precisely by acknowledging and allowing the effects of the interventive property. I discuss several different ways in which this can happen. I should note that while these examples show that it is at least sometimes possible to maintain descriptive truth, this possibility still needs to be *understood*. In other words, it must still be explained *how* it is possible, how this possibility works and makes sense. As the book proceeds, I argue that Plato offers a way to understand this possibility and its implications for the nature of thinking and of the world.

In particular, the following examples rely on two possibilities that are actually main theses of this book and so will be developed as the book proceeds: first, that descriptive truth and its self-interfering effects can be or become entirely separate from, entirely external to each other; and second, that one can focus entirely away from a truth in a way that is *also* relevant to it. I have already given some indication in Idea 1 (especially 1.2) that different dimensions of the same truth (in this case, descriptive truth and its effects) can be purely external while also internally relevant to each other (the "sometimes always" logic again). But I argue primarily in Idea 8.1 that this kind of relation is possible. Here I concentrate on exploring some practical ways of trying to establish that separation between these dimensions of truth, to give an idea of the concrete possibility of what I argue (mainly) in Idea 8.1 is also logically possible and ultimately comprehensible (so that, for example, my interpretation of these examples just below would not be automatically mistaken, would not necessarily create at best only the illusion of making sense).

In the course of these examples, I begin to focus on the relevance of the fact that truth also has a truth, that there is truth about truth itself: that truth itself has conditions that as the conditions *for truth,* enter into the character of the truth they condition.

In an interpersonal context, one way in which we can have a true description, the knowledge of which would otherwise change what it is knowledge about, is by holding or presenting it in such a way that it can be ignored. For example, "I know you don't want to discuss this, and I think you're right not to want to, so just let me say something about it and then we'll talk about something else and not mention this again." In this kind of case we can take the bite out of the effects of what we say precisely by allowing those effects and acknowledging their significance. Now, this is purely a matter of tact; but that does not diminish its value. On the contrary, it means that tact is not only an ornament or smoothing of truth but can also be fundamental to establishing it.[23]

A second way in which we can have such a true description is by saying or thinking it wrongly, in a way that lets it be known that it is wrong. This can be done, for example, with humor, or in the very pedestrian way of simply saying that it is wrong and leaving it that way.

In the *Symposium,* Plato shows Socrates making a very feeble joke to reassure Aristodemus that he can come to a drinking party or symposium hosted by Agathon (translatable as "Goodman") uninvited.[24] The joke is a mangling of a proverbial saying about attending feasts, a mangling that confuses what is good and bad relevant to social appropriateness and leaves the truth about them in suspense:

> "I know [says Socrates] you haven't been invited to the dinner; how would you like to come anyway?"
>
> And Aristodemus answered, "I'll do whatever you say."
>
> "Come with me then," Socrates said, "and we shall prove the proverb wrong [the proverb states, 'Good men go uninvited to an inferior man's feast']25; the truth is, 'Good men go uninvited to Goodman's feast.' Even Homer, when you think about it, did not much like this proverb; he not only disregarded it, he violated it. Agamemnon, of course, is one of his great warriors, while he describes Menelaus as a 'limp spearman.' And yet, when Agamemnon offers a sacrifice and gives a feast, Homer has the weak Menelaus arrive uninvited at his superior's table."26

Socrates reassuringly accomplishes a suspense of socially appropriate good and bad with respect to his own social presence, by telling an obviously feeble joke in the course of presenting himself as knowing what is socially appropriate. The joke also makes a point that is an obvious mistake (to an audience steeped in Homer, as Plato's was) in two different ways: first, the comparison between Aristodemus's and Menelaus's situations is hardly apt;[27] and second, the point he does make contradicts his purported intention of putting Aristodemus at ease, since it evokes exactly the painful point of inferiority, as Aristodemus's reply below shows. Socrates intensifies this suspense of appropriateness by elaborating, still feebly and wrongly, on the wrongness of the message given by his wrong version of the point. In contrast with what he achieves by the (descriptive) content of the joke, he accomplishes this suspense more fully by virtue of the effects of what he does in expressing the content, that is, by intervention. And suspending what is relevantly good and bad is also just what he does, interventively, in his own actions, by taking the initiative in inviting Aristodemus and so suspending the pertinent formal rules of partygoing.

Aristodemus's next statement shows not only that arriving late is a concern for him, so that reassurance is needed, but also that he is too feisty or too worried to accept direct and simple reassurance:

> "Socrates, I am afraid Homer's description is bound to fit me better than yours. Mine is a case of an obvious inferior arriving uninvited at the table of a man of letters. I think you'd better figure out a good excuse for bringing me along, because, you know, I won't admit I've come without an invitation. I'll say I'm your guest."[28]

Direct reassurance would therefore force him to deal with an uncomfortable concern in an uncomfortable way, achieving the opposite of reassurance. The reassurance would be a descriptive truth, whose acknowledgment would achieve the opposite of the aim that motivated the statement of the truth. The statement would remain descriptively true but would no longer be a true act, true to the situation and to its aim.

More than this, however, truth itself has a truth, that extends beyond its immediate presentation to its justification and its place in the order of purposes and things. Consequently, if the statement is not true to the situation and its aim, the descriptive truth of the statement is *itself* vitiated. Its describable aim, the unstated part of it that says, "*you can be reassured* because . . . ," would in fact now be false, exactly in consequence of the stating of the descriptive truth itself. Aristodemus would no longer be able to take the description as a reassurance, because the description itself would prevent that. Further, that unstated aim is not only itself describable but is implicitly involved in the stated content of the truth statement that has that aim. The aim is part of the context of the description, and, like any piece of language, the description without its context and aim simply does not have the same meaning that it has with them.[29] It is simply not the same descriptive truth.

Socrates' self-interfering, interventive way of saying the descriptive truth, on the other hand, saying it wrongly in several obvious ways and leaving it so, holds the truth itself in suspense and so removes its impact. It is the interventive, self-interfering property of truth that works against itself here to *allow* its descriptive property to be maintained unchanged.

That Plato shows this being done by means of a misquoted saying and references to fiction (Homer's poetry) on Socrates' part—and that this happens on Socrates' very first appearance in the dialogue—might suggest that we should consider the corresponding features of Plato's dialogue itself. It is fictional, and is structured as a series of speeches that Plato himself could never have heard even if they had been real, so that he could only be misquoting them.[30] Furthermore, it is presented as a series of quoted accounts of quoted accounts of the event. This initial framing, the prominent initial placing of Socrates' efficacious misquotational foolery, and the way this foolery achieves its effects all suggest that these features of the dialogue may well be relevant in some way to the truth claims in it. There is a great deal of further support for this suggestion in the composition of the dialogue: two of the formal speeches in the *Symposium* are given by a comic and a tragic poet respectively; the tragic poet is Agathon, mentioned in Socrates' mangled proverb, and whom the party honors; Socrates is shown at the end discussing the capabilities of tragic and comic poets with these two characters (they discuss whether one person can write both kinds of work); and most of Socrates' own formal speech at the party consists in a complete fiction involving his own fictional quotations of his fictional teacher Diotima. I return to this interweaving of fiction and truth below.

Because the episode from the *Symposium* that I have discussed here is purely a social interaction, and in a context apparently unrelated to the main theme of the dialogue—the theme of love—it may seem that it really has no bearing on the metaphysical truths—truths about the nature of reality—with which Plato is thought to be concerned or on the essential questions about knowledge that I am using it to exemplify. But the entire pervasive setting of the dialogue has to do with a social event, after which, after all, the dialogue is named.[31] Judging by the name, the protagonist of this drama is a social event, and a frivolous one at that.[32] And the episode I discuss *is* related to the theme of love, is in fact an exhibition of loving action on Socrates' part, and all the more so because it is not grandiose. In fact it has to do with erotic love, which is specifically the kind of love addressed in the dialogue. By this point in the dialogue, Aristodemus has already been described as having gone "to the party because, I think, he was obsessed with Socrates—one of the worst cases at that time."[33] I shall return to these dimensions of the *Symposium* as well.

A third way of maintaining a true description in the face of its interventive character is an extreme form of the last one: to make a false statement or know falsely. This may not appear to be a way of solving the problem of true description, since it involves simple falsehood. But, as I have already begun to indicate, there are contexts in which the interventive character of knowledge is such that the falsehood actually disappears as relevant and, as it were, emerges on the side of truth.

For example, an angry person may say "I am not angry" or act as if s/he were not angry in order to allow a resolution of her/his anger and/or the situation that caused it (despite the unconscious and fairly widespread crassness of taking the truths of psychotherapy out of their very limited context). This might be appropriate in a case where, for example, if the anger is simply stated, the other person's own emotions would cause her/him to misinterpret its focus or significance, or where if the angry person stated her/his anger, just that small release of it would make it all-consuming. A statement of the descriptive truth, then, would alter the situation it describes, making the truth undecidable. (Similarly, when Socrates says, "I know nothing," this is patently not true as it stands; but saying he does know something would certainly mislead an audience with a different conception of knowledge itself from his own, and might also provoke his audience, in either case removing the conditions for establishing the truth that he knows.) Later the conditions for deciding relevant truth or falsehood may be established, so that statements relevant to the context can be made without immediately changing what they describe—so that they *can be* false or true. The statement "I am not angry" does then become a past falsehood. But at that same later point the contrasting truth can be made known and is no longer relevant: the falsehood is therefore both irrelevant and what allowed the truth to emerge. Once the situation is such that statements can be true or false, rather than abuse or defense or productive of more falsehood than truth, the past falsehood is closer to being a true statement than to being a false one. We are back here to something closer to the second way of maintaining descriptive truth discussed above: something said wrongly rather than falsely.

It is the falsehood alone, then, that provides the conditions for the possibility of saying and thereby realizing (making real, both subjectively and objectively) the truth at all in the pertinent connection. It is, therefore, in fact neither true nor false at the time, given (I give another example almost immediately below) that the truth of a statement also involves broader considerations of how a truth is placed in the order of its own purposes, validations, justifications, and effects. Given, that is, that there is truth about truth itself, that truth *about* is essentially connected with truth *to* a situation and purpose. (In this connection, see also the discussion of the relevance of the truth of the knower in Idea 4.2.)

This is again a matter of taking the interventive property of truth into account *for the sake of* its descriptive property. Because of its interventive property, the statement or action that said "I am angry" would have said many other things that would have remained false and would have had effects, including the removal of the possibility of correcting the false impressions. These false impressions then acquire a life of their own and become true subsequently and independently. Like truth, falsehood has interventive effects, and here they would be the consequence of the true statement in the wrong place. Further, even at the time of the statement the impressions would have been false indicators of the truth of the anger itself—after all, one becomes angry with someone one likes partly because of contrasting feelings, such as the importance to one of the other's actions and statements. On the other hand, again, by taking that interventive property seriously one is able (sometimes) to avoid those other present and future falsehoods and establish the conditions in which the original true statement can be said.

In fact, later the "lying" person shows him/herself to have behaved more in accordance with not being angry than with being angry, since at the time s/he acted so as to make her/his anger irrelevant rather than to give it prime importance in the situation. It follows that the person later turns out to have been telling the descriptive truth in the first place. This is so even though it can be acknowledged at the later point, without risk of yet greater falsehood, that that initial description at the earlier time, as seen from the later time, was a lie. The underpinning for this was given in Idea 1 (which one expresses or represents the truth about one's feelings more: being angry as one is or the desire to overcome that anger, a desire that is itself the opposite of an angry feeling?).

Again, the interventive character of the description here is what allows its descriptive character to remain unchanged, rather than being what changes it. The context of assessment for interventive descriptions includes not only what the description describes, as with simple descriptions, but also the future outcome of the intervention, the future change in what is described that results from the description of it.[34] It can also happen that the outcome does not allow a retrospective (and, knowledge here being interventive, a retroactive) consideration of the initial situation. My point is only that it can; and because it can, this possibility needs to be taken into account from the start. Consequently the future retroactive establishment of the present truth needs to be taken into account from the start, whether or not the outcome ultimately turns out to allow it.

A fourth way of maintaining a true description in the face of its interventive character is to say or know the thing in an unrelated, irrelevant context: at another time or when a different mood prevails. This is perhaps a variant of the first way, saying the truth in such a way that it can be ignored. But it does depend, again, on the possible conflict between a truth and the conditions that make that truth what it is.

A fifth way is to say something irrelevant to the truth in question. This may seem not to be a way of maintaining the description in question, since in fact it says something by definition irrelevant to it. But in the light of the previous discussions, it should be clear that one not only comes close to saying the thing but does already say part of what is involved in saying it, by maintaining the conditions under which it can be said at some point. A dimension of this is that in circumstances where one cannot say something without coming closer in that act to belying the intention involved in saying it in the first place, one has discharged one's responsibility for saying it by not participating in a gainsaying of it.

An example from *Sense and Sensibility:* Miss Steele has just gaily confessed to Elinor that she eavesdropped to get information about how Elinor's not-so-secretly beloved Edward has been trapped into marriage to someone else. Miss Steele then prattles on at great length about the details of the forthcoming marriage as they affect her own most trivial concerns, ending with the following:

> "Good gracious! (giggling as she spoke) I'd lay my life I know what my
> cousins will say, when they hear of it. They will tell me I should write to the
> Doctor [someone Miss Steele likes to take every opportunity of linking with
> herself], to get Edward the curacy of his new living. . . . 'La!' I shall say

directly, 'I wonder how you could think of such a thing. *I* write to the Doctor, indeed!' "

"Well," said Elinor, "it is a comfort to be prepared against the worst. You have got your answer ready." (274, my insertion)

Here Elinor responds exclusively to the irrelevant triviality with which Miss Steele consummates her wrongdoing and self-absorption. By taking seriously only the immediate content of the indirections in what Miss Steele is saying and not the preoccupations they point to, Elinor expresses the message: "these preoccupations should not have been spoken, and I should not have heard them, and the things I am concerned with do not occur in this context."[35]

It is of course possible to combine these and other ways of maintaining interventive truth as descriptive truth.

All of these ways involve what I called the metalevel of conduct in Idea 1. They all take into account the possible self-interfering effects of the right actions themselves, and so they avoid or alter situations in which the right behavior would also be wrong. That is, they take into account the conditions of the truth of situations and of rightness itself.

IDEA 3

A Philosophical Rhetoric

The third general idea I believe is basic to Plato concerns the nature of a philosophical rhetoric. All the ways of maintaining descriptive truth through interventive truth have to do with the *presentation* of truth or knowledge, including its presentation to oneself. Now, the presentation of truth involves, for example, its orientation to particular audiences or compositional and stylistic choices of sequence, syntax, phrasing, and word type. Even where one is concerned purely with the content of the arguments that are presented, one can—and, I argue, often must—consider the particular choices of issues that are being argued for. Further, since the same point can be demonstrated or suggested equally well through an indefinite variety of arguments, one can consider why the particular presented lines of argument are chosen. All of these considerations belong to the field of rhetoric, traditionally defined as the art of persuasion or, a little later, as the art of speaking well.[1]

These particular kinds of rhetorical considerations are independent with respect to the truth: one can present a glittering, intricately composed, and persuasive argument that is thoroughly flawed with respect to logic and evidence. (In fact, rhetoric has very often been understood to include or be included by reasoned argumentation or the forms of *legitimate* persuasion, what Plato calls dialectic. As already discussed, Plato himself understands rhetoric as part of truth-seeking discussion in the *Phaedrus* (though not, I should note, in most of his work). But I shall use the term here to refer only to those dimensions of rhetoric that are independent with respect to truth or at least to descriptive truth.)[2] The ways of maintaining descriptive truth through interventive truth, therefore, have a connection with rhetoric, which in turn is independent with respect to the truth.

But since all these ways of maintaining interventive truth as descriptive truth also have to do with the possibility of truth itself, they are also more than rhetorical. In fact, as I try to show here, their connection with rhetoric, specifically in the respects in which it is independent of a concern for truth, *is* their connection with the possibility of truth itself. Differently put, rhetoric is not *simply* external to truth, simply added on to it, but is also essential or organic to it, involved in its very nature.[3] Let me stress that this is not to say that truth is reduced to rhetoric but that rhetoric plays a part in truth while *also* being external to it, so that they are *also* independent of and irrelevant to each other.

Rhetoric is often taken to refer to public speaking, but like Plato in the *Phaedrus,* I use the term to refer to all kinds of presentation of thought.[4]

One important example of the organic relation of rhetorical or presentational considerations to truth is the requirement *not* to present the truth as one sees it, either to oneself or to the other person, until s/he has come to see that truth for him/herself. As I discuss in Idea 4 and Idea 7, truth involves an element of risk on the knower's part.[5] Accordingly, if one is to make room for truth for the other person, one has to leave room for his/her own risk. As Hans-Georg Gadamer writes:

> All testing sets up the proposition to be tested not as something for one person to defend, as belonging to him or her, and for the other person to attack, as belonging to the other, but as something "in the middle." And the understanding that emerges is not primarily an understanding resulting from agreement with others but an understanding with oneself. Only people who have reached an understanding with themselves can be in agreement with others.[6]

If one does not make room for the other person's risk, then the conditions of truth, the truth about truth, are in conflict with the content of the truth, and one no more has truth than one does not have it, as in some of the examples in Idea 2. Until the other person has taken her/his risk, either to confirm or disconfirm one's view of the truth, one can only take the risk for oneself. This means that one does *not* know for both parties, and therefore cannot rightly *simply* present this truth as established truth *to oneself* either, as long as one is engaging with the other person's position. Since the other person is in the same position, the simple agreement on the truth may have to occur via, for example, a series of approximations on both sides until the noninfluenced mutuality is *indirectly* evident. At that point the rhetorical considerations become irrelevant, and one can, for example, simply say the content without maintaining a tension between it and the conditions of its being truly said, and without the specific presentation mattering. So the audience can then correct one's own mistakes in presenting one's own truth.

(This importance of the other's understanding should not be taken to presuppose that truth is relative.[7] As I began to argue in Idea 1 and discuss in the concluding chapter of the book, what is at issue here is a kind of thought that need not always oppose relativism and absolutism, or even always use those categories meaningfully at all. Here one's truth is absolute for oneself and the other person—in one's own view—at this time *and* absolutely invalid for both parties from the other point of view. This is not a relativism but more like two absolutisms. But both mutually exclusive absolutisms are in one position, that which discusses the other two and is the one being argued in this book. Accordingly, we need to think both absolutisms at the same time, each from its own point of view. In this context, therefore, the relative/absolute opposition is inadequate to think the issues it purports to grasp.)

The organic relation of rhetoric to truth can also be shown in a different way. Thinking that aims at truth intervenes in its environment and is affected by it. It is therefore also a *negotiation* of truth. It "negotiates" both in the sense of "making its way through obstacles" and in the sense of "bargaining or compromising for its place with counterconcerns." This negotiation is the rhetorical and stylistic dimension of thinking that aims at truth. Because the rhetoric of this kind of thinking negotiates truth, it illuminates it in various ways. It shows, directly or indirectly, the circumstances and concerns involved in truth, and also shows something about the *nature* of those circumstances and concerns. It shows them accurately in the degree that it negotiates them *well*. Much more important, however, because rhetoric and style constitute the negotiation of truth, they are *part of* the general working to get and therefore the working *of* truth. They could not help in the search for truth if they themselves were not already part of the truth, if they were not "truthful." Accordingly they are *part of* the nature of the circumstances and concerns that, *in addition,* they illuminate. That, again, is why they are able to negotiate and illuminate *truth.*

In general, as I argue, truth itself has a truth that involves conditions other than the content of the particular truth at issue. This truth of the truth can conflict with the particular truth in ways catalyzed or obviated by presentation, as in the examples in Idea 2. Again, then, the rhetorical activity of selecting ways of presenting truth is therefore of the essence of, is internal to, truth itself.[8]

That is why, perhaps paradoxically, it is crucial to establish the validity of *external* connections at the very foundations of truth itself. Otherwise the interventive property of knowledge as it operates in the presentation or rhetoric of knowledge (even in its presentation to oneself) is *simply* organically or internally involved in the nature of knowledge and must interfere with *any* possibility of simply descriptive knowledge also. I tried above to show the validity of external connections for (internal) logic in discussing the nature of essence and artificiality.

In fact, rhetoric, as means of persuasion or mechanics of discourse rather than means of achieving truth, is commonly seen either as simply external to truth or as simply internal to and successfully destructive of it. In this second view, logic and rigorous method are just other kinds of persuasion or mechanics of meaning, and so give no truth.[9] My claim, by contrast, is that rhetoric and truth can be external to each other, but only *on the basis of* their essential, internal connection, and in fact vice versa, as I have argued of nature and artifice.

The examples in Idea 2 of ways of maintaining the descriptive property of truth also demonstrate the validity of external and in fact specifically rhetorical connections in establishing and maintaining descriptive truth. When someone makes the rhetorical choice of saying something in a way that is wrong (the Socrates example), a different point has really been expressed, and so the actual point has been missed. Here is an external connection between what is said or thought and the subject matter of the statement or thought. The same is clearly true when someone says something irrelevant to the subject matter (the Elinor example). The discussion of each of these examples linked these external, rhetorical connections with both the content of the truth at issue and the level of the truth of that truth. This linking of the conditions for truth with the particular truth whose nature they condition involves a turning of truth against itself. And the examples show that this self-incompatibility of truth, that is, its difference from *itself* or its externality to itself (its internal externality), itself solves the fundamental problems that arise from it. That is, the interventive property of truth, which alters itself, makes itself different from itself, is invoked to alter and undo that alteration in turn. It is the self-externality of truth that *allows* its self-internality, its being simply what it is, and vice versa. And part of what is (internally) external to truth in this self-undoing way that allows its simplicity here is its modes of presentation, its rhetorical dimensions.

When Plato and his characters, then, are more rhetorical than not—ironic, frivolous, or indirect, for example—their triviality and indirection need not necessarily be explained away in order to rescue their commitment to truth. Nor need these rhetorical features be recognized at the expense of that commitment. In contrast with both of these alternatives, the frivolity, triviality, and indirection of the characters and author may carry out and demonstrate their commitment to truth.[10] Correspondingly, if these features were not there, their absence might demonstrate a lack of depth of rigor in that commitment.

Rhetoric taken as the art of persuasion, of influencing, producing an impression on and communicating with people, relies on the interventive property of truth or knowledge. By contrast, I call the ways of maintaining descriptive truth *through* interventive truth, essential rhetoric.

IDEA 4

Knowledge as Intervention: Advantages

The fourth idea basic to Plato concerns some simply positive aspects of the interventive dimension of knowledge and truth.

4.1. KNOWING IS DOING

First, given that truth and having knowledge themselves have effects, knowledge has practical value even before its applications to specific activities. The most purely theoretical knowledge already *is* concretely effective just in being what it is, without any extra application. This is not to say that there is no such thing as disinterested, purely theoretical knowledge. On the contrary, as I argued in Idea 2, the interventive property of truth *allows* its purely descriptive property. My point is rather that one variety of being practical is simply being something, including being theoretical knowledge. It is not that theoretical knowledge has value only because of its applications (it is not, for example, that "all knowledge can serve political interests"). Rather, applications themselves must be differently understood as including a kind that already occurs in what is purely theoretical, descriptive, and disinterested. Being is itself a kind of doing, and is very different from kinds of doing that are above and beyond the agent's being who or what s/he or it is. An account of this part of the practical relevance of knowledge would only need to trace out what knowledge already is, what difference it makes just by existing. I try to show in detail below how Plato does this.

One example of the difference knowledge makes simply by existing is that recognizing oneself as being a certain kind of person is itself already a change from being that kind of person. The very act of recognizing oneself adds a dimension to oneself that is independent of what it recognizes. And this dimension occurs before any effects of the knowledge that is the recognition: it is simply the existence of that knowledge.[1] In addition, the recognition also has effects, and intervenes in the truth of the self it recognizes.

So, for instance, returning to the issue of the selfish or prejudiced people discussed in Idea 1, recognition that one is selfish or prejudiced is itself a margin of oneself that is beyond being selfish or prejudiced.

It is, of course, possible, as I am arguing, to find ways of maintaining the purely descriptive dimension of one's self-recognition. But the interventive dimension of knowledge means that it is possible for it to be transformative simply by being the knowledge it is.

4.2. THE RELEVANCE OF THE TRUTH OF THE KNOWER

Second, that being is a kind of doing is true not only of the being of knowledge states or statements but also of the being, the truth, of the people who know or try to know.

It follows from the discussion of the interventive dimension of knowledge that knowing (thinking truly) involves being truly. Insofar as descriptive truth is often possible only given recognition of and active participation in its interventive dimensions, it *is* what it is only by taking into account and being in keeping with the nature of its interventions. Therefore truly knowing certain things presupposes, partly *is, being* true to them in certain ways. As Socrates is made to suggest in the *Laches*, it is unsatisfactory if "our deeds are not in accordance with our words."[2] This principle is stated by the famous "Socratic paradox" that virtue *is* knowledge, that to know what is good is to do what is good. Plato and Socrates do not overestimate human virtue in holding this, as many critics have it; rather, the critics misestimate human knowledge in seeing it as independent of how one is.

At the turning point in Plato's *Meno*, where Meno has been reduced to perplexity in trying to define virtue, he presents the following paradox with respect to learning, or gaining knowledge: "how will you look for something when you don't in the least know what it is? . . . even if you come right up against it, how will you know that what you have found is the thing you didn't know?"[3] Socrates initially answers this difficulty by giving a mythical description of the existence of the soul before the present bodily life. The soul has already learned everything in the past and therefore needs only to recollect rather than learn. Now, for one thing, this description does not solve the difficulty: we still need to know how the soul could have learned anything in the past.[4] Second, Socrates introduces the description as one he has "heard from men and women who understand the truths of religion," and from "poets who are divinely inspired."[5] As we know from the

Ion and the *Apology*, Plato's Socrates offers reasons for thinking that it is at least highly questionable whether such inspirations have the status of knowledge.[6] I think, then, that his answer indicates the questionableness of descriptive truth. But it is important that it does so in its indirect way.

I suggest that if, as is often done, we treat the indirect myth or fiction as a metaphor that needs to be interpreted and accordingly translate it into directly descriptive conceptual terms,[7] we miss the point that is made by its form of a myth or fiction. And I suggest that this point is that description on its own lacks the status of knowledge. The form of concepts, being purely descriptive, does not present the interventive dimension borne by a truth in being what it is and in acting as what it is. Accordingly, when we translate the truth of a myth or fiction into conceptual form, we lose the indication that this truth is also such as to put itself in question and perhaps invalidate itself. The mythical or fictional form, in contrast, both presents a description and suspends its status, leaves it undecided as to its truth.[8]

Socrates proceeds to introduce the interventive dimension of knowledge:

> we ought not then to be led astray by the contentious argument. . . . It would make us lazy, and is music in the ears of weaklings. The other doctrine produces energetic seekers after knowledge, and being convinced of its truth, I am ready, with your help, to inquire into the nature of virtue.[9]

The interventive dimension here is referred specifically to the nature of the person seeking knowledge. And this is both a nature it affects and a nature from which its effects partly derive (it can already be "music" to its "ears" or, presumably, sound unpleasant to a stronger nature and so affect it differently).[10] The topic of the dialogue is, after all, virtue.

Finally, Socrates exemplifies his point for Meno by getting one of Meno's slaves to take the risk of trying to think actively on the basis of Socrates' assumption that learning is possible, and the slave succeeds in getting his answer. That is, Socrates shows the overcoming of the descriptive problem by the interventive effects of a description. At the end of the exhibition, Socrates says of the myth of the immortality of the soul and recollection:

> I shouldn't like to take my oath on the whole story, but one thing I am ready to fight for as long as I can, in word and act—that is, that we shall be better, braver, and more active men if we believe it right to look for what we don't know than if we believe there is no point in looking because what we don't know we can never discover.[11]

Socrates is not committed to the descriptive truth of the story, but he *is* committed to its interventive dimension. As Jacob Klein writes, "the emphasis on that courage and that tireless effort is more relevant to him than anything else in the story we have just heard him telling."[12]

It is worth noting that, as Klein also points out, the practical or interventive import of taking the story's description as true is also that one would seek knowledge within one's own soul, by trying to "recollect."[13] Here again the truth of or already in the person's nature, self, or being is brought into play.

It follows from this discussion that there are limits to the principle offered in the *Phaedrus*, that one should take statements of truth under consideration irrespective of their source.[14] The person who considers the truth is part of reality, of what truly is. Consequently truth is also in accordance with the person and not only the other way round. This, I believe, is what underlies the importance of what Gregory Vlastos has called Plato's "say what you believe" requirement.[15] If the person cannot honestly grasp the truth in question or live in accordance with it, it is pointless with respect to truth to pretend to pursue it. This is not merely pragmatic but a matter of *truth*. Pursuing the truth in question here introduces a different kind of falsehood. Because the person, with her/his social or personal constraints, is part of what is true, there is a sense in which what s/he can honestly espouse is as fundamentally of the truth as is the truth when it is considered without taking her/his person into account[16]—and correspondingly, espousing what s/he cannot honestly espouse introduces a real, though different, falsehood.

Of course, that there is a sense in which what one can honestly espouse is fundamentally of the truth does not mean that this is the same as truth considered without taking one's person into account. But here we are differentiating ways of being of the truth rather than differentiating truth from subjectivity. And I argued above that the dimension of "being true *to*" is internally related to the dimension of "being true *about*" (see Idea 2.3). An additional aspect of this internal relation between the truth of the person and the impersonal truth is that true descriptions themselves make up part of the being of the person who makes them. The person's thoughts, including her/his descriptions, are parts of the reality of his/her subjectivity. And the interventive dimensions of these descriptions, these parts of the person, relate them internally to the truths they describe.

There is a contrast here with the discussion of interventive truth in Idea 2. Several of the examples there show that the interventive dimension of true descriptions can affect the truths they describe in such a way that falsehoods and mistakes become the right way to get at truth. In the present discussion of honesty or personal truth, however, the (internally connecting) effects of the interventive dimension are entirely a result of what is *true* about the descriptions (or the effects simply *are* that truth).

Plato himself offers the alternative principle, among other places, in his *Gorgias*:

> if I cannot produce in you yourself a single witness in agreement with my views, I consider that I have accomplished nothing worth speaking of in the matter under debate; and the same, I think, is true for you also, if I, one solitary witness, do not testify for you and if you do not leave all these others out of account.[17]

Similarly, in the *Protagoras*: "it isn't this 'if you like' . . . that I want us to examine," says Socrates, "but you and me ourselves."[18]

Perhaps all of this is why Socrates is made to say in the *Phaedrus*: "I've not yet succeeded in obeying the Delphic injunction to 'know myself,' and it seems to me absurd to consider problems about other beings while I am still in ignorance about my own nature. So I . . . make myself . . . the object of my investigations."[19]

Referring this connection of being and knowing to the discussion of being angry in Idea 2.3—or, as an alternative example, to a Marlene Dietrich–type "vamp" telling the man she loves that she has no interest in him because secretly she believes she would be bad for him—in certain kinds of descriptive falsehood there is a strong element or kernel of being true to who one is. This element or kernel requires, if one respects truth, a special kind of respect. This is not romanticism. What confirms, and adds a poignant and telling twist to it, is that it holds all the more true given a respect for thoroughgoingly impersonal or disinterested truth, rightly appreciated.

There is evidence for this in the nature of what modern psychology calls defenses. Insofar as defenses protect something true of the person and something that could not survive without those defenses, they are an indispensable condition of the person's being who s/he truly is. That is, they are bound up in the truth of the person. In this respect they are less accurately described as defenses than, for example, as expressions and actions of a commitment to certain values. Or perhaps they should be described in both ways at once. An implication of this line of thought—or, if this thought is valid, of this state of affairs—is that removal of "defenses" will not typically reveal "the real person behind," because the real person is a combination of the defenses and what they protect. What will be revealed, then, is a different combination of what the defenses protect and the commitment they express. (The nature of this combination cannot be predicted, because its components themselves would change their nature on being differently co-ordinated and in order to be differently coordinated.) Now, it cannot be established whether defenses are also true commitments without a prior sus-pension of judgment on the matter, that is, without the kind of risk-taking engagement of the inquirer's own truth and being discussed above. The es-tablishment of even the most subjective and personal truths, then, presup-poses a commitment to impartiality. And what this impartiality can show is that some kinds of descriptive falsehood involve an element or kernel of being true to who one is. That is, honesty, truth to oneself, can also involve the interventive dimensions of truth and so its externality to itself.

Because the truth of the person, or various dimensions of honesty, are fundamentally involved in the nature of truth, the decision as to whether the exploration of an assumption validates that assumption rightly comes in part from what satisfies the seeker. The subjectivity of the inquirer is there-fore not only sometimes an obstacle to finding truth but also at some of those same times its means. Again this is not a merely a pragmatic point: the subjectivity of the person is the means of establishing truth in the most fundamental way, since that subjectivity *is* either part of or internally related to the truth being found. And again, just because it is internally related to truth in this profoundly helpful way, it becomes a self-intervening problem that is resolved only by theoretically and practically recognizing that the person's subjectivity is also and equally fundamentally externally related to truth in general and to this particular truth.[20]

In view of these considerations, personal honesty is a necessary part of establishing truth in general. The truth of the inquiring self is part of the truth it seeks, since the truth of that self is one of the general conditions of there being a truth for the inquiring self at all and since the self is part of the reality of the specific situation in which it seeks that truth. Given the interventive dimension of truth, this is also true for what we call impersonal truth, because the truth of the inquiring self, even a self that successfully puts its concerns and biases aside, is part of the conditions of truth in general, part of the truth of truth.

We are right, nonetheless, to call impersonal truth impersonal. (It is right to say both that truth should be considered irrespective of who states it *and* that it depends on who states it.) Factors other than the self are equally parts of the truth of truth, and there is consequently no reason to declare one kind of part to be more significant than the other, in advance of examining particular cases. The distinction between personal and impersonal ways of considering events has a meaning in many kinds of particular situation, and what has so far been said gives no grounds for declaring that meaning unjustified.

Plato has Socrates present dialectic, the reasoned dialogue between opposed points of view, as the final form of knowledge. Aristotle regards dialectic as only probable, because it finds only the best of a number of viewpoints. It does not show that there are no unstated viewpoints that are closer to the truth, and still less does it show that the best viewpoint presents the truth exactly. Aristotle offers as the final form of knowledge what he calls demonstration, knowledge that begins from unquestionable first principles and arrives at its viewpoint by showing what unquestionably follows from those.[21] But if truth is partly constituted by the truth of the inquirer, then dialectic, which can engage with particular viewpoints as held by particular inquirers, is not always only probable but is also the final form of knowledge. And demonstration then partly misses the point. In addition, demonstration does not, of course, allow the nature of the unquestionable principles themselves to be investigated. Aristotle himself admits that the principles of demonstration can themselves be reached only by means of dialectic and nondemonstrative inquiry.[22] While it is true that for him, "dialectic and empirical inquiry are simply means of discovery, not essential for justification . . . of a principle,"[23] if there is any unclarity or disagreement about a principle, these less certain means of inquiry are the only medium in which it can be resolved. Dialectic in the context Plato presents, by contrast, is able to investigate the nature and worth of knowledge itself in a way that, as I argued above, can question and justify its own foundations, and is also not merely probable, since it engages truth itself.

Approaching the issue of honesty from the opposite direction, because honesty involves engaging the truth of oneself, dimensions of truth are necessarily involved in being honest. In particular, any honest interpretation of Plato will necessarily involve dimensions of truth. But the truth that Plato tries to present is primarily the truth about truth itself, the truth about the foundations of truth. Consequently any illumination of truth will engage with it, including those of honest attempts at interpretation. More particularly, an honest interpretation will present not only some truth about the interpreter, but also some *directly relevant* truth about the interpreted work as it affects the interpreter. If the interpretation is honest, it will show directly how the work in question affects this kind of interpreter. These comments, of course, also apply to *honest* interpretations that read Plato in different ways.

Again, this is not a relativism; nor is it *simply* that "one cannot decide between good interpretations," that "some contrasting interpretations are equally right." For one reason, given that the truth of an interpretation is partly in its honesty, interpretations are only seen truly as what they are and for what they have to offer from their own viewpoint, in their own terms, from "inside." What they *are* is partly an "inside," an awareness or set of insights that *are* partly "subjective." This means that at certain crucial points *there is no comparison* between interpretations. When certain points of considering them are reached, they simply do not share the "insides" that offer part of their truth. *The very question* of their relative truth is therefore *meaningless* at those points. It makes no sense to ask the question. Consequently it makes no sense to come up with answers that their comparative truth is relative or not.[24]

This argument against relativism is not the end of the story. Part of my discussion has been that external connections are essential to truth, and this means that things that precisely are *not* shared are essentially (or "internally") meaningful to each other. Consequently the issue of relativism arises again. Nonetheless, the external connections are important exactly *as external* connections, so this argument against relativism retains its truth. The problem is to establish how these incompatible dimensions of truth coordinate with each other. Since that is the central problem of this book, I develop it as the discussion continues.

4.3. THE ACTIVITY OF THE OBJECT OF KNOWLEDGE

The third positive aspect of interventive knowledge I want to discuss is that knowledge or truth actively helps its seeker to find it, because knowledge, and therefore all the more so truth, has effects just by being what it is. The thing that knowledge attempts to know (or, if it is preferred, the truth of the thing) has effects simply in being the truth that it is. The truth of the thing is active. The attempt to get knowledge therefore has not only intellect or subjective capacities as a resource but also what it tries to get knowledge about.

In other words, the problem of getting or justifying knowledge is not (only) one of the mind as opposed to the nonmental world, or of one part or level of the mind as opposed to another, but a problem of a negotiation or dialogue, cooperative and not only conflictual or mutually indifferent, between them.

4.4. DIALOGUE ACROSS INCOMPATIBLE IDEAS OF TRUTH

Fourth, the interventive dimensions of knowledge and truth allow engagement of one view of knowledge or truth by another, fundamentally different or incompatible one. By "fundamentally" different, I mean a view with different principles and different standards for what counts as evidence for truth, and not simply having reached different conclusions on the basis of the same principles. In the case of fundamentally different knowledges, one can even reach what look like identical conclusions, that nonetheless have radically different meanings because they are supported on radically different kinds of foundation. These foundations can include, for example, different values, priorities, and kinds of evidence accepted as significant.[25]

As discussed above, because the interventive property of knowledge has the effect that knowledge of the truth changes the truth, that is, that truth itself changes, truth and knowledge are partly different from themselves or external to themselves. It is part of being knowledge to be external to itself, not to coincide with itself. Consequently, knowledge inherently already has access to what it excludes. It is possible, then, for a form of knowledge to have access to a view of truth that it entirely excludes. That is, one is not necessarily caught in the circularity of one's own assumptions, but one can be affected by knowledge based on different assumptions, and so get to understand it.

And if one wants to establish the truth here, as in the case of balancing decisions about the nature of something discussed in Idea 1,[26] both conflicting descriptions and both sets of assumptions, of standards for what makes a description true, for what counts as good reasons, have to be taken into account (otherwise we have not taken into account everything that is necessary to establish the truth). That is, incompatible principles both can and need to be simultaneously explored.[27]

This in turn means that they have to be successfully presented.[28] But because the conflicting positions have different conceptions of truth itself, and of what follows from what, they will construe the "same" presentations differently. As a result, as in the examples in Idea 2, one may have to say things wrongly or through logically irrelevant connections in order to say them rightly, and so allow both views to be understood and balanced. Again, then, the rhetorical dimension, that of taking styles of presentation and the nature of the audience into account, is also properly the dimension of truth.

I discuss this kind of mixture of principles and the complex rhetorical negotiation it requires in Idea 8.

IDEA 5

The Variegated Texture of Truth

5.1. THE VARIEGATED TEXTURE OF TRUTH

The fifth idea I believe is basic to Plato concerns the nature of truth as a whole, truth considered in general. As I discussed in Idea 2 and Idea 3, if one takes into account the truth of truth itself, the self-incompatibility and self-externality of truth emerge. But a consideration of truth in general must include the truth of truth itself, since truth is one of the "things" that have a truth. Consequently, any statement or thought about truth in general must be self-incompatible and/or self-external. That is, it must contain statements or thoughts that are mutually opposed and/or mutually irrelevant. One may say, perhaps, that the consistency or texture of truth considered in general is variegated or uneven.

Of course, this must include the present statement, which is, after all, about truth as a whole or in general. In other words, the unity of the world must sometimes be truly described, for example, as simply additive (in which case the "texture" of the truth of that unity is simply heterogeneous), sometimes as simply organic or conceptual (in which case the "texture" of its truth is simply homogeneous), and sometimes, as above, as various kinds of combination, that is, heterogeneous *and/or* homogeneous. And each case, as I discussed above, entirely excludes the validity of the others. I shall use the terms "variegated" and "uneven" for this combination of mutually exclusive alternatives.

In Idea 1, I quoted the following statement from the *Sophist*. Speaking about some of the basic aspects of reality, the Stranger says, "one of these alternatives must be true—either all will blend, or none, or some will and some will not."[1] As I argued in Idea 1, these alternatives exclude each other. Since they are alternatives about the basic aspects of reality, they are alternatives about what structures reality itself, including the very viewpoints that think about these alternatives. Consequently, each makes the very viewpoint that thinks about them different, with the result that each excludes the possibility of thinking from the viewpoints of the other alternatives. But the kind of thinking that considers these alternatives must itself allow all of them, and all of them as they are. That is, it must allow all of them in their mutually exclusive incompatibility.

A little further on in the *Sophist*, the Stranger describes the philosopher's art, dialectic, as follows (I should note that his description is in the tentative form of questions):

> Dividing according to kinds, not taking the same form [or Idea] for a different one or a different one for the same—is not that the business of the science of dialectic? . . . And the man who can do that discerns clearly *one* form [or Idea] everywhere extended throughout many, where each one lies apart, and *many* forms [or Ideas], different from one another, embraced from without by one form, and again *one* form connected in a unity through many wholes, and *many* forms, entirely marked off apart. That means knowing how to distinguish, kind by kind, in what ways the several kinds can or cannot combine.²

I suggest that this statement identifies both the internal and the external relations sometimes found between Ideas and hence between things at the level of their true being. In Idea 8 I discuss the emphasis, not much further on in the *Sophist*, placed on nonbeing and hence on a connection that is not simply organic but has some nonconnection essential to it.

To explore the idea of variegated truth, let us start by assuming, on the one hand, that there is no truth about the world as a whole, that the world does not constitute a unity. Different parts or dimensions of the world will then have no internal relation to each other. That is, what makes one part of the world what it is will be entirely different from what makes another part of the world what it is. So, for example, how I am in one mood will be different from how I am in another mood, and there is no connection between the two except that I am liable to both moods. Even if there is a third factor connecting these moods—say, my perspective on the fact that I have moods—this third factor alone provides the unity, and the moods are themselves still disconnected from each other. Each must be understood in a way entirely unrelated to how the other is understood. And that means that in the context of each, truth must be understood in a way that is entirely unrelated to how it is understood in the other. *Entirely* unrelated: that means that when we consider truth in one of these contexts, there is no alternative way to understand truth that can be related to the current view of truth. In each different context, truth is exclusively and universally as it is understood there. On this assumption, then, truth in general would have what I called a variegated or uneven "texture" or consistency.

If, on the other hand, we were to start by assuming that there *is* a truth about the world in general or as a whole, then, apart from the paradoxes I have already discussed, one has to acknowledge the possibility of alternative understandings of the world as a whole. And for reasons similar to those I gave in connection with the confrontation of differing views of essence in Idea 2, and in connection with the engagement of fundamentally different positions at the end of Idea 4, there is no way simply to decide between such alternative views. I say "simply" because I am arguing that one *can* sometimes decide *nonsimply.* Let me stress that this impossibility of simple decision includes the impossibility of simply deciding in advance that none of these views is valid, or that only one is valid, or that more than one is valid.

One cannot use any agreed-on part of the world as a criterion to help the decision. What is at issue here is the truth about the world as a whole. Consequently, no part of the world *will* be agreed on, since all parts are given their meaning by the context of the differing and disputed views of the whole.

One is left, again, with the necessity of maintaining a fundamental indecision and exploring the directions given by assumptions. As I suggested in Idea 4, because of the interventive character of knowledge, one *can* learn—be taught—and explore views following incompatible or incommensurable assumptions. One is not caught in the circularity of validating one's assumptions on the basis of those same assumptions. The fundamental indecision puts one in a position to take advantage of this possibility.

Because this process is part of the reality of the world—in fact, part of the working of knowledge and hence of truth themselves—the truth or nature of the indecision between externally related views of the world in general is part of what must be included in a description of truth in general. That is, again, the truth about truth in general is that it has a variegated or uneven texture.

Now, it is *truth* we are talking about. What is true about truth is true about what it is the truth of. And what truth is true of, that which is true, is what is real. Truth in general, then, is the truth of reality in general. It follows that if truth in general has a variegated texture, then reality in general has a variegated texture.

5.2. IRONY AND THE VARIEGATED TEXTURE OF TRUTH

In the *Republic*, Plato has Socrates say the following about democracies in the course of arguing that they are the second worst kind of political system:

> Possibly, said I, this is the most beautiful of polities: as a garment of many colors [ποικίλον], embroidered with all kinds of hues, so this, decked and diversified with every type of character, would appear the most beautiful. . . . and it is the fit place, my good friend, in which to look for a constitution. . . . Because, owing to this license, it includes all kinds, and it seems likely that anyone who wishes to organize a state . . . must find his way to a democratic city and select the model that pleases him, as if in a bazaar of constitutions.[3]

Adeimantus replies, "Perhaps, at any rate . . . he would not be at a loss for patterns [παραδειγμάτων]." There are many ironic indications here that Socrates despises this gaudy political dispensation. But the thinking in the *Republic* itself partly arises in a democracy, whether it is Socrates' or Plato's thinking. And Socrates is at pains throughout the discussion to point out the connection between a polity and the kind of people in it. Democracy (among other polities) helped to produce Socrates and Plato, the latter a philosopher not at a loss for "patterns," as he sometimes describes the Ideas. Further, the texture of Plato's dialogues is very much "embroidered with all kinds of hues," of styles and kinds of metaphor, and very much "decked and diversified with every kind of character."[4] All of this suggests that Socrates is being ironic in rejecting a patchwork of "patterns."

Democracy, the social context that partly produced Plato's kind of philosophy, is described here as many-colored. In one of the passages from the *Phaedrus* that I quoted in the general Introduction, Socrates is made to use the same word when insisting that a speaker who knows what s/he is doing "must . . . discover what type of speech is suitable for each type of soul. . . . addressing a simple speech to a simple soul, but to those which are more complex something of greater complexity [ποικίλη μὲν ποικίλους ψυχῇ] which embraces the whole range of tones."[5] Perhaps, then, this image of being many-colored is an image of the truly variegated consistency of truth in general, of its being structured by the contexts of particular truths, for which I am arguing.[6]

Further, if, as I argue in Idea 7, Plato does not think that the (democratic) Athenians are simply to be blamed for putting Socrates to death, there is further reason to believe that the irony in Socrates' words turns on itself also, and on the entire argument against democracy. And yet another, very different consideration also gives reason to suspect thoroughgoing irony in this context. The *Republic* (and most of Plato's dialogues) contains just the kind of poetry that Plato has Socrates condemn at great length in the *Republic,* including the imitation of bad, even the worst, characters. Clearly something other than what meets the eye is happening here.

Perhaps Plato is merely being frivolous while discussing serious things, fooling around in the course of demonstrating the wrongness of an argument, in this case an ironic one, by taking it to its absurd logical conclusions.[7] He presents Socrates as being with friends, after all, and on a festival night. Why not combine seriousness and entertainment by succeeding in saying the right thing backwards? The democratic values he espouses would really be what he is arguing for, since they would be the criteria by which one understands that he is being humorously ironic even about his own irony.[8] They would be present as the standards for making sense.

In fact, as I have already begun to argue, it is likely that the values that Plato has Socrates espouse include the value of questioning those values. Consequently, he would necessarily adopt an irony that also puts *itself* in question, that ironizes itself and the values on which it depends, *at the same time as* separately relying on those values to make its ironic point. This irony is so thoroughgoing that the contrasting meaning it conveys in turn itself also means the first, literal meaning. Differently put, the irony is also directed at itself, canceling itself to retain the original meaning; but what it already exists as, in order to cancel itself, is the expression of the ironic meaning. That is, it is *both* meanings.[9] And since each cancels the other, it is each to the exclusion of the other. At a second level, since the self-cancellation is part of its ironic effect, its being turned on itself also cancels that cancellation, so *also* retaining the ironic direction of meaning away from the literal meanings. *Both meanings are intended, and both indirectly, through each other.*

In other words, this irony is a way of exploring a presupposition while also presenting an indecision as to whether the presupposition has any viable meaning at all. It wholly inhabits the viewpoint enabled by the presupposition, and *also* inhabits an indecision as to the meaning of the presupposition that the presupposition necessarily excludes (our "sometimes" logic again).[10] In accomplishing this, the self-ironizing ironic humor would be a necessary and integral part of the serious discussion and not simply an optional addition (and a possibly confusing and perhaps even surprisingly frivolous one, at that). Perhaps, then, the political dispensation that the *Republic* puts forward is one that differs from others primarily in the attitude or perspective with which it takes up its commitments and specifically by taking irony and hence a particular kind of self-perspective seriously.[11]

Differently put, to return to the discussion of irony in the introduction to this book, the principles of this political dispensation might include a coordination of other-sensibility (inhabiting indecision as to one's own foundations) and other-insensibility (wholly inhabiting one's presuppositions), so that both these mutually exclusive modes of awareness are sometimes maintained simultaneously with respect to the same things.[12]

This passage from the *Republic,* then, suggests that a "many-colored" context fits with Plato's philosophy. The comment in the passage remains true that, like anything else, "bright-colored things"—like Plato's dialogues themselves—can be fascinating for entirely misguided reasons. But it is precisely the most important things that are worst or most damaging to misunderstand. It makes sense, therefore, that Plato's strongest irony and his strongest affirmation would be focused on the same subject matter at the same time. This is also true if his subject matter is really the balancing of incompatible views, including views (some opposed to his own) *on how to balance views,* rather than simply the philosophical view taken to be valid without questioning and justifying it. And in the *Gorgias,* for example, Socrates stresses the need to balance the philosophical method of testing views itself against alternative methods: "Now here is one form of refutation accepted by you and by many others, but there is also another according to my opinion. Let us compare them."[13] A "philosophical" view simply presupposed as the right approach, then, would be just another among "bright-colored things" and not a considered view at all.

If Plato's subject matter includes or *is* this balancing, then, again, his humor would uphold both sides of the irony, which is ironic both about its immediate content and about itself.

5.3. THE (EXTERNAL) ORIENTATION TOWARD TRUTH

The attitude or posture required by understanding truth in general as unevenly textured is given by Socrates in the *Apology*:

> I reflected. . . . Well, I am certainly wiser than this man. It is only too likely that neither of us has any knowledge to boast of, but he thinks that he knows

something which he does not know, whereas I am quite conscious of my
ignorance. . . . The truth of the matter . . . is pretty certainly . . . that . . .
human wisdom has little or no value.[14]

As a result, Socrates considers philosophy not to mean the upholding or
presenting of true descriptions, of truths that can simply be stated, but to
mean the "the philosophical life, examining myself and others."[15] He contrasts himself with the Sophists, who are "qualified to teach":[16] "Presumably
the geniuses I mentioned just now are wise in a wisdom that is more than
human. I do not know how else to account for it. I certainly have no
knowledge of such wisdom, and anyone who says that I have is a liar and a
wilful slanderer."[17] He does not merely disclaim knowledge that can simply
be taught but is insulted by being described as having it.[18] And he insists: "I
have never set up as any man's teacher . . . I have never promised or im-
parted any teaching to anybody."[19]

Further, Socrates is shown to maintain himself in a posture of fundamental indecision, and then to explore the directions offered by particular assumptions. In the *Charmides,* for example, he says:

> you're treating me as if I'm maintaining that I know what I'm asking about,
> and as if I'll agree with you if I really want to. But it's not like that. In fact,
> I'm going along with you in investigating whatever proposition is made,
> because I myself am in ignorance. So, when I've considered it, I'm prepared
> to tell you whether or not I agree with you.[20]

And as the discussion of Meno's paradox in Idea 4 shows, for Plato, the
character or truth of the inquirer, and not merely the descriptive content of
statements about the subject of inquiry, is part of what will allow the inquiry
to terminate in establishing truth. Perhaps this is why Socrates is shown to
insist in the *Apology* that he will:

> go on saying, in my usual way. . . . Are you not ashamed that you . . . give
> no attention or thought to truth and understanding and the perfection of
> your soul? . . . I spend all my time going about trying to persuade you . . .
> to make your first and chief concern . . . for the highest welfare of your
> souls.[21]

What Plato, like the Socrates he portrays, teaches is not a descriptive
truth. It is the right—true and "virtuous" (having to do also with excellence
of character or being and not purely of thought)—attitude or posture and
way (amounting to a way of life) to attain descriptive truths, given the possi-

bly variegated texture of truth and the part the person's self plays in truth itself. That is, he teaches how to live in accordance with the coordination of the descriptive and interventive dimensions of knowledge and truth. This, presumably, is why he presents his truth always in the form of an unresolved dialogue between radically different positions. In this situation, the interventive dimension of truth and the limitations of its descriptive dimension are exceptionally prominent. And the reader is forced to make an intervention to reach a descriptive truth, engaging the truth of her/his own being, rather than having a descriptive truth offered to him/her in a way that obscures the interventive dimension.

This posture or attitude that Plato teaches is partly one of externality to truth. Socrates is explicit about the need for this externality in the *Protagoras*:

> When you buy food and drink . . . you can . . . take the advice of an expert as to what you should eat and drink . . . and how much . . . and when. . . . But knowledge cannot be taken away in a parcel. When you have paid for it you must receive it straight into the soul. You go away having learned it and are benefited or harmed accordingly. So I suggest we give this matter some thought.[22]

Philosophy begins with and bases itself on not knowledge or a definite idea but critical thought about knowledge or a definite idea, maintaining an indecision as to the genuineness of that knowledge or definite idea.

If the discussion so far is right, a posture is most fundamentally of the truth in also being rigorously external to it. This externality allows an orientation toward the truth, a being poised with respect to it, rather than simply being of it. And this external orientation is essential to being simply of the truth for at least two reasons. First, it allows truth to be established rather than, for example, pursuing a "truth" that is arbitrarily already presupposed without question, without distance. That is, this externality is a condition for truth, and in that way it is simply of the truth. I mean "established" here in both the senses of being discovered or confirmed and—since the inquirer is in one way or another part of the truth into which s/he inquires and since s/he changes in learning something new—in the sense of being made real in being found and confirmed. Second, as in the discussion in Idea 1, the truth is itself external to itself, so that being organically of the truth involves also being artificial and external to oneself.

"Philosophy" means, literally, the love of wisdom. That is, as Socrates reports Diotima arguing in the *Symposium*, philosophy is at a distance from, external to, wisdom itself, so that it yearns for it rather than being it.[23] And the quest of Plato's Socrates is knowledge of self.[24] Since he claims always to be in search of this knowledge, he claims also never to have it. That is, he claims always to be at a distance from himself. This state is what he describes as the life of the philosopher, the lover of wisdom. Presumably if he is truly at a distance from himself, if he truly does not know himself, then he is also at a distance from, ignorant of, what he is and knows *as a philosopher*. His philosophical distance from being is, as in the discussion in Idea 1 again, also part of his being. This means that he is at a distance also from his own being at a distance, so that he does know and is himself also, as well as not knowing and not being himself.

This externality to the truth includes the need to leave open the possibility in any given case, as well as in the case of truth in general, that the truth may be homogeneous, single and *not* self-external, in a way that does not require externality in any respect; differently put, that it does *not* require an orientation that is open to the possibility of having to shift to discrepant orientations. In other words the meaning of the "uneven texture" or self-externality of truth includes the "unevenness" of this characterization itself, so that in granting the sense of this idea at all, one already grants the possibility of a truth one can *simply* "go along with."

This argument gives the sense of my statement in Idea 2 that the assumption one pursues in the context of fundamental indecision is not simply unconnected to that indecision, but that they are both aspects of the same thing.[25] The fundamental indecision has to be undecided about itself also, leaving room for the truth of a simple assumption and its implications. In fact, because of the radical nature of this indecision, one should rather say that the indecision and the assumption are *sometimes* aspects of the same thing—or something like that.

The orientation or "poising with respect to" that I discuss here is what I had in mind in the Preface and the general Introduction, where I wrote of a delicately poised ungainliness. The previous paragraph should indicate why this poise is necessarily and ideally ungainly, and why this apt and true ungainliness means that the poise is all the more delicate and elegant.

The means of attaining this posture is a certain kind of questioning. This questioning reduces the questioned person to perplexity and resourcelessness, to the unusability of her/his current conceptual equipment to solve the problem at issue. Plato uses the word "*aporia*" to describe this state. During the demonstration to the slave in the *Meno*, Socrates makes the following comments about the slave's progress:

"Now . . . he does feel perplexed [ἀπορεῖν]. . . . Do you suppose . . . he would have attempted to look for, or learn, what he thought he knew, though he did not, before he was thrown into perplexity, became aware of his ignorance, and felt a desire to know? . . . Now notice what, starting from this state of perplexity, he will discover by seeking the truth in company with me, though I simply ask him questions without teaching him.[26]

And the questioner also can and ought to be oneself.

I suggest that the need to be oriented toward the elsewhere where truth is or to be oriented toward truth from elsewhere, rather than simply to be of the truth, is also repeatedly and graphically exemplified in Plato's dialogues by their fictional dialogic form, by the role of Socrates' *daimonion*, and by his reliance on fictional sources and myths, as in the *Meno* passage discussed previously.[27] Socrates also occasionally takes direction from invented or real dreams. For example, in the *Theaetetus* he introduces an important phase of the argument with: "here is my dream, . . . I have the impression that I have heard a theory."[28] These are not, I suggest, sources that are antirational or an alternative to rationality but indicate the dimension of indecision in the place from which rationality thinks.

Rationality can only be purely rational given this place that is other than it. The principle of rationality is to accept only what is justified by reasons, and if this is to be completely carried out, rationality itself must be justified by reasons. That is, the giving of reasons must itself be justified, and for this to be done without a vicious circle, the activity of giving reasons must draw its justification, its further reasons, from suspending itself and balancing itself against nonreasoned thought. I suggest that the *daimonion* and other nonrational or not fully or properly rational sources provide this suspension that makes rationality properly rational.[29] They are resources of rational indecision.

Consequently, they do not directly give truth, nor are they taken by Plato to do so. In the *Timaeus*, Plato makes Timaeus say:

he who would understand what he remembers to have been said . . . by the prophetic and inspired nature . . . must first recover his wits. . . . And for this reason it is customary to appoint interpreters to be judges of the true inspiration. . . . they are only the expositors of dark sayings and visions, and are not to be called prophets at all, but only interpreters of prophecy.[30]

Nonrational sources, then, do not give truth itself. But because they give a dimension of the source of truth, of its conditions of possibility, they are *more fundamental* to truth than the rationality that does give truth or falsehood.

The truth that is connected with them, I suggest, then, is to be found not in what these sources say but in the conclusion that is arrived at and the effects achieved after the exploration of the assumptions that they offer. Their only significant content is the offering of the assumption, the offering of a possibility, and their offering it *as* an assumption or possibility. They emphasize the nature of possibility or assumption itself. Accordingly, they offer a risk to be taken, not a conclusion to be accepted. Perhaps philosophical thought is often regarded as abstract just because of this posture of considering possibilities. In fact, my argument, since it concerns the conditions for truth in general, implies that philosophical thought is neither concrete nor abstract but the condition for the fullest form of both.

It is worth noting that Socrates takes these nonrational indications no more seriously than he takes the suggestions that come from his interlocutors. And like those latter suggestions, they are followed by an exploration that ends no less tentatively than his other explorations do. The nonrational indications are part and parcel of the purely philosophical process, both less adequate than reasoned discussion, because they are baseless, and more adequate, because they are resources for providing the basis for reasoned bases in general. Through them, Socrates obviously only pretends to have a worthwhile source, and so says through irony, "I cannot justify this, I am taking a risk in pursuing this direction"; and through them simultaneously also says nonironically, "but this applies to you too, you also have no initial absolute basis for your contrasting claims: we need to step back and approach the issue again."

I shall return to the issue of risk in Idea 7.

IDEA 6

The Artificiality of Rigorous Thought and the Artificial Dimensions of Reality

The sixth idea I want to discuss as basic to Plato is that the more rigorous thought is, the more artificial it is.[1] That is, it is more redundant, adds less with respect to the truth of its subject matter, and to that degree is an unnecessary, artificial addition to what is naturally given. Here I want to elaborate and generalize what I said in section 2.2 about the meaninglessness of radically rigorous thought. By rigorous thought, I mean thought that tries consistently to establish or engage with the truth of its subject matter, and does so consistently enough that it thinks not only about its subject matter but also about itself and the validity of its consistency. The artificiality I want to discuss is true of thought whether considered in its descriptive or its interventive aspects. And part of what this artificiality involves is that rigorous thought is meaningless: which, I am arguing, is its strength. It cancels itself, in this way doing away with the problematic interference of its descriptive and interventive dimensions. And it cancels itself productively.[2]

By way of anticipation, let me note that the main discussion in Plato's *Sophist* is motivated by the need to make sense of the idea that true speech or thought, no less than false, "is not" or involves "what is not," since it "is not" what it speaks about.[3] Accordingly, if rigorous speech or thought is to make sense, we need a way of talking about "what is not" as "what is." The *Sophist* suggests, then, that if rigorous, truth-seeking speech or thought exists, its very substance involves a kind of fundamental nonsense.

6.1. THE ARTIFICIALITY OF RIGOROUS THOUGHT

One dimension of rigorous or fundamental thinking is that it moves from a starting point (its subject matter, something given) to establish a particular kind of truth of the starting point, one that explains or accounts for its nature. This truth is new: it was not evidently connected with the starting point before, or there would have been no need for hard thinking to reach it. This new something is then taken as the starting point or guide in thinking about the old starting point.[4] But the old starting point, the thing being explained, has to remain the final guide, the measure of the rules or logic by which the new something, its truth, is thought, otherwise the new something stops referring to it.[5] (I develop this point more fully in Chapter 1 of Part II, section 1.1.2.)

Now, part of what it is to have a certain nature, to be something, is to be describable only in accordance with certain kinds of rules or logic and not others. Consequently, if what gives something its truth does not itself operate with the right kind of logic, it is really the truth of something else, or of nothing. In that case the new something is not the truth of its particular starting point. The explanation has changed the subject of discussion and now explains something else. Rigorous thinking of this kind is therefore either nonsensically false, having changed the subject midstream in its discussion, or, since the measure of the truth it establishes must remain the knowledge of the thing with which it began, it adds nothing with respect to the truth or nature of the thing; it is a redundant artificiality. As I pointed out in the general Introduction, these are the two criticisms Aristotle makes of Plato's theory of Ideas.

This generalizes to rigorous thought as a whole. All explanation depends on a grasp of what it is that is being explained. Asking "why" presupposes knowing "what" is being explained or at least is simultaneous with it.[6] And *any* consistently pursued questions are given their sense only in the context or medium of grasping "what" the question is about (as with the discussion of the "nature" of a thing in Idea 1). Consequently, *all* rigorous thought internally involves this dimension of redundant, nonsensical artificiality. Further, what makes rigorous thought rigorous is ultimately that it accounts for itself. Now, "rigorous thought" refers to that which consistently attempts to gain truth. At the level of accounting for rigorous thought itself and in general, then, there is nowhere to look for its truth other than itself. That is, an account of rigorous thought itself can only be the kind of redundancy I am discussing. What makes rigorous thought rigorous, then, itself consists in this kind of redundancy. Consequently, all rigorous thought, again, ultimately consists in this redundant artificiality.

One might object to this whole line of thought that what we try to explain cannot be so easily separated from our descriptions and attempts to understand it in the first place. Consequently, there is no "something" independent of our "new" starting point to measure or test our thinking by. But as both Wittgenstein and Derrida point out, if this is true, then we cannot measure our thinking about *it* either, since our thinking about our thinking would also not be neatly separated from the thinking it thinks about.[7] There is then no measure or test to ensure that we are speaking the truth about our thinking when we say it is not neatly separated from what it thinks about. The truth of these statements then becomes undecidable. And that brings us back to the point I am making. The argument has intervened in itself to become meaningless, and we are now justified in beginning again by exploring the alternatives. I shall therefore continue to do so.

Many language-analytic philosophers have taken this kind of argument to show that the only valid explanation of subjects that, like human behavior or society, are themselves characterized by or are internally connected to logical thought (or thought constrained by the requirements of truth) is description of them in their usual connections.[8] By a different route, phenomenology also insists that only this noninterfering kind of description is ultimately valid.[9] One problem with this view is that such description makes exactly the same kind of unusual or nonapparent addition, something new that does not evidently belong to the described thing when we start with it. This kind of description is itself a novel activity, and makes connections with the thing that are themselves novel with respect to it, at least by being carefully thought and ordered in some way. Such description is usual or apparent only in philosophical or theoretical work, and it is the meaning of precisely that work that is in question here. Consequently, we cannot refer to what is usual or apparent only in the context of such work in order to establish that we are adding nothing to the subject matter in its usual or apparent connections.

My suggestion is that this kind of thinking *is* redundant and nonsensical and, like all rigorous thought, for that very reason tremendously important. For one thing, reality often involves what is nonsensical and redundant. Rigorous thought itself, after all, even if it is a mistaken activity, is part of reality. Even the above views acknowledge this by exposing and so demonstrating the existence of extensive examples of such nonsense and redundancy in both thought and practice. Further, presumably no one would deny that how one thinks is involved in how one acts, or that there are nonsensical and redundant acts. And coming to understand or grasp in general, which is achieved through rigorous thought and so itself involves this kind of nonsensical falsehood or redundancy, is an important part of reality, and so itself requires to be understood. But in order to be properly understood, the subject matter—here, "coming to understand"—must give the logic by which it is to be understood. Accordingly, coming to understand requires that its own kind of nonsense and redundancy is recognized and taken seriously if its truth is to be established. It requires, that is, that the "logic" by which it is understood be nonsensical and redundant.[10] And in any event, the coming to understand *of* coming to understand *will be* nonsensical and redundant, since *it* is also a coming to understand. This kind of redundant artificiality, then, is necessary if we are to grasp important parts of reality.

In fact, since it is important specifically in order to grasp what coming to understand is, it is important for grasping *any* aspect of reality. We cannot have a genuine grasp of anything without also grasping what understanding is itself.

Let me emphasize that, as I argued in a different connection in Idea 2, the artificiality of rigorous thought fully thought through extends also to the rigorous establishment of its artificiality. In other words, this artificiality rigorously establishes the possibility that rigorous thought is *not* artificial. It intervenes in and cancels itself. As I discussed in Idea 2, it brings us to the point of undecidability or indecision that allows inquiry in the directions given by particular assumptions without necessarily imposing those assumptions circularly on the subject matter of the inquiry.

By way of acknowledgment, let me say that I believe that this idea, perhaps like everything fundamental in my discussion, was already Wittgenstein's, although expressed entirely differently in his work.[11] Many of his interpreters would certainly disagree, but I shall not argue the point here.

6.2. UNIVERSALS AND THE ARTIFICIAL DIMENSIONS OF REALITY

It will be helpful, in order to explore the relation of rigorous thought to realities other than knowledge itself, to discuss what is traditionally called a universal. A universal is or expresses the truth of a thing that remains constant in all times and places. The individual tree and the truth of that tree, what can be said of the tree as long as it is a tree, are not at all the same as each other. The individual tree can change and, for example, burn, but the truth of what that tree is, as long as it is a tree and not something else, cannot change or be set on fire. That truth is the essence of the tree, its very being. It is also what is true of all trees, insofar as they are trees and not something else: it is what distinguishes them all as being trees, distinguishes them from other things in their being what they are. Accordingly, truth is given by a universal, that is common to all of the kind of thing of which it is the universal, and that remains constant irrespective of time and place.

I suggest that the idea of a universal repeats the redundancy and nonsense found in shifting from the subject of rigorous thought to its explaining truths, but here includes a shifting between different instances of the same thing. And I shall try to show that as a result, the nonsensical redundancy of rigorous thought, as well as the nonsense involved in changing the subject of discussion midstream by moving from the thing to be explained to what explains it, together make up the foundation of universals.

The discussion of the artificiality of rigorous thought in section 6.1 already implicitly presents the problem of how the universal that makes this tree the tree it is, that which gives its truth, can also be radically different from it in nature.[12] Now, the additional "horizontal" axis of artificiality presents the problem of how that which makes this tree what it is can also make another individual tree what *it* is. Surely that would make all individual trees the same tree?[13] In fact, what I described in Idea 5 as the truth of the world as a whole can also tentatively be described as the concept of the world as a whole or the universal that is specific to the world grasped as a whole. Given the discussion in Idea 5, then, one can say that universals have an uneven or variegated texture, sometimes entirely here and sometimes entirely there. Here I am arguing in the reverse direction, that one arrives at the variegated texture of truth by considering the nature of universals and the concepts that they make up.[14]

I suggest that the fact of the redundancy of rigorously achieved truth allows the giving of the truth of the thing, and the fact of the changing of the subject involved in rigorous thought allows that same truth to be given elsewhere, in another instance of the kind of thing. What makes it the *same* truth that is given is that the redundancy and changing of subject are different dimensions of the same fact, the artificiality of rigor. In redundantly repeating the truth of the thing in what rigorously explains it, one also moves to talking about something of a different nature from that of the individual thing, its truth. But in moving to talk about the truth whose nature is different from that of the thing, one repeats, redundantly, its truth, its true nature.[15] Accordingly, one changes the subject to the same subject. In other words, the pure artificiality of rigorous thought is what allows a universal, what belongs equally to the truth of different things, to be thought.[16]

In Plato's *Theaetetus,* Socrates asks Theaetetus what knowledge is. Theaetetus's first answer consists in a variety of separate departments of knowledge, "geometry . . . and also cobblery and the other craftsmen's arts; each and all of these are nothing else but knowledge." Socrates points out that "when you are asked for one thing you give many, and a variety of things instead of a simple answer," and Theaetetus is puzzled: "What do you mean by that, Socrates?" Socrates then explains how to give a general definition. Giving particular examples does not answer the question, because one cannot understand the examples without first understanding what they are examples *of.* We do not know what "arithmetic" is, as a "knowledge of working with numbers," until we know what "knowledge" is. "Or does anyone, do you think, understand the name of anything when he does not know what the thing is?"[17] The general definition Socrates is made to ask for is what he sometimes gives the name "Idea." These later come to be understood as "universals." Aristotle understands Plato's Ideas to be universals (and he rejects Plato's understanding of the Ideas on the basis of his, Aristotle's, own understanding of the nature of universals).[18]

Now, universals are not simply thoughts. As the discussions in Idea 1 and the start of Idea 2 indicate, they are also something in reality (however we may understand that something). Things really are what they are partly in being what other things are. In any event, if there is any truth to the thoughts about the natures that things share, then there is truth to the natures themselves. Certainly, these kinds of thoughts have real effects on our experience—for example, the concept of identity, personal and otherwise. Accordingly, then, the purely artificial dimension of reality, and not only of pure thought, is what allows a universal to be.

Perhaps we could further specify what I am calling the uneven or variegated texture of truth by saying that corresponding to the posture or position of fundamental indecision (of absence even of decided grasp of the issue) in rigorous thought, there is something like a firm hesitancy in the nature of things.[19] Perhaps this is what it means that sunsets and sunrises are so serenely tremendous. There is an inconceivable display of peculiarly glorious vastness, all concentrated as an ungraspably huge and tentative disappearance, together with smaller, firm departures and appearances, for example of hues and moods. And that sunrises and sunsets are so very different from each other and from day to day indicates that even what is ungraspable is not one indistinguishable "thing" untouchable by human experience. In fact the ungraspable frequently offers an indefinite variety of things to be understood and explored.

In any event, it follows that the fundamental indecision or rigorously achieved nonknowledge or confusion that I discussed above is itself, in combination with the exploration of a decisive assumption, *directly descriptive knowledge*. Often in very subtle ways, the world involves moments or aspects of what is unknown, even to the extent of its being unknown quite whether they are unknown. One concrete example is the experience of deciding whether or not one's view is mistaken. The indecision and assumption together are a form of awareness, or, more accurately, a human posture, that directly articulates the undecided structure of these aspects of reality. Plato's indirection and irony do not, I suggest, exclude direct knowledge, expression, and description. Rather, they give the context in which directness and simple description are soundly established as truly that; and sometimes indirection and irony are themselves already directness and simple description.[20]

Now, since truth itself has the self-divided "sometimes" nature (or the "sometimes" self-divided nature) that I discussed above, the fundamental indecision and external or indirect approach to truth is therefore *also, and precisely in being indirect*, a direct and simple articulation of truth. Accordingly, this indirectness itself accounts for the "sometimes" possibility of simple directness just as it accounts for the "sometimes" necessity of indirectness. Again, this is not a relativism. Truth *itself* is variegated; what is accounted for here is precisely the simplicity and *not* the relativity of direct graspings of truth. What needs to be reunderstood is not so much the status of these claims to truth but rather the meanings of "sometimes" and "in some respects."

Expressing the same point differently, as I argued of rhetoric in Idea 3, externality of meaning is what makes possible the rigorous establishment of internality of meaning. Or: variegation of truth or artificiality of universals is itself what makes possible their simple homogeneous truth, rather than involving relativity or unreality. And this includes the internality of referring to and describing externality itself. It also includes the internality of describing the indecision between internality and externality, or between directness and indirectness, itself. Internality and externality, directness and indirectness, and universality and relativity sometimes go together, with implications that are not straightforward.

There is no reason why there should not be many different kinds of these moments or features of artificiality and indecision in the world. Accordingly, there is no reason why there should not be many different kinds of the awareness, responding to those moments or features, that is fundamental indecision together with an assumption. In other words, there may be many kinds of wonder, which both Plato and Aristotle claim is the beginning of philosophy.

6.3. PARTICULARS, PERTINENCE, AND ARTIFICIALITY

A second dimension of rigorous thought is that it focuses on one aspect of a thing at a time, and on one topic in particular to the exclusion of all that is otherwise relevant to that thing or topic at that time. So in the *Republic*, for example, the argument at one point considers the craftsman precisely (ἀκριβῶς), that is, only insofar as he is exercising his craft, so that if he makes a mistake he is not being a craftsman at all.[21] This precise focus is what makes it possible to be concerned with the truth of a thing. Without differentiating what one is specifically trying to understand from other things, there *is* nothing in particular one is trying to understand. And without following one line of thought rather than another, there is no line of thought one is following. But, as I have discussed, the context of a thing (or of a topic) is an internal part of its truth. That is, the mixture of aspects that make the thing or topic what it is interventively reconstitute each other, so that even the single aspect considered on its own is incorrectly understood, is artificial. Consequently, what rigorous thought considers must be reinserted in the mixture of aspects before even the single aspect is properly grasped. Both of these moments, the artificiality and the reinsertion, are necessary to rigorous thinking. The first recognizes the coherence and distinctions that are to be found in things, and the second recognizes the organic and/or additive interconnections of those distinctions themselves.

It should be noted that both extremes, the consistent order of rigorous thought and the consistent disorder of finding or making no distinctions at all, are purely artificial, since we begin with a mixture, at that point indeterminate, of these two aspects of organizing or disorganizing principle themselves.[22]

The same problem and solution involved in universals reappear with this dimension of the artificiality of rigorous thought. What one is dealing with in this single focus on a single aspect is a universal, that which reappears identically in many other cases. And what one is dealing with in the reconnection of aspects is the coordination of universals or complex universal traditionally known as the concept of the specific thing. (The man in the *Republic* is skilled *and* animal *and* thinking *and* two-legged, and so on.) Consequently, the artificiality of focusing exclusively on a single aspect and the reinsertion of that aspect into the mixture correspond respectively to the moment of the difference of the universal from the thing whose truth it is and the moment of the redundant identity of the universal and the thing.

Because the artificiality that is the nature of universals is in some sense in the world and not only in thought—or, said differently, because the world involves moments or aspects of fundamental self-canceling confusion and incoherence—the purely artificial moments of thought can be strictly true as they stand, but in very limited contexts and senses. There are contexts, then, in which they do not need to be reinserted in the mixture of aspects in order to be understood truly. That this is so accords with the idea that this pure artificiality is such as reflexively to include its own artificiality itself as artificial, so that it is also not artificial at all.

Differently put, the artificiality of thought, as artificial, is also externally related to what the thought is about—this artificiality is external, irrelevant to, the truth of the thing—and the moments or dimensions of artificiality in things are also externally related to the other moments and not simply and in every sense organically related to them so as to be meaningless if considered independently of them.

In addition, in the context of the discussion of the externality of truth to itself, it makes sense that the truth of a thing can be given *only* by something, like the universal, that is fundamentally (also) external to the thing and to itself and not only identical with the thing and itself.[23] It is therefore a mark of the adequacy rather than (as Aristotle would have it) the refutability of the universal as the truth of the thing that it is both redundantly the same as the thing and, having changed the subject of discussion, nonsensically irrelevant to it.

6.4. THE THEORY OF IDEAS

I suggest that Plato's theory of Ideas is developed on the basis of an awareness of the artificiality of rigorous thought and of the nature of that artificiality. Because rigorous thought is inevitably wrong, taken on its own, the theory of Ideas is inevitably wrong, taken on its own. But because of this particularly radical or fundamental kind of wrongness or artificiality, the theory can cancel itself so as to return us to the concrete mixture of the externally, immediately grasped sensuous things themselves. And because pure sensuality is itself artificial in this way, involving as it does various ideas of what things are and how they fit together, it is *only* through a passage through artificial wrongness that one can grasp sensuous things truly. The theory of Ideas, like novelistic fiction, is a thoroughgoing and profound wrongness of this kind, and accordingly returns us to a thoroughgoing and profound grasp of sensuous things. In the light of this thesis, it makes sense that Plato's dialogues are permeated with various kinds of sensuousness and sensuality, both in description and in attitude and interaction of the characters.

In fact, the nature of the ideas expresses this movement precisely. For example, as Socrates is made to insist in the *Phaedo,* the beauty in things must be explained by Beauty itself, which is not the same as any particular beauty.[24] The ideas literally point toward the thing they explain *as* a pointing away from it.

I argued in Idea 5 that Socrates' irony in the dialogues at least sometimes turns on itself, creating a space of simply fooling around, which is also a space in which the genuine values toward which Socrates is oriented stand out, and stand out as questionable. I also argued there that the nonrational elements in the dialogues, including this frivolity and Socrates' *daimonion,* are crucial to the philosophical elements. I argued that the philosophical elements themselves require that they themselves be reasonably justified, and the nonrational elements create the necessary distance from careful thought and hence the space in which careful thought can be justified in a noncircular way. The "Socratic" philosophy presented in the dialogues *is only philosophy at all with the inclusion of the nonphilosophical elements.* Now I am arguing that Plato's writing as a whole, including the "non–Socratic" contributions, is ironic in just this way, including, and especially, his most rigorous thought, the theory of Ideas. Plato's wit and indirection are of the essence of his philosophical thought and practice. Not only do the fictional and frivolous (and sensuous) components of the dialogues belong together with the components of rigorous thought, but these two aspects are parts of each other, make each other what they are.

This interpretation indicates why a thinker as conceptually adept as Plato would frame his discussions of the conceptual foundations of truth, including the nature and implications of the ideas, in conceptually clumsy metaphorical and mythological terms. By doing so, he writes into the very surface of the presentation of the ideas that they are not only inadequate to the capturing of truth but *hopelessly* inadequate, *completely* the wrong kind of thing. He writes the ideas as purely oblique, in the way of mythology, and as both purely and sensuously fictional. Since they are also the point of purest conceptual thinking in his dialogues, it seems that they are oblique and fictional precisely in being purely conceptually rigorous.

This conclusion makes further sense if one considers that the ideas are supposed to give ("supposed" here should be read technically as well as conventionally) the truth of, among other things, sensible/sensuous things. Accordingly the sensuous metaphors and the sensuous images of the myths via which Plato presents the ideas do not *only* show the inadequacy of the ideas. Because these inadequate images are expressions of the idea, they do make that inadequacy clear. But because they are also sensuous, they show at once both the inadequacy of turning away from sensuous things *and* the sensuous things themselves, whose contrasting truth emerges because it is the measure that allows one to register the inadequacy of turning away from them.

And as I argued just above, the things themselves can be known *only* upon having been turned away from, since initially what is simply artificial in appearances is unclear. The sensuous things themselves are truly shown in, approximately speaking, both turning away from them, which establishes them in the limits of what they truly are, and turning away from that turning away in the right manner, which cancels the extraneous effects of having established those limits.

Differently put, the interventive property of knowledge can intervene in itself to produce descriptive truth. Here, the sensuous metaphors and images that present the ideas offer directly the sensuous/sensible truth the ideas are supposed to offer, and they do so because it is the ideas, and not the sensuous truth, that they present (that is, because of their indirection, their focus away from the sensuous truth they thereby directly present). At the highest level of rigor, the ideas cancel themselves immediately. Their inadequacy at its rigorous extreme is their success.

Because the adequacy of the ideas consists in their inadequacy, one is always left with more to know about the truth of the things they are ideas of. And the way to find out more is to think through to the ideas, or something like them, again.

Putting these conclusions differently, the immediate grasp of sensuous intuition—immediately internal to the thing and thinking its truth in being purely external to and thoughtless about it—and the universal, partly distant connections of conceptual thought—purely external to and thoughtless about the thing in being purely internal to it and thinking its truth—are at their extremes the same, while each is also itself indifferently to the other.[25]

IDEA 7

The Risk of Rigorous Thought

The seventh idea basic to Plato concerns the risk dimension of establishing truth. Because the initial thing to be explained gives the measure for the explaining principles and factors, as I discussed in Idea 6, one can find truth only after encountering the things that need to be explained. But, as Meno points out, even to recognize the facts, one must already know something of the truth about them. The standard of that truth, however, is still given by the things it is the truth of, the things we encounter that it explains. As a result, one finds the truth of the thing or issue only after the fact, but one also finds it out only by trying out assumptions one already has. That is, one finds it out only by taking risks.

Expressing this differently, all truth is in a sense a posteriori, all truth comes after investigating the facts. But this does not mean that there is no a priori truth, truth before one comes to investigate the facts. I suggest, rather, that there is a priori truth but that even a priori truth, truth before facts, in a sense comes after the fact.[1] We need to understand truth, and the relation between a posteriori and a priori, differently—I suggest with an element of confusion and artificiality in our understanding. This is the same problem in a different dimension as the problem of universals' being the truth of the thing and yet other than the thing. Since universals are the truth or essence of the thing, the thing *depends on* them to be what it is. As a result, they precede any example of the thing, are more truly what the thing is than any example of the thing we might investigate. But it is *the thing* whose truth they are: *it* gives their measure. In discussing universals, then, I have already begun to elaborate this different way of thinking what precedes and what is posterior.

Because one finds the truth of the thing or issue only after the fact, then, one finds out only by taking risks, trying out assumptions. While this involves much of the same behavior as a dogmatist's, that is, the person who simply proceeds on the basis of assumptions that are not questioned in their turn, and while it can lead to the same conclusions as the dogmatist's, there is a different attitude and different attendant behavior and statements. There is also a different marginal rhetoric: that is, for example, the kinds of qualifications one makes and spaces one makes for subsequent inquiry. When one encounters situations that are essentially the same as situations one has encountered before, then one can be assured in advance. But even here one's knowledge is based on a prior process of risk-taking or putting to the test. Consequently there is an at least subtly different attitude and marginal rhetoric from the dogmatist's here as well.

As I discussed in Idea 1, moral assessment of one's actions in unfamiliar situations does not always or only depend simply on the truth of the immediate situation but also sometimes on the metalevel of awareness of built-in risk in establishing the truth of that situation. Hence, for example, Socrates' accusers, who had him put to death by the city-state of Athens on charges of impiety and corrupting the youth, are not necessarily in the wrong, even if the charges were false. As with all rigorous knowledge, in this case knowledge about a whole way of life, they would have had to take certain risks to learn enough to know even that they had something to learn: and these risks would have been *risks*, with no assured justification for taking them. Perhaps the *Apology*, which is Plato's version of Socrates' defense at his trial before the people of Athens, is very much a classical tragedy, in which there are two equally weighted necessities rather than a simple wrong and right. As it happens, there are a number of friendly allusions to Socrates' trial in Plato's dialogues. In the *Symposium*, for example, Alcibiades, very drunk, jokes about putting Socrates on trial for his arrogance in not having sex with him. It is a joke in a very festive and humorous situation, and there is no indication whatsoever that Plato did not find it delightful and want to portray it that way:

> I slipped underneath the cloak and put my arms around this man—this utterly unnatural, this truly extraordinary man—and spent the whole night next to him. . . . But in spite of all my efforts, this hopelessly arrogant, this unbelievably insolent man—he turned me down! He spurned my beauty, of which I was so proud, members of the jury—for this is really what you are: you're here to sit in judgment of Socrates' amazing arrogance and pride.[2]

Alcibiades is portrayed as at least admiring Socrates and possibly loving him. Plato presents no evident ugly feeling about Socrates' trial here. One might see this as a poignant reference to Socrates' trial, highlighting its bitter injustice by contrast with the present sweet situation, but even that possibility would surely remain ambiguous, given the festive frivolity of the context.

As discussed in Ideas 3 and 4, the knowledge-establishing risk is not only an intellectual one but also an engagement and risk of one's being, in a greater or lesser degree.[3] One's own truth, the truth of who one is, enters into the establishment of truth. And as discussed in Idea 6, this is all the more true the more purely artificial or rigorous the thinking is. The most rigorous thought is most thoroughly external to one's bases, and consequently puts the *whole* of one's position in question. Being interventive, it offers the possibility of changing one's whole position, of a radical transformation of one's being.

But there is no reason or call *within* one's position to change in this way. This is true by definition, since now it is the whole of one's position that is put in question, so that the reason can only come from outside one's position, from some wholly different position. That is, thinking rigorously is itself a risk, merely a chance one takes, in that there is no justification for it from the standpoint that undertakes it. Accordingly, rigorous thinking or knowing is not something to be done lightly. The motive that justifies rigorous thinking or knowing is that one honestly (truly) wants to: in which case one is already outside as well as inside one's position, in accordance with the discussion of spontaneity in Idea 1.

Again, then, the thoughtless view of life grasps the situation rightly. Thinking is a peculiar activity that itself requires justification, and there is often the best of reasons not to engage in it.

Paradoxically, that one should not think rigorously without good reason is part of the solution to the problem of gaining assured knowledge given in Idea 4 in terms of honesty. When one reaches the point at which one does not honestly want to think about a thing or issue, one's own truth is asserting itself. If one is searching for truth, then truth has found oneself, and one has succeeded in one's aim. Hence again, perhaps, Socrates' insistence that what is primary in his search for knowledge is knowledge of himself.[4]

Contemporary language-analytic philosophy, like Aristotle, recognizes a form of this principle in disqualifying some paths of thought as meaningless in terms of ordinary language usage, since we cannot mean anything if we depart too far from the familiar meanings of our words. We would be pretending to be other than what we in fact are. It is worth noting that this is not necessarily a stance that keeps us essentially static.[5] Marxists, feminists, and gay/queer liberationists, for example, do the same thing with respect to what the meanings of the present (ordinary usage) indicate about *alternative ordinary* meanings. Here the familiar usages are disqualified by contrast with alternative familiar or becoming-familiar usages.

Further, the proper identification of which "ordinary" usage is the one to be relied on requires a prior (even if it is a posterior prior) balancing or indecision about what we could meaningfully consider ordinary or familiar. But in identifying anything in this rigorous way as ordinary, as falling within the limits of what is meaningful and known, we have already established a whole position, a view of the totality of meaning. And this, as discussed above, is itself purely artificial. It therefore already places us outside as well as inside this ordinariness. And our doing this *also* legitimates the exploration of *other*, "nonordinary" artificial positions, even ones opposed to ours.

On the other hand, this exploration can simply return us to the original position, knowing it better and more confirmed in it. Whatever a priori legitimation of our position we come to will come, again, only after the fact. My point is that we *can* come to a priori, nonrelative truths, and *also* that these truths, even about the same things, may differ even in the final analysis. One first has to risk before one can know, and no one, not even an outside observer, whether Hegelian or therapist, can know prior to the pertinent risk and its outcome.

I suggest, then, that Plato's dialogues do not contain a Socrates who knows best, on the one hand, and foolish interlocutors on the other. I suggest that they present Socrates' attempt to establish the preconditions for someone to know, to establish the conditions for the risk of establishing knowledge by maintaining the purely artificial posture of externality to and orientation towards truth.[6] Accordingly, what Plato has to teach us is not philosophical doctrine, but a philosophical doctrine about the establishment of any kind of doctrine.

If there is universal and unchanging truth, it is inextricably linked with the uncertainty and risks of perishable life. The problem of how to understand this linkage is traditionally regarded as part of our inheritance from Plato's theory of Ideas. I discussed this problem above in the context of the problem of universals. Here the question runs: How can inherently changing and contradictory things and events be thought to connect with—in Plato's phrase, "participate in"—the entirely different nature of the inherently unchanging and self-consistent Ideas that give them their truth and reality? This problem is traditionally seen either as the flaw that invalidates the theory of Ideas or as the profound legacy that Plato leaves us to work on.

I suggest that this problem is in fact the genuine crux of his thinking. But in answering that question, one comes to understand the nature of truth itself very differently. And as a result, one comes to understand the nature of the quest for truth very differently. The problem is not really whether there is a theory of Ideas. The problem is rather what this theory might mean, and I have been arguing that this meaning is to be found not in what the theory says, but in its indirection, the tension between what it says and the kind of life and approach that it orients.

The truth of the Ideas themselves, that is, lies at a distance from the Ideas and the things and events they explain. It lies in the (external) approach to them and to those things. That is why I have devoted so much space to what I have called provisional ideas.

IDEA 8

Mixture and Purity

The eighth idea I believe is basic to Plato concerns the importance of the confused mixture of considerations, meanings, dimensions, characteristics, and viewpoints in which thinking (and acting) begins. In Idea 6 I argued that rigorous thought is artificial because it departs from the thing it explains or makes sense of and because it focuses on only one aspect of that thing at a time, although any aspect of a thing exists as what it is only in a mixture of many aspects. I argued further that rigorous thought nonetheless gives the truth of the thing. It can do so directly, because the thing itself exists partly or sometimes as a confusion or hesitation as to whether it is external to itself—"departed" and isolated from itself and its context—or simply at one with itself. Or it can do so indirectly, since the artificiality of rigorous thought is itself artificial and so ultimately cancels itself.

Here I want to emphasize that the recognition and articulation of the context of thought as a confused mixture of aspects is itself a product of careful thinking; it is a decision about the truth of what is basically real. It is therefore itself artificial. Consequently, as with the "sometimes" logic I discussed previously, one needs to achieve the posture of not thinking in terms of either a simple contrast or a simple lack of contrast between mixture and purity. Differently put, one has to think mixture through until its own self-intervening externality to itself becomes evident, just as I have tried to think the artificial character of careful thought through rigorously to the same point. One arrives, for example, at an understanding of mixture as being a mixture of mixture itself and purity.

As a result, mixture itself involves and so is what *allows* purity of thought and truth. This includes the purity of what I have called the artificiality of thought. And the confusion and uncertainty of life themselves involve and so are what allow clarity and assurance. In Plato's language, the perishable world itself involves the sense of the ideas that are so very different from it.

8.1. PURITY THROUGH MIXTURE

Let me begin with the mixture. It is arguably only because one's thinking is challenged or provoked by a thinking inconsistent with one's own thinking—a thinking that mixes with it, that makes one mixed up—that one thinks actively at all. And we always return to the mixture. What gives the measure of the truth of rigorous explanation of a thing is the mixture of aspects which is that thing.[1]

But this mixture is not simply a mixture of aspects. Understanding the mixture as a mixture involves understanding the aspects purely as aspects, independent of the mixture (otherwise there is nothing to think of as mixed), and also understanding their mixture purely as a mixture, independent of the particular aspects that make it up (otherwise there is no *mixture*). That is, what we understand as the mixture is not only a mixture of aspects but also a mixture of the purity of the aspects and the purity of the sense of mixture itself that rigorous explanation or thought about it gives. Rigorously understood, mixture includes a mixture of mixture itself and purity (independence of mixture). What it means to say that one is part of the mixture, then, is that one is also sometimes and/or in some respects not part of the mixture.[2] Just as to say that one is exercising the purity of thought also means that, precisely in doing so, one is sometimes and/or in some respects outside the purity of thought. And just as one truly describes the essence of thing by such thought, since an essence is such as sometimes and/or in some respects to be one with and also outside of itself.

As I mentioned previously, a large part of the discussion in the *Sophist* is an attempt to find a way of talking and thinking about nonbeing, leading up to the inquiry into how the different aspects of reality do or do not "blend."[3] The problem is that it seems immediately self-contradictory to say something about what is not, since such a statement says that what is not, is, simply by virtue of talking about it. But it is necessary to talk about what is not, in order to distinguish falsehood, which refers to what is not, from truth, which refers to what is. Without that distinction, we cannot talk about truth. What is more, since *talk about* true things is itself "not" what it talks about, true statements themselves already involve (are already mixed with) what is not.[4] The result so far is that we have no sense-making statements at all.[5]

The Stranger is made to propose the following solution to the problem of talking about nonbeing. Knowledge, he argues, is separated out into different fields. Difference, too, is "parceled out, in the same way as knowledge," but with reference to a field it is not in. For example, "whenever we use the expression 'not beautiful,' the thing we mean is precisely that which is different from the nature of the beautiful. . . . May we not say that the *existence* of the not-beautiful is constituted by its being marked off from a single definite kind among existing things?" Accordingly, "the contrast" between "a part of the nature of the different and a part of the nature of the existent" is real, and "this is just that 'what-is-not' which we were seeking."[6] What is not, then, or difference itself, exists in such a way that it is, but not where it is. Also, difference itself is real as "a single form to be reckoned among the many realities."[7] And although Plato does not make this connection explicit, both as single and as something that exists, it "participates" in sameness, since "everything partakes of the same [sameness]";[8] that is, it is the same as itself. But this self which it is the same as consists in not being the same as itself, since it *is* difference itself: its existence is constituted as being something other than what is. That is, it is self-external.

But difference or nonbeing itself not only is real but is a special kind of reality that allows us to speak about truth and what is, in distinction from it. Nothingness, understood in this way, must therefore be taken into account together with and as fundamentally as truth in understanding reality.

As the Stranger points out, the argument implies that "the contrast is, if it be permissible to say so, as much a reality as existence itself: it does not mean what is contrary to 'existent,' but only what is different from that existent."[9] Later he insists that "so far as any contrary of the existent is concerned, we have . . . said good-by to the question whether there is such a thing or not and whether any account can be given of it or none whatsoever."[10] What is not is not simply the contrary of what is, it is not simply exclusive of "is," but can mix with it.

This curious kind of "not-ness," which is not simply an exclusive contrary to what it is not, also describes Socrates' relation to his interlocutors. Or, since Socrates is presented as an image of a philosopher, it describes philosophy's relation to what is not philosophy. I have suggested that his position is one of considering or balancing both views, his own and his interlocutor's, each considered on its own terms. That is, among other views, he balances different views of "what is," for each of which what the other understands by "what is" is understood as not what is. But he balances each of these views considered on its own terms. Consequently, for this balancing of views, what is not is not simply exclusive of what is.

In contrast, if each view is not considered on its own terms, a circular and so arbitrary rejection of one view and acceptance of the other would result. As Socrates is made to point out in the *Crito,* when there can be "no agreement in principle," the parties "must always feel contempt when they observe one another's decisions."[11] And in the *Phaedo,* at a point stressed by a dramatic interruption of the narrative thread, Socrates insists that we "refuse to mix . . . things together by discussing both the principle and its consequences."[12] Let me suggest, provisionally, some reasons for this, supported by the observation in the *Crito.* If one is exploring particular topics, one should refuse to discuss the principles that give one's topics their meaning for that exploration. Such a discussion would simply put in question or change the meaning of the topics, change the subject; that is, it would be an arbitrary change of the entire discussion. Consequently one can only explore a position at all on the basis of its own principles. And if one discusses the principles, one should refuse to discuss the particular topics whose exploration those principles support. Those topics are given their meaning by the principles and therefore cannot help but circularly support the validity of the principles. Consequently one can only explore a position as a whole by ignoring its own content. Neither of these mixtures of principles and consequences together, being either simply arbitrary or simply circular, achieves anything. Instead, as I argued above, we need both to be exclusively inside the position, based only on its principles, and also exclusively outside the position, ignoring its content.

By way of support for this as an interpretation of what Plato presents here, let me note that when Socrates speaks here against mixture, as he does, this is a possibility that is itself given by this fundamental kind of mixture, a mixture itself mixed and so not only mixture. When, for example, Socrates speaks in the *Crito* for *both* positions as understandably despising the other, he is, precisely, speaking *from both positions* and not only of one position in its exclusive purity. This means that he speaks from a position that allows at once both the mixture of incompatible positions with their incompatible meanings and the two purities of each position considered on its own.

Socrates, then, is in general both *entirely* opposed and *entirely* not opposed to his interlocutors. As the statement from the *Crito* shows, he is aware that the opposing party would be in the same position as his of necessarily rejecting the opposing view, in this case his own. This is perhaps one motive for the statement that arguments must be accepted or rejected because they are true or false, and not because Socrates or anyone else says so. "As for you, if you will take my advice," says Socrates in the *Phaedo,* "you will think very little of Socrates, and much more of the truth. If you think that anything I say is true, you must agree with me; if not, oppose it with every argument that you have."[13]

I have suggested that the balancing of ideas and positions in Plato's dialogues is not simply preparation for conclusions that can be stated later in a doctrine and that are really what is important. But I suggest that sometimes it is *also* exclusively this preparation for conclusions that are really what is important, for pure viewpoints that *exclude* this balancing. I suggest, then, that it is both of these incompatible things, sometimes in a unified way, as different dimensions of the same thing, sometimes separately, or externally to each other, and sometimes in both of these ways. This is a result of the sometimes self-canceling indeterminacy of the mixture.

It follows that there is no infinite regress here. The "sometimes" logic applies to itself as well, so that the unevenly uneven combination of these principles is the condition for conclusive certainty no less than for indefinite rebeginning and questioning.

Given the nature of mixture as mixed even in its nature as mixture, then, theoretical discourse, or an articulated line of thought, is not less purely theoretical because it is always involved in a mixture of motives, considerations, positions, and figurative and literal meanings. Rather, pure theory is established *as pure* precisely in such a mixture. And the undecidabilities of truth and falsehood discussed in Ideas 2 and 3, which occur in one position's confronting another one fairly and therefore trying to be true in a mixed way to the principles of both positions, are accordingly the basis for clear simplicity, and not simply the reason for its impossibility. The Stranger in the *Sophist,* for example, in fact continues the discussion by relating what has been said about the being of nonbeing to discourse, to "securing the position of discourse as one of the kinds of things that exist. To rob us of discourse would be to rob us of philosophy."[14]

In the case of action, too, the fact that our motives are not pure does not prevent us from acting purely but rather, given the mixed context, makes acting on a pure motive an achievement and therefore admirable. That is, mixed motives can add to the virtue of the pure motives among them. What is more, they can also allow the pure motives to be *established*, in both senses of being known to be there and being stably achieved. Because contrasting motives are present, one can *tell* that one is acting on one motive rather than another. And this in turn allows one to ensure that one is doing so and that one continues to do so.

In the traditional reading of the theory of ideas, the link between the single, selfsame ideas and the many and differing particular things whose truth they are is explained by a fundamental "indeterminate" or "indefinite dyad," or twoness. The theory resolves the indeterminate dyad into determinacy and definition by reference to the principle of the Good or One. As I understand it, the indeterminate dyad is cofoundational or "cofirst" with that first principle, so much so that they are parts of each other.[15] Together, these two mutually exclusive and mixed principles express what I am calling the mixture or the variegated consistency of truth.

All of this is a more detailed statement of the definition I am suggesting of philosophical thinking as a fundamental indecision together with the exploration of a particular assumption.

8.2. THE *PHAEDO*

8.2.1. *Mixture in the* Phaedo

Plato has Socrates emphasize in the *Phaedo* the importance of the mixture as a basis for thinking. Interestingly enough, he does so almost exactly in the middle of this lengthy dialogue. And this is the first and only time Socrates talks with Phaedo in the dialogue named after Phaedo and that Phaedo largely narrates. Socrates explains here why people lose their faith in argument, through an analogy with becoming disappointed in other people: "misology [dislike of argument] and misanthropy arise in just the same way. Misanthropy is induced by believing in somebody quite uncritically. You assume that a person is absolutely truthful and sincere and reliable, and a little later you find that he is shoddy and unreliable."[16] As a result of assuming that people are purely what one expects, one loses faith in them. But, Socrates continues, "'Isn't it obvious that such a person is trying to form human relationships without any critical understanding of human nature? Otherwise he would surely recognize the truth: that there are not many very good or very bad people, but the great majority are something between the two.'" And he explains:

> Can you think of anything more unusual than coming across a very large or small man, or dog, or any other creature? Or one which is very swift or slow, ugly or beautiful, white or black? Have you never realized that extreme instances are few and rare, while intermediate ones are many and plentiful?[17]

In addition, Socrates begins this brief discussion by insisting that "no greater misfortune could happen to anyone than that of developing a dislike for argument."[18] The precautions against this misfortune are therefore the most important precautions in human life. And, as Socrates insists in this passage, these precautions are those of thinking on the basis of mixed cases.

It may seem odd to choose the *Phaedo* as a reference for the idea of mixture, since this dialogue is one of the main sources for the traditional interpretation of the theory of ideas. For almost the entire dialogue, Socrates is made to argue the purity of the ideas, their independence from the things of sense, their primary reality with respect to those things, and the eternity of their pure selfsameness. The philosopher welcomes death, he argues, because in death one is freed from precisely the distracting mixing of things that the senses and bodily emotions and experiences necessarily involve. Further, one will be immortal, because the soul on its own is pure, like the ideas, and consequently cannot be destroyed, having, for example, no parts to break up into. For these reasons the philosopher's life is in fact a practice of death: "true philosophers make dying their profession."[19]

I suggest, however, that Socrates does not mean what he says for most of the dialogue.[20] First, he is talking to Pythagorean philosophers,[21] Simmias and Cebes, and defending a classically Pythagorean view of the relations of body, soul, and truth. But the dialogue, as I mentioned above, is named after and largely narrated by Phaedo, one of Socrates' circle.[22] And Phaedo does not speak during these discussions, so we are prompted to wonder what he might think of these un-Socratic, Pythagorean arguments.

Second, Phaedo is part of the discussion only when Socrates insists that mixture, rather than purity of soul and being, is a basis for thought, a moment that is stressed by Plato in several ways. As I mentioned above, Phaedo's entry into the discussion occurs almost exactly in the middle of the dialogue.[23] It is also immediately preceded by a breaking of the narrative thread. For most of the dialogue so far, Phaedo has been narrating the discussion, which takes place in Socrates' prison cell between Socrates and his Pythagorean friends. Now Phaedo is interrupted by the circle of friends to whom he is telling the story—at another time and in another place—and who are dismayed by the objections raised against Socrates' arguments by his Pythagorean interlocutors. (It is also noteworthy that Socrates encourages such objections throughout the dialogue.)

What is more, when Phaedo returns to his account to explain how Socrates dealt with this crisis, he tells us that Socrates' first response is to address Phaedo for the first time, and to do so with reference to Phaedo's body:

he laid his hand on my head and gathered up the curls on my neck—he never missed a chance of teasing me about my curls—and said "to-morrow,

I suppose, Phaedo, you will cut off this beautiful hair [in mourning for Socrates]." "I expect so, Socrates," I said. [Socrates replied,] "Not if you take my advice."[24]

The narrative of the discussion in the jail has already been interrupted by Phaedo's listeners; now, on returning to the jail setting, the thread of the discussion *within* that narrative is itself broken by Socrates. And surely it cannot be unimportant that he breaks the thread of a discussion about the desirable freeing of the soul from the body by speaking lovingly and encouragingly of Phaedo's body.[25]

In fact, this interruption itself is also interrupted, by Phaedo's questioning Socrates' suggestion that the "great majority" are between the extremes of good and bad. After his various examples showing that extremes are rare, Socrates says, "however, you have led me into a digression."[26] This "digression" in fact consists in the grounds for Socrates' suggestion that extremes are unusual: that is, that particular passage is what is singled out by this peculiar interruption within an interruption.

Third, this emphasized moment in the dialogue itself includes a number of indications that Socrates does not mean what he says in the rest of it. In addition to his initial interest in Phaedo's body, his argument that extremes are unusual consists entirely in a series of references to sense observation: large and small, white and black, ugly and beautiful. That is, Socrates bases his claim about the foundations of thinking on the bodily senses. And this, again, is the passage that is doubly emphasized by the interruption within an interruption.

Further, immediately after the mention of Phaedo's hair, Socrates compares the relationship between himself and Phaedo to the relationship between Hercules and his comrade Iolaus and places Socrates' Pythagorean interlocutors in the role of their opponents.[27] Phaedo and therefore Phaedo's part in the dialogue are put on Socrates' side as against the Pythagoreans.

And finally, Socrates makes the extremely surprising claim in this passage that the greatest misfortune is not death, which has been the subject of discussion so far, but dislike for argument.[28] This seems a strong indication that the discussion he is now having with Phaedo is more fundamental than the Pythagorean discussion about immortality, and that this latter discussion is therefore fundamentally misguided in taking death as the essential philosophical issue.[29]

There is a very robust humor and patience here, since the discussion about immortality takes up almost the entirety of the dialogue before and after this extraordinary interruption, which contains a foundational inter-ruption/digression that itself follows an interruption of the entire setting. Plato makes his point with a huge and, as I shall argue, hugely constructive indelicacy.

It is nice for my overall thesis that Socrates describes the grounds for his suggestion that mixed cases are usual as a digression.[30] This can be taken as either an ironic way to emphasize its importance, or a way to undermine its importance, or perhaps both.

8.2.2. *Mixture and Socratic Method in the* Phaedo

If this interpretation is right so far, then Plato is offering us another typical Socratic dialogue. Inadequate arguments—here Socrates' own—are made by Socrates to yield clues to a more adequate starting presupposition, but the clues are given indirectly. Socrates does not take up the clue, drops the thread, so that the reader is forced to do the thinking for her/himself. In this case the (so far) inadequate arguments are those containing the theory of ideas.

The link with what is traditionally taken to be Socratic thought goes much further. Near the start of the *Phaedo,* Socrates expresses surprise that Cebes and Simmias have not heard certain philosophical tenets (what "they say") from their Pythagorean teacher Philolaus.[31] In this way he sets himself up to defend a view indistinguishable from the Pythagorean view. But shortly afterwards he associates his argument with his defense during the trial that brought him to prison. "You mean, I suppose, that I must make a formal defense against this charge. . . . Very well then, let me try to make a more convincing defense to you than I made at my trial."[32] He ends this phase of the discussion with a similar reference.[33] The Socratic wisdom we are presented with in the defense in the *Apology* is one of ignorance about such fundamental issues as the immortality of the soul.[34] And in the *Phaedo,* Socrates ends the crucial central conversation with Phaedo by reasserting exactly this position. What he says presupposes that he does not know either way:

> You know how, in an argument, people who have no real education care nothing for the facts of the case, and are only anxious to get their point of view accepted by the audience? Well, I feel that at this present moment I am as bad as they are. . . . This is how I weigh the position [λογίζομαι: the idea of weighing is not literally in the Greek]. . . . If my theory is really true, it is

right to believe it; while, even if death is extinction, at any rate during this time before my death I shall be less likely to distress my companions . . . and this folly of mine will not live on with me (which would be a calamity).

And he concludes:

That, my dear Simmias and Cebes, is the spirit in which I am prepared to approach the discussion [ἔρχομαι ἐπὶ τὸν λόγον]. As for you, if you take my advice, you will think very little of Socrates, and much more of the truth. . . . You must not allow me . . . to deceive both myself and you.[35]

Again Socrates shifts the entire focus of the discussion. First he shifted the theme of fundamental misfortune from death to dislike of argument. Here he shifts the entire way of proceeding from a defense of a single, given truth to an exploration of the relevant alternatives, on the basis of an indecision.

One implication of this shift is that we are dealing not with a "Platonic" dialogue as opposed to a "Socratic" dialogue but with a Socratic dialogue in the deep sense of a thoughtful exploration consistently based on rigorous ignorance. Another implication is that Plato, through Socrates, is not rejecting the Pythagorean view nor, with it, the theory of ideas. He is presenting this view as something that needs to be thought about, and needs to be thought about in balance with the alternative, the thinking on the basis of mixture. And if the entire dialogue is taken as a unity, as Socrates' last statement summing up the philosopher's life, then he is presenting philosophy as a combination—or mixed mixture—of fundamental indecision and the rigorously pure exploration of an assumption.

It is, after all, only because the theory of ideas is thoroughly explored and its limitations discovered, that mixture can be established as a necessary starting point. And it is also only because mixture can be a starting point that a pure point of view can be fairly explored without circularly and therefore arbitrarily either simply accepting or rejecting it.

Differently put, in a sense the philosopher's life *is* a practice of death, as Socrates claims to the Pythagoreans: truth is external to itself, so that the truth about life is external to life. But this externality to life *is* life. Accordingly *this* practice of death is exactly the opposite, as well as being itself.

If this dialogue sums up Socrates' philosophical life, Plato is also presenting philosophy as a combination—or mixed mixture—of fiction and rigorous thought. That is, it is a combination of what can be thought and what excludes thought, what is specifically not thought (such as the directives of Socrates' *daimonion* and of his dreams, and the Wittgensteinian "I want to say . . ." discussed in the introductory section to this part of the book. At the start of the *Phaedo,* for example, Socrates says that he is adapting Aesop's fables because of a dream that recurred through his life). And he is also presenting philosophy as a mixture of interventive and descriptive truth, with respect to both feelings and thought. He is being true both to his own principle and to the dogmatic Pythagorean principle of his interlocutors, offering both simply a reasoned dogma and the mixture of indecision plus explored assumption, and allowing them to unsettle each other and perhaps as a result resettle each other or one or the other in the reader. In the act of doing this, he avoids presenting and acting on his own undogmatic mixture as itself simply a reasoned dogma, that is, without fair consideration and exploration of the dogmatic alternative to it.

But one possible outcome is that the truth of the theory of ideas as presented to the Pythagoreans becomes legitimately settled for the reader. This Socratic dialogue, then (like any other, I believe), is also a traditionally Platonic dialogue, precisely in being purely Socratic.

While the second half of the dialogue pursues exactly the same Pythagorean themes as the first, it does so now with the Socratic attitude or posture. What Plato teaches is not primarily a content, a theory or doctrine, but "the spirit in which . . . to approach the discussion" ("ἔρχομαι ἐπὶ τὸν λόγον"): how to "go toward" the discussion. In other words, he teaches that and how one's thinking needs to approach itself: that is, from outside itself. Rigorous thought and truth, as I argued above, are partly external to themselves.

In this case, the truth of the mixture in whose context thinking begins itself involves the purity that it also excludes. That is, its own nature allows the possibility of purity. Just so, the typicality of intermediate cases that, Socrates warns Phaedo, should tell us to think, to be critical, does not simply exclude the possibility of pure cases. In fact the very thinking that the mixed cases advise is what makes the establishment of pure cases possible. Without the caution of that thinking, we become disillusioned and give up, while with it we are able to avoid being fooled by false arguments:

> "Well, then, Phaedo, . . . supposing that there is an argument which is true and valid and capable of being discovered, if anyone nevertheless . . . was finally content to shift the blame from himself to the arguments, and spend the rest of his life loathing and decrying them, and so missed the chance of knowing the truth about reality; would it not be a deplorable thing?"
> "It would indeed," I said.[36]

The enormous indelicacy, then, with which Plato dismisses almost the entirety of the dialogue via the little central discussion with Phaedo at the same time and with equal cogency repositions *itself,* replaces itself with nothing. It is a deliberate and elaborate performance of tripping itself up, or pulling itself out from underneath itself. It is a humorous clumsiness or ungainliness, and with perfect precision or poise: it involves the detailed presentation of each incompatible standpoint, dismisses each presentation, and dismisses its dismissal, so that it neither does nor does not weigh on a particular side. Its clumsiness allows this balance to bring out something very subtle (what I am calling the "sometimes" logic and the attitude that recognizes it) clearly into the open, and to do so with truth to the interventive rhetorical necessities involved in the truth of this something, given this particular (mixed) audience. Accordingly, its clumsiness *is* its poise, and its humor is at one and the same time perfect seriousness.[37]

8.2.3. *Mixture and the Approach to Truth in the* Phaedo

As is evident in a variety of ways, the second half of the *Phaedo* proceeds on the basis of fundamental mixture. For a start, the interruption by Phaedo's audience occurs just after Phaedo has related how Simmias and Cebes each presented objections to Socrates' arguments about the immortality of the soul. Now, after the conversation with Phaedo, Socrates first establishes to Simmias's satisfaction that his objection was a result exactly of the careless approach to thinking that Socrates has insisted is responsible for dislike of arguments. Simmias's argument "appealed to me," Simmias says, "without any proof to support it, as being based on plausible analogy; which is why most people find it attractive. But I realize that theories which rest their proof upon plausibility are imposters, and unless you are on your guard, they deceive you properly."[38]

Socrates then goes on to address Cebes' objection, and he does so, "after spending some time in reflection,"[39] by giving an account of his own intellectual history. Socrates' trial and therefore Plato's *Apology* are evoked earlier in the dialogue. Here there is another parallel, in that Socrates gives his intellectual history in the *Apology*, too. He does so there in order to explain why he is a philosopher, that is, someone who questions because s/he knows nothing fundamental. Here he explains that he came to find the tradition of explanations found in the natural philosophy (philosophy of nature) of his predecessors unsatisfactory, because these explanations led to inconsistencies and contradictions. Socrates specifies further and at length that in the case of Anaxagoras, the kind of explanation he gives confuses one kind of being with another. The equivalent explanation of Socrates' presence in prison, for example, would be in terms of the contractions of his muscles that brought him there, rather than in terms of the social and ethical actions and convictions that were involved.[40] That is, the meaning of the thing being explained is missed: the subject of discussion is changed in the way I discussed in Idea 6.

Socrates offers his own method of explanation, "a haphazard [or "confused"] method of my own."[41] This method is based on maintaining a distance from the thing being investigated:

> it occurred to me that I must guard against the same sort of risk which people run when they watch and study an eclipse of the sun; they really do sometimes injure their eyes, unless they study its reflection. . . . So I decided that I must have recourse to theories [or "words," or "arguments," or "reasons": "λόγους"], and use them in trying to discover the truth about things. Perhaps my illustration is not quite apt; because I do not at all admit that an inquiry by means of theory employs "images" any more than one which confines itself to facts. But however that may be . . . .[42]

The risk here is the same one Socrates warned against when discussing dislike of arguments: being taken in by arguments by being too uncritical in the first place. Differently put, one risks an intervention in one's organs of knowledge (or, since this is an analogy, in the conditions of one's knowledge) by the direct truth of what one's inquiry should be investigating, rather than finding a considered description of that truth.[43] But as I argued above, such an intervention is both inescapable and indispensable in undertaking true description. The remedy is an initial external approach. This approach consists in acknowledging the risk of being taken in by the thing being investigated, and so maintaining an undecided, indirect relation to it, and in that context, "in every case I first lay down [ὑποθέμενος] the theory which I judge to be soundest; and then whatever seems to agree with it . . . I assume to be true, and whatever does not I assume not to be true."[44] A fundamental indecision together with an assumption or hypothesis.

Once this general external approach has been achieved, Socrates offers a two-step exploration. There is a lot of disagreement among Plato scholars about the kind of explanation Socrates is aiming at with this and related explorations in other dialogues. As Benson notes, "Most of these commentators have argued that what Socrates has in mind is something like a logical cause or what Aristotle called a formal cause. Others have suggested that Socrates has in mind something closer to Aristotle's efficient cause."[45] In the language I am using, this is a disagreement about whether Socrates is looking for a cause that is internally or externally related to what he is explaining. In keeping with my discussion so far, I shall try to show that both sides of the disagreement are right.[46]

The first step consists in a "safe" explanation of something: that it is what it is because of what makes it what it is. For example, "it is by Beauty that beautiful things are beautiful."[47] As Socrates' criticism of Anaxagoras suggests, this "safe" answer ensures that we are dealing with the appropriate kind of being, that we are not changing the subject while claiming to explain it. As Vlastos notes, "If this were to strike us as uninformative, Plato would agree . . . but insist that it is not useless on that account, for it would save us from misdirecting our search for *aitiai* [causes or explanatory factors] to irrelevant factors."[48] It ensures, among other things, that we keep meaning what we think we mean. As the Stranger in the *Sophist* suggests, "dividing according to kinds, not taking the same form for a different one or a different one for the same—is not that the business of the [philosophical] science of dialectic?"[49] This explanation, then, is purely internal to the thing being explained, entirely identical with it: beauty is explained by Beauty. As I argued above, however, and as Socrates exemplifies by his history of his own thought, we are brought to recognize the need for this internality by the externality, the uncommitted caution, with which we approach thinking. The presentation of this "safe" step, this thinking that is purely internal to its subject matter, ends with Socrates' insistence on not mixing the levels of the principle and its consequences. In an important sense, this involves not mixing the different kinds of being that make up rigorous discourse.

Now, there are, of course, principles involved in Socrates' present discussion, including his comments on how to discuss principles. And as I mentioned above, this insistence on not mixing principle and consequence is immediately followed and so stressed by the second interruption of the narrative by Phaedo's audience. The content of that interruption is perhaps also relevant to the issue of principles. Echecrates, one of Phaedo's listeners, says, "It seems to me that Socrates made his meaning extraordinarily clear to even a limited intelligence," and Phaedo replies, "That was certainly the feeling of all of us who were present, Echecrates."[50] Is it the same meaning that is clear to (the possibly Pythagorean) Echecrates and to (the presumably Socratic) Phaedo? It would fit nicely with my interpretation if it is not. The *Phaedo* itself contains an explicit illustration of this kind of conflict of understanding. Early on, when Socrates suggests that true philosophers are preparing themselves for death, Simmias laughs and says, "most people would think . . . that it was a very good hit at the philosophers to say that they are half dead already, and that they, the normal people, are quite aware that death would serve the philosophers right."[51] Socrates answers:

> And they would be quite correct, Simmias; except in thinking that they are "quite aware." They are not at all aware in what sense true philosophers are half dead, or in what sense they deserve death, or what sort of death they deserve. But let us dismiss them and talk among ourselves.[52]

Here we have two different and, within limits, very clear understandings of the same fundamental issue, each based on different principles.

It is important, I think, that Socrates' brusque dismissal of the opposing "normal" view is itself true to the principle of that other view: it is a principle of being unthinking. Given the discussion in this Part about incompatible principles and the establishment of truth, it is not an unphilosophical response.

But presumably Socrates' *own* audience, the Pythagorean Simmias and Cebes, have a different understanding of the issues they discuss from Socrates'. And Socrates' example of un-Socratic reasoned dogmatism—the pursuing of the consequences of an hypothesis without also at some point mixing this pursuit with a questioning of its principle—through most of his discussion with the Pythagoreans is true to their principle in turn. With Phaedo, as I discussed above, he behaves differently.

I suggest that Phaedo, as a silent (and Socratic) listener through most of the dialogue, like Socrates in the *Sophist,* is not other-insensible, and is therefore able to hear both what Socrates and what the others hear in the same statements—or at least to be aware of that possible distinction. Accordingly, he would also hear what in Socrates is response to the differences in meaning and in the principles that make those meanings what they are. Plato makes Phaedo teach us, his readers, not directly but by example, requiring an inference on the reader's part and hence action on the basis of truth, which is something freely established, and not on the basis of uncritical and so arbitrary acceptance.[53]

The second step in the kind of exploration Socrates proposes consists in exactly the kind of recourse to unrelated kinds of being that Socrates criticized in Anaxagoras:

> don't answer in the exact terms of the question. . . . I say this because besides the "safe answer" that I described at first, as the result of this discussion I

now see another means of safety. Suppose, for instance, that you ask me what must be present in body to make it hot, I shall not return the safe but ingenuous answer that it is heat, but a more sophisticated one . . . namely that it is fire.[54]

A quality, which cannot exist independently of something whose quality it is, is now explained as being what it is by means of an independent thing, which has a different kind of being from a quality. This is a kind of explanation that is external to what it explains. The first kind is tautological, redundant; the second is nonsensically false of the subject of inquiry: Aristotle's criticisms of the theory of ideas.

I suggest that both steps go together, however. The first ensures that we are talking about the thing we are supposed to be talking about. The second then invokes the different kind of being only in the context of the subject at hand: that is, this being is evoked only in those respects in which it is relevant to the meaning of the thing being explained. That a different kind of being *can* be relevant at all, however, is mysterious. But the self-canceling nature of rigorous artificiality justifies this possibility: the difference of nature cancels itself into relevance, just as the redundancy cancels itself into difference. And this self-canceling character explains, at the level of the nature of truth itself, why the two-step procedure is preceded by an external, or artificial, "approach": it is only by canceling something inappropriate that one achieves appropriateness. The two steps of redundancy and nonsensical irrelevance, then, work together to cancel each other into sense and substance. And because of these misdirected steps, the sense and substance are established, are rigorous. Just so, in the *Sophist* the Stranger is made to argue that difference (or nonbeing) and sameness go into making each other what they are, and this is what allows us to speak truly about things.[55]

In social contexts the foundational indirection would be, for example, a tactful approach. This kind of approach makes space for the inquirer to correct ways in which the fact of inquiry might mislead its subject with respect, for example, to what the inquiry implies, and so to what response is called for. And it also makes space for its subject to correct the misshaping effects of the inquiry, even to the point of avoiding it altogether.

The rest of the discussion about the immortality of the soul in the *Phaedo* is conducted by means of this two-step method, based on this external or indirect approach. But the discussion is not only *approached* from the position of fundamental mixture, of Socratic indecision plus assumption or hypothesis: the explanations themselves are a mixture of pure—and, I argued above, artificial—concepts or universals and sensible or substantial things. This means that the theory of ideas is used together with the sensible things it excludes. Both the Pythagorean and the Socratic positions are used, in tandem. That is, the Socratic method is external to itself as well as being internal to itself.

That explanation necessarily and rightly involves a mixture of the theory of ideas with sensible things is explicitly argued in the *Sophist*. There the Stranger is made to argue that both of two views are inadequate: the view that "real existence belongs only to that which can be handled and offers resistance to the touch," and the view that "true reality consists in certain intelligible and bodiless forms."[56] The Stranger is made to insist that:

> only one course is open to the philosopher. . . . He must refuse to accept from the champions either of the one or of the many forms the doctrine that reality is changeless, and he must turn a deaf ear to the other party who represent reality as everywhere changing. . . . He must declare that reality or the sum of things is both at once—all that is unchangeable and all that is in change.[57]

Neither the theory of ideas nor the opposite, but both at once. While this version of the combination of both views is almost immediately refuted in the dialogue, it is replaced, as I argue in Part II, Chapter 4, with a more sophisticated version of the same combination.[58]

The *Timaeus* offers a description of the construction of the universe that also supports the necessity of this combination. The eternal, unchanging ideas are said to be connected with the changing, perishing things of sense that are their images through what is named "space" or "place" ("*chora*"), whose role is described as follows:

> there is a third nature, which is space and is eternal, . . . and provides a home for all created things. . . . For an image, since the reality after which it is modeled does not belong to it . . . must be inferred to be in another [that is, in space], grasping existence in some way or another, or it could not be at all. But true and exact reason, vindicating the nature of true being, maintains that while two things [that is, the image and space] are different they cannot exist one of them in the other and so be one and also two at the same time.[59]

This peculiar "third nature," mixing both what is eternal and what is not, is required by the theory of ideas. Otherwise the ideas cannot be linked to the sensible things that are fundamentally different from them. That is, they would not be able to explain sensible things, although they are only understood to exist at all because they are supposed to explain them.

But the "third nature" in turn cannot help sharing the incoherence of mixing these incompatible natures. Plato was clearly aware of that: it

> is apprehended, when all sense is absent, by a kind of spurious reason, and is hardly real—which we, beholding as in a dream, say of all existence that it must of necessity be in some place and occupy a space. . . . Of these and other things of the same kind . . . we are unable to . . . determine the truth about them.[60]

That is, Plato holds consciously to a theory with consequences that are both central to the theory and directly contradict the aim of the theory. The theory aims for pure self-consistency; its consequences are a "kind of nature" unthinkable by self-consistent thought, by "true and exact reason."

One could argue that Plato simply and nobly acknowledges the limitations of human understanding here. But then it is absurd for him to maintain the theory of ideas, which presupposes perfection of knowledge, except in order to show more clearly its own failure and consequently the limitations of human thought. I argued above, however, that he does both this *and* keeps rigorously to the inconclusiveness of the "third kind." In this case, if "space" (*"chora"*) is unthinkable, then we do not know if it invalidates the possibility of assured knowledge. Neither the theory of ideas nor the opposite, but (sometimes) both (sometimes) at once.[61]

On this reading, if I may say so, though it is couched in an utterly different style and by an utterly different personality, Plato's is a thoroughly Wittgensteinian way of thinking.[62]

8.3. GOODNESS, TRUTH, AND MIXTURE

Socrates begins his explanation of his own method in the *Phaedo* by describing his excitement on discovering that Anaxagoras emphasized Mind as an explanation of the universe. This was important to him, Socrates says, because:

> if this is so, Mind in producing order sets everything in order and arranges each individual thing in the way that is best for it. . . . On this view there was only one thing for a man to consider, with regard both to himself and to anything else, namely the best and highest good; although this would nec-

essarily imply knowing what is less good, since both were covered by the same knowledge.[63]

In the ensuing discussion, as I noted above, Socrates, disappointed by Anaxagoras's neglect of his own explanatory principle, insists on investigating things with strict reference to their meaning. What is best for a thing, then, is what the thing is, what it means to be that thing.

In the *Republic* Socrates is made to describe justice as follows: "we laid down . . . that each one man must perform one social service in the state for which his nature was best adapted. . . . This . . . if taken in a certain sense appears to be justice, this principle of doing one's own business."[64] Here, too, in the social context, living out the person's nature, what or who s/he is, is identified with what is good.

The idea of the Good is said in the *Republic* to be what ultimately gives being and truth and knowledge to everything else. This idea is not directly explained there, nor anywhere else. I suggest that this idea is what I argued to be the "nothing further to know" (in note 37, in connection with Socrates' explanation of what supports the earth), the fundamental indecision and/or hesitation, the fact of the ironic and self-ironizing and so fundamentally indirect self-displacement or self-tabling of rigorous thought by which it renders itself beside the point. As I argued above, the truth of the inquirer is involved in the truth of the subject of inquiry. Consequently, a subjective ethical discipline (including, for example, honesty) and way of life are required to allow the things of the world to show themselves as they are. And this discipline involves a fundamental indecision, corresponding in things and events to a fundamental hesitancy of being.[65] The idea of the Good, then, is not (always) the One, as the recent tradition I discussed in the general Introduction argues, but is rather the mixture of the principles of the selfsame One and the self-external Indeterminate Dyad.

In fact, then, the idea of the Good *is* directly presented in the *Republic,* in the mixed form, directly expressing its own mixed character, of being both explicitly asserted and only indirectly explained.

8.4. TRUTH BEYOND RIGOROUS THOUGHT

Given the identification of what is with what is best, it is interesting that Socrates goes on to talk about what he thought Anaxagoras would say about the earth, including that "if he asserted that the earth was in the centre, he would explain in detail that it was better for it to be there."[66] As I mentioned above (see note 37), in the myth near the end of the *Phaedo* Socrates argues that if the earth is in the center, it needs no explanation for how it stays there. I suggest, again, that this is an image for what I argued corresponds in the world to the ungainly poise or elegantly poised clumsiness, the displacement of indecision by indecision itself, in finding an explanation of the being of a thing (or justification of an action), in grasping what it is and how it is as it is. For at that point, when explanation has been pursued to the point of showing how it sweeps itself out of the way, showing itself to be beside the point, one needs no further explanation or moral justification than the simple grasp of the thing or situation, which is an explanation without explanation. When one has that grasp, one has, simply, understood the thing. One does not even need "nothing further" at that point: the concept of explanation itself becomes meaningless, and with it, the very concept of going further.[67]

Differently put, the *relevance of explanation itself* disappears, and with it the sense of the problems that arise from requiring an explanation. A later tradition (Hegel's) will say, "one has made the transition to grasping the concept of the thing," although part of my argument is that the idea of "concept" is not adequate. This grasp does not need that or any kind of category: it grasps the thing in simple externality to other things, and also to the act of grasping or knowing it. The explanatory ideas and factors, whether pure ideas or sensible or substantial things, disappear as in any way relevant.

It is at the point at which one grasps the thing in its externality—and because this is externality also to one's very act of grasping it, this is the point at which one's grasp of the thing is itself also external to the thing— that knowledge or understanding is achieved. This external grasp *is* understanding of the thing, as it is beyond (external to) the meanings for rigorous thought of both internality and externality. And it is achieved by the double engagement of externality and internality that the ideas and sensual or sensible things and factors artificially involve.

Rigorous thought in general, I suggest, is made in order to vanish. That is why it is not simply a problem but also an advantage that it is perhaps never quite clear whether pure rigor of thought is ever quite there in the first place. And that it is never quite clear whether it is ever quite not there, also. And these formulations, too, sometimes, have only their limited truth.

PART II

Truth and Love

When someone asks me "What colour is the book over there?," and I say "Red," and then he asks "What made you call this colour 'red'?," I shall in most cases have to say: "Nothing *makes* me call it red; that is, *no reason.* I just looked at it and said 'it's red.'" . . .

When we philosophize about this sort of thing we almost invariably do something of this sort: we repeat to ourselves a certain experience, say by looking fixedly at a certain object and trying to "read off" as it were the name of its colour. And it is quite natural that doing so again and again we should be inclined to say, "something particular happens while we say the word 'blue.'" For we are aware of going again and again through the same process. But ask yourself: Is this also the process which we usually go through when on various occasions—not philosophizing—we name the colour of an object?

—Wittgenstein, *The Blue and Brown Books,* 148, 150

If anyone should think he has solved the problem of life and feel like telling himself that everything is quite easy now, he can see that he is wrong just by recalling that there was a time when this "solution" had not been discovered; but it must have been possible to live *then* too and the solution which has now been discovered seems fortuitous in relation to how things were then. And it is the same in the study of logic. If there were a "solution" to the problems of logic (philosophy) we should only need to caution ourselves that there was a time when they had not been solved (and even at that time people must have known how to live and think).

—Wittgenstein, *Culture and Value,* 4e

CHAPTER 1

What Plato Is About: An Overview

I argued in Part I that what Plato's works are about is not *simply* a content we can describe, but also involves an interventive dimension that we realize (in both senses of the word) by our own thinking, actions, and attitudes. And this interventive dimension will sometimes rightly falsify the descriptive content, including the descriptions I am giving in this chapter.

With that in mind, I propose that Plato's achievement lies in showing how to let things be what they are without any explanation or understanding. Since this is a letting-be of what things are, it is a relation to the truth of things. And as an explicit relation to this truth, it is an understanding. My proposal means, then, that Plato shows how to understand things without understanding them. Now, I have been arguing that Plato's work makes visible what is really true of truth-seeking thought generally. That is, this understanding without understanding is ultimately what truth-oriented thinking in general achieves, even dry and matter-of-fact scientific thinking.

A sort of understanding without understanding is sometimes seen as the work of spiritual insight or of the fine arts. In this chapter I summarize why I think it is also the work of truth-seeking thinking, what it involves, how it makes sense, and, in a general way, how it appears in Plato's works. In chapters 2 to 4, I explore and test this interpretation of Plato in more detail, by looking at the whole of a short dialogue and at details of the overall structure of some long dialogues. In the brief concluding chapter I make some very general remarks about the significance of Plato's framework.

Now I turn to my explanation of what I mean by Plato's achievement.

1.1. OVERVIEW OF PLATO'S STANDPOINT

1.1.1. Explanation Cancels Itself

As I argued in Idea 6.1, one begins thinking with what one sees at first glance. One begins, then, with things that are not yet explained or understood. The purpose of thinking is to move on from the surface where one begins. But it is the surface that one is aiming to explain or understand. It is *this surface* that must be accounted for at the deepest depths. And, as I argued in Idea 6, this surface must be grasped *as what it is on the surface,* so that one explains *it* and not something else. What one sees at first glance must therefore be retained right through to the deepest depths. This is the principle motivating phenomenology, which is explicitly and deliberately descriptive and not explanatory. It also motivates, I believe, the contemporary emphasis on conceptual analysis in analytic philosophy.[1]

The deepest explanation or understanding, then, is still an explanation or understanding *of the surface thing* being explained. And that surface thing is precisely something not explained or understood. The deepest and only adequate explanation therefore explains the thing as it is *before it has been explained.* Differently put, explanation or the act of gaining knowledge alters or intervenes in its own object, and this intervention must be eliminated in turn before one has adequate knowledge of that object (as I argued in Idea 2).

We always arrive at things with something like an interpretive framework already, and this involves an understanding or explanation. As Plato constantly emphasizes, the prejudices this framework involves need to be worked away, even if to allow their validity ultimately to be confirmed (that is, to discover whether they are in fact prejudices). Now, it may not be possible to eliminate our initial interpretive framework entirely or even for the most part. But it is also unnecessary and undesirable to eliminate it.

It is *unnecessary* because we can let the thing be unexplained in certain respects only. In fact, absence of explanation itself is meaningful only in the context of a lot of explained features. Otherwise we would not even recognize the thing as a particular thing distinguished or distinguishable from other things. It follows that what it *means* to let something be unexplained *is* partly to have a context of a lot of explained features.

On the other hand, it is *undesirable* to eliminate our initial framework entirely. Given that knowledge-seeking overcomes its own intervention by allowing that intervention to carry through to intervening in itself, this framework is also the means by which it itself is eliminated. Differently put, self-cancellation involves *something that is canceled* in the relevant respects. And if it is true that knowledge-seeking intervenes in its object and overcomes this problem by intervening in itself in turn, using itself to cancel itself, then our initial assumptions and prejudices are not *simply* prejudices but also the means to truth and even the truth itself. I discuss this further in the following chapters.

Innocence, then, or the absence of interfering experience, is achieved, not *simply* natural. And it involves both knowing *and* not knowing *at all*. The former gets itself out of its own way by being recognized and developed to its fullest. Since it is in this way that it makes itself *fully* external to, uninterfering with, what it knows, it is external or irrelevant to what it knows *in and by* its full relevance or internal relation to it.

It is worth noting that, as I suggested in Idea 4.1, even if we just recognize our assumptions, while we may not get rid of their effects simply by doing that, we are *already* occupying a place that is not limited to our assumptions. In a way, the present discussion is an account of this subtle partial transcendence of assumptions and its implications. Self-awareness involves an externality to, a difference from, self and hence from what self depends on, as I discussed above.

1.1.2. *The Surface Reappears in the Depths*

There are two kinds of case in which the explanation or understanding must offer us something different from the surface thing. First, the surface thing may be a true appearance, the subjective awareness of something that corresponds to something that is really there, but in a different form from the appearance. For example, in one of our contemporary theories, colors are the subjective awareness of different frequencies of light waves that are not absorbed by the object we see. We do not see frequencies, but the colors we do see really correspond to different frequencies. Second, the surface thing may be a false appearance, an illusion, like mirages of water on the road. According to our contemporary theory, we in fact see a bit of the sky in the wrong place because of how our subjective perceptual apparatus works.

But first, in the case of true appearance, what is true about it reappears as the basis of the adequate explanation. For example, the differences between colors do reappear as differences in frequencies. But the facts of the particular colors themselves, which do not reappear in the explanation, remain to be explained. And in fact our explanation by means of pigments in the eyes does not treat the particular colors themselves, in their nature as *colors,* as true appearances. The colors themselves do not accurately record anything "in" the object but are entirely explained by properties of our subjective perceptual apparatus, the pigments in our eyes.

Second, the equivalent kind of reappearance in the explanatory depths of what is true about the surface thing being explained is necessary in the case of illusions. In their case, their surface appearance already involves error. A number of equivalently "first" glances, say using different senses, will not show anything like the same thing. *The possibility or the structure of error* must therefore reappear in the explanation. Otherwise the error has not been explained, and the explanation of the thing is incomplete.[2] The illusion needs to be explained in terms of some explanatory thing's having in itself the capacity, as it were, not to coincide properly with itself, to differ from itself. The explanatory something must have in itself something at a distance from itself. In our contemporary theory, mirages are possible because light *moving in a straight line* is our contact with the object, and when this line (not the light, but the line) *varies from itself* (it moves from the sky to the ground and, when the light bounces, it changes its angle), we see wrongly. Our seeing is the result of a self-variance independent of us.

It follows from my argument, however, and is explicit in Plato, that as long as this self-variance is not located in the object itself, illusion has not yet been explained successfully. Our contemporary theory locates it in the properties of light, which is only the medium through which we see the object itself. In the passages I quoted in Idea 8.1, when Plato has the Stranger in the *Sophist* argue that nonbeing exists in its own right in some sense, is part of reality itself, he does so specifically to account for the possibility of falsehood.[3] The character of the surface must reappear in the depths. It is this requirement that motivates the Stranger's argument that the Ideas themselves, the basis of the being, truth, and explanation of things, have self-otherness in them.

In fact, as I argued in Idea 6, *any* explanation already departs from the thing being explained. More than this, when we simply notice the thing as something needing to be explained, we have set up the truth of it as it stands, as incomplete.[4] One inquires into something only if there is a question about it. We have set up a separation between its truth as it stands and its further truth. Our noticing it as in need of explanation has already identified its being as uncertain in some respect and therefore as not simply what it is, as not quite coinciding with itself. That is, our act of wondering, of recognizing that we need to seek its truth, has intervened in its truth. And the inquiry then needs to undo that interventive distance from the truth of the thing that it itself presupposes and establishes. That is, the inquiry needs to end at the surface thing as it is *before one even approached it inquiringly.*

Approaching this point differently: the inquiry needs to identify and eliminate the contrasting possible accounts that are wrong. And if this is done fully, it eliminates *any* accounts, including the right one, since without meaningful contrasts, no account stands out. Again, then, explanation and understanding aim to grasp the surface thing in a way for which explanation and understanding are themselves meaningless.

As I argued in Idea 2, then, rigorous inquiry is itself a kind of mistake with respect to its aim. But it succeeds precisely by recognizing that and recognizing how it is a mistake. Consequently a rigorous being-mistaken is part of the working of truth, is itself a fundamental kind of truth, both internally and externally related to direct valid insight.

Ideas that have meaning in the process of finding truth, like Plato's Ideas, then, disappear entirely as meaningful when the truth is gained. But since this self-canceling structure is part of the roots of truth, explanatory ideas *truly do* refer to something when they are there and *truly* do not when they are not there. I elaborated this "variegated texture of truth" in Idea 5. Differently put, as I argued in Idea 3, the rhetorical dimensions of truth—the fact that truth needs to be expressed differently in different contexts and for different aims (say, in terms of Ideas at one time and so that the notion of Ideas has no meaning at all at another)—are rhetorical dimensions of *truth*, and not simply rhetorical devices simply external to truth and leaving it unaffected.

Approaching this self-cancellation of explanation from the other direction, it is the structure of self-externality, including its self-cancellation, at the roots of truth itself that makes the self-cancellation of explanation both possible and necessary. I argued this in Ideas 5 and 6. But one can also make this point by applying this discussion of explanation to explanation itself. The surface fact of explanation or of the search for understanding itself, the surface fact that it already departs from or alters the truth of its object from the start just by seeking to understand it, must reappear at the roots of the explanation of that fact itself. Now, truth itself is the aim of the process of inquiry and so partly makes that process what it is. And in general, truth also includes the truth *of* the process of inquiry. The nature of truth is, then, part of what directly accounts for the nature of explanation. The surface self-externality of the inquiry into truth itself must therefore reappear at the basis of the account of discovered truth itself. Truth itself must be understood as self-external and so also self-canceling. And since truth is the truth of what is, of being (which, oddly, does not exclude what is not, as the discussion in the *Sophist* quoted in Idea 8 argues), being, too, is self-external in a self-canceling way. The self-canceling self-disparity of explanation is therefore both possible and necessary.

1.2. OVERVIEW OF THE STRUCTURE AND RHETORIC OF PLATO'S DIALOGUES

Accordingly, then, Plato offers us what from the point of view of achieved knowledge are sequences of mistakes. As I mentioned above, his dialogues are famously full of misleading arguments.[5] I suggest that he necessarily presents these sequences of mistakes, since the process of explanation is still present and so is interfering with the thing being explained. I shall try to show that these mistakes approximate more and more closely to the truth as it is once knowledge has gotten itself and its effects out of the way and rendered itself meaningless. And somewhere in this approximating series, the process leaps furthest away from the relevant truth in order to intervene in itself, in its own intervening process. For instance, the dialogues often have a digression that sheds unexpected light on the discussion, usually neatly in the middle, like the one in the *Phaedo* that I discussed in Idea 8.2.1 and 8.2.2. I argue shortly below that one example of this leap is Plato's discussion of the Idea of the Good, which is itself part of an explicit digression in the *Republic*.[6]

1.2.1. The Ideas and Particular Things

Plato's Ideas then (genuinely) exist for the sake of knowledge but no longer exist when the knowledge is gained. They undo themselves, are self-canceling. They are objects of knowledge while the inquiry is in progress, since the inquiry orients itself toward them as the truth it seeks. And as I argued above, they *really do exist* as these objects at the time. But once the inquiry has found that truth, the Ideas exist not as objects of knowledge but as the vanishing points that are its self-intervening, self-canceling source. And again, then their existence *really has changed*.

In the *Republic* Plato has Socrates describe the Idea of the Good as the source of all knowledge and being.[7] That is, it is the source of truth in both its subjective and objective aspects.[8] As I mentioned in the Introduction to this book, there are contemporary arguments that the Idea of the Good is not an Idea, being more fundamental than the Ideas. But Plato does have Socrates call it an Idea here. I suggest that it is both an Idea *and* more fundamental than that.[9] And in this way it is like all the Ideas. Since it is the basis of everything, it is the basis of the being or truth of all the Ideas, all the beings and truths. It makes sense that what is true of the Ideas in general, including their coherent self-disparity or self-contradictoriness, should appear most acutely and noticeably in the Idea of the Good. I discuss this extreme character of the Good more fully shortly below. But what makes this and all the Ideas more fundamental than themselves is that their very existence or being consists in disappearing in favor of the truth of the things that they allow to be understood. Their more fundamental dimension is their disappearance together with the emergence of the truth of the particular things they explain.

Socrates' typical emphasis on the simple self-consistency or unity of the Ideas in the dialogues makes sense as a rhetorical or interventive truth. He is typically facing opinions that are by their very nature thoughtlessly universalizing: that is, they unify thoughtlessly. One result is that they are insensible to and so hide genuine unities that thoughtfulness finds, and they do so especially because these unities involve an internal relation to disunity or self-externality. This intervening nature of opinions will prevent any real comprehension and so discussion of alternative understandings until it is brought to awareness. Socrates therefore needs to show their nature as thoughtless unification before he does anything else. Consequently he insists on thinking their self-consistent unity through, at which point this unity itself can show its self-contradiction, its real disunity.

And then Socrates is typically made to indicate, in one way or another, a different understanding of unity as *also* involving disunity in a rigorously self-canceling way. At this point the dialogue *as a whole,* including the rhetorical context it involves, and *not* just Socrates' position, gives the truth of a fundamental coordination of unity and disunity, and of this coordination with a fundamental coordination of thoughtlessness and thoughtfulness. In the dialogue as a whole, the thoughtless unity and hence also the thoughtless disunity engaged by opinion are juxtaposed with and related (internally and externally) by self-canceling dialogue to the rigorous unity and hence also to the rigorous disunity engaged by rigorous thought.[10] The inquiry into truth cancels itself in favor of at least part of the truth it inquires after, and its mistaken, partially thoughtless history is precipitated as part of this truth.

As I discuss in Chapter 4, the dialogues sometimes give a different rhetorical context in which this coordination, rather than *simple* unity or *simple* thoughtfulness, can be articulated. The *Sophist* and *Statesman,* for example, emphasize a method of division of the Ideas from each other rather than a drawing out of the self-consistent meanings of one Idea, and they emphasize both the importance and the faultiness of this method.

Since the Ideas are the truths of particular things, including sensible things and universals that are less universal or less rigorously thought through than the Ideas, particular things are (in this respect, in this rhetorical context) essentially like the Ideas. But the Ideas are the truth of particular things as it must be understood when this truth is *in question*. Accordingly, when this truth is *gained,* it is the particular thing that is known, and not the Idea. Particular things are not like the Ideas, then, in that their *known* truth does not involve the rigorous process of testing the nature and consistency of their compatibility with and relation to a variety of other things and contexts. That process of unification, sorting, and relating disappears with the end of the process of inquiry, and what is left is the particular thing, precisely as a *particular* thing. That is, it is left on its own, without respect to its relation to other things. The universality of the Ideas serves, by its rigorous self-cancellation, to gain a more adequate relation to the particularity of the explained things.

As I argued above, what is to be explained or understood on the surface is retained at the depths of the explanation or understanding. It follows that the Ideas can explain self-identically particular and changing things only by retaining selfsame particularity and change in themselves. And as I previously quoted from the *Sophist,* the Stranger is made to argue there that they are both unchanging and in motion, both selfsame and self-differing.[11] But more, if the Ideas are to explain sensible things, they must retain sensible properties, too. I suggest they do this by having in themselves their own self-cancellation as mere steps on the way to the truth of a particular thing. In existing as and in order to be self-canceling as such steps, they already refer to the sensible qualities that they are steps toward. Differently put, they contain in themselves as tangential vanishing points the truth of the sensible properties they also exclude.[12] The extremely sensual and colorful metaphors, allusions, and stories, then, in which Plato couches his discussions of the Ideas are not only metaphors. Their sensuality captures something simply true about the Ideas.

Of course, read one way, this is nonsense. But my point is that the Ideas have to be read a very particular way if they are to make sense at all (given, for example, Aristotle's criticisms). And if they are read that way, they offer solutions—and to problems for which we have no alternative solutions. The Ideas are not three-dimensional objects, which cannot exist as self-canceling. They are the truth of particular truths, or the truth of adequately truth-oriented thinking (the truth of truth can meaningfully be said to exist only in the context of that thinking). And that is a very different, purely intelligible kettle of fish, rather than one that works simply in accordance with the properties of physical things reported by the senses.

1.2.2. The Idea of the Good and "Nothing Further to Know"

The Idea of the Good is presented as the truth of truth in general. (And we should not forget that this truth is presented this way in the very particular rhetorical articulation of the *Republic*. Even if it is a true presentation there, it may be false in different contexts and circumstances.) Since this Idea is the truth of all the Ideas, it must and does, as I mentioned above, contain the fact of self-cancellation most acutely. Plato has Socrates present it as the "highest matter for learning," on which all other knowledge rests, and claims not to know it and to be unable to discuss it. What he mentions as his grasp on it, which he could perhaps offer to a different audience or at another time, he calls an opinion ("δοκοῦντος ἐμοὶ"), in a context immediately preceded by one of many very strong statements that opinion is inadequate to capture truth.[13] The Idea of the Good is mentioned but does not emerge. I suggest that this is because it exists precisely *as* something that does not emerge.[14]

The Idea of the Good in the *Republic,* I propose, has the same significance as the moments of *aporia,* or fundamental indecision, in other dialogues. It has nothing to do with the particular truth being sought but has everything to do with the nature of truth in general and of seeking for it. It orients the seeker toward truth by rigorously establishing fundamental indecision and is accordingly the source of truth. More than this, it *actively* has nothing to do with the particular truth being sought. It orients the seeker toward the truth of truth in general and so away from the object of the inquiry. In this way it is the source of undoing the falsifying effects on the object of the act of seeking its truth.

In Idea 2 I discussed various ways in which interventive truth can get around itself by focusing on things irrelevant to what it is truth about. The Idea of the Good is such a focus, but in connection with knowledge in general rather than in direct connection with particular points that knowledge is about. It is the source of rigorous self-cancellation, including its own. It is the point at which one recognizes in action that the act itself of seeking truth departs from truth of the thing one seeks truth about. And being interventive as well as descriptive, it is also the point at which one *does* something about that by *actively and fully* departing from the search in order to investigate the departure *that is knowledge-seeking itself* and take it into account.

Plato, then, offers us knowledge of particular things, including sensible things, and only *on the basis of* the failure of knowledge of the foundations of the whole.[15] The Ideas are the real objects of knowledge in the sense that once they have vanished, once their redundancy has been recognized, we have *already* understood. The moment of their self-cancellation does not simply precede the moment of insight but *is* the moment of insight. The Ideas are the vanishing tangential points at which knowledge is able to get out of its own way and precipitate, as this very act, one's truer relation to the particulars. The Idea of the Good, *as Plato presents, or does not present, it,* is one articulation *of that truth about the Ideas and their significance* and one *way of carrying that significance through* in the practice of rigorous thought. It is a tangent to the tangents that are the other Ideas.

The Idea of the Good needs no further tangent or intervening and self-canceling thought to cancel its own intervention and so justify its descriptive truth and give it a foundation. What its self-cancellation shows is the truth of the interventive aspects of the other Ideas. This intervention is what it intervenes in, and this self-canceling showing is its intervention. That is, the Idea of the Good intervenes by showing that the truth of the Ideas is undecidable. It shows their getting in the way of their own aim of gaining truth. And this act itself shows that the Idea of the Good is undecidable too, since, as an Idea, it is subject to the same criticisms. What it makes the Ideas into by intervening in them is therefore itself already the further thought that intervenes in and justifies its own descriptive truth. As I discussed in Idea 8.3, the Idea of the Good is already the moment of "nothing further to know." I return to this justification of an explanatory moment by what it justifies below and in the following chapters.

But in fact *this* description of the grounding of the Idea of the Good is an example of how the careful search for truth itself falsifies just by virtue of its existence as (in part) a focus on a line of thought and away from the object of inquiry. In thinking through the nature of the Ideas so as to find their truth, one departs from them to yet another, deeper and so different, Idea, the Idea of the Good. But the Ideas are already *constituted as what they are* by being self-canceling. Consequently the Idea of the Good, which cancels them, is nothing but their self-intervention, clumsily expressed as separate from them. Properly understood, the Idea of the Good does not exist separately in its own right but is already part of the nature of the Ideas properly understood. The very attempt to explore the truth of the Ideas leads us away from them and falsifies our understanding of them.

It is this clumsiness, however, that allows us to see this dimension of the Ideas in its full significance, and the recognition of the clumsiness is what in turn allows us to eliminate it and return to the Ideas, seeing this dimension truly *as* a dimension of the Ideas rather than as something separate. That is, the clumsy separation of the truth of the Ideas is what allows its insight-bringing, truth-establishing self-cancellation. In accordance with the discussion of the rhetorical context of truth above, then, and since the self-canceling structure is part of the nature of truth itself, this clumsy expression is simply *true* and not clumsy while the inquiry toward establishing its clumsiness is in process. The Idea of the Good therefore has different being at different moments of the inquiry into the Ideas. At one point it does have separate existence in its own right; and it ends by vanishing. Similarly with the being of the other Ideas when particular things are being explored through them.

The process of establishing truth works partly by moving externally and irrelevantly to the object of inquiry. And again, truth and being themselves work that way, truth and being themselves are partly a clumsy and perfect movement or shift that is external and irrelevant to themselves.

As I said in Idea 6.4, the character of the Ideas expresses this movement precisely. Socrates insists in the *Phaedo,* for example, that the beauty in things must be explained by Beauty itself, while Beauty itself is not the same as any particular beauty. The Ideas literally point toward the thing they explain *as* a pointing away from it.

1.2.3. *Everything Simply as It Is*

In this light, it might make intuitive sense that the dialogues consistently jumble the level of explanation or of reasoning *about* something and the level of the something being explained, despite Socrates' insistence in the *Phaedo* that one should not confuse them (see Idea 8.1). At the extremes of conceptual thought, they suddenly elaborate sensual images, or mythic allusions, or sociocultural metaphors. This is not, I suggest, *simply* cuteness on Socrates' part or *simply* Plato's emphasizing fundamental mistakes for the careful reader's sake. I think it is *also* a rhetoric true to the self-externality within the consistency of fundamental thought and truth. Differently put, it is true to the recognition that "mixture" of conceptual levels and areas *is* the locus of conceptual purity at these fundamental levels.

I suggest, further, that we need to be careful not to let the rhetoric of the Ideas, or any purely consistent rhetoric, acquire undue importance.[16] The Ideas are *one* articulation Plato develops of the working of truth. But he offers us a very wide variety of forms of expression, developed in various different ways: thinking as wrestling, or going out to sea, or moving in and out of a cave, or sculpting statues in the *Republic*; philosophy as midwifery in the *Theaetetus* and as medical practice in many dialogues; philosophy as one-to-one erotic interaction in the *Phaedrus* and as public erotic interaction in the *Symposium*; philosophy as banqueting or feasting in the *Republic, the Timaeus,* the *Symposium,* the *Gorgias*; and so on. Plato's work contains an extensive vocabulary of sensibility, both physical and attitudinal. And its stylistic texture is thoroughly variegated in kind of style, metaphor, and character. As I have argued, it is the theory of Ideas above all that should teach us how to use these renderings of sensibility and, collectively, of self-variation philosophically.

By way of oversimple illustration of all this, in the *Symposium* (or "drinking party"), largely a series of speeches by different characters on love, Socrates takes us on a ladder from the love of particular physical beauties to the love of Beauty "itself by itself with itself,"[17] relating to nothing but itself. As Aristotle says of the Ideas, this absolute beauty explains no actual beauty, being entirely remote from anything but itself. It is entirely empty. What it does by its combination of ultimacy and emptiness, however, is rigorously to displace and trivialize all our existing forms of knowledge of actual beauty. This allows us to appreciate actual beauties and also our preconceptions of them freshly.[18] With our preconceptions trivialized in general, actual beauties are now more fully able to impress upon us what each of them has to offer as what it uniquely is. And our preconceptions of beauty themselves can be more clearly seen and appreciated both for what they offer and what they prevent. Expressing the same thing differently, the "ladder" suggests the nullity of what is *strictly* or rigorously in common and related in the various appreciable aspects of particular beauties: beauty itself. And the grasp of this particular nullity *is,* then, a grasp of the truth, the actuality, of beauty in each of its unique instances, as it is prior to our preconceptions. The *Symposium* is, in fact, largely a presentation of a series of particular characters and styles, each loveable, and so each beautiful, in a very different way. And further, rather than connecting and ordering them in a definitely established way, Socrates' discussion leaves them exactly in the combination of ordered connection and of partial disorder and partially external, loose relation to one another that they present at first glance.

There are, then, both an objective and a subjective dimension of the achievement of letting things be what they are without understanding, the first being the rigorous self-cancellation or "firm hesitancy" of their Idea, and the second the *aporia* that is fundamental indecision. And *aporia,* achieved through the objective self-cancellation of something like the Idea, gives us an orientation to our own subjective truth in relation to the thing as well as to the context and aims with which we inquire into it.

The objective and subjective dimensions have a relation to each other that itself involves a "firm hesitancy." Knowledge and the capacities that allow knowledge are conceptually different from the kinds of thing knowledge knows: that is, they need to be understood according to a different logic. Like the Ideas in relation to more particular objects, then, the subjective and objective dimensions can relate to each other only by means of the kind of self-cancellation and tangential character for which I have argued.[19]

Accordingly, the Ideas and their equivalents are about our particular relation in our particular circumstances to the particular thing in its particular circumstances. These particularities may include the actual existence of universals and even Ideas. But the particularities we inquire into must be allowed to tell us if and how this is so, since *they* are what we inquire into.

The thing being explained gives the measure of what explains it. Further, thinking and explanation themselves can be put into question and so explained only from the standpoint of what is different to what they are. That is, as I argued in Idea 5.3, the irrational and arational dimensions of life are essential to the rigor of rigorous thinking. The Ideas give the truth of particular things, and particular things give the truth of the Ideas. This is possible in a noncircular way because the giving of truth, in either case, is self-canceling. It appears circular because it seems that the truth of particular things, for example, must be given before the truth of the Ideas, which depends on it, can be given. And the truth of the particular things depends on the truth of the Ideas, which must therefore be given first. But in fact the circle of these mutually dependent explanations does not close smoothly. At the point at which it closes, it vanishes, since, as I argued above, at that point explanation takes its own nature fully into account and becomes evident as artificial and empty. Consequently both explanations rest on a partial *nothing*—a fundamental ignorance or indecision or hesitation between the principles of explanation and the principles of what it explains—that is given by and as self-cancellation.[20]

The trivia in which particulars consist, then, are not only essential to the being of the most profound, the metaphysical (the deepest nature of reality), but are also its deepest foundation. They are *also* the *most* profound, the *most* metaphysical, and that at which the profoundest thinking, including metaphysics, aims.

And given my discussion of the significance of external or superficial relations, trivia are these things precisely in being trivial. Even as trivial, they are certainly a cause for wonder. These trivia include the minutest social interactions, like Socrates' silly humor in talking to Aristodemus near the start of the *Symposium*, which I discussed in Idea 2.3. Socrates is typically made to address his interlocutors, foolish or otherwise, in grand and superlative terms.[21] He is certainly being ironic, but this irony itself expresses a literal ironic truth. His interlocutors *are* grand precisely in their trivial and distinctively flawed particularities.

When Plato was growing up, the very influential comic poet Aristophanes treated the same things with both extreme ridicule and extreme pathos and earnestness. In this way he achieved an appreciative simultaneity of incompatible attitudes. Plato had precedent, then, for developing an irony that enacts a warm appreciation of particularity, and not despite, but together with his work toward universality.

As I argued above, the objective dimension of letting things be what they are extends beyond thinking to the thing itself being thought about. I argued in Idea 6.2 that something corresponds in the thing to fundamental indecision, and I called it a firm hesitancy in the nature of things. In the *Sophist,* after Plato has had the Stranger identify the subject matter, the Sophist, in a number of conflicting ways, Theaetetus is made to say that he is in a state of *aporia* ("ἀπορῶ"). The Stranger is made to respond, "No wonder. . . . But it is fair to suppose that by this time he is still more at a loss ("ἀπορεῖν") to know how he can any longer elude our argument; for the proverb is right which says it is not easy to escape all the wrestler's grips."[22] Both the inquirer and the subject matter of the inquiry are said to be in a state of *aporia.*

As I suggested above, the Ideas are partly the logical conclusion of customary opinions, ideas held in common and in abstraction from careful engagement with the particularities of their objects, and preventing us from seeing their objects for their own sakes. The point is to refute these opinions and in that way genuinely to overcome our blinders. The Ideas, by taking opinions to their logical conclusions, make their refutation possible by showing their inadequacies most clearly in a pure form. When Socrates has finished his universalizing speech in the *Symposium,* Plato has Alcibiades, Socrates' beloved, arrive at the party unexpectedly and drunk. Inspired by love and explicitly uncaring about customary social appropriateness and opinion, which he nonetheless mixes into his speech in delightfully revealing ways ("this unbelievably insolent man . . . spurned my beauty"),[23] Alcibiades makes a final speech. And this unexpected final speech is in praise of Socrates in particular instead of love in general.[24] Alcibiades provides, as it were, the comic catastrophe or downfall that gives the kind of truth that Socrates' movement to the Idea is constituted to precipitate.

But it is crucial to note that opinion is not generally worth less than knowledge. As I argued above, rigorous thought itself requires irrational or strictly unrigorous elements like opinion. And sometimes there is no need to relate further to truth than is already the case. Sometimes it is destructive, false to the requirements of the situation and the conditions of truth, to pursue the issue of truth. In which case one is not, in pursuing truth, really pursuing it at all.

And this truth about truth in particular situations is itself also established by self-canceling rigor like that of the Ideas.

1.2.4. Why We Should Bother

1.2.4.1. Truth, Well-Being, and Justice

Even if this account of Plato is correct, one still needs to ask: Why be concerned with truth? One answer is that significant falsehoods, whether we hold them ourselves or others succeed in imposing them on us, affect us in our very being. One contemporary psychological way of thinking the effects of falsehood is that we deprive ourselves of our own energy, both by avoiding parts of ourselves that are sources of energy and by expending energy avoiding them. But the experience and the fact are far deeper and more harmful than this. Since our very being is affected, our sources of energy and means of using the energy themselves are affected. Consequently, even if we get more energy, we cannot integrate and use it properly.

Fundamental falsehood is not a matter of acting on assumptions and explanations that are not properly thought through and checked. It is a matter of our holding and acting on our beliefs while we take for granted that alternative views are not really possible, so that the issue of thinking through and checking cannot even arise. The very conditions of truth are falsified. In the *Republic,* Plato has Socrates describe the "veritable lie" as "deception in the soul . . . , to have been deceived and to be blindly ignorant and . . . hold the falsehood there."[25] This blind ignorance is given a central role in many dialogues as ignorance even of one's own ignorance. In the Introduction, I called this attitude other-insensibility.

In fact, as I argued there, what it means to take something for granted is that for that sensibility, this activity or attitude does not even exist meaningfully, and so is *not* something that is happening. It exists, and more particularly exists as an activity or attitude, only if it makes sense that one can take responsibility for one's fundamental thinking, thinking that includes thinking about the nature of thinking.

An idea one knows is right or wrong because one has conclusive evidence or reasons already involves the awareness that alternatives are conceivable. One can have tried to find justification for it only given an awareness that its justification makes sense, that is, that alternatives are possible. On the other hand, even if an assumption is descriptively true, it is perhaps all the more falsifying when it is held without awareness that alternatives are possible. For, while it still enacts a blind, foundationally insensitive force, it is harder to distinguish from the same assumption fairly held. The very different effects, on oneself and others, produced by mere awareness of conceivable alternatives, indicate another dimension of the subtle transcendence achieved by awareness of our assumptions that I mentioned near the start of this chapter.

There is a palpable difference between an assertion, opinion, attitude, or action accompanied by awareness that alternatives are conceivable and one without that awareness. The latter suffocates (oneself and others) at the level of a person's being. *Fundamental* falsehood does not simply distort. It replaces and so completely eliminates the being it presents as it does, even if its presentation is superficially accurate. It eliminates the very idea of justification, of the described thing's establishing the true connections with other things and with its context by which it is partly established as being what it is. In contrast, even a blatant falsehood presented with awareness that justification of our ideas is meaningful shows its awareness of its possible limits and so of the possibility that it is blind to something it replaces. It does not simply eliminate.

Falsehood that is unaware of the conditions of truth is suffocating for two mutually reinforcing reasons. First, it makes no room for *resisting* falsehood, for the described thing to assert its being. Second, significant falsehood about humans forces the described person to *make* that space, even though it is the describer who is responsible for artificially occluding it. This is doubly hard rhetorically and in direct reality because the challenge to the falsehood, if it is to intervene effectively in the situation, must engage with the artificiality of the describer's assertion, separated as this assertion is from the conditions of its truth. Since this artificiality is unacknowledged, the challenging engagement with it must seem responsible for gratuitously introducing implausibly artificial concerns. Plato's *Republic* deals with a paradigm case of such mistaken descriptions, exploring the case of the just person's appearing entirely unjust and the unjust person's appearing entirely just.

These factors, really variations on the interventive dimension of truth, explain the apparent artificiality and contradictoriness that challenges to other-insensible oppression often seem to show at first glance. For example, feminists must insist on making an issue of their specific gender in order to explain why it is but ought not to be an issue.[26] Feminists also argue both for the absence of politically important differences between men and women and that those differences explain why men need to dominate in the first place, or that these differences should be given positive value for women. Similar apparent contradictions are produced by queer activists and race and ethnic theorists.[27]

Since falsehood affects the falsifier, whose relation to his/her own truth is vitiated by connections with falsehood, significant falsehood in the case of the inanimate world is the human knower's loss, even if not that of the things known. Though I would argue that things function differently and so *are* different in a world in which they are related to differently.

For other-sensibility it does make sense to take rigorous responsibility for one's own thinking. But of course that sensibility cannot simply force its sense on the other, otherwise it is being false to itself and simply doing the same other-insensible thing. Further, as I argued above, elements of thoughtless nonrationality are fundamental to rigorous thinking itself. Plato shows the nature of rigorous negotiations of truth in the interaction of the two sensibilities (a dimension of the mixture of truth; see Idea 8) through a number of his Sophists and their students.[28] I discussed this kind of negotiation between different sensibilities as a kind of opposition between fundamentally different positions that is also not an opposition in Idea 8.1, in connection with the presentation of the being of difference in the *Sophist*.

The statement that Plato frequently has Socrates insist on, that virtue is knowledge, begins to make sense here.[29] The disciplined attempt to establish truth is also the disciplined attempt to relate to the being of other people and things, and to oneself, responsibly. And a genuine attempt to relate responsibly to the being of oneself and others *is* the attempt to relate to truth.

A rigorous negotiation of truth, then, is also a rigorously responsible social and political practice.

1.2.4.2. Truth and Love

Why, then, worry about being irresponsible, about harming ourselves and others? In the end the reason can only be love,[30] and presumably that is one reason why love features so prominently in Plato. Plato offers a way to seek truth, I suggest, because it is a way to love adequately and to continue learning to love better. The *Symposium,* for example, is devoted to the theme of love and foregrounds a social event as its context for this theme. And Socrates is shown to do there what a good participant does in an event devoted to social enjoyment: he helps to make room for everyone to be themselves and to enjoy and be enjoyed that way.[31] I tried to show an aspect of this attempt in discussing Socrates' interaction with Aristodemus in Idea 2.3. This interaction is also Socrates' first appearance in the dialogue and consequently, in all its triviality, it sets the tone for the rest.

In the *Phaedrus,* Socrates is made to describe love in a lengthy myth as a kind of madness, divinely given, the deepest form of which is the "love of wisdom," the literal meaning of philosophy.[32] And in the *Republic,* Plato has Socrates begin his lengthy discussion of what philosophers are by distinguishing between different kinds of love.[33] Toward the end of the dialogue, Socrates is made to present even the tyrant, the worst of people, as motivated by love, but love that he does not take care of, to the extent that he allows it to become self-defeating.[34] The nature of one's life, then, perhaps depends most fundamentally on one's love and one's relation to it.

It follows that the first problem for the philosopher, as for the psychoanalyst, is to establish what the love, the *eros,* is with which s/he is dealing, and the relation that s/he or others have to their love. The philosopher cannot go deeper than that, or rather, there is nowhere deeper to go. S/he cannot meaningfully question people's basic loves except to ask what they are and identify their self-questionings, if any. Her/his own activity of questioning is itself based on nothing more fundamental from which to put them in question. In Idea 5.3, I noted Diotima's emphasis in the *Symposium* on the lack of wisdom that the phrase "love of wisdom" implies, and the external relation to the truth even of oneself that follows from that lack. Ultimate questioning, and so finding ultimate answers, is first set in motion by a love that therefore itself involves none of those questions or answers. The philosopher can only establish the nature of people's basic loves, including her/ his own, and go on from there.

The ultimacy of eros in the risk or decision that orients a person does not mean that either its truth or the truths it orients one toward are "subjective" in the sense that "anything goes," "anything is right." One's eros, like all truths, is established by means of fundamental indecision, that is, by careful investigation of the coherence of and evidence for more than one view.

1.2.5. Love and Justice

It is important that love involves both a distance from what it loves, even if it is love of self, and a deep connection with it. It is both an internal and an external relation to what it is love of. Issues like that of the meaning of justice appear very differently on this understanding from, say, an under-standing of self-love as entirely involved or entirely uninvolved in love of others.

The *Gorgias* presents a savage struggle between Socrates and two admirers of Gorgias, the Sophist (that is, a paid teacher of persuasive rhetoric), over the question of whether principled justice is better than self-indulgent injustice. But it seems to me that the dialogue shows that the more fundamental struggle is between indulgence of a self that is understood simply superficially and indulgence of a self understood not *simply* superficially, which (the second) is also a carrying out of principled justice. Differently put, it is a struggle between a loving life and a loveless or love-defeating life.[35]

Gorgias himself is shown as being committed to principled virtue, including justice. While Socrates shares this commitment, he finds Gorgias's sophistic method of living it out inadequate. Gorgias's self-supposed admirers, Polus and Callicles, on the other hand, are presented as rejecting virtue, extolling self-indulgent savagery, and tearing without restraint into Gorgias's and Socrates' commitments. In the course of the confrontation, Socrates refers to erotic love, in a trivial way, several times. First, when Callicles, the most savage of his interlocutors, enters the discussion, having found Socrates' statements shocking, Socrates begins by noting that they have both experienced erotic love: "I with Alcibiades . . . and philosophy, and you . . . with . . . the Athenian demos and Demos, son of Pyrilampes."[36] He uses this fact to make the point that he is not guided by his own designs to make his statements but by philosophy, as a lover is seduced to think what the beloved favors. He makes the same point later, this time exclusively about

Callicles' being seduced by the demos or people.[37] This witty couching or ornamentation of his point is tangential to his focus, and Callicles ignores it on both occasions, without any counterinsistence from Socrates.

Now, if Callicles had taken this suggestion seriously and investigated the nature of his own eros, the discussion would have taken a very different turn. The erotic fact immediately suggests that neither Socrates nor Callicles is simply guided by his own designs, so that the nature and benefit of their lifestyles depend on the nature of their guides. And Callicles is guided by people he claims to be above. More generally and importantly, however, the erotic fact shows that a "self" is not *simply* separate from other selves and is not *simply* itself. Consequently, not indulging a separate self may in fact already *be* not indulging one's own self. But Socrates leaves the fact as a trivial rhetorical device for introducing his point.

The triviality is important in itself. It is not for Socrates to condemn the loveless or love-defeating position of his interlocutors. Any condemnation from Socrates' position would presuppose his own eros, his motivation to his own particular risk. Because his eros is the basis of his entire position, he is not in a position to justify it against a different eros. Consequently he is not in a position to condemn his interlocutors' standpoint fairly. A discussion about the fundamentals of the thinking of the opposed parties can only be meaningful if the parties share the relevant priorities.[38] Here, as I mentioned above, they do not even agree on how to discuss, on how to establish any truth in the first place.[39] Socrates insists, for example, that "if I cannot produce in you yourself a single witness in agreement with my views, I consider that I have accomplished nothing worth speaking of in the matter under debate,"[40] while for Polus, justification is a matter of producing "many reputable witnesses."[41] As a result, as Socrates comments, "here is one form of refutation accepted by you and by many others, but there is also another according to my opinion. Let us compare them, then, and consider whether there is any difference between them."[42] And the *Gorgias* in fact contains Plato's most detailed discussion of the way in which fundamentally opposed positions need to debate. Socrates, then, given his commitment to rigorous truth, cannot fairly persuade his interlocutors that his eros and hence fair discussion are appropriate, and so he cannot attempt to persuade them on that issue at all. But he can fairly present that issue for them irrelevantly. And he does so, by presenting it as a witty triviality that they are able successfully to ignore. Their own *erotes* (the plural of eros) will then motivate them to pursue that presentation further if, uninterfered with by Socrates, it happens to be spontaneously directed that way.

For the rest, Socrates is true to their own principle of savagery by refuting and humiliating them, so that at the deepest level he does not challenge them; that is, he does not unequivocally challenge their principle of savagery itself. And he is also true to his own position for which, first, he retains room by defending himself. And second, because he does not interfere illegitimately with their most basic motivating principle, their self-defeating eros, he is not being *fundamentally* savage, and so he is also fundamentally true to his own, loving principle. It is possible that his interlocutors will subsequently look at their own motivational foundations. But if they choose to look in that direction, that is *their* act; Socrates does not point there in any persuasive way.[43]

Eric Voegelin is representative of the tone of a lot of Plato scholarship in statements such as the following. Discussing the *Gorgias,* he describes Callicles as "co-responsible, through his conniving conduct, for the murder of Socrates and perhaps of Plato himself." He goes on to mention:

> those among us who find ourselves in the Platonic position and who recognize in the men with whom we associate today the intellectual pimps for power who will connive in our murder tomorrow. It would be too much of an honor, however, to burden Callicles personally with the guilt of murder. The whole society is corrupt.[44]

It is true that Socrates was put to death by Athenian society. Plato was not, although Voegelin is referring to a kind of spiritual murder by unjust treatment. The discussion above should make it clear that my account is very much at odds with the kind of attitude Voegelin represents. On my account, Plato does not simply condemn the Athenians, and in fact shows that the philosopher, then or now, does not *simply* know better than her/his associates.

To give only the most obvious points telling against Voegelin's attitude, Plato has Socrates insist in several places, including the *Gorgias,*[45] that injustice is not fundamentally bad for its *victim.* And the *Apology* ends with Socrates insisting that only the god knows whether Socrates or his judges are better off.[46] Voegelin's decisive condemnation seems distinctly *un*-Platonic. As Plato frequently makes clear, only a small proportion of people are suited to philosophy. It follows that the rest cannot be blamed for not thinking and living like philosophers, and so for necessarily misunderstanding philosophers. In fact, presumably, they would be blameworthy if they tried to live and make decisions falsely as philosophers.

Voegelin's tone does respect the real seriousness of the issues. But I think the point is that the issues are far *more* serious than this tone recognizes. Moral indignation or self-righteousness can be *part* of an appropriate tone, but on their own, I think, they are sadly inadequate. I suggest the issues are tragic in the sense of Greek tragedy, bigger than we and our insight are. And that is where the humorous or comic dimension comes in. The *Symposium,* for example, as I mentioned above, includes both Agathon the tragic poet and Aristophanes the comic poet and ends with Socrates arguing to them that the same person can write both comic and tragic poetry. I suggest that the tone of this kind of Plato scholarship needs to be resituated in a context of sympathetic self-irony.

This kind of sympathetic self-irony is crucial not only for scholarship but for living truly, too. As I argued with reference to the posture of fundamental indecision, the attitude or posture or tone with which we approach truth *is already* our relation to truth, and conditions our further progress in and toward it.

1.2.6. Truth and the Variegated Texture of Love

To continue with the theme of love: love is a relation to the being of what it loves. It relates to what it loves purely for the sake of what that thing is. As Socrates argues in the *Lysis,* if we always love something for the sake of something else, we would then love that something else for the sake of yet another thing, and that one for the sake of another, and so on. As a result, we would never get to the point of actually loving. So it must be true that, "With that . . . to which we are truly friendly [τὸ φίλον; equally, 'what we love,' used here in the sense of friendship or social bonds, but in the context of a lengthy, explicitly erotic setting earlier in the dialogue],[47] we are not friendly for the sake of any other thing to which we are friendly."[48] As a relation to the being of what it loves, love involves the same discipline as the search for knowledge, which is what relates us to the truth and so the being of things. Love, then, is a discipline of letting things be what they are uninterfered with by the love.

This means that love relates to the depths of its object by only just touching its surface at a vanishing point, tangentially. It relates to the very being of its object by being at a distance from it, rigorously external to it. Differently put, if we want to relate to the being of the other person or ourselves, we need to be true to our lack of knowledge of her/him and ourselves.

Otherwise we interfere, unlovingly, with the being of what we love. It is this distance, this recognition by partial nonrecognition, that allows love to let its object be what it is and to sustain that letting be.

This letting be is the deepest nourishment. It supports, for example, the being of the person that makes him/her *want* and find meaningful other kinds of nourishment, like food. Love, then, or relating to things for their own sake and not for some further purpose, is the source of true practice, because it nourishes what makes practice meaningful, the *being* of love's object. It is, therefore, the most basic practice.

The externality that is part of love means that love is sometimes and/or in some respects most personal by being impersonal. By contrast, for example, "Marianne . . . turned her eyes towards Elinor to see how she bore these attacks, with an earnestness that gave Elinor far more pain than could arise from such common-place raillery."[49] This impersonality is the living out of fundamental indecision that leaves room for the beloved to be and to become what he/she/it is, and to be related to that way. As the *Gorgias* may show, for example, love need not be warm. In fact, hating can be a way of loving, given the need to negotiate the rhetorical dimensions of one's relation to the truth of oneself and others.

In a sense, then, one relates to the immediacy of oneself or another by relating, instead, to the slightly and self-cancelingly removed Idea or truth of the person.[50]

Differently put, because self-identity involves self-externality, one is complete by being incomplete, one's knowledge is complete by being incomplete, and one relates to oneself or another completely by relating incompletely, if one does so in the right way. The nonrecognition essential to recognition is *also* a direct recognition itself (see Idea 6.2). It is the recognition of the self-externality of the other person and/or of oneself.

Like the pervasive (but not exclusive) mood in Plato, *this* impersonality can be a kind of warmly personal humor. It is an self-ironizing irony, among many other things, which subverts in order to sustain as best as possible, given what is.[51] Against Hegel and Marx, fully self-knowing and self-transparent nonalienation from self and world *is* partly alienation from self and world. True nonalienation, on the other hand, *is* "sometimes always" a certain kind of alienation, like the feeling of cosiness in a snug, well-lit room while the cold wind blows in the night outside, or like the competent feeling of walking in the rain under an umbrella.

And in turn, the externality, the internal *irrelevance*, of these "sometimes" to the times or respects in which true nonalienation is not at all a certain kind of alienation is fundamentally important to *those* times, in the same way that impersonality is important to the personal character of love.

1.2.7. Truth, the Variegated Consistency of Selfhood, and Risk

To focus for the moment on the individual self alone, the conflicted soul that is presented as a model of human being in the *Republic* is not essentially conflicted if the internal significance of external connections is recognized. As I argued of fundamental truth generally, the truths of externality and of conflict both ultimately have a "sometimes always" character. Differently put, they are variegated or self-disparate, as I argued in Idea 5.3. Unqualified conflict can be in the service of harmony, just as hate can be in the service of love, and vice versa. And conversely, given the externality of internal connections, the "conflicted" character of the soul, appropriately lived, is not something that creates a problem for self-unity but sometimes (*sometimes*, but then, and only then, rightly invalidating any contrasting "truths" of other times) *is* the way a self is purely and simply unified.

If one's fundamental commitment is to live in accordance with one's truth, that is, to love that truth and to learn to love it more fully, the conflicts become means of letting oneself be what one is more deeply than one has been able to do so far. This also means letting one's conflicts, which are part of what one is, be what they are more deeply. In keeping with the logic of self-externality, accepting conflicts, as with recognizing assumptions, is, in the act of letting them be what they are, *also* a subtle transcending of them and an alteration of their meaning and effects. Hence, perhaps, Socrates' suggestion almost at the end of the *Republic,* despite the conclusions he has apparently already reached about the divided nature of the soul, that if we think about the soul most truly, "one might see whether in its real nature it is manifold or single in its simplicity, or what is the truth about it and how."[52]

I argued, for example in Ideas 4.2 and 7, that the subjectivity of the knowledge-seeker is involved in the establishment (again in both the subjective and objective senses of this word) of truth. And, as I noted above in section 1.2.3, the state of *aporia,* fundamental indecision, is the subjective dimension of the self-cancellation of the Ideas and their equivalents. Fundamental indecision *is,* then, the living out of the truth of the Ideas. The workings of such subjective things as love and personal attitudes and tones therefore have a very intimate relation to the workings of objective truth, and vice versa.

One's access to these subjective things is honesty, letting oneself be and relating to oneself as what one is. (This should give a more specific context for the arguments in Ideas 4.2 and 7 that personal honesty is fundamental to truth-seeking.) Honesty, or truth to one's own experience, connects with truth at its deepest even if one makes a mistake about oneself, because, as I argued above, the structure of error is given its possibility at the roots of being.[53] An honest mistake about oneself still orients one directly to truth because it consists in that structure. A dishonesty, even one that involves a true description, conceals that structure and so points one away from it. The only way to correct a dishonesty is to approach the issue again, start again entirely. An honest mistake gives its own orientation as to how to go the right way: it has already started one off.

But honesty also works with the self-canceling tangential logic of truth. When one is trying to make a decision or find out about the whole orientation of one's life in some way—this can happen in apparently trivial connections, for example in wondering about one's clothing or gestural style, or in considering changing one of these—one does have to accept that one simply either is what one wants to be, or one is not. If one tries to make or see oneself as something one is not, one allows oneself to be what one really is all the more uncontrolledly. One's attention is then directed to the artificially maintained self, so that one's actual self is not directly restrained. And if one tries to make oneself what one is, one does not really engage with one's life, since one is occupied with artificially maintaining one's self. But the same is true if one does *not* try to make or see oneself as something, since what one is beforehand may be the artificial self. I discussed the logic of this in Ideas 1 and 2. Accordingly, in order to be honest, one has to achieve a fundamental indecision about one's being in the relevant respect. But this fundamental indecision, which maintains both alternatives together, still has to maintain the contrasting exclusive logic that one simply is the thing or one is not, but not both together. This indecision in fact already does include both logics, since it is indecision about itself also. Given that indecision, then, one can rigorously explore either alternative and allow oneself to show oneself which, or which other alternative, is true of one.

There are times when the *very act* of taking a risk shows the risk to be validated. It shows that one does in fact have a particular eros. So, the risk of wearing a certain kind of clothes shows one's desire to wear that kind of clothes, which in turn shows that in an important sense, wearing those clothes is in keeping with who one is. (Similarly, I argued in Idea 1.1 that the desire to be artificial is not itself artificial.) Or the effort of trying to use hating feelings for caring purposes (for example, by apologizing for them) may show that the hating feelings are not the fundamental ones; or the act of risking that one can get knowledge makes it possible for one to get knowledge (as Socrates insists in the passages from the *Meno* that I discussed in Idea 4.2). The fundamental indecision does not only allow the object of knowledge to impress itself upon the knower in its own right (see Idea 4.3); it also lets the knower impress him/herself upon her/himself in his/her own right.

The indecision, being fundamental, does not affect or remains completely external to what subsequently impresses itself on it or is done in its context. It is like the "artificial"/artificial decisions I discussed above that risk both making things a certain way and also making them other ways, all entirely excluded as possibilities by each other. The indecision already makes room, with "sometimes always" logic, for the alternatives each considered wholly exclusively in its own terms. And precisely because of this externality to the decision between them, it is what allows those things to be established genuinely. Because of both this fundamental indecision and the different "sometimes always" dimensions that its context allows, then, honesty, relating to oneself as one is, can and sometimes must include departures from letting oneself be and relating to oneself as what one is.

Of course, one cannot try, for example, to wear those clothes *in order to validate* that one is the kind of person who wears those clothes. Then one is no longer taking a risk (or one is taking a different kind of risk, with a wholly different logic and effect). One is no longer operating in accordance with a fundamental indecision. Instead one is trying to achieve an outcome decided on in advance, not letting oneself be what one is, and so not engaging with one's truth. One is not doing the thing for its own sake, and is forcing rather than loving. But one can, nonetheless, be *aware that* the genuine risk will validate itself, without affecting the risk. This is one of the consequences of the externality of self-identity.

One result of the fundamental self-disparity of rigorous thought is that one cannot *simply* have an idea of the outcome of fundamental inquiry and debate. In fact, one cannot have *any* accurate idea of this kind of outcome *at all*. At the same time, however, this complete lack of accurate anticipation works *in and by* having rigorous ideas about that outcome. Because of the dimension of thorough ignorance, the commitment to rigorous inquiry or debate essentially involves risk. One's choice of taking the risk of a possible solution by undertaking rigorous thought, or of taking the risk of the impossibility of solutions by declining rigorous thought, then, says something about the truth of one's own commitments.

The same considerations apply to relating to other people's fundamental decisions about and understanding of themselves. Fundamental indecision is therefore crucial to relations to other people for this reason also. This often involves all sorts of rhetorical complexities. One may need to resist, in a decided way, someone else's refusal to be loving in this way toward themselves, in order to avoid being decidedly unloving oneself. And that resistance may need to take harsh forms ("tough love"). In fact, being tenderly loving toward the person may itself be the harsh form it takes, since it would very painfully invalidate, for example, a self-hating person's self-structuring. Or one may need *not* to invalidate the person's self-structuring, which may also take harsh forms, as with Socrates' treatment of his interlocutors in the *Gorgias*. Here pleasant forms would really be harsher, since they *would* implicitly invalidate the person's self-structuring.

1.2.8. Surface and Depth of the Dialogues

Plato needs to and does take the same kind of rhetorical care with his readers. This is already apparent in the *Gorgias,* since readers are left free to find what *their* own *erotes* decide without fundamental persuasion by Plato.

But I suggest, further, that Plato presents a two-layered rhetoric in all his dialogues. In the Introduction I wrote that:

> nonironic readings of the dialogues result in views that *approximate, in the results of acting on them,* the view that a self-critical ironic reading presents as *descriptive statements.* In accordance with another tradition of Plato interpretation, then, I suggest an 'esoteric' and 'exoteric' level of the dialogues. But I shall argue that these levels are in an important sense the same.

I briefly made this argument in discussing the *Meno* in Idea 4.2, where I pointed out that taking the recollection myth at face value amounts to looking to oneself to establish truth, just as taking it as a fiction does in the context of Socrates' other suggestions to Meno.

In the case of the theory of Ideas, taken at face value it has the effect of orienting one so as to live at a distance from oneself, precisely because it is clumsily unworkable. One is continually in a posture of indecision when considering fundamental truth, because the rigorous attempt to attain the Ideas taken at face value consistently refutes itself. As a result, one is constantly in a position to be freshly impressed by features of what one explores.

This clumsiness, together with its effects, precisely images the delicate precision of what I take to be the more rigorous understanding of the Ideas as the act of rigorous self-cancellation, or of something like self-eluding elusiveness. They both turn the interventive dimension of knowledge against itself to achieve a justly reached relation to or orientation toward truth.

In Plato's *Seventh Letter* he writes about "the subjects to which I devote myself":

> I do not . . . think the attempt to tell mankind of these matters a good thing, except in the case of some few who are capable of discovering the truth for themselves with a little guidance. In the case of the rest to do so would excite in some an unjustified contempt in a thoroughly offensive fashion, in others certain lofty and vain hopes, as if they had acquired some awesome lore.[54]

Now, while no descriptive truths can be attained nonmythically or non-fictionally when the Ideas are taken "exoterically" at face value (although one can *act* truthfully), the truths that can be attained on the deep, "esoteric" self-cancellation understanding *also* have precisely and literally "nothing" to do with what Plato calls "awesome lore" here. On the contrary, these truths are found exactly by the rigorous collapsing of "awesome lore."

Conversely, Plato often has Socrates say that "there is just one small thing" he wonders about in what he has just heard. In the *Protagoras*, for example, he says, "To have heard what Protagoras has just said is something I value very highly . . . . There is just one small thing holding me back, which Protagoras I know will easily explain."[55] Now, although Socrates is being ironic, I suggest that he is not *simply* being ironic. The "small thing" always turns out to be very big for the understanding Socrates is questioning, but the understanding itself also turns out to be too self-impressed, too big for its object, so that the issue really is small for it. The attempt to understand and the achievement of understanding have to be gotten out of their own way, made truly trivial, so that the whole issue is at that point genuinely unimportant.

The self-ironizing irony of Socrates' "one small thing," then, is initially both an ironic false and an ironic true description, and later a nonironic true description (see Idea 2.3 for this kind of shift), letting the understood thing and the limits of the questioned understanding stand out against each other. This self-ironizing irony is an expression of the coherently and fruitfully self-canceling "sometimes always" logic that is spread out over the course of each Platonic dialogue.

1.3. Summary

I suggest, then, first, that Plato's work is about showing how to let things be what they are, rigorously without any explanation or understanding. Second, that he is about this in order to teach how to love, and so to be, better, in a "sometimes always various" world of disparate fundamental loves and fundamental kinds of beings. And third, that he achieves this, as I suggested in the Preface, by a delicately poised clumsiness, or a perfect, ungainly poised elegance.

CHAPTER 2

Charmides: *Lust, Love, and the Problem of Knowledge*

In this chapter I look at the whole of Plato's *Charmides*. In the next chapter I explore some details of the overall structure of the argument of the *Republic*, and in Chapter 4, I look similarly at the trilogy of dialogues consisting of the *Theaetetus, Sophist,* and *Statesman*. Before I discuss the *Charmides,* I shall make some comments on the dialogue form of Plato's work in general.

2.1. THE DIALOGUE FORM

Plato's philosophy is always presented in the form of dialogue, typically with Socrates as one of the participants.[1] This choice of form is not fully explained by saying, for example, that Plato followed Socrates' example of engaging in dialogues. Socrates' choice of dialogue for his philosophical activity itself needs to be understood before it can explain Plato's motivation to imitate it. And Plato's choice of dialogue is also not sufficiently explained by saying, for instance, that Plato was continuing the cultural tradition of tragic and comic plays in ancient Athens. For one thing, there were other traditional forms Plato could have taken up. One of the traditional options for presenting philosophy itself, for example, was in the form of monologic poems.

Plato's choice of dialogue, typically with Socrates participating, foregrounds two very basic facts about Plato's view of philosophy. First, the dialogues include a wide variety of non- and antiphilosophical standpoints. And the dialogues also keep reminding us, more or less explicitly, that Athenian society ultimately put Socrates to death for philosophizing. That is, philosophy exists as one among many very seriously conflicting human commitments. Second, philosophy exists as an activity carried out by particular human beings in this conflicted context. Plato's dialogues, then, present philosophy first and foremost in its individual and social context.

Much of the content of the dialogues, however, is oriented very firmly away from this individual and social context into all sorts of technicalities of meanings and conceptual relations. And the philosophical participant is often made to be explicit about the irrelevance and negative status of the individual and social context. The dialogue form functions very differently in connection with these technicalities, which the explicit content foregrounds as what is exclusively essential. Typically, it is not even clear if the dialogue *is* a genuine dialogue in these contexts. The philosopher's interlocutor often seems just to be going along with the flow, with a very lengthy and unrelieved series of affirmatives such as "yes," "of course," "certainly." The prominently foregrounded social and individual context, then, is presented just as prominently as being external to the philosophical content.

I argued above that particular, trivial circumstances are the essence of the deepest, most universal truth, and vice versa. And I argued that this "being the essence" occurs partly and fundamentally by virtue of externality. Philosophy is only genuine philosophy to the extent that it questions itself, and only the standpoints that are external to and conflict with it allow that questioning. Philosophy, then, is only what it is in the context of those standpoints that conflict with it. It is therefore both externally and internally related to them, and in the same respects in each case.

Like so much else in Plato, then, the conflicting mutual externality of the foregrounded dimensions of his dialogues is both a literal presentation of their relation and an ironic one. And because this externality is *fully* both of these mutually exclusive things, the irony is ironic about itself, too. I shall try to show this more concretely as I explore particular dialogues.

2.2. THE *CHARMIDES*

Since the sequence of descriptions and discussions with which Plato presents the *Charmides* is one of his rhetorical choices, I discuss the dialogue following his order of presentation. This should allow to emerge what this sequence of presentation shows both about the topic of the dialogue and about rhetorical sequence itself.

2.2.1. General Considerations

Plato presents the *Charmides,* like many of his dialogues, as narrated by Socrates: that is, it is a monologue in the form of a dialogue. Its most basic structure is therefore undecided as to whether it is two (or more) stand-points or one. As I argued above, this is precisely the structure of rigorous knowledge-seeking indecision between alternative standpoints. It is also the structure of reality, as reality is in the context of its relation to rigorous thought. In order to establish the reality the dialogue seeks, as that reality is in the context of life independently of the peculiar activity of rigorous thought, this structure will have to cancel itself into irrelevance. And as I argued in general, it does so when and only when one takes its issues up and resolves them for oneself.

The form of the dialogue is not the only relevant indecision. The ad-dressee of Socrates' speech is unknown. And it is left undecided as to whether the reader is placed in this unknown position or, rather, in the posi-tion of remaining known to her/himself while privy to Socrates' conversa-tion with someone else. Together with the truth of what the reader aims to understand, the truth of the reader him/herself is put into question by the first alternative; and so is that putting in question itself, by the second. As I argued above, these subjective and objective and thoughtful and thoughtless dimensions of truth-seeking are (internally and externally related) parts of the same thing.

Socrates is made to narrate the dialogue the day after it happened.[2] He reports that he had just returned from war[3] and was introduced to the young and extremely beautiful Charmides by Charmides' cousin and guardian, Critias.[4] About thirty years later, well before Plato wrote the dialogue, Charmides would serve a group known as the Thirty Tyrants, who were responsible for extremes of injustice in Athens during their short rule. They were led by Critias.[5] The topic of the dialogue, as it will turn out, is relevant both to the causes and conduct of war and to these later events. It is the nature of *sophrosyne*, variously translated as self-control or temperance.

The dialogue, then, is also undecided as to when it is situated in time. It is narrated "today," but its main events occurred "yesterday," and it refers to events that have not happened yet. Its meanings are not simply locatable in time. That is, the indecision as to time sets the dialogue, like any fiction, not quite in time. And by participating in the meanings of this fiction, the reader is also not quite in time, and so can get a perspective on time itself. In this way, I suggest, a fundamental indecision is established with respect to the reader's own historical and social context, so that this context need not simply determine her/his understanding. Like assumptions, this context is partly *transcended in and by* being recognized in contrast with the *Char-mides'* fictional context. But it is partly transcended in and by *being recognized for what it is, a constraining context.* The reader's context itself is *fundamentally* undecided, then, undecided even as to whether it is undecided, even as to whether it does not simply determine understanding.

This indecision as to the reader's position in time with respect to the dialogue also establishes an indecision as to whether the rhetorical sequence of presentation in the dialogue is significant at all or whether what is presented can rather be grasped in a single moment of understanding.

2.2.2. Setting up the External Orientation toward Truth

The dialogue begins, as I mentioned above, with Socrates' report that he had just returned from war and a description of how he answered questions about the "very hard-fought" battle, in which "many people we knew . . . died."[6] And, as I also mentioned, his main conversation partners later became well-known as political monsters. The topic, then, is presented as a very serious and moving one. In contrast with Charmides' present innocence and beauty, we are reminded of the reality of death in the immediate past and Charmides' own murderous injustice in the future.

Socrates is made to begin his description of Charmides by noting that he, Socrates, is incapable of discrimination when it comes to the beauty of young men: they all seem beautiful to him. As will become significant given the topic of self-control, this is not the mark of an erotically disciplined or temperate man. But even despite his lack of discrimination, he says, Charmides "at that moment" seemed extraordinarily lovely to him.[7] Socrates' intemperance is additionally suggested by this "at that moment." As well as being generally excessive, Socrates' lusts are liable to wayward surges.

Nevertheless, Plato has him report that he then suggested to Critias that they examine Charmides' soul before his body, since the "just one other little thing" of having a fine soul would make him "irresistible."[8] This trivializing description of the soul or temperament as "just one other little thing" is of course ironic, since the nature of a person's soul or temperament explains how s/he lives her/his life and so affects her/himself and others. But I think it is also simply an accurate description. From the standpoint of the kind of people Critias and Charmides would become, for example, a temperate soul is not highly regarded. For this standpoint, among many others, the difference in virtue between souls or temperaments is in fact trivial.[9] And there are no grounds in the discussion so far for dismissing these standpoints.

Plato is typically regarded as rejecting this latter kind of standpoint. Accordingly he is typically regarded as *simply* ironic in this kind of context. But this seems to me to miss the point. Given Plato's frequent care elsewhere to establish the difference between the philosophical way and unreasoned adherence to customary belief, and given the detailed attention he gives to untangling the silliest of arguments, it would surely be an extraordinary inconsistency if he were to reject a standpoint in advance without the least consideration of its grounds or even its possible statement. What is more, it would be blatantly irresponsible of him, both as a teacher and a citizen, to reject a standpoint of tremendous social force without any consideration. I suggest, then, that here Socrates' irony presents and models a contextualized maintaining of a fundamental indecision between two standpoints, one in which soul or temperament is an essential consideration and one in which it is trivial.

Plato then has Socrates report that, on his suggestion, Critias called Charmides over on a false pretext Critias invented: that Socrates was a doctor who had a cure for Charmides' headache. Socrates went along with this pretense. The initial meeting, then, was established on the basis of a lie.

When Charmides sat next to him, Socrates is made to recount, he was overcome by lust for Charmides: "I was on fire, I lost my head."[10] Socrates was now subject to an extreme loss of self-control. Given the importance he had just given to the soul in contrast to the body, and given that self-control would turn out to be the topic of the dialogue, this is a nicely humorous moment. A good-humored, broadly comic tone had in fact already just been set when the beautiful Charmides sat down:

> he caused a great deal of laughter: each of us who were sitting down tried to make room for him by pushing his neighbour away in a frantic attempt to have the boy sit next to him, until we forced the man sitting at one end of the row to stand up and tipped the man at the other off sideways.[11]

The search for truth that was about to begin, then, was set up in the context both of literally deadly seriousness, as I discussed above, and of various relaxed, good-humored incongruities, most of them involving trivialities: slapstick conduct, a lie, Socrates' lust, and, as I shall discuss shortly below, an elaborate fiction.

Specifically, what was out of control at this point was Socrates' eros, his motivating foundation. He managed, however, to explain that his cure for the headache involved both a leaf and a charm to be chanted. Just as part of the body can only be successfully treated together with the whole body, he explained, so the body can only be successfully treated together with the soul. While the leaf treated the body, the charm treated the soul by producing self-control in it. And Socrates' self-control returned when Charmides agreed to the "principle" [τοῦ λόγου] of the first part of this reasoning, concerning the body:[12] that is, Charmides agreed to the principle that the part cannot be treated independently of the whole.

Perhaps, then, this principle, in Plato's so-far-unargued view, is basic to self-control. Socrates says that after "losing his head," he felt he was "as a fawn in the presence of a lion."[13] It was Charmides who had endangered Socrates' self-control, and it was Charmides' acknowledgment of the principle of the dependence of parts on their whole that had allowed Socrates to regain self-control.

This in turn allowed Socrates to complete his argument so as to present the soul, and hence a quality of the soul such as self-control, as essential to the body. Perhaps it was the possibility of communicating this completion of the argument, rather than the acknowledgment of the principle on its own, that had restored Socrates' self-control. Either way, perhaps Plato is suggesting that the basis of self-control lies in both the self-controlled person *and* whom or what, *external* to him/herself, s/he is relevantly in relation to, a relation of which the individual person is only a part. It is not only truth-seeking, after all, that involves full consideration of opposed standpoints. Established truth and reality themselves, in all their practical significance, involve the indecision between and rhetorical constraints imposed by such standpoints when they are relevant.

Socrates, with his self-control returned, however, went on to do more than complete his argument. He wove it into what is presumably a fiction about an exotic Thracian doctor who gave him the cure and explained it to him in partly mythological terms: " " " 'Our king Zalmoxis," he said, "who is a god, says . . .' " " "[14] (in connection with the distance Plato, and here Socrates, maintain from the truth of their own statements, it is worth noting the necessity of multiple nested quotation marks here). Now, as Socrates is made to relate, Charmides had already shown that he was not taken in by the pretense that Socrates was a doctor, although he was willing to go along with it. After Socrates had mentioned the leaf and the charm, he had called Socrates by name in saying that he would take the charm from him, and explained that "there's a great deal of talk about you among the boys of my age, and I remember your being with Critias here when I was a child."[15] With his exotic fiction, then, Socrates elaborated and so emphasized the dimension of pretense for Charmides.

In a related way, the *Charmides* itself, like all of Plato's dialogues, is elaborated and emphasized for the reader as first and foremost an evident fiction and pretense. Plato pretends to be someone else narrating events at which he was not or could not have been present. Often these are events that could not have occurred, because of obviously incompatible dates and places. Hence, for example, the annoying but built-in necessity for varieties of "Plato has Socrates tell us that someone said" in order to present the dialogue accurately.

Critias then assured Socrates, Plato has Socrates tell us, that Charmides was generally considered to be superlatively self-controlled for his age. Accordingly, Socrates set out to establish whether Charmides already had enough self-control to make the charm unnecessary. He began, he reports, by asking Charmides directly: "Tell me yourself, then, whether you agree with Critias and say that you already have enough self-control, or whether you say that you are deficient in it."[16] Charmides "gave a not ignoble answer":

> "If," he said, "I say I'm not self-controlled, it's absurd that one should say such things against oneself, and at the same time I'll make a liar of Critias here and of many others too, who, according to him, think I'm self-controlled. On the other hand, if I say I am, I praise myself, which will perhaps seem rather bad form. So I don't know what answer to give you."[17]

Charmides identified a paradox: the act of answering the question contradicts whatever the content of the answer might be. That is, the answer to the question is interventive as well as descriptive, and its interventive property falsifies whatever its descriptive truth might be.

This paradox is related to one that originally precipitated Socrates' philosophy. As Plato has Socrates tell the story in the *Apology*,[18] the oracle of Apollo at Delphi had said that Socrates was the wisest of people. The oracle's pronouncement was made to Chaerephon, whose notable presence is also mentioned at the start of the *Charmides*: everyone else "hailed me from a distance . . . ; but Chaerephon, like the mad creature that he is, jumped up . . . and ran to me."[19] Plato has Socrates explain his reaction to the oracle as follows:

> I said to myself, What does the god mean? Why does he not use plain language? I am only too conscious that I have no claim to wisdom, great or small. So what can he mean by asserting that I am the wisest man in the world? He cannot be telling a lie; that would not be right for him.[20]

Sallis plausibly infers from this and the rest of Socrates' explanation the interpretation that if, on the one hand, Socrates accepted the oracle's declaration, he would be unwisely hubristic, stepping beyond the bounds of his human limits. But if, on the other hand, he rejected the declaration, he would be opposing divinity, again unwisely stepping beyond his human limits.[21] With or without this elaboration, however, any response to the oracle's description is interventive in a way that falsifies the content of the response.

Socrates, as the *Apology* has him tell us, responded by talking to supposedly knowledgeable people and investigating their wisdom, and found a solution. He was wisest because he recognized the limits of his wisdom while others thought they knew what they did not know. And "[t]hat is why I still go about seeking and searching in obedience to the divine command, if I think that anyone is wise . . . , and when I think that any person is not wise, I try to help the cause of God by proving that he is not."[22] Socrates was in an *aporia,* and he resolved it by learning not to try simply to decide between its alternatives, but rather to occupy the indecision between them by thinking and talking partly about the dilemma in its own right. This maintaining of and thinking and talking about the dilemma resulted in the solution: he was wise, and his wisdom consisted in his recognition of his lack of wisdom. The meanings of the very terms on which the problem was based, "wise" and "unwise," were able to shift as a result of maintaining the self-incompatible problem and thinking and talking partly in the terms given by the character of the problem itself.

Differently put, the self-interventive property of the responses to the oracle's declaration was fully acknowledged rather than being eliminated or avoided. And it was consequently able to intervene in, alter, even the nature of its own paradox-producing intervention in itself. The result was its self-cancellation and the emergence of a solution tangentially related to the alternative responses, both beyond their reach and presupposing them. It was a new starting point that involved a different, tangentially related, unforeseeable coordination of the elements of the old starting point and so different, tangentially related, unforeseeable meanings of those elements. And this new starting point was precipitated by the self-cancellation of the old coordination and meanings. That is, the problem, *as a problem,* became *part* of the solution, which involved a different understanding of what it is to be a problem or a solution itself. Differently expressed, the new starting point was both internally and externally connected to the old meanings and their coordination (see Idea 1.2).

Plato shows Charmides dealing with his dilemma similarly. Instead of trying to decide between the alternatives of the dilemma, he spoke about the dilemma itself. In this way he allowed the interventive properties of his response to intervene in and cancel themselves. And his very doing so showed the descriptive answer. It was a "not ignoble" answer: he dealt reasonably with a difficult situation: he was self-controlled. Charmides followed one of the ways of maintaining descriptive truth against its interventive dimension, which I presented in Idea 2.3. He said it so that it could be ignored, or in a manner irrelevant to the direct aim of the question.

Socrates, Plato has him report, responded as follows:

> What you're saying seems reasonable to me, Charmides. I think . . . that together we ought to consider whether or not you do possess what I'm asking about, to make sure that you're not forced to say things you don't want, and that I don't resort to medicine without due consideration. So if it's all right with you, I'd like to consider the question with you; but if it's not, we'll leave it be.[23]

Socrates suggested, then, that the solution was to be found in dialogue "together." This particular truth about Charmides' self was to be found not simply by virtue of Charmides' own resources but by virtue of those resources in relation to someone else's. This is also how Socrates had gone about finding his solution to his own dilemma: he had spoken with and questioned other people. In fact, the issue of Charmides' nature had arisen in the first place only because someone else, Socrates, had raised it. The whole that is a person, then, is adequately treated only by also treating the greater whole, partly external to it (or, in the same senses in which it is fundamentally internal to it, *also* fully external to it), of which it is a part.[24]

Plato has Socrates present himself as having been careful not to force even the very search for this truth on its object. Clearly, if he had, he would have distorted the results of the inquiry. Pressure would have had indeterminate effects on Charmides' answer: the search for truth would have intervened in its own process. Socrates is presented as having been clear that it was his own wish ("ἐθέλω") to pursue this inquiry. His own motives, for which Charmides need not take responsibility, were involved. And he asked Charmides to do it if, literally, it was a "love to him" ("σοι φίλον"): that is, if it was called for by Charmides' own truth, by the basis of his own motivations or commitments.

In fact, as I noted above, Socrates had begun the inquiry with a lie and had emphasized this fact for Charmides by elaborating it into an extended fiction. This is another of the ways of maintaining descriptive truth against its interventive properties that I offered in Idea 2.3: presenting the truth in a form in which it is obviously wrong. And he had also trivialized it in this way, so that it was also made essentially irrelevant. Socrates did not only keep open the standpoint from which the whole concern for temperance is unimportant; he also kept open the standpoint for which the whole concern for truth is unimportant. Plato presents him as having consistently negotiated not only the content but also the orienting structure of the situation in a way that allowed the interventive properties of descriptive truth to cancel themselves, including the interventive properties of truth about truth itself. In related ways, Plato does this for the reader too.

Socrates' and Plato's fiction and pretense, then, point themselves out, and do so in a way that establishes the conditions for truth. In both these respects, they are *also* literal and honest precisely in their extreme playfulness. They are ironic in a way that cancels even itself as irony. In this light, the humorous dimension of the dialogue is the palpable working of its fundamental rigor or cogent logic. It is the freeing and active absence, by and as its own self-cancellation, of careless imposition. As I argue below, Socrates' lust also turns out to be part of this fundamental humorousness.

On Charmides' prompting, we are told, Socrates then suggested that Charmides try to give an opinion about self-control, since if it were in him, he would have some perception of it that he could then express.[25] The rest of the dialogue does not address the question of whether Charmides is self-controlled, but the question of the nature of self-control. On the assumption that if self-control were in Charmides, he would be able to define it, the second question *does* address the first. But I suggest that this shift to an indirect address in fact approaches the first question without reference to this assumption, but does so instead through the self-cancellation of the interventive dimensions of that address.

2.2.3. Consequences of the External (or Tangential) Orientation toward Truth

These interventive dimensions had already been intervened in and canceled by Charmides' shift away from the question to acknowledging and focusing on them themselves. But the issue is now addressed more fully while still (and because) tangentially, in that, I try to show below, the way in which Charmides deals with the other question establishes the answer. And since the issue is addressed tangentially, focusing away from it, the fact of the inquiry itself will not interfere with the aim of the inquiry. That is, the issue is now addressed as it was prior to being the subject of an inquiry in the first place. The dialogue as a whole here rejoins Socrates' rigorously truth-seeking beginning in the indecision of evident, and so self-canceling, pretense and fiction.

Similarly, the focus away from Charmides himself and his own resources to the joining of resources in dialogue is in fact what allows the focus properly on Charmides himself. Having suggested they deal with the problem together, Socrates promptly asked Charmides to deal with it by looking in himself and reporting what he finds. In thinking carefully on his own about himself, Charmides would still have been departing from himself artificially, this, as I argued above, being the nature of disciplined thought. But having been being provoked by Socrates, that is, in an explicitly external way, to think about himself, he was in a much better position to come to recognize this artificiality. This is especially so given, again, the basis of the inquiry on a known lie and fiction. Consequently, he was in a much better position to avoid being caught up in the interventive properties of disciplined thought about himself.

The main point here is not that rigorous thinking genuinely happens only in dialogue with another, ironic person but that it occurs only with the kind of self-externality and artificiality that this kind of dialogue and irony makes explicit. Again, then, in general, a whole and a part of a whole are treated fully and primarily in their own right by also treating the greater whole that extends beyond them, is partly external to them.

Similarly, the truths of Plato's dialogues themselves are thoughtfully approached by also taking into account the truth of the reader, who is external to them, and not only what is reported inside Socrates' or Plato's memory and thinking.

Given that, as I show more fully as we proceed, the act of tangential focusing away *is* the act of focusing *on,* the *aporia* or fundamental indecision between alternatives that allows the justified decision for one of them does not occur only as a subjective experience but also between objectively contrasting elements of the situation such as the effects of different directions of focus, or such as speech or stated thought, on the one hand, and what action contrastingly shows, on the other. Differently put, not only thinking but also reality occurs as Platonic dialogue.

Bearing in mind that this indecision or hesitancy is undecided even as to its own indecision, each element of the situation *is what it is to the exclusion of the possibility of the other, of the other's even having any meaning,* and this is so on the basis of the indecision between them. This is the "sometimes always" logic that I discussed in Idea 1.2. The partners in the dialogue, as it were, are in a very fundamental way externally as well as internally related to each other, in the same respects. That is, they are what they are, exclusively of each other's possibility, while and in being dependent on each other. They are what they are tangentially. They are treated *primarily* and *in their own right* by being focused away from. And as I argued above, they are ultimately *only* established, in thought and reality, as what they independently are while and in being dependent in this way.

That is, they are *sometimes and/or in some respects* only established that way. What is ultimate or most fundamental is, for one thing, self-canceling. It undoes its own fundamental character in order to establish what it establishes without intervening in and distorting it. For another, it is ultimately dependent on the superficialities that also depend on it, and it is also as fundamentally externally as internally related to them. Consequently, the nature of the establishment of the truths of superficial thought cannot *simply* be reduced to that of the truths of fundamental thought.

This fundamental self-disparity of the truth of things is directly relevant to self-control itself. As I argued in Chapter 1 in connection with the *Gorgias* (sec. 1.2.5) and with the conflicted soul in the *Republic* (sec. 1.2.7), a self is what it is partly in other selves and disparately from itself. Consequently self-control, rigorously considered (bearing in mind, again, that rigorous consideration "sometimes always" cancels itself), is not *simply or always* a matter of subordination of parts of a self to other parts but *is sometimes and/or in some respects already* the self simply as what it is. In this light, the question of whether Charmides has self-control is the same as the question of whether he is truly a self at all. Or, differently put, whether he lives his (whole) self truly.

It follows, then, that self-control itself, as a matter of the truth of the self, is fundamentally self-canceling, with the same "sometimes" consequences.

2.2.4. Self-Control, Self-Externality, and Knowledge

Charmides gave three answers to the question of what self-control is: quietness,[26] modesty,[27] and doing one's own job.[28] Socrates proceeded to refute them by drawing out, in each case, other meanings associated with self-control and establishing, with Charmides, that his original answers did not correspond consistently with those meanings. So, for example, self-control is something honorable, and quickness is often associated with honorable skills. But quickness conflicts with what Charmides meant by quietness.[29] This procedure of following associated or united meanings will itself have to come into question, as the undecided dialogue/monologue (separated/ united) form of Plato's overall presentation already indirectly suggests. As I shall try to show, that line of questioning is already prepared in the external- ity of internal union itself.

It seems that Charmides had really heard the third answer, that self- control is doing one's own job, previously from Critias. Socrates explains that he himself was convinced that this was the case, and he reports that Critias was very eager to defend the answer.[30] Critias consequently replaced Charmides in the dialogue at this point. The focus is now at yet a further remove from Charmides, who is no longer involved in the inquiry at all, either as agent or object.

It is perhaps important that the dialogue is named after Charmides, though it is questionable whether Plato gave the dialogue this name. If Plato did give the dialogue its name, Charmides is the focus of the dialogue, even if this focus works by being a focus away from him. Critias, after all, was an important part of his life, being his guardian and apparently an influential model for him. And here Critias was apparently one of the sources of Char- mides' opinions. Again, something is treated as what it is and in its own right by the additional treatment of other parts of the greater whole that extends beyond it, parts that are external to it.

Critias responded to Socrates' initial questions to him by modifying the definition of self-control. "Doing one's own job" became "the doing of good things"[31] on the grounds that "only such things" are "our proper con- cerns."[32] Again Socrates drew out the associated meanings, this time associ- ated with the meaning of "doing good things," so as to show that one can do good things and not know it. In his example, a doctor can be helpful, which is one variety of doing a good thing, without knowing that his treat- ment in fact worked.[33] On Critias's definition, then, one can be self- controlled and not know it. Critias rejected this conclusion:

> if you think that that must follow as a result of what I admitted earlier, I'd
> rather retract part of that admission—and I'd not be ashamed to say that I
> was wrong—than ever allow that a man who does not know himself is self-
> controlled. Indeed, I'd almost say that is what self-control really is, knowing
> oneself.[34]

Critias did not rebel against the reasoning, even though it was adverse to a case he was eager to defend, but rather corrected himself quite radically. This seems to indicate an impressive degree of self-control on his part.

Having continued to correct himself at some clever and artificial length (to which I shall return), however, Critias immediately gave a first indication that he understood knowledge, in turn, as simply exclusive of self-questioning and ignorance. That is, he understood it as what I would call homogeneously textured: "Now . . . I'm willing to explain this fully to you, unless you do agree that self-control is knowing oneself."[35] His knowledge was something he possessed fully and only needed to be explained, not perhaps justified against legitimate questions. Socrates presented his own different understanding of and relation to knowledge in response:

> But, Critias, . . . you're treating me as if I'm maintaining that I know what I'm asking about, and as if I'll agree with you if I really want to. But it's not like that. In fact, I'm going along with you in investigating whatever proposition is made, because I myself am in ignorance. So, when I've considered it, I'm prepared to tell you whether or not I agree with you.[36]

And Socrates' immediately following procedure was simply to consider, by drawing out the meanings united with "knowing oneself": that is, he inquired rather than immediately aiming at an achieved result of inquiry. He maintained an indecision about the kind of result he was looking for.

If one thinks of the theory in the *Meno* that in seeking knowledge one recollects what one already knows, one can conceive of this as an indecision not only between alternative answers but even between whether or not one already knows the answer, or whether or not one already has the relevant knowledge. (Even if the *Meno* was written later, it allows us to think of the *Charmides* as fitting into the general Platonic framework in this way.) This possibility fits with a recognition that one already approaches a problem with assumptions from the start, and that one needs to leave room both for what one's current assumptions exclude from even having meaning, and for the incompatible possibility that one's assumptions are the appropriate ones. I suggest, then, that Socrates maintained his indecision between *mutually but not simply or homogeneously (not simply "always") exclusive* knowledge and ignorance.

Let me stress that in referring to knowledge as not simply exclusive of ignorance, I do not mean that there are degrees between knowledge and ignorance.[37] In keeping with the "sometimes always" logic I am developing here, I mean that *as well as* sometimes involving degrees, knowledge also *both entirely excludes* ignorance *and also* makes room for it. It makes room for what it excludes from even having meaning (and for what is excluded in turn by that making room for what is excluded: the degrees between knowledge and ignorance).

Like Socrates' procedure of inquiry, I suggest that his self-control was also rigorous, and that it was so because he was aware, as his initial reaction to Charmides gloriously emphasizes, of what was *not* self-controlled in him. This awareness, first, allows the identification of what needs to be controlled and, by the contrast, allows one to be sure about what is already controlled. Second, it *is already part* of the establishment of control: in being aware of what is not controlled, one already occupies a position that extends beyond one's uncontrolled areas. Because of this extra extension, this position both reduces the significance of these areas and gives an external standpoint from which to negotiate them. Self-control involves knowledge of uncontrolled elements of the self. And self-knowledge, as Socrates constantly insists, essentially involves recognizing one's ignorance of oneself. Self-control, then, involves both uncontrolled elements of the self and a self-knowledge that is equally and fundamentally a self-ignorance. Again, then, the solution *is* in part the problem, maintained *as* a problem, and stably recognized and lived as self-canceling. And again, something is what it is by also being other parts of a whole that extends, partly externally, beyond it.

In fact, as the dialogue continues to suggest, a dimension of rigorous knowledge is that it is a practice of its own partial dependence on what extends externally and heterogeneously or incompatibly beyond it. Consequently, rigorous knowledge *is already* rigorous self-control. It relates to its object as what it is, that is, as it is in its own limits. It is, then, *already* a restrained treating of the immediately given part, in the light of its greater whole. As the Platonic tradition has it, virtue is knowledge.

Critias, Plato has Socrates tell us, went on to explain that "knowing oneself" means "the knowledge both of the other knowledges and of its own self."[38] The knowledge that is self-control has no object other than knowledge itself.[39] It is knowledge exclusively of knowledge. And Critias is made to continue to show the homogeneity of his knowledge of knowledge (that is, his lack of what I have argued rigorous knowledge to be). After explaining his new meaning, he accused Socrates of being "well aware" of this meaning and so of ignoring what he knew simply in order to refute Critias.[40] Since knowledge, in Critias's understanding, is simply there or not there, without qualification, and since Socrates is someone with knowledge, then if Critias believes he knows something, he must also believe Socrates knows the same thing. Disagreement with Critias in general, on this view, can only be simple ignorance or pretense. (That is, Critias was other-insensible.)

Socrates is made to report that he responded again with his own rigorous view of knowledge and his relation to it: "if I'm trying my hardest to refute you," it is for the same reason "for which I'd investigate what I say myself! You see, my great fear is that I may some time not notice that I'm thinking I know something when in fact I don't."[41]

Plato has Socrates relate that he continued, "Never mind whether it's Critias or Socrates who is the one refuted. Just concentrate on the argument itself, and consider what on earth will become of it if it is examined."[42] Again, as I argued above and try to show further below, it is in and by this focus away from the particular persons that their particular truths are fully established in both thought and reality in their own right.

Socrates is made to continue that he proceeded to bring Critias to admit that knowledge of knowledge, involving no knowledge of an object of knowledge, seems unlikely to make sense, for example on the analogy of the senses. It makes no sense to speak of physically seeing physical vision itself.[43] Critias's definition seems to require that knowledge have the knowable properties that belong to an object of knowledge rather than to knowledge, and this is troublesome.

In fact, the view of knowledge Socrates is made to present is that it *does* have such properties: it is something that can be investigated and its limits considered. This is certainly clear from the passages in the *Apology* discussed above. And Plato has Socrates report that he asked a little later in the *Charmides*:

> does knowing knowledge and ignorance, which is what we are now dis-
> covering self-control to be, bring the following advantage, that the man who
> possesses this knowledge will more easily learn whatever else he learns, and
> everything will appear clearer to him inasmuch as he will see, in addition to
> each thing he learns, its knowledge?[44]

But if knowledge can be the object of knowledge, it is then also true that knowledge, rigorously considered, is not simply limitless and exclusive of ignorance. That knowledge has limits is part of what it is to be knowledge, in contrast to, for example, taking unquestioned assumptions for granted or with blind presumption. Approaching the same point differently, if one can investigate the nature of knowledge, one can be ignorant about the nature of knowledge, and this in turn means that knowledge of that ignorance is a kind of knowledge about one's own knowledge, or at the very least that knowledge can enter into a significant relation with ignorance. And in fact Critias agreed that his definition meant that self-control was also a knowledge of ignorance.[45] But Critias's (indirectly indicated) understanding of knowledge as simply exclusive of ignorance does not allow ignorance to enter into knowledge in this way. Accordingly, it is his own understanding of knowledge as homogeneous that does not allow knowledge to have the limits that go with being an object of knowledge.

It is not, in this context, that Critias's definition is wrong, but that his understanding of the meanings of the definition was, rigorously considered, wrong. Differently put, his standpoint is not what is rigorously refuted here, but his understanding of his standpoint. Rigorously considered, he was not defending what he thought he was defending.

But given that what he was defending was in fact an unrigorous understanding of knowledge and hence of self-control, it was *by and as* not rigorously understanding what he defended that he was consistently true to it and consistently defended it. His homogeneous understanding of knowledge as exclusive of ignorance is also an understanding of mistakes about knowledge as not occurring. Consistency to this understanding means that his *rigorously* visible mistakes about knowledge are not corrected but stay there. Given his commitment to careless thinking, this *rigorously* visible stable inconsistency *is* consistency. And, as I argued above, part of what is structured into the dialogue is that the commitment to rigorous or careful thinking cannot be assumed to be valid in advance. The alternative must be given its fair consideration also.

Critias, Plato has Socrates say, tried to bluff his way past the difficulties he was now in: "conscious that he had a reputation to keep up, he felt ashamed in front of the others and was unwilling to admit to me that he was unable to determine the points on which I was challenging him. He said nothing clear, in an attempt to conceal his difficulties."[46] When what he thought of as his perfect knowledge failed, he had nothing left but pretense. At that point he had no substantial self-control, and no means of establishing genuine knowledge. And each of these lacks, I have argued the *Charmides* shows, is the (internally related) partial expression and (externally related) partial cause of the other.

In fact, in the way he handled the question about his own self-control, Charmides had already shown he knew better than Critias with respect to knowledge of self or, as Critias had explained it, knowledge of knowledge. Critias's confident definition of self-control as self-knowledge or knowledge of knowledge indicates again that unlike Charmides, Critias was apparently unaware of the self-interventive dimension of knowledge, that is, of the troublesome, paradoxical nature of an idea like "knowledge of knowledge" or "self-knowledge." He was necessarily also unaware, then, of the inherent self-interfering limitations of knowledge of knowledge. And as a result, he was necessarily also unaware of the possibility, and still less the necessity, of using those self-interventive limitations to cancel and transcend themselves. Differently put, he was, again unlike Charmides, apparently unaware of the place of the limits of knowledge, of ignorance, as part of (successfully complete) self-knowledge and knowledge of knowledge. Whatever Critias's self-control may have been, then, he identified it with an unrigorous idea of knowledge as homogeneously unlimited in its ability to know its subject, or as not consisting partly in an externality to and questioning of its own nature.

Charmides, in contrast, had known that he was unable to answer—and hence to know at all in that context—whether he was self-controlled or not because the answer would have intervened in and falsified itself. And he had shown himself to be self-controlled in and by this rigorously established self-ignorance or indecision, rather than in *simple or homogeneous* self-knowledge.

The focus away from Charmides onto Critias and onto the issue of knowledge of knowledge now allows Charmides' own self-control to be seen in fuller perspective. In contrast with Critias's self-control, which involved an awareness only of knowledge without limits, Charmides' self-control had emerged only as an awareness of ignorance without knowledge. He had known the limitations of his knowledge, but with no sense of the relevance of those limitations to knowledge of their subject. That is, his self-control had emerged as also, like Critias's, an unrigorous thinking, but one for which self-ignorance and the limits of knowledge relevantly exist, although they exist as simply independent of knowledge. And where Critias's sensibility was too completely, too self-sufficiently formed to cancel itself and so get a perspective on itself, Charmides' was as yet too unformed either to cancel itself or to be the subsequent object of a perspective.

Charmides is shown, then, not to have been shaped enough, not to have developed his own meanings enough, to be able to *be* a defined particular, that is, a self to be self-controlled, properly on his own. In the terms I am developing, he had not sufficiently developed his externality to himself, not sufficiently developed the meanings of himself into the further meanings united with them, not established enough of the artificiality of thought in himself. In contrast, Critias had too much of this kind of artificiality to be properly a particular and so a self to be self-controlled. When he had first modified his definition of self-control, he made a very clever and learned distinction between usually synonymous meanings, based on a line of the well-known poet Hesiod, in order to establish which united meanings he was defending.[47] And when he later changed his definition, he had given a long speech basing his self-correction on another clever interpretation, this time of the well-known inscriptions at the oracle of Delphi.[48] Critias, then, had too much developed but un-self-questioning or un-self-canceling thought, that is, too much or too simple artificiality, to be sincerely himself, to be properly a particular on his own, either. He did not recognize or live his artificiality as artificiality, but based himself unthinkingly on an identity with ultimately unquestioned conventions. In this respect he was something like a customary universal. Let me stress that this is not simply a metaphor: as I argued above in various ways, one *is* in part one's thinking.[49]

I should emphasize that these unrigorous kinds of artificiality and universality are not necessarily less adequate, in general, than rigorous kinds. This is true for the same reasons that superficial truths are not necessarily less adequate, in general, than fundamental ones. But rigor and nonrigor do have different consequences nonetheless.

Plato has Socrates say that he went on to argue that even if knowledge of knowledge in Critias's sense had been possible, it would have been valueless for two reasons. First, it would have been empty. (This is the moment of empty focus on knowledge itself and entirely away from its subject matter that I discussed as the ultimate "tangent to the tangents" in Chapter 1 at section 1.2.2, in connection with the Idea of the Good.) Since it is knowledge of knowledge without an object, it is really knowledge of no particular knowledge, which is always knowledge of something other than itself. This means that Critias's knowledge of knowledge is at most knowledge *that* something is knowledge, or not, but not *what* it is knowledge of.[50] But further, it also follows that Critias's knowledge of knowledge cannot even be knowledge *that* something is knowledge or not. A knowledge *is* only knowledge at all as knowledge *of* its objects. Without knowing those objects, one cannot know if the knowledge of them is really a knowledge or not.[51]

Second, even if Critias's version of knowledge of knowledge had not been empty, it would not have been the right *kind* of knowledge to have value on its own. Socrates is made to report that he introduced his argument here with:

> I'm sure I'm talking nonsense. . . . All the same, one must examine any
> thought that occurs to one and not dismiss it without due consideration, if

one has even a little respect for oneself. . . . Listen to my dream, then, . . . and see whether it's come through the Gate of Horn [through which true dreams were said to come] or of Ivory [through which false dreams were said to come].[52]

Even when Socrates gave his potentially decisive refutation, he situated it on a basis of nonsense and dreams, which have no rational grounds; that is, he continued to present his position in the context of fundamental indecision.

Socrates went on to argue that it is living according to knowledge specifically of good and bad that makes "one do well and be happy."[53] (And here, at this point of discussing the empty knowledge of knowledge, we have an explicit reference if not to the Idea of the Good, at least to goodness.) Without that specific knowledge, we cannot know if any other knowledge, including knowledge of knowledge—that is, the basis of rigorous knowledge—is beneficial or harmful. Even if self-control could be knowledge of knowledge in Critias's or any homogeneous sense, then, "it is the producer of no benefit."[54]

Here Plato has Socrates make explicit, beyond the limits of the context of Critias's claims, that the worth of the knowledge that simply rigorous thought gives is not itself given in advance. Rather, it needs to be established in accordance with a more specific kind of knowledge, a knowledge, that is, that is less universal, less comprehensive. As less comprehensive, this knowledge does not reflect fully on its own status as part of knowledge in general. The worth of fully rigorous thought is therefore at least *also* established, rigorously considered, by a less rigorous and less fundamental knowledge than that which fully rigorous thought gives. This specific knowledge is that of good and bad.

As I argued in Idea 8.3 in connection with the *Phaedo,* what is most fundamentally good is for a thing to be what it is. What is good for something depends on the truth of what it is. And knowledge of what a thing is that does not interfere with that thing, that does not intervene in it to make it something other than itself, is an already-canceled knowledge. At this point of already-cancellation, even the entire context of aiming at knowledge has been canceled, has become meaningless. It is an achieved point of "there is nothing further to know, knowledge is irrelevant." In fact, as I argued in Idea 8.4, even the idea of "nothing further" becomes meaningless at this point: the very idea of explanation becomes meaningless, and with it the idea of going or not going further.

To behave well toward oneself and/or others, that is, to behave with a view to the good, then, as I argued in Chapter 1, is to let oneself and/or others be what they are without the interference of explanation or understanding. And this letting-be is precisely the self-canceling process of drawing out united meanings in which Socrates engages. This process, as Aristotle argues, is both redundant and nonsensically false. It is a self-canceling artificiality. And this self-canceling artificiality takes one to the knowledge that is the irrelevance of knowledge, the "nothing further to know."

But because it is self-canceling, it is not *simply* a process of drawing out united meanings, but rather *also* a process of establishing, *by and as* that drawing out of unity or sameness, the *disunified externality* internal to that unity itself. In this case, Socrates (we are fictionally told) showed the emptiness, the pure artificiality, of homogeneous (unified), universal knowledge of knowledge: precisely, that is, of the homogeneously self-unified kind of knowledge Critias was (implicitly) practicing. In other words, Socrates showed how this knowledge cancels itself. And *by and as this focus* on universal knowledge, that is, *by staying within* it, Socrates offered a rigorous knowledge, *external* to that focus, of Critias's own, implicit, particular knowledge, as essentially limited and so essentially requiring self-intervening questioning. And again, because of that internal externality, he did so without forcing him or the reader simply to accept or even to follow his demonstration. Further, his procedure (and Plato's) does not even force one to follow or accept the principle of being rigorous itself. In fact, as the rest of the dialogue shows, Critias retained his commitment to nonrigor to the end. That is, Socrates also established, by and as this process, that his *own, specifically rigorous* knowledge of his knowledge was limited in the same way. The nature of both particular knowledges, then, was established *by (externally) and as (internally)* the rigorous self-cancellation of universal knowledge.

Now, expressing this process differently, the self-cancellation established the sense and worth of the particular knowledges, but they, in turn, as the results or fruits that were all that remained of it, also established its own sense and worth. In other words, Socrates also exercised, by and as this process, the knowledge that establishes value, the uninterfering knowledge of good and bad that he argued to be primary. As my argument so far implies, this knowledge is both internally and externally related to the greater whole of knowledge in general of which it is a part. This knowledge was therefore exercised as the entire sympathetically good-humored, fundamentally self-canceling process of the dialogue as a whole.

The particular knowledge that Socrates ultimately offered to establish was the initial topic of the dialogue: whether Charmides had self-control. Socrates is shown to have approached it by focusing first on a different, more universal topic: what self-control in general is. And he approached this topic in turn by focusing away yet again, via a different interlocutor and still more universally, on knowledge of knowledge in general, that is, on what is basic to all topics in general. Further, he focused away from an answer to the topic even more definitively here by arguing for the impossibility of this most basic knowledge. If knowledge cannot be known in general, no particular knowledge can be known. In other words, no answers can then be known to be justified. But the establishment of this universal impossibility allows the particular issue that is in question, and the assumptions, categories, and context with which it was initially approached, to be fundamentally reassessed. Differently put, it allows a reunderstanding of the knower and the foundations of knowledge in general, and allows the particular issue to precipitate this deep reunderstanding without the interference of preconceptions. And this, if pursued (uniquely by each particular knower, of course), is what in turn would allow genuine knowledge of the particular issue.

The dialogue establishes, then, what I have called rigorous understanding without understanding. It rigorously establishes the superficial, un-thought-out features of the topic as the basis for rigorous knowledge of it. And it does so by also establishing the unrigorous, fictional, partial foundation of rigor itself. And again, because this establishment of unrigor at the basis of rigor gives, precisely, rigorous understanding, it also reestablishes the successful rigorousness of rigor itself.

In fact, as I argued above, this tangential process is *part of* reunderstanding and knowledge itself. This knowledge of knowledge, being "sometimes always" self-canceling, consists partly in a configuration of particular awarenesses and lack of awarenesses both internally and externally related in the same respects. That is, it consists partly in these elements as both simultaneous and separated nonimmediately connected parts of a sequence or process. And similarly, it consists partly in a partially external positioning or positionings of the particular knower with respect to his/her particular contexts at various times. This positioning or stance is expressed as, for example, the knower's perspective, attitude, experience, and conduct.

For example, what guarantees that Socrates' knowledge of his own knowledge is permanently established is not that he has it immediately available in his head to present directly in other contexts. Rather, it is that it is clear that he knows that it is *not* in his head, and that he will have to establish it freshly in each new particular context by his conduct and other dimensions of himself, just as he starts afresh with each of Charmides' and Critias's definitions. His knowledge lies not simply in the descriptions and responses he knows how to make but also in his positioning or orientation toward the truth of the issues in particular contexts.

Differently expressed, again, the problem of knowledge and of self-control, recognized and honestly lived, *is* part of the solution. Each fresh establishing will tell him more about his knowledge of his knowledge, and establish him more in his own being, precisely because it starts from the beginning again. Because he starts from the beginning, so that his knowledge itself, in general, is rigorously put in question, each time he will come to know more deeply and widely. That is, he will become more deeply and widely oriented toward truth. And he will become more deeply and widely self-controlled. And each development will involve equally a deeper and wider ignorance and ability to start over with knowledge and a deeper and wider recognition of where he is not self-controlled.

The old criticism of philosophy that it "reinvents the wheel" in fact misses the nature of human life, rigorously considered, and the things that are meaningful in it. The most fundamental "getting somewhere" occurs in staying in exactly the same place, exploring and, in and as the act of exploring, establishing (both subjectively and objectively) the nature or reality of that place. One brings oneself, and where one is, to be more fully what they are. Again, "knowledge" and "getting somewhere" themselves are exactly what they are by (also) only becoming what they are, that is, by (also) being external to themselves in order to become themselves: in other words, by (also) being other parts of the wholes that include but extend beyond them.

2.2.5. The Legitimacy of Unrigor and Directness

In fact, as I argued above, the *fundamental* ignorance whose coordination with knowledge Socrates presents *also* justifies the possibility of the "*simply getting somewhere*" kind of knowledge that Critias, for example, understands knowledge to be. It justifies, even as part of careful thinking, the possibility of descriptive knowledge homogeneously exclusive of ignorance and directly, not tangentially, related to its object. It even justifies the possibility of simply and directly descriptive knowledge of knowledge itself.

First, if it did not, it would just be another kind of self-homogeneity, instead of engaging with fundamental indecision.

Second, once the idea of the variegated texture of truth is understood (the legitimacy of that idea is a separate issue), a simple and direct description will (sometimes) be understood as *already* self-canceling, which is (sometimes) what allows the description simply to convey what it aims to convey. This is not simply to gloss over interventive and indirect features of the description that are always really implicitly there but are now taken for granted rather than actually having vanished. The rhetorical context, here the one involved simply in this different understanding of truth, or at this different moment of our discussion, is itself part of the truth of the situation, and a change in rhetorical context means a change in the truth itself. And this not only allows but requires a different kind of expression. After all, if descriptions can intervene in a situation so as to falsify themselves simply by virtue of being descriptions, then carrying out even the trivial intervention of exploring a different description of description does genuinely change the truth of the situation.

Third, the *indirect* address of the topic via the relevance of the truth of the knower, the context, and the process of inquiry *is itself already* partly a direct address of the topic, is itself already partly simple description of it. As I argued above, *truth and being themselves, including those of the topic, are partly self-external, self-indirect.* An indirect address of them is therefore already partly (or "sometimes always") a direct address. It is only partly so because, as I argued, they are only partly self-external. Since this self-externality is *fundamental,* it is also external even to its own self-externality, directed away even from its self-indirectness, so as to be *also* simply self-identical. One way, then, in which the indirectly relevant descriptive truth of the elements of the topic's situation can be directly relevant to the topic is precisely in describing the topic's own characteristic of self-canceling self-externality. That is, an indirectly relevant description can directly describe the way in which the topic or the thing the topic names is simply and self-identically itself in not being itself. Charmides and Socrates, for example, are only adequately *directly* described in *also* describing their interactions with and relations to the significant elements of the greater wholes that are their contexts (like Critias, in Charmides' case).

The dialogue, then, offers a rigorous understanding without understanding by and as also offering direct, simple understanding, homogeneous with itself. That is, it also establishes the simply homogeneous, superficial, unrigorous elements of rigor itself.

This can be seen in the relation of the dialogue to the initial paradox that Charmides identified in answering whether or not he was self-controlled.

As I argued in Idea 2.2, knowledge of knowledge involves self-falsifying paradoxes that can be resolved by allowing that self-intervention to intervene so fully that it cancels itself. Charmides' speaking about the paradox directly described how its opposed alternatives turn themselves into each other, its inherent character of being at variance from itself. This in turn required a similarly self-disparate process, focusing away from these alternatives in order to decide between them. Both his description of the paradox's self-disparity and the self-disparate process it required could then in turn be described (as I did), to decide between the alternatives, his being self-controlled or not.

This description then turned out to show a self-disparity of self-control, the topic, itself, as partly dependent on uncontrolled elements and, like knowledge, on parts of a whole beyond itself. As a result, the indirectness of addressing the topic, via the self-disparity of the paradox and then of the focus elsewhere, neither *simply* prevented a direct address of the topic nor *simply* disappeared in favor of an entirely different address. Rather, it itself, *as* indirect, became part of the directness of the homogeneously descriptive truth of the self-disparate topic. The indirect approach, then, also focused away from *itself*: that is, it approached even itself indirectly, and as a result made its own indirection explicit, an indirection that it shared with the truth of its topic and so directly reflected. Differently put, it intervened in its own indirectness and so canceled itself into directness.

The very act of philosophical "getting nowhere," of "reinventing the wheel," then, is *also* sometimes and/or in some respects *simply* a getting-somewhere-new, since new contexts can internally affect the truth of the thing being "rediscovered." In fact, at the most fundamental level, it is (sometimes) the *only* getting-somewhere-new, since other kinds of new discoveries are made on the basis of assumptions that only fundamental thinking (or fundamentally thoughtful activity) reworks.

For rigorous thought, then, the knowledge of knowledge, which is included in rigorous knowledge, *is* possible and worthwhile, and *is* self-control, restraint from uncontrolled imposition, as Critias suggested. But it is knowledge, and self-control, because it transcends itself, is partly but also pervasively (in the "sometimes always" sense, completely) external to itself, and establishes its limits by intervening in itself in a *fundamentally* self-canceling way so that it also in turn cancels that limiting intervention.

If Critias had learned by the end that he did not know what knowledge was, he would have become self-controlled (without necessarily knowing it) because he would have included ignorance in the constitution or texture of his knowledge. And he would have learned precisely by virtue of the limitations of truth-oriented thinking: he would have learned by rigorously establishing his mistakes. The sequence of spelling out his ideas until their contradictions emerged would have allowed him to know that a reunderstanding was necessary and would have given him some indications as to how to start again. And this in turn would have allowed him to understand that mistakes are not simply opposed to knowledge. The mistakes in the process of thinking are part of the knowledge they aim at: like Charmides' paradox, they cancel themselves so as to become reoriented and part of the solution.

2.2.6. Love, Lust, and Knowledge

That Critias did not learn that he did not know what knowledge was is a matter of his eros, his motivation to risk. And Socrates made room for that. At the end of the discussion, Socrates blamed himself for the unsatisfactory outcome of the investigation, although it was in fact Critias's definition that had led to this outcome. Socrates also offered no reasoned or persuasive alternative to Critias's position, and in fact behaved as if there were no such alternative. More, he proceeded to build on that last impression: "I'm . . . annoyed . . . for you, Charmides . . . because you, who have such good looks and are in addition very self-controlled, will not profit from that self-control."[55] Exploring the possibility of an alternative position for either Charmides or Critias needed to be initiated, if at all, by their own respective *erotes*, otherwise Socrates would have been imposing his own eros or motivation to risk a different commitment.

Socrates provided only the opportunity for their *erotes* to show different directions or be confirmed in their current directions by establishing a *fundamental* indecision in Charmides and Critias. That is, again, he established an indecision even as to whether there was an indecision. So, in building on the assumption that there was no alternative position to Critias's, he returned to his initial and known fiction: "I'm even more annoyed about the charm I learned from the Thracian—that I went on taking great pains to learn the charm for a thing which is worth nothing."[56] Socrates claimed to be most deeply distressed—about nothing that happened. The learning of the charm was a fiction. Here he indirectly but explicitly treats the outcome of his argument as a fiction of no significance, just as he had done with its beginning and its concluding moment (the "dream"). And he then gave support to Critias's and Charmides' beliefs as whatever they had been before his refutation: "In fact, I really . . . think . . . that I'm an awful investigator—because I do think that self-control is a great good . . . if you do possess it, I'd advise you . . . to consider me a fool . . . and yourself the happier the more self-controlled you are."[57]

Socrates did not impose a "good" on Critias and Charmides. He lived out or practiced knowledge of good and bad as involving ignorance of what is good or bad.

As I discuss in Chapter 3, this "early Socratic" dialogue, then, ultimately does exactly what the "middle Platonic" *Republic* does. It shows the intervention of rigorous thinking in itself so as to cancel itself and produce tangential knowledge of particulars. The point of complete self-cancellation is the point of established impossibility of knowledge. In the *Charmides*, it is knowledge of knowledge that is impossible. And the real worth of this knowledge depends on knowledge of what is good. In the *Republic*, it is the Idea of the Good that is beyond knowledge. And it is knowledge of knowledge that nevertheless gives the truth and right orientation of goodness, the "highest matter for learning." It makes sense, given the discussion so far, that the impossibility of knowledge of knowledge in the *Charmides* allows the foregrounding of knowledge of good, on which it depends, while the impossibility of knowledge of good in the *Republic* allows foregrounding of knowledge of knowledge, on which it similarly depends. Insight is partly but pervasively (or in the "sometimes always" sense, completely) self-external and tangential to its object.

It is worth noting that the *Meno* (see Idea 4.2) and the *Phaedo* (see Idea 8.2.1), which are "early middle" dialogues, also include central digressions from investigating the topic to investigating the nature and possibility of knowledge in general.

Perhaps it is not, then, that Plato has a metaphysics, a theory about the nature of reality, where Socrates had only a method focused on ethics, but that different particular questions, contexts, and commitments require and allow completely different, even incompatible, and yet universal metaphysics and also sometimes the irrelevance of metaphysics, in accordance with the good-humored, variegated texture of truth. Both Socrates and Plato may have had many different metaphysics and nonmetaphysics, and the diversity of the dialogues is possibly partly meant to emphasize the significance of exactly that.

As I argued in Chapter 1, the letting-be without understanding in which Socrates engages with Critias and Charmides is ultimately the work of non-self-defeating love, of relating to things for their own sake. Socrates left Charmides in a state of indecision or *aporia:* "I [Charmides] don't know whether I possess it [self-control] or whether I don't."[58] And, as I argued above, he succeeded in doing this not only despite his initial uncontrolled lust for Charmides, but also partly because of it. This *aporia* allowed Charmides to begin to establish, without interference and without its being unquestionable and so irrevocable, a direction of his own desire or eros that had not been established before: "Still, I don't really believe you at all, Socrates, and I really do think I need the charm [*epoides*]; and as far as I am concerned, there's no reason why I shouldn't be charmed [*epaidesthai*] by you every day, until you say I've had enough."[59]

The dialogue ends, as it begins, in uncertainty not only as to the topic, but as to the status and worth of the philosophical approach itself. Charmides, as we see here, continued to play along with Socrates' fiction about the charm, which gave him a transparent pretext for talking more with Socrates. And he added his own erotic twist to it: "there's no reason why I shouldn't be charmed by you every day." But when Critias encouraged Charmides in this flirtatious play, he responded, "I'd be behaving terribly if I didn't obey you, my guardian, and didn't do what you tell me."[60] In the face of his admission of his own somewhat erotic motive for pursuing Socrates, Charmides playfully and charmingly pretended that he was pursuing Socrates out of a sense of duty.

Critias went along with him, and Socrates, joining in the play, asked what they were plotting. " 'Nothing,' said Charmides. 'We've done our plotting.' " Then Socrates: "Are you going to resort to the use of force, without even giving me a preliminary hearing in court?"[61] " 'I certainly am,' he replied, 'since Critias here orders me to.' "[62] This is a full evocation of the later careers of Critias and Charmides as, respectively, leader and follower of the Thirty Tyrants, more unjust and intemperate even than the democracy that at least gave Socrates a trial. But this evocation of the Thirty Tyrants is *also* charmingly playful and pleasant. The talk of force here, even by the intemperately forceful characters, is a way of expressing and engaging in love, by focusing away from it.

And Plato has Socrates report that he accepted this topic, attitude, and manner. Charmides explained that, since he was plotting to use force on Socrates, "*you* should plot what *you'll* do." "But," Socrates responded, " 'once you're intent on doing something and are resorting to the use of force, no man alive will be able to resist you.' 'Well then,' he said, 'don't you resist me either.' 'I won't,' I said."[63]

Plato, then, even given his hindsight, is true to the noninterfering lack of knowledge about the status and outcome of fundamental inquiry.

Plato leaves it entirely unclear whether the rigorously thoughtful—philosophical—side of Socrates' engagement with Charmides and Critias has achieved anything at all. And this allows the reader to think about the topic, the relevance of her/his own context and commitments, and all three of the particular characters without a ready-made decision or judgment either way. That is, the reader can approach the particulars, including her/his own particular assumptions, and including the particular worth of this philosophical approach itself, for the first time (and, by rereading the dialogue, for the first time repeatedly) without an already-operative understanding. And this is achieved not by the simple absence of understanding, but by fundamental indecision between more than one rigorously developed understanding.

The particular characters and issues can make a truthful impact on the reader, in the particularity of the reader's own truth, because rigorous indecision is achieved with respect to all of these elements of the situation. And the reader is shown how to resolve these indecisions on the model of Charmides' and Socrates' resolution of Charmides' initial paradox. The paradox or indecision is established and recognized, and this established recognition *is,* as it turns out, part of the tangential resolution of the indecision or paradox. Differently put, establishing the structure of indecision *is already* its transcendence into some relevant-to-the-topic, justifiable decisions, including relevant decisions about the process of indecision and deciding itself. One knows partly in knowing how not to know. And similarly, one is responsibly self-controlled partly in knowing and drawing on one's uncontrolled, thoughtless elements, specifically in their *externality* to rigorous responsibility and rigorous thought, and in knowing that one's knowledge of them is limited.

The indecisions that the dialogue structures in foundationally from the start, then—indecisions about whether the dialogue is basically one unified monologic line of thought or really more than one, about who the reader is, about whether or not historical and social context determine the reader's understanding and possibilities, about whether the sequence of presentation is ultimately significant or whether what is presented can be grasped in a single moment of understanding—these indecisions cancel themselves into irrelevance not *simply* by disappearing, but *also* by staying exactly as they are. Their self-cancellation *is* the emergence of truthful decision. Consequently their self-cancellation *is itself stably part* of the enduring solution.

These indecisions, entirely canceled as the *problem*, remain as part of the essentially ("sometimes always") self-testing, and essentially ("sometimes always") eros-based, and so ("sometimes always") self-external *solution*, both to the topic and to the problem of how the topic is dealt with.

The establishment of indecision with respect to the topic *is* initially the knowledge of *at least two different, mutually exclusive senses of self-control*. That is what makes an indecision possible. One has to grasp something, and about at least two conflicting construals of the topic, otherwise one either does not know enough even to be undecided, or one is not undecided about that topic but about which topic to consider. One sense of self-control here is self-control as it is in a carefully thoughtful life, and the other sense is self-control as it is in one kind of conventional, comparatively thoughtless life. This fundamental indecision allows self-control to stand out not only in its particularity, but in being more than one particular. And these particular senses of self-control are known in their relation to the particular characters for whom they make sense in their particular contexts. In understanding them, and understanding ourselves in our particular contexts in relation to them, we can relate truly and effectively to them and ourselves. And we can then come to further decisions rigorously on that basis.

It seems to me, then, that the most fundamental alternatives between which the indecision about the topic occurs are not, for example, whether Charmides' and Critias's standpoints with respect to knowledge and self-control are simply valid or invalid. If one accepts the validity of responsible thinking, that decision is made: they are clearly simply invalid. What Plato contributes beyond this result of careful thinking, however, is that they may be valid if one accepts the validity of irresponsible or careless thinking. And this kind of thinking *is* valid if one begins on the basis of a self-defeating eros, one that does not set about letting itself or what it loves be what it is independently of the eros's intervention. The most fundamental undecided alternatives, then, are between Socrates' standpoint, in which careful thinking and responsibility are fundamentally important and valid, and Charmides' and Critias's standpoints, in which careful thinking and responsibility are trivial and invalid, while careless superficiality is important. (This feature of their standpoints has the result that they carelessly understand careful thinking and responsibility as both impossible and unlimited.)

That is a much more subtle and difficult issue. And the answer presupposes an already given eros or commitment or risk or motivation in the particular decider, either toward thinking responsibly or not. This eros is part of what ultimately needs to be established.

As I argued above, this indecision between careful and careless thought does not simply mean that truth is relative. Rather, it is what allows the full justification, that is, the full rigor itself, of careful thinking, whether relativist *or* absolutist, and responsibility themselves. This justification requires a standpoint external to rigor, and that standpoint is something like careless superficiality. Rigorous thought and responsibility, then, essentially or foundationally *include* careless superficiality.

Furthermore, it is essential to rigorous thought and practice, including self-control, not to impose themselves, but to deal with things as they are independently of or prior to the depth rigor brings. Consequently, as I argued above, rigorous avoidance of imposition or distorting intervention requires active thoughtlessness or absence of rigorous discipline in a variety of possible ways.

For the rigorous standpoint, then, rigorous knowledge and responsibility, including self-control, are ultimately each *already* more than one particular kind of thing. But because they are so in being (partly or "sometimes always") a single self-canceling indecision, they are each also only one particular kind of thing. Careful thinking and responsibility are treated *as what they are* by *also* treating parts of a greater whole that are external to them. To mangle Browning, philosophy, or rigorously thoughtful life, grasps itself by exceeding its own grasp.

The *Charmides,* I suggest, tries most fundamentally to show and justify to careful thinking the nature and importance of the delicately ungainly and precise negotiation, both rhetorical and logical, that this self-canceling indecision between careful and careless thinking requires. And it does so by exploring both decisions in their mutually exclusive ways.

CHAPTER 3

Republic: *Justice, Knowledge, and the Problem of Love*

In this chapter, I discuss some details of the overall structure of the argument of the *Republic*. Like the *Theaetetus,* which I discuss in Chapter 4, this dialogue is widely regarded as written in Plato's "middle" period. Together with the *Theaetetus* I shall discuss the *Sophist* and *Statesman,* and these are widely regarded as "late" dialogues. While I aim to show, among other things, that these distinctions need not make any important difference, my point is not *simply* that Plato presents the same philosophy in all of his dialogues. Rather, I aim to show that Plato's philosophy is selfsame partly in that it shows the significance of staying undecided between what is selfsame and what is other, and also staying undecided about that indecision itself. That is, as I argued above, his philosophy shows an occasional, and sometimes only an occasional, identity of the internal and external connections that a thing has with itself and with other things. I suggest that his dialogues are related accordingly.

In my view, then, his dialogues present the same philosophy partly by being fundamentally different from each other in an indefinite variety of ways. And some of these differences themselves are, in different but equally fundamental respects, similarities. Even if the division of his dialogues into different periods has some truth to it, therefore, on my view it is hopelessly oversimple.

The *Republic* is famously taken to be about the nature and worth of justice as illuminated by Plato's idea of the best political state.[1] These topics are certainly centrally discussed in the dialogue. As some of the sources I cite below indicate, it has also been strongly argued that Plato's presentation of this state as the best is ironic. I argue, however, that the dialogue examines not only its topic, but equally the nature and worth of the activity of examining itself, and the mutual relevance of the topic and its examination. I also try to show that Plato's presentation of the best state is tied to this multiple concern so as to be both fully ironic and fully literal, in the same respects.

I try to show that the *Republic* argues, first, that the nature and worth of justice in fact lie in both its internal and external relations to the philosophical inquiry into it. And second, that the nature and worth of philosophical inquiry in turn lie in its internal and external relation to love. Accordingly, in dealing with justice, the *Republic* deals as fundamentally with knowledge and love.

The dialogue of the *Republic,* like that of the *Charmides,* is narrated in a monologue by Socrates. Like the form of the *Charmides,* then, it is undecided as to whether it is two things or one. Again like the dialogue in the *Charmides,* it takes place "yesterday" and alludes to events that have not yet happened. And as in the *Charmides,* Socrates' addressee(s) is/are unknown. The reader is again placed in an indecision with respect to who s/he is, and when, with respect to the dialogue.

3.1. DISCUSSIONS OF JUSTICE, SOCRATES' EXAMPLE, AND SELF-EXTERNALITY

Near the start of the *Republic,* Socrates refutes two definitions of justice. He does so by drawing out the meanings united with each of them and showing that in each case these meanings do not fit with each other, so that the definitions do not make sense.

The first definition is that justice is helping one's friends and harming one's enemies; this definition is defended by the host of the discussion, Polemarchus. Socrates argues, to Polemarchus's satisfaction, that harming one's enemies is unjust, since harming them means making them worse, and this in turn means that they become more unjust. And only injustice, not justice, can produce injustice.[2] The dialogue emphasizes this conclusion with some fuss:

> "It is not then the function of the just man . . . to harm . . . anyone . . . ,
> but of his opposite, the unjust." "I think you are altogether right, Socrates."
> "If, then, anyone affirms that . . . harm is what is due to his enemies from
> the just man . . . he was no truly wise man who said it. For what he meant
> was not true. For it has been made clear to us that in no case is it just to
> harm anyone." "I concede it," he said. "We will take up arms against him,
> then, . . . if anyone affirms that . . . any . . . of the wise . . . said such a thing."
> "I . . . am ready to join the battle with you."[3]

And a bit more is made of it before they go on. As I show below, this emphasis will turn out to be significant.

Socrates' own argument is based on falsely uniting two disparate meanings: he confuses apparent and real harm. Later he himself will argue, for example, that just punishment is only apparent harm. And in this earlier context, he asks Polemarchus to distinguish between appearance and reality, but in connection with apparent and real friends and enemies rather than in connection with harm.[4] Plato emphasizes this distinction in one of the ways I discussed in Idea 2.3, that is, in a way capable of being irrelevant to the discussion. He does so in an interruption of another discussion (that is, through the structure or composition of the dialogue): Polemarchus interrupts Socrates' subsequent discussion with Thrasymachus to emphasize a distinction between real and apparent advantage.[5] Polemarchus's definition, then, is only refuted superficially. But just because this superficial refutation succeeds, Polemarchus's method and level of dealing with the definition are refuted. They are too superficial to deal even superficially with the issues they involve.

Because Socrates presents this refutation in a way that can be ignored, he does not impose the principle of careful thought on Polemarchus. That is, he does not arbitrarily insist that rigor is more appropriate than superficiality to someone committed to a nonrigorous principle but presents the rigorous refutation so that only those already committed to rigorous inquiry will notice it.

The importance of the appearance/reality distinction, I suggest, is that without it, knowledge is entirely unproblematic. What one sees simply is as one sees it. And this is what I have called other-insensibility. Given an other-insensible standpoint, fundamental learning, or growth in one's being, is impossible, since mistakes are unthinkable. Further, reassessment of impressions is similarly impossible, while conflict between impressions, including one's own, is inevitable.[6] Consequently irresolvable personal and social conflict is inevitable. Here it is worth noting that the dialogue begins with Polemarchus's mock threat to detain Socrates and Glaucon by force, while Socrates offers "the alternative of our persuading you to let us go."[7] But as Polemarchus suggests in response, he could not be persuaded if he refused to listen.

Like the *Charmides,* then, the *Republic* presents the possibility of a standpoint that is, perhaps, ultimately committed to rigorous questioning, including self-questioning, and the possibility of another standpoint that is, perhaps, ultimately committed to careless superficiality. But it is also worth noting that Socrates himself is made to engage in superficial thinking, and with rigorous results.

The second definition, that justice is the advantage of the stronger, is given and defended by Thrasymachus, a Sophist, a practitioner and teacher of persuasive rhetoric. Thrasymachus is typical of the Sophists as Plato presents them. He is egotistical and very certain that he has the right answer.[8] Like Polemarchus and perhaps Socrates, Thrasymachus turns out to confuse what is apparent with what is real: the stronger may mistakenly enforce laws that appear advantageous to them but are really not so.[9] He corrects this confusion by connecting expert knowledge with what he means by strength. Accordingly, the stronger cannot be said to make mistakes as long as their strength is the point at issue, which it is here.[10]

But then Socrates shows Thrasymachus's argument to be contradictory in reality and not only in appearance. Thrasymachus does not understand that knowledge, political or otherwise, is expertly successful only because it is guided by the nature of its object. Expert knowledge is therefore guided by what is advantageous for its object rather than by its own independent interests.[11] The issues that guide rigorous knowledge, making it what it is, are precisely not its own. That is, Thrasymachus, like Critias in the *Charmides,* does not understand that rigorous knowledge is what it is by being external to itself.

Further, Socrates argues, if justice is taken to be the advantage of the stronger/expertly-knowing, to the homogeneous exclusion of the advantage of others, then the stronger/expertly-knowing could not cooperate. Each of them would work against the others to her/his own exclusive advantage.[12] Even more, a single person operating in this way would be paralyzed by the conflict of his/her own contrary inclinations. S/he would work each of these, too, to its own advantage exclusively of that of the others.[13] In fact, this definition of justice, as Thrasymachus himself boldly notes, is really a definition of injustice (which he sees as rightfully replacing justice as a virtue). Rigorously considered, then, homogeneously self-consistent strength and knowledge that are not at all self-external are self-defeatingly self-contradictory precisely in being homogeneously self-consistent.

The importance of the self-externality of rigorous knowledge, I suggest, is the same as that of the appearance/reality distinction. As I argued in Chapter 1 at the end of 1.1.2, the latter expresses the self-externality of reality itself, which involves and requires the self-externality of rigorous knowledge, both because knowledge is part of reality and because such knowledge must be guided by reality.

Thrasymachus finds ways, although with difficulty, to resist accepting or to trivialize Socrates' refutations all the way through: for example, near the end of this discussion, "Revel in your discourse . . . for I shall not oppose you, so as not to offend your partisans here,"[14] and, "So it appears . . . by your reasoning."[15] The rigorous standpoint, then, is not imposed on him.

Glaucon and Adeimantus (Plato's brothers) then ask Socrates to defend justice against the common opinion that while justice is necessary, it is a necessary evil. It is a burden, while injustice brings all sorts of advantages. They make clear that this and related common opinions are taught by the poets, from whom conventional religious learning primarily comes, by parents and teachers, and by the public at large. And they take the distinction between reality and appearance fully into account. In fact, they ask that justice be discussed as if it has the appearance of injustice, and vice versa, so that the real worth of each can be investigated without the interference of their superficial appearances and reputations.[16]

Setting up this reversal of appearances asks the question: Is justice *so* much better than injustice that it is *always* worth choosing justice over injustice, whatever the circumstances? That is, is justice *essentially* and so *universally* better than injustice? As Adeimantus puts it, the question is what each, justice and injustice, is "in itself, by its own inherent force."[17]

In response, Socrates sets out to identify what justice is and so to prepare to establish whether it is more advantageous than injustice. In order to do so, he creates a city-state "in theory" (or in speech: τῷ λόγῳ),[18] since, he suggests, justice will be more easily apprehended in a city-state than in individual people, who are much smaller.[19] In keeping with his aim, he builds this city-state so that it will be just. And he ensures this not by drawing out united meanings, but by having his interlocutors, Glaucon and Adeimantus, confirm at each point that he is correctly identifying what is just, which they do.

This process is clearly viciously circular. Socrates is claiming to *establish* what is just by relying uncritically on his interlocutor's *already given conclusions* about what is just.[20] The most he can do in this way is to establish that there are common opinions about justice that contradict the unfavorable common opinions that Glaucon and Adeimantus initially present. But this does not justify one set of opinions against the other. As I try to show, it will turn out that this process is not only viciously circular, but is also inadequate in other ways, including being self-contradictory. And it is all of these things for reasons Socrates himself gives and emphasizes but without also making explicit that these reasons conflict with the argument he is presenting.

Socrates bases his creation of the city-state on the principle that:

the origin of the city . . . is to be found in the fact that we do not severally suffice for our own needs, but each of us lacks many things. . . . As a result of this . . . between one man and another there is an interchange of giving, if it so happens, and taking, because each supposes this to be better for himself.[21]

That is, one not only takes but also gives for one's own sake. One lacks some necessities and so, just as in the *Charmides,* one is complete partly in what is other than, external to, oneself. This rules out the advantageousness of injustice already. Mistreatment of others is mistreatment of oneself. But Socrates does not mention this already-available result, here or later. I discuss below his possible motives for leaving it implicit once the process he does explicitly pursue has become clearer.

The first stage of the city-state Socrates arrives at is a pure fiction, a rustic idyll that, as Glaucon then points out, is as subhuman as a "city of pigs."[22] Like the *Charmides,* then, the main discussion of the *Republic* begins with a recognized fiction.

In response to Glaucon's reaction, Socrates builds on this fictional city-state to arrive at one acceptable to his interlocutors, in which he finds justice. This city-state is divided into three classes, rulers (guardians), military protectors (auxiliaries), and a class consisting of workers such as artisans, merchants, and farmers. The auxiliaries protect because they have a disposition and training to help friends and harm enemies.[23] The rulers rule because they are the best of the military protectors, "the most regardful of the state."[24]

Socrates claims to find justice in this city-state by elimination. He finds wisdom, courage, and self-control and then finds justice as what is left over.[25] Justice turns out to be "doing one's own business"[26] (and not interfering in others'), if this phrase is "taken in a certain sense."[27] Socrates then proceeds to establish whether the individual soul corresponds to the city-state so that justice as it is in the city-state is also justice as it is in the individual person.

He finds that the city-state and the individual soul do correspond in the relevant ways. The individual soul also has three parts, the rational, the spirited, and the desiring ("ἐπιθυμητικόν"), and they correspond respectively to the ruling, protecting, and laboring classes in the city-state.[28] Justice is therefore a doing of one's own business in which "a man must not suffer the principles in his soul to do each the work of some other and interfere and meddle with one another."[29] Injustice, then, is a mutual interference of the principles of the soul, and so is a kind of ruinous disease more serious even than "a ruined constitution of body."[30]

At this point, Socrates is about to describe four kinds of inferior city-states in order to clarify that justice is essentially better than injustice.[31] But he manages only to explain his intention before Polemarchus indirectly interrupts him. It was Polemarchus who had initiated the encounter with Socrates at the start of the dialogue: he had sent a slave after him, and the slave had stopped Socrates by grabbing his cloak from behind. Now Polemarchus takes Adeimantus's cloak from behind to consult with him about whether to interrupt Socrates, and Adeimantus does the interrupting.[32] This repetition of the initiating structure suggests a new beginning.[33] And in fact Socrates is made to go back to features of his city-state that he had argued were necessary for the best polity, but now to show that they are also possible.

This account, which, when it ends, Socrates calls a digression,[34] takes up almost a third of the dialogue and it offers a new foundation for the city-state and so for the topic of the nature of justice. Socrates now argues that the city-state that has so far been assumed to be just is only possible if the ruler is also a philosopher.[35] Only a philosopher knows enough to establish such a city-state. At this point, as part of the digression, then, it is made explicit that the account of the city-state in which justice was identified is inadequate.[36]

In fact, even if the account of the polity were adequate, the method of finding justice in it by elimination is glaringly absurd. For a start, there are more than four virtues according to the opinion of Plato's time and even in his dialogues. Piety, for example, could hardly be considered a secondary virtue in a dialogue that takes religion seriously, as the *Republic* does. The elimination, then, is not really an elimination. Second, even if there were only four virtues, removing the other three has no connection with finding justice. Their removal does not leave any definite area to investigate. The metaphors Socrates was made to use there make this quite clear:

> "Now . . . is the time for us like huntsmen to surround the covert and keep close watch. . . . It plainly must be somewhere hereabouts [where exactly is "hereabouts"?]. . . . Pray for success, then. . . ." And I caught a view and gave a halloo and said . . . "I think we have found its trail."[37]

There is no connection whatsoever here between finding justice and anything in the preceding discussion, including the elimination of the other virtues.

Further, when Socrates came to compare the city-state and the individual soul to establish whether their relevant "parts" correspond, he stated explicitly that "in my opinion we shall never apprehend this matter accurately from such methods as we are now employing in discussion. For there is another longer and harder way that conducts to this."[38] Even if the account of the city-state were adequate, then, Socrates made it clear that he believed they lacked the methods to make adequate use of it.

More than being inadequate, however, the account of the city-state has already turned out to be self-contradictory in several ways, without this having been said explicitly. First, the military protectors, and the corresponding part of the soul, are supposed to help friends and harm enemies. But Socrates had already argued with much emphasizing fuss, as I noted above, that harming enemies is unjust. And although that argument might apply only to apparent harm, the discussion of the protectors makes no mention of the difference between apparent and real harm.[39] In fact, Socrates refers ironically during that discussion to the gap between the kind of knowledge the protectors would need to be able to establish that difference and the knowledge they actually have as discussed so far. Using the analogy of a dog who is angered by the sight of an unknown person and who fawns on a familiar person, he argues, "But surely that is an exquisite trait of his nature and one that shows a true love of wisdom. . . . How, I ask you, can the love of learning be denied to a creature whose criterion of the friendly and the alien is intelligence and ignorance?"[40] This analogy does not speak well for the sophisticated capacity of the protectors to discriminate between real and apparent harm or even real and apparent enemies. The defining function of the protectors, who are the most valued part of the city-state[41] and from whom the rulers are chosen, can therefore only be carried out in a way that is by their own definition unjust. And since they may mistake friends and enemies for each other and so mistreat them as easily as not, it is unjust with or without Socrates' qualifying distinction between real and apparent harm.

Second, the comparison between city-state and individual is incoherent. Socrates did warn at the time that:

> if something different manifests itself in the individual, we will return again to the state and test it there and it may be that, by examining them side by side and rubbing them against one another, as it were from the fire sticks we may cause the spark of justice to flash forth, and when it is thus revealed confirm it in our own minds.[42]

That is, this comparison might force us to rethink the results of the account of the city-state, like fire sticks rubbing together to produce a spark different from either of them. The three classes of the city-state are differentiated by virtue of the three different characteristics shared respectively by their individual members. But the individual soul has all three of these character-istics, and these are required to be in the same relation to each other in all souls. This means that every individual in every class has the characteristics of all three classes, and has them in the same way, so that the classes are no longer different. Alternatively, one could argue that different parts of the soul are better developed in different individuals. But then the comparison with the city-state collapses from the other end. Justice, each part doing its own business, in the individual would no longer be like justice in the city-state at all. The parts in the individual simply would not function in relation to each other in the ways they do in the city-state.

Third, it is clear that the "just" city-state is radically unlike Plato's fic-tional version of the actual, current city-state of Athens, as represented by the assembled company. The features of the "just" city-state that Polemar-chus wants Socrates to revisit include, for example, that the auxiliaries have no possessions "save the indispensable,"[43] women and children are possessed in common among all the men,[44] and women are given the same training and roles as men.[45] But this utterly different "just" city-state was "built" under the guidance of the opinions about virtue most generally held in the actual city-state. Glaucon and Adeimantus made it clear that these are the opinions taught by religion, parents, teachers, and society at large. The dia-logue shows the currently held opinions about virtue and justice, then, to be *revolutionary* with respect to themselves. When employed in a sustained way, they abolish the social structure that produces them and that they are supposed to represent and maintain. That is, they are self-contradictory. And since they are ideas of *justice* that contradict themselves, this in turn means that they are unjust on their own grounds.

There is an important further consequence of this point. The current opinions represented here are not just a particular selection of opinions but those taught by society both in its various aspects and at large—common opinion *in general*. Plato does not only show, then, that uncritical ultimate reliance on particular common opinions in order to establish the truth of their subject is inadequate, viciously circular, and, in particular details, self-contradictory. What he also suggests, if not shows, is that common opinion is *in general and so inherently* self-contradictory and self-subversive.

The process the dialogue has so far presented consists of the following phases. First, a particular opinion on the topic at hand was explicitly refuted by drawing out its united meanings. Then a new starting point, a second particular opinion on the topic at hand, was given, and the mistake both opinions had in common was implicitly identified and avoided. This mistake was that of failing to distinguish appearance from reality. As a result, the second opinion was improved into a better starting point, since it now avoided this mistake. It was then also explicitly refuted by drawing out its united meanings, and a new mistake was shown: failure to recognize that knowledge is self-external, guided by the nature of its objects rather than circularly or homogeneously by its own independent interests. Then yet another opinion was given as a new starting point, this time with two important new features. First, it was the most thoroughgoing of this kind of starting point: it was opinion *in general* on the topic at hand—what is taught by religion, parents, teachers, and society at large. Second, it was given in a way that altogether and explicitly avoided the first mistake of confusing appearance and reality. Opinion *in general* on this topic was then *implicitly* refuted, without drawing out united meanings, and *implicitly* shown to share the second mistake. It tried to guide knowledge by what was taken to be homogeneously selfsame: accepted opinion.

I suggest that the implicitness here is essential. As in the *Gorgias* and the *Charmides,* Socrates cannot legitimately *simply* refute conventional opinion in general, opinion as such. Opinion is what it is by virtue of its not engaging in rigorous examination: that is, the other-insensibility involved both in identifying appearance with reality and in identifying knowledge with itself as simply its own, unquestionable guide is essential to opinion's being what it is. Consequently Socrates cannot fairly engage with opinion as such simply by means of rigorous thought. If he does so, he has already distorted it, and has himself forced his standpoint on it in an other-insensible way. He can therefore only offer the option of rigorous thought, in a way that does not force opinion-committed people to engage in it. I suggest that he did this here by presenting the option only implicitly.

But in fact, if Socrates is concerned with truth, he was *also* obliged to present the *rigorous* option, for at least two reasons. First, his own truth was part of the truth of the situation, and so had to be presented. Second, as in the case I discussed in Idea 1.1, it was not yet clear what his interlocutors' *erotes* were. To relate truly to them, then, Socrates was obliged to allow for fundamental indecision about those *erotes.* Consequently, he had to present the relevant issues as they were in his standpoint but not in his interlocutors' standpoints, so that both standpoints could be represented between which the possible indecision would be. Socrates, then, had to find a way of operating simultaneously in accordance with both mutually exclusive standpoints, in order to maintain the indecision instead of illegitimately forcing a decision either way. The *erotes*, the ultimate commitments, of his hearers and readers would then determine, without Socrates' interference, what option they took up.

Socrates did explicitly raise the appearance/reality distinction and the self-externality of knowledge when he was dealing with *particular* opinions. And that was appropriate and necessary. It was appropriate because the relevance of these issues to opinion *as such*, and hence to the difference in *standpoints as such*, was not yet at stake. And it was necessary because explicitly raising these issues in connection with particular opinions allowed him to work *toward establishing* fundamental indecision, indecision about the knower's very standpoint. This is what would give his interlocutors access to the rigorous standpoint if they were motivated that way, without forcing them into it in advance.

This indecision was established for Glaucon and Adeimantus: they presented the standpoint of opinion in general while also differentiating fully between appearance and reality. But having established that indecision, Socrates would then have to work to *maintain* it, as I argued above that he did, until his interlocutors resolved it. His initial explicitness established the conditions for his later implicitness. Accordingly, the implicitness combined with the indirectly relevant explicit indications was his way of operating in both mutually exclusive standpoints simultaneously.

Perhaps, then, in giving the explicit indications only when they had indirect relevance, Socrates was maintaining descriptive truth in the face of its interventive property in the way that I described in Idea 2.3 as saying it in an unrelated context. Similarly, in his earlier discussion with Polemarchus, he presented the distinction that might refute him but did so only in the context of discussing a different issue. Something said implicitly, then, is not always the same thing at all as when it is said explicitly. Even for this reason alone, Socrates' implicit presentations are not always *simply* ironic, requiring the reader to "catch on." On the contrary, they may require the reader precisely *not* to consider them explicitly in some circumstances, both in the context of reading the dialogue and in carrying its lessons elsewhere.

And Socrates does more than this kind of displacement here. As I argued above, Socrates coordinates direct, indirect, and displaced modes of presentation, in order to operate truthfully with simultaneous, mutually exclusive, and mutually intervening standpoints. In doing that, he is also, *in and as all of* that combination, *directly* presenting the mixed truth of the situation he is in, involving, as it does on these occasions, conflicting principles and their conflicting consequences. That is, this coordination, this dimension of the dialogue's composition, is an image of what I am calling the variegated texture of truth, or "sometimes always" logic.

3.2. THE SELF-EXTERNALITY OF KNOWLEDGE, LOVE, AND JUSTICE

At this point of the process, then, opinion in general has been implicitly refuted and implicitly shown to involve the mistake of taking knowledge to be guided circularly by itself. It is here that Socrates, in continuing to pursue opinion in general on the topic of justice, introduces the necessity that the ruler be a philosopher. That is, he introduces an examination of the nature of knowledge itself, involving an explicit inquiry into the difference between knowledge and opinion. As I argue below, the *rigorous* dimensions of this inquiry will not be made explicit. The rigorous relevance of this distinction to the implicit dimensions of the discussion so far—and hence to Socrates' interlocutors' fundamental commitments—will therefore also remain implicit. The second mistake, taking knowledge to be guided homogeneously or circularly by itself, to work the same way as opinion, will now be avoided, still implicitly, repeating the whole process with appropriate adjustments for its more fundamental level.

After an initial discussion of the philosopher as a lover, to which I return below, Socrates explains that philosophers have true knowledge as opposed to opinion. They "contemplate the very things themselves in each case, ever remaining the same,"[46] as opposed, for example, to the many beautiful things that, unlike beauty itself, are self-contradictory, being ugly in some contexts and in some comparisons.[47] These particular things, objects of opinion, are as much not what they are said to be as they are: they are "midway between existence or essence [οὐσίας] and the *not to be*."[48] Since, then, philosophers can "fix their eyes on the absolute truth, and always with reference to that ideal . . . establish in this world also the laws of the beautiful, the just, and the good," they should be the rulers.[49]

This seems to remove the difficulty that the protectors would not know the difference between apparent and real harm to enemies. And the path of achieving philosophical knowledge that Socrates goes on to explain seems to avoid the mistake of trying to base knowledge on customary opinion. Genuine knowledge, rather, is based on ensuring that the thought being pursued does not contradict itself (the principle of noncontradiction is first introduced earlier at 436B, when the individual soul is compared with the city-state), but deals with what is "ever remaining the same."

Rigorously considered, the circular and self-contradictory nature of opinion-based thought has allowed its own cancellation and transcendence, first in part, in the form of various particular opinions, and then as a whole. And the principle in accordance with which this process is negotiated has been made explicit: the principle of noncontradiction. The second mistake, that of circularity or of proceeding homogeneously on assumptions without realizing it, is avoided by drawing out the united meanings or implications of opinions to see where they contradict themselves. One begins not with opinions, but in a new way with a principle by which opinions are measured. A wholly new *kind* of starting point is established.

But this explicit presentation of the contrast between philosophical knowledge and opinion is then itself implicitly refuted. This knowledge, according to Socrates' presentation, depends on knowledge of the Idea of the Good.[50] And Socrates states that "we have no adequate knowledge of it,"[51] declares himself unable to present this knowledge in that context, and suggests that he is incapable of it in any context. When asked to give his opinion (this is the word used) of the Idea of the Good, he answers, with much emphasizing fuss, "do you think it right to speak as having knowledge about things one does not know?"[52] And when, after Socrates agrees to approximate an explanation by the inadequate means they have used so far, Glaucon says Socrates will "pay" him the proper explanation another time, Socrates replies, "I could wish . . . that I were able to make and you to receive the payment."[53] Philosophical knowledge, then, depends on a knowledge that is not justified in the dialogue and that, it is suggested, is unjustifiable. In fact, Socrates speaks of his subsequent approach to hinting at the nature of the Idea of the Good as his "opinions" (δοκοῦντα).[54] The dialogue bases the distinction between knowledge and opinion on opinion.

Further, Socrates, as I mentioned above, introduces this discussion of knowledge by explaining the philosopher as a lover, beginning with the example of lovers of male bodies.[55] In explaining the love—the *"philia"* or *"eros"*—of wisdom that is philosophy, he uses the word *"epithymeten,"*[56] referring to the same kind of desire that gave its name to the part of the soul furthest removed from the rational part. This introductory emphasis on the erotic and even irrational dimension of the philosopher suggests that it is important that the philosopher is not simply wise, but a lover of wisdom. The philosopher does not know the nature or Idea of the Good, which is the basis of knowledge. Consequently s/he is a lover of knowledge, not its possessor. The ruling guardian-philosophers, by contrast, are supposed simply to know what is best. Further, their education occurs in the light of common *opinions* about what is best, as confirmed by Glaucon and Adeimantus. Rigorously considered, then, the guardians are claimants to possess and teach unself-questioning *opinions*, knowledge understood as homogeneously simply established and understood to be knowledge of what gives itself homogeneously and simply to be known. In other words, they are Sophists, like Thrasymachus (who had argued near the start of the dialogue that a ruler makes no mistakes when ruling)[57] or like the Sophist-influenced Critias (Socrates was reminded of the Sophist Prodicus in talking to him)[58] in the *Charmides.*

Since the new starting point that Polemarchus's interruption provoked involves the homogeneously knowing guardians and their replacement with the philosopher, and so the emergence of a difference between philosophy and homogeneous knowledge, it implies fresh inadequacies in the previous account of the city-state. But it also gives some positive indications, now, toward an adequate account. The philosopher is not essentially someone rational, but someone desiring rationality. Her/his characteristics are therefore located not simply at the rational top of the hierarchy of the three-part soul but at least at the desiring bottom as well as the top.[59] (As I noted above, Plato has Socrates use variants of the same word for desire, *epithymia*, in both contexts.) Analogously, if philosophy is the ruling principle, the ruling characteristics of the city are no longer located simply in the ruling class, but at least also in the bottom class as well as the guardian class. We have shifted to some kind of democratic principle.[60]

This kind of principle is also at least suggested by the fact of dialogue with which we are literally constantly presented. This suggestion is especially strong when, later, Socrates points out that philosophical training does not *give* anyone the capacity to "see" (know), but that *everyone already has* that capacity and philosophical training only turns it in the right direction: "there might be an art . . . of . . . shifting . . . of the soul, not an art of producing vision in it, but on the assumption that it possesses vision but does not rightly direct it . . . of bringing this about."[61] Perhaps the location of the ruling principle can be expressed as being in the desire of all the citizens to be wise.

This in turn suggests that the new starting point, in which philosophy rules, is not *simply* one of a rigorous principle of noncontradiction by which opinions are measured. Rather, it is a starting point involving opinions, which belong to the nonphilosophical part of the soul, *together with* (externally and internally) the rigorous principle that measures them, which belongs to *only* one part even of the philosopher's soul and, therefore, of her/his being. The procedure of drawing out united meanings to detect the circularity that contradicts the aims of rigor needs to be inherently questionable, fundamentally self-disparate, itself. Otherwise it shares the ultimate unrigorous self-contradiction (in contrast with rigorous self-contradiction, like that involved in self-cancellation) of simply homogeneous thought. This single-and/or-double use of principle and opinion is what Socrates has been practicing all along. And the process itself of practicing it (I return to this process below) has implicitly given the justification for doing so. In the terms of the cave image that Plato has Socrates use, we start, and continue, neither in the cave of opinion nor out of it but in both places at once.

I suggest, then, that the Idea of the Good, the foundation of knowledge, is unknowable beyond opinions and images not because it is beyond them, but because knowledge itself occurs, and occurs genuinely as *knowledge,* distinct from opinions and images, partly *in and as* the medium of opinions and images. As I argued in Chapter 1, the Idea of the Good focuses us away from the topic of the inquiry and onto the fact of inquiry, in this way canceling the interventive effects of the fact of inquiry itself. But *that* interventive effect then needs to be undone, and the Idea of the Good does that by also canceling *itself,* as something beyond opinion. Its emptiness returns us to the topic of the inquiry, as it is in the medium of everyday opinion. But in contrast to *simple* opinion, we are now able to see that topic differently because we can see it without simply being caught up in the circle of our starting assumptions.

The problem of the foundations of knowledge is in fact addressed. But it is addressed, like Socrates' and Charmides' paradoxes of self-knowledge, by recognizing it, and recognizing that it applies to itself also, that it makes it a problem even whether there is a problem. As a result, it is established that we need to begin differently, at a tangent, with a fundamental indecision between the problem and the solution of knowledge in general (that is, not just the problem and solution of the particular topic but of knowledge as such). And this in turn, as I argue shortly, allows a further tangent, which is the recognition that this first tangent, the indecision between the problem and solution of knowledge in general, is already partly a direct address of the topic of the inquiry: What is justice, and is it more profitable than injustice? This kind of "tangent," as I argued above, is itself fundamentally self-external, is itself and also not itself, a direction away and a direction toward in one act and in separate acts.

The process the *Republic* shows now consists of the following phases. A particular opinion on the topic at hand is refuted by drawing out its united meanings. As a result, a new starting point, a new particular opinion, is developed. The mistake both opinions have in common—that they fail to distinguish between reality and appearance—is identified, and as a result, the new opinion is modified into a better starting point. That opinion is refuted in the same way, and a second mistake identified—that it fails to recognize the self-externality of knowledge. Yet another opinion is developed. This opinion is the best starting point of that kind, since it is opinion in general on the topic. The mistake *all* opinion has in common is identified—that is, that it is *inherently* self-contradictory, inherently failing properly to carry through the appearance/reality distinction and the insight into the self-externality of knowledge (as Socrates already shows of homogeneous knowledge in his earlier debate with Thrasymachus). As a result, opinion itself in general is refuted as a viable medium for thought, but not by explicitly drawing out united meanings. And also as a result, a yet better, different *kind* of starting point is established, consisting in a combination of opinion and knowledge based on the principle of noncontradiction. This combination is in fact undecidable, because, as I discussed, it is opinion that establishes the difference between itself and knowledge: it rejects itself on its own basis in favor of knowledge, and so is calling itself a liar. If this description of itself is true, it is false, and vice versa.[62]

The mistake common to all such homogeneously noncontradictory knowledge is then identified: that it fails to recognize its full difference in kind from opinion. This difference is that knowledge is essentially self-questioningly rigorous or fundamental. It both distinguishes between reality and appearance, other-sensibly, *and* questions the status of that distinction itself. And it also both recognizes that knowledge is guided by its objects, is self-external, *and* questions that self-externality itself. Accordingly, as I elaborate in the rest of this chapter, knowledge allows and involves *rigorous* self-contradiction, including simultaneous internal and external relations to its objects, among which is opinion itself, in the same respects. As a result an even better starting point is established, involving two aspects. First, with respect to the external relation between knowledge and opinions of its object, the undecidability is maintained as involved in something *fully* different in kind from opinion, such that in its context even "difference in kind" and "refutation" themselves mean something different. Second, with respect to the internal relation between knowledge and opinions of its object, these different meanings are self-canceling in the context of this undecidability, and so are tangentially related to—upon being canceled resolve into—the corresponding meanings in the context of opinion. The undecidability is therefore resolved precisely by being maintained. Fundamental difference, that is, difference in kind, and fundamental refutation itself, that is, refutation of a standpoint as a whole, such as the standpoint of opinion in general, cancel themselves. And they cancel themselves into fundamental identity and justification, that is, identity and justification of a standpoint as a whole.

As I argued above, in this context the rigorous thought about opinion in general, the fundamental thought dealing with a distinction between rigorous and unrigorous standpoints *as such,* is necessarily made explicit only when it is only indirectly relevant, in the medium of opinion that does not recognize that distinction or its own character as such. And it is necessarily given only implicitly when it would be directly relevant, in the medium of rigorous thought that does recognize it. Again, then, the rigorous option is not imposed. In this process the reader is first given explicit models for rigorous thought, consisting in drawing out united meanings and checking for contradiction, and is then required actively to take up those models if the implicit refutation is to be established. If the reader's own truth or eros is engaged, it is without unjust imposition. If the reader is spontaneously moved to careful thought, the means for pursuing that path are there. If the reader is spontaneously moved not to think carefully, the means for pursuing that inconsistent path are also there, in the unrefuted text.

At the end of the digression on the new starting point—or establishment of the tangent to the old one—Plato has Socrates proceed as though the earlier findings were still unaffected, as though the city-state could retain exactly the same hierarchical organization despite the radical difference between philosophical rule and the rule of simple knowledge. He then argues that the rulers of the original city-state necessarily have inadequate knowledge (although he argued previously that their philosophical knowledge is perfect, he does not now suggest they have a different *kind* of knowledge from his earlier description, but just insists on a mysteriously arising inadequacy) and that a deterioration of this best state is a necessary result of this inadequacy.[63] In fact, he argues that the city-state necessarily deteriorates through several types of city-state, including democracy, until it becomes an entirely unjust tyranny. This tyranny is thoroughly self-defeating and punishing for all its members and especially the tyrant him/herself, for just the reasons Socrates gave Thrasymachus near the start of the dialogue, and now exemplifies in detail.[64]

Plato has Socrates argue, then, that the state run by the philosopher-king, as that state and as philosophy are explicitly (but not implicitly) presented, necessarily becomes an entirely unjust, self-defeating tyranny. This is another point not particularly favorable to the idea that the explicitly presented state of the philosopher-king is the best and most just. I suggest, again, that the *Republic* is ironic and aporetic just in the way the "early" Socratic dialogues are.

One positive alternative indication as to how the city-state and philosophy might make sense, it seems to me, is given by Socrates' repeated and elaborate emphasis on the tyrant's being motivated by unrestrained love, eros.[65] After elaborately comparing the tyrant's soul to the state s/he rules, Socrates asks, "is not this analogy . . . the reason why Love has long since been called a tyrant?"[66] A little later he speaks of "all the doings of those whose souls are entirely swayed by the indwelling tyrant Eros."[67] Plato has Socrates emphasize the fundamental place of love, then, in the constitutions of both philosophers and tyrants. Just as in the *Gorgias,* the same thing is the source both of good and bad directions.[68] What allows someone to be a philosopher also allows her/him to be a tyrant. In order to show why this is a positive indication of a viable alternative, which I do just below, I need to note a second indication of how the city-state and philosophy might make sense.

This other positive indication is that Socrates, in describing the start of the philosopher's education, explains that contradictions, even those given by sense-awareness, are the means by which the soul is provoked to think and so is turned toward what truly is.[69] Contradiction, then, is part of the philosophical process, is in fact its source or motor, and is not only what the process aims to avoid. The *Republic* itself is a process of contradiction, even in its dialogic/monologic form. The reader is provoked to think by contradiction right from the start. In fact, as I argued above, the very contradiction between unrigorous opinion and rigorous knowledge itself is also *internal* to rigorous knowledge itself. The rigorous self-canceling process of learning by mistakes and self-contradiction comes to include—that is, part of the process includes—(internally and externally) its own history as a stably self-canceling part of its result.

I suggest, then, that the philosopher's political position is in the self-canceling contradictory tension or indecision between, on the one hand, the homogeneously and simply knowing and controlled ruler wrongly placed in the position of the guardians and, on the other hand, the homogeneously and simply inconsistent and uncontrolled tyrant.[70] This is structurally identical to the position of self-control as presented in the *Charmides*. One way this works is that one can recognize the good only by contrast with the bad impulses and directions, just as one learns the right path by correcting mistakes. And one can carry out that recognition in practice by steering away from the wrong impulses and ways and directions. A simple positive, as it were, is given only by the deeper combination of a positive and a negative. Socrates' lust in the *Charmides* illustrates this in connection with self-control. Similarly, knowledge is given by the simply direct opinion established by fundamental indecision and which establishes fundamental indecision with respect to itself.

Living out this position constitutes rigorous justice. It is truth to the firm hesitancy of self, other, and the relation between self and other, and so establishes and lives out what is appropriate to all of these. In the case of people, their truth is given by their *erotes,* as Socrates is made to indicate in the case of each of the different kinds of city-state, the citizens of each of which are made what they are by a specific kind of love. Justice, then, as truth to people's selves, is a truth to people's love, including one's own. Accordingly, justice can only be the carrying out of kinds of love. And since it is a being true, this justice must be not only a kind of love but more specifically a desire for or an orientation to truth. That is, it is a love of truth, or wisdom. It is philosophy, or knowledge, in Plato's sense.

Like self-control, then, justice, too, if it succeeds in coming about, is rigorous knowledge. And if piety, one of the virtues Socrates is made to leave out of his justice-seeking elimination of virtues, is living in accordance with one's being partially constituted by, partly owing one's being to, a whole greater than oneself, then piety also is rigorous knowledge. Virtue, again, is rigorous knowledge.

Plato has Socrates argue the deterioration of the city-state by developing (without explicitly mentioning) the principle of reciprocal dependence between people that he started with (a principle he also presents in the *Charmides* in connection with parts and their greater context) and that I quoted above:

> the origin of the city . . . is to be found in the fact that we do not severally suffice for our own needs, but each of us lacks many things. . . . As a result of this . . . between one man and another there is an interchange of giving, if it so happens, and taking, because each supposes this to be better for himself.[71]

Each individual lacks certain necessities and so is complete only in a combination of other individuals. Here Socrates shows in detail in each stage of the polity's decline how the individual and the organized collection of individuals, the city-state, are each what they are only in relation to the other. The initial question, then, of whether justice is *essentially* more profitable than injustice, is answered by putting the just or unjust person in the context in which s/he is what s/he is, the context of social life, a political community.

This allows two things to become clear. First, the effects of a just or un-just act on the agent's environment are also effects on the agent her/himself, since the agent's being is what it is partly in its connection to that environment. Second, since it is the agent's very being or nature that is affected, these effects precede and govern any other kinds of effect, so that the appearances really do make only a secondary difference.

Socrates had said that he would treat justice first in the city-state rather than the individual because it would be easier to see in the bigger form. Clearly, this makes no sense: justice does not have a physical size. The result of his treatment, however, is that the essential or fundamental dimension of the individual's connection with her/his social environment becomes evident. Perhaps Socrates lied about his motive, then, in order to be more fundamentally truthful by not illegitimately imposing what belongs to the rigorous, fundamental standpoint on his interlocutors and so removing the very conditions for truth themselves. He would have done so had he explicitly presented and demonstrated an essential relation between individual and society, where relations as understood by opinion are, in contrast, (simply) external. As I mentioned above, he did in fact present the principle of that internal relation, in the form of reciprocal dependence, at the start of his discussion, but at no point made its consequences for the topic explicit.

In addition to not imposing, his presentation allowed him to show, even in the medium of opinion, the relevant importance of social environment to the individual: that is, he found an external, if false, relation—comparison in size and structure—that perhaps approximates an internal, true one enough to convey something of the rigorous truth. Perhaps, then, he followed the way of maintaining descriptive truth in the face of its interventive property that I described in Idea 2.3 as saying it by means of a false statement.

Justice, then, turns out to be essentially or fundamentally more profitable than injustice. It allows one to live out one's eros by recognizing its (one's eros's) contradictions and taking them meaningfully into account, instead of not taking them into account and consequently allowing them to defeat each other. I suggest that this self-contradictory dimension, too, is already implicit in the principle on which Socrates bases his account of the city: that what we are in ourselves is something not self-sufficient, and so we do not only take but also give for our own sakes. We are *essentially* self-contradictory; we destroy ourselves by trying to be consistently or homogeneously ourselves; but we can live successfully and homogeneously by negotiating our self-contradictions.

One of the things Greek tragedy expresses is that the nature of human existence is such that it allows us to be caught in the contradiction between mutually exclusive and equally valid fundamental obligations. Plato adds (internally and externally) a comic dimension to this insight.[72] As Edward G. Ballard puts it, "the admission of self-ignorance forestalls exorbitant claims. Thus it prevents the initiation of tragedy and places one in the way of moving through the foreseen and controlled catastrophes of comedy."[73] I would replace "foreseen" here, however, with "made room for." This respect for the unforeseen turns lack of control itself into a kind of tangential coordination of control and lack of control.

Again, the love whose living out constitutes philosophy has exactly the kind of self-external nature of justice. It is satisfied by the benefit of people or things that is sometimes incompatible with its own benefit. The problematic process of the inquiry into the nature of justice and whether it is more profitable than injustice, then, has canceled itself into being the answer to these questions. The problems have not *simply* disappeared, but they have become, *as* problems, the medium of the essentially or fundamentally *self-questioning solution*.

As I argued above of self-control, the just negotiation of our contradictions is not *simply* an externally imposed discipline. We are *essentially* self-contradictory, *essentially* tragic, so that even our self-contradiction or tragedy itself, fully entered into, does not remain consistent or unconflicted but is contradicted. As a result, entering fully into the contradiction that we are means also entering into our homogeneous simplicity, as I argued in Chapter 1 in connection with the "conflicted" soul in the *Republic*. Further, we are simply what we are partly by being external to ourselves. Similarly, conversely, then, entering fully into our spontaneous and natural simplicity *means* contradictorily moving externally and artificially with respect to it. Accordingly, Socrates can still be made to keep as an open question, almost at the end of the dialogue, that if we saw the soul in its own proper context, we might see "whether in its real nature it is manifold or single in its simplicity, or what is the truth about it and how."[74] The discipline that is justice, like self-control, is spontaneous *in being* an external imposition. Just as knowledge is a full engagement with what is given in being purely external to it, artificial.

3.3. THE SELF-CANCELLATION OF THE *REPUBLIC* AND OF PHILOSOPHY

Near the end of the dialogue, Socrates is made to argue at length that poetic imitation, and especially tragedy, is seriously misleading to "all listeners who do not possess as an antidote a knowledge of its real nature"[75] and so it should be exiled from the best state. The nature of poetic imitation is that of "appearance . . . but not the reality and the truth."[76] That is, poetic imitation makes the mistake rigorously identified at the start of the dialogue. In "building" the city-state ruled by the guardians, Socrates has already been made to argue against poetic imitation of shameful or bad behavior. Such behavior includes that of "bad men . . . reviling and lampooning one another . . . and in other ways sinning against themselves and others in word and deed."[77] But in fact, Plato had Socrates imitate the reviling and lampooning Thrasymachus near the start of the dialogue. What is more, the whole *Republic* is a poetic imitation that is just an appearance. The very end of the dialogue rubs the point in by presenting a lengthy fiction about the afterlife, the story of Er. In other words, Plato warns us that one of the lessons of the *Republic* is how to read it itself without being seriously misled.

Socrates has already warned his interlocutors at the turn toward the new kind of starting point, the philosophical way, that he does not have simple access to truth and so might mislead them. Glaucon had just encouraged Socrates to introduce his new considerations: "Do not shrink . . . for your hearers will not be inconsiderate nor distrustful nor hostile."[78] Socrates replied:

> The fear is . . . lest, missing the truth, I fall down and drag my friends with me. . . . So I salute Nemesis . . . in what I am about to say. . . . For . . . I believe that involuntary homicide is a lesser fault than to mislead opinion about the honorable, the good, and the just. This is a risk that it is better to run with enemies than with friends, so that your encouragement is none.[79]

The *Republic*, and therefore the activity of philosophy as the *Republic* poetically imitates it, then, needs and is an antidote to itself. It is as a whole self-canceling, existing in order to remove itself. The first stage of the city-state, as revisions of which the rest are constructed, is a recognized idyllic fiction. The imperatives for the city-state are systematically and directly contradicted, both explicitly and implicitly, by their giver. And then, at the end, the entire work within which those imperatives, their justification, their contradictions, the justification of those contradictions, and their social context occurs is raised into relief as itself wholly a fiction. In being identified as a fiction, it is made an element of its own discussion, and in fact it is situated at the fictional, unrigorous start of its own disciplined movement from unrigorous self-contradiction to (rigorously self-contradictory) self-knowledge and self-transcendence or fundamental growth. It is made artificial, an appearance that is "not the reality and the truth."

But this artificiality, simply appearing to be what it is not, and so an unrigorous self-contradiction, is what opens the question of its reality and truth. It is, rigorously considered, such as to be undecided about. If it is purely appearance, it requires us to consider whether its character as only appearance is itself only appearance. Its very artificiality, in the context of the indecision that it requires if taken *rigorously,* is itself artificial, so that it itself rigorously opens the possibility that it in fact expresses or engages with what is real and true.

We are left with both opinion being questionable and the alternative that questions it, philosophy, being questionable. That is, opinion is questionable and the reasons for thinking it is questionable are themselves questionable. Opinion, then, is perhaps simply valid. Socrates does leave the option open that imitative poetry "may . . . justly return from . . . exile after she has pleaded her defence,"[80] if this defense is successful. Further, at the very start of the discussion of justice, Cephalus, Polemarchus's old father, had offered as his view a conventional acceptance of the need to earn rewards and avoid punishments in the afterlife. Socrates began to question him about this idea of wisdom, and that is how the discussion of justice started.[81] The story of Er at the end restores just the kind of conventional considerations Cephalus had offered at the beginning. And this is not only done in the form of a purely poetic story; that story is preceded by Socrates' reasoned proof that the soul is immortal. Philosophy itself here is in the service of traditional opinion.

We are left, accordingly, not simply with an alternative to opinion, but with opinion and an internally and, in the same respects, externally related, rigorously established indecision about an alternative to opinion. This is the simultaneity of fundamental indecision and an assumption to be followed that I first discussed in Idea 2.1.

The philosophical dialogue that is the *Republic,* after all, like all of Plato's dialogues, is manifestly nothing but a dialogue between opinion and philosophy. That is, philosophy itself is manifestly presented in and as these dialogues *as* a dialogue between itself and opinion. Philosophy is a whole of which it is only one of the parts. Differently put, philosophy includes in itself the context that includes philosophy in *itself.* Philosophy is both inside and outside itself, both relying on itself and questioning its own worth.

Modifying the terms of Socrates' first distinction between knowledge and opinion, we are left with opinion, which engages with what is in a sense midway between what is and what is not, and philosophy or rigorous thought, which is simultaneously on both (mutually exclusive) ends of, on the one hand, what is between what is and what is not, and, on the other hand, what is.

The *Republic,* then, teaches and leaves one with a fundamental indecision, undecided even about itself as an indecision, so that it is an indecision that is also a specific decision or explored assumption. In not simply imposing itself homogeneously and blindly on its topic or object, this indecision plus assumption also allows its topic or object to stand out and make impressions beyond the assumption, impressions that are uninterfered with, unexplained, not already understood. In this respect it is, then, an uninterfered-with engagement with or relation to the truth of the thing being thought about. That is, this assumption plus fundamental indecision is a knowledge without knowledge.

The indecision is awareness that the assumption is an assumption. This is already a knowledge about the limitations of one's thinking about a topic. In this respect, it is concrete knowledge of a specific ignorance. That is, it is a knowledge that is a coordination of ignorance and knowledge. In contrast with the unrigorously considered, simply external relation between ignorance and knowledge, it is a kind of coordination of ignorance and knowledge in which they partly, but also essentially or in a sense completely, *are* each other. And *both* the rigorous and unrigorous kinds of knowledge and coordinations of knowledge and ignorance themselves are involved in this rigorous kind of coordination. Rigorously considered, and *only* then, they too are (externally and internally related) parts of the same thing.

It is part of the rigorous philosophical solution, then, that even at the end of the dialogue, the city-state and the individual soul are still understood on a basis largely caught up in conventional, unrigorous opinion. It emerges that from the point of view of *opinion* as it is engaged by philosophy, justice is essentially better than injustice. But the self-canceling indecision between philosophy and opinion is all that is needed. Questions only meaningfully respond to their occasion for being asked, that is, to their rhetorical context. As is always the case, the superficial level on which the question is asked, here the level of conventional opinion, precedes whatever deeper thinking through might answer it. If the question is to be satisfied, it must be satisfied on the level that gives it its context and meaning. The answer must therefore be addressed, in the end, to a level of thought that is superficial with respect to the greater depth achieved in trying to answer it. Otherwise, as I argued in Chapter 1, the question is not answered but is, rather, illegitimately replaced with a different one.

A truly rigorous answer, then, as always, is one that cancels its rigorous depth into meaninglessness or irrelevance. Differently put, a truly rigorous answer is one that becomes purely empty rhetoric, so that it gets its own interference out of the way. As a result of this self-canceling activity, the superficiality that preceded the rigor, here the superficiality of opinion, can then offer the answer.

In the *particular* context of this *particular* question about justice, it is simply essentially and so *universally* true that justice is better than injustice. It is "sometimes always" true, and this is one of the times when it is always true. And whether this is a relative or an absolute truth can and must be differently answered, depending, in turn, on the particular context of *that* particular question.

Putting into question the worth and validity of the philosophical or carefully thoughtful way, then, is not only necessary to engage the reader's or listener's truth without imposition and to establish relevant fundamental indecision. It is also itself already part of the resulting truth of the topic. Differently put, not only is the rhetorical context part of the conditions of truth, but the self-cancellation of the rhetorical context, including the carefully thoughtful response within it, is part of the resulting truth.

Rigorous thought, then, does not simply "get somewhere" contrasted with the opinions with which it begins. Rather, it gets to a better understanding and appreciation of, and relation to, what it begins with.[82]

It follows from all of this that the explicit city-state, ruled by the homogeneously knowing philosopher-king, is not presented *only* ironically. Rigorous knowledge and justice occur in the self-canceling contradictory tension between, on the one hand, homogeneous knowledge, which, as the *Republic* shows, is unrigorously self-contradictory, and so is also homogeneously uncontrolled unrigor, and on the other hand, self-external, rigorously self-contradictory knowledge. That is, they occur by and as the dialogue between homogeneous knowledge and rigorous self-cancellation itself. This self-cancellation includes themselves, rigorous thought and rigorous justice. Consequently the rigorous city-state is sometimes and/or in some respects and/or elements the explicit, unrigorous city-state, just as it stands.

If, on the other hand, the explicit city-state is taken seriously in the standpoint of pure opinion, it can only be aimed at and never reached. It depends ultimately on knowledge of the Idea of the Good, which is not accessible to opinion. Its truth is then realized interventively rather than descriptively, *because* it is taken simply descriptively, at face value. As I argued of the truth of the Ideas at the end of Chapter 1, this purely interventive truth closely approximates the rigorously established truth. The citizens of the explicit city-state will always maintain a fundamental indecision between their real circumstances and the ideal at which they aim.

It also follows from all of this that Socrates, as the philosophical leader of the little dialogic community of characters in the *Republic*, has maintained a structure in which he is guided by them as fundamentally as he guides them. And this guidance is such, in its self-canceling self-disparity, that everyone can *also* fully exercise her/his own "business," without interfering with anyone else's otherwise incompatible "business." That is, it is a just community, both rigorously *and* unrigorously considered.

3.4. LOVE, THE MEANING OF LIFE, AND SELF-EXTERNAL VIRTUE

In relating rigorously to the truth of the thing known, one relates to it for its own sake. One appreciates or enjoys or celebrates it, or at least, in relating specifically to its truth, takes it very seriously for what it is simply because that is what it is. That is, one loves it. As José Ortega y Gasset expresses this:

> Contemplation . . . to seek in a thing what it has of the absolute and to cut off all other partial interest of my own toward it, to cease to make use of it, to cease to wish that it serves me, but to serve it myself as an impartial eye so that it may see itself and find itself and be its very own self and for itself . . . is this not love?[83]

And he links this thought to Plato's "idea about the erotic origin of knowledge."[84]

This relation to the thing for its own sake can allow one to learn from the thing too, which in turn can deepen and broaden one's capacity to relate generally to the truth of things. That is, it can deepen and broaden one's capacity to appreciate, enjoy, love things. And since relating to the truth of things also involves, in each case, relating to our own particular truth and the truth of our particular circumstances, this relating is also an expression of what we are. The deepening and broadening of this relating is consequently the deepening and broadening of being what we are.

The ultimate aim of rigorous thought, of philosophy, as of life, then, is being what it is, is itself. And in being this aim, it gives the source and orientation of all other aims. It is for its own sake: it is empty, self-canceling, and so returns us to any and all other aims, but now oriented to their truth. And what aims at this general aim of "for its own sake" is love in general.

Elements of other dialogues resonate with this idea. In the *Lysis,* for example, Socrates argues in favor of a controlling and manipulative relation to the object of love, and ends up showing in a variety of ways that this kind of relation to the beloved does not make sense. In other words, it does not engage with or relate to the truth of what it aims at. As a result, it is self-defeating. In showing this, Socrates argues, as I mentioned in Chapter 1 at section 1.2.7, that if we are to make sense of love, we need to take into account something that is loved for its own sake. Otherwise we have an infinite chain of ulterior motives for loving something, and since the chain is infinite, none of the motives is love.[85] Differently put, love could then never have begun to occur. Accordingly, love is ultimately love of something for its own sake.

In the *Phaedrus,* Plato has Socrates state in the form of a myth that beauty is what inspires love,[86] because beauty is the visible emergence of truth, and truth offers the nourishment that the best in people requires.[87] Similarly, according to Socrates in the *Republic,* what philosophers love is truth.[88] The truth of truth itself, as Socrates goes on to present the philosopher's goal there, is the Idea of the Good. The true, the good (what nourishes the best), and the beautiful, then, are ultimately all names for different dimensions of the same thing, and are what inspire desire and love.

Just before Socrates reintroduces the issue of imitation near the end of the *Republic,* Glaucon points out that "the city whose establishment we have described" has its "home . . . in the ideal [ἐν λόγοις: "in words"], for I think that it can be found nowhere on earth."[89] Socrates replies in the following wonderfully brave and strong way:

Well . . . perhaps there is a pattern of it laid up in heaven for him who wishes to contemplate it and so beholding to constitute himself its citizen. But it makes no difference whether it exists now or ever will come into being. The politics of this city only will be his and of none other.[90]

But the remainder of the dialogue puts poetic imitation into question as dangerously misleading—and Socrates, and this reply, are poetic imitations by Plato—and reasserts the claims of customary opinion by reasoned argument and then, finally, by a poetic story.

Socrates' reply is open to construal in a variety of ways. It supports the traditional reading of a theory of Ideas that exist in another and, in Plato's view, better world. It also supports a reading of these Ideas as being vivid metaphors (a kind of *logoi*, words) for ideals that guide us without actually existing themselves. On this view the Ideas, if they are good metaphors, make up an edifying sort of fiction. I argued above, however, that the "pattern" Socrates presents is not *simply* the city-state Glaucon refers to. Rather, I argued that Socrates presents, with the help of this city-state, a loving, truth-oriented, and ongoing process of establishing organizations in the context of a fundamental indecision. If this interpretation is right, then it is this stance and process that the Ideas would orient, and the corresponding "firmly hesitant," "sometimes always self-canceling" reality that they would exist as.

I have argued that the Ideas are (sometimes always) metaphors that engage us, in the disciplined process they orient, with "betterness," with what is good, true, and beautiful for its own sake in the world. Whether they are real or fictional is, at the end of the inquiry they orient, irrelevant. What is governed by the Ideas exists in heaven, "perhaps," and "it makes no difference whether it exists now or will ever come into being." But, as I argued, it is precisely *by* that (self-canceling) irrelevance that the Ideas engage us, tangentially, with what is good for its own sake. And that tangential, or externally internal, engagement with what is good *is,* once its irrelevance is established, full and direct engagement with what is good, true, and beautiful. Accordingly, I suggest, this self-canceling tangential engagement is itself the truth and essential nature of goodness. That is, it is the Idea of the Good.

It is also the attempted participation of particular acts in this Idea that *is* its realization or establishment (in both the objective and subjective senses of these words).[91] Taking the risk that one is doing something good—that is, that one is participating in the Idea of the Good—is itself, as a good motive, something good. That is, it introduces the Idea of the Good into the world.

And the initial falsehood or truth of this Idea makes no difference to that. In fact, it is only the lived recognition of the possibility that it is false, a fundamental indecision with respect to whether there is intrinsic goodness in the world, that makes the attempt to participate in it a real attempt to be good. Otherwise one is simply being irresponsible or ignorant, imposing what one does not know as though one does. The Idea of the Good, and Plato's dialogues, are truer for being fictions. Their fictional nature is what allows the orientation toward truth that is the self-externality of truth itself.

The Idea of the Good, rigorous thought and conduct, and these dialogues, then, are self-canceling tangents directed away from the things in the world, and whose focus away from things allows and is our direct relation to things for their own sakes. They take us away from the conventional, taken-for-granted opinions about things in which we necessarily start relating to them, and return us to those same opinions, now freshly appreciated as the context in which the things they are about are what they are, and can be recognized simply as what they are.

In this light, what Socrates bravely and strongly declares himself committed to, in the passage about the heavenly pattern of the city-state, is the willingness fundamentally to rethink what he is committed to.

This is a commitment that can also rethink *itself*, that is, that can cancel itself. And among the things that it can rethink is what it is to be brave and strong. Near the start of the dialogue, Thrasymachus accuses Socrates of needing "a nurse . . . because she lets her little snotty run about driveling and doesn't wipe your face clean."[92] This insult is provoked by Socrates' failure, as Thrasymachus sees it, to recognize that "injustice . . . is a stronger, freer, and more masterful thing than justice."[93] I suggest that for Socrates, instead, rigorous courage and strength, like justice, self-control, piety, and wisdom, sometimes or partly involve a lack of mastery, a kind of weakness, a fundamental indecision (which is *also* commitment to a decision and so is not even always successfully undecided) about what they themselves are.[94]

Certainly, courage in general is partly knowledge. As Socrates is made to propose in the *Protagoras*, "those who are . . . ignorantly confident show themselves not courageous but mad."[95] *Rigorous* confidence, then, is partly rigorous knowledge, which consists partly, but essentially or in a sense completely, in fundamental indecision. And the risk dimensions of fundamental indecision and rigorous knowledge mean that they in turn *are* partly courage.

In the light of this self-externality of virtue, its being fully what it is by being disparate from itself and inadequate, incomplete, the kind of poetic model of a philosopher or the kind of hero that Plato presents Socrates as is one we are fully taken with only when we are partly left unmoved. And he is one we genuinely identify with only when we partly do not identify with him at all. There is a nonknowledge with which we are required to relate to him. And because he himself is partly but essentially ignorant, that non-knowledge *is* also a direct and simple relation. His ignorance is part of what constitutes him as what he is, so that ignorance about him is what directly identifies with the significant nonknowledge that partly *is* him.

In tragic and comic drama, we either identify with their heroes, or find them ridiculous, or are left entirely unmoved, but not all at once in the same respects. Plato, then, presents a dramatic form and hero that are tangentially related to both tragic and comic drama and their heroes.

But these complexities and tangents to what is heroic or despicable are not simply opposed to simple clarity. As I argued in Idea 1.2, indecision about what we should be proud of and what we should be ashamed of is what establishes the possibility of simple pride and shame. This "metacon-duct," conduct dealing with our conduct and its conditions, is itself some-times what we should be proud of. And sometimes what it establishes is that we should be proud when we would otherwise be partly proud and partly ashamed, and that we should sometimes be ashamed in a similar way. That is, recognizing that pride is sometimes complex, and living it with that rec-ognition, can *be* its simplicity.

The *Republic,* then (like the *Symposium*),[96] argues that we love and con-tribute to others and ourselves in a rigorously prideworthy way, directly, fully, and successfully, when we do so tangentially, when we focus away from or beyond what we love into what becomes an empty artificiality: which then returns us, for the first time, and repeatedly for the first time, to the particulars we aim to love.

3.5. POETRY AND WHAT JUSTICE IS

Accordingly, it seems to me, the particular issue the *Republic* itself leaves us relating truly to is the nature of relating well to others and ourselves, or—not surprisingly—the nature of justice. And it does this through a metapre-sentation, a presentation about presentation. That is, it shows the nature of presenting models of how to relate to others and ourselves (for example, in its discussion of the effects of poetry), and also puts models in general in question (for example, in its discussion of the inadequacy of images). Differently put, it presents a model of what is involved in aiming at models while questioning whether one should be aiming at models. What emerges is that a rigorously just member of society is someone who presents models of truth in word and action,[97] orientations toward truth, and in the same act, *through* the same models, avoids misleading others *by* those models, and similarly avoids being misled by others or her/himself.[98] That is, s/he presents models of truth that intervene in themselves, that include in themselves a perspective that is outside of them.[99] They have a dimension that is something like explicit fiction.

In this way truth, and so what is truly best for everyone, is allowed to operate. These descriptive models that intervene in their own interventive dimensions precipitate simply true descriptions in two ways. First, they do so as (ultimately) simple descriptions of what they present. And second, they do so in the very process of their self-canceling self-intervention, as simple descriptions of the self-canceling conditions and/or nature of the truth of what they present, which I began discussing in Idea 2.

Let me emphasize again that since truth is fundamentally self-external, this commitment to truth also involves the irrelevance of truth. It involves this irrelevance partly or sometimes internally, as part of itself, and partly or sometimes externally, as simply separate from itself.[100]

When most poetry and drama are rejected in the *Republic* because of the models they give us to imitate, then, they *are* rejected, but they are *also* called for. They are rejected so that how they are called for can be rightly grasped. And in fact their necessary contribution is their being there to be rejected. They offer an initial fiction—or not—that as questionable is external to itself in either case, and so allows orientation toward truth. Artful presentations understood *as artful presentations*, then, are necessary for truth-seekers.[101] It is when they are understood to be *simply* homogeneously true that they are destructive. And to understand them not as homogeneously true requires, not that poetry be banished, but that *truth* be understood as (sometimes always) not homogeneous.

CHAPTER 4

Theaetetus, Sophist, *and* Statesman: *The Tragicomedy of Knowledge, Reality, and Responsible Conduct*

In this chapter I explore some details of the general structure of the arguments presented in the *Theaetetus, Sophist,* and *Statesman.*[1] In doing so, I
leave out a great deal that is both rich and relevant in these dialogues, but
the more specific focus should be solid enough to support and illustrate my
interpretation. Before looking at these details, I shall make some comments
on the context in which these dialogues place themselves, that of Socrates'
trial.[2] I also return to this context after discussing the arguments.

4.1. THE CONTEXT: SOCRATES' TRIAL

The three dialogues are presented as consecutive discussions. The *Theaetetus*
is named after Socrates' dialogue partner and is set on the day of Socrates'
indictment, the preparation for his trial. The *Sophist* and *Statesman* are both
set on the next day. In the *Sophist,* a Stranger from Elea is Theaetetus's dialogue partner, and in the *Statesman,* the Stranger is the partner of Theaetetus's friend, young Socrates. At the start of the *Sophist,* the old Socrates asks
the Stranger whether he considers the philosopher, the Sophist, and the
statesman to be different or the same. The Stranger sets out to answer by
trying to establish the nature of each, while old Socrates listens in silence
throughout. The *Sophist* and the *Statesman,* then, respectively ask what a
Sophist and a statesman are, while the question about the philosopher seems
not to be taken up.

Socrates is about to go on trial for his life, on charges of corrupting the
minds of the youth by his teaching and of impiously introducing new gods.[3]
The first of these charges assimilates Socrates to the Sophists, who claimed

knowledge that they could teach, most pertinently knowledge of virtue.[4] The second assimilates him to some of the philosophers who preceded him.[5]

The investigation of the relation between the philosopher and the Sophist is clearly relevant to the first charge. And a large part of the *Theaetetus*, whose topic is the nature of knowledge, is devoted to criticizing the great Sophist Protagoras. Again, if one takes the statesperson as a specialist in producing good citizens, the investigation of the relation between the philosopher and statesman is relevant to the charge of corrupting minds as well as to the charge of impiety.

A large part of the *Theaetetus* is also devoted to criticizing Heraclitus, one of Socrates' two most formidable philosophical predecessors. And a large part of the *Sophist* is devoted to criticizing Parmenides, Socrates' other most formidable philosophical predecessor, as well as various other preceding philosophers, and to reworking the foundations of philosophy on the basis of that criticism. In fact, Elea, the Stranger's home, was also famously the home of Parmenides and his followers. These investigations of the philosophies of Socrates' predecessors in relation to his own philosophy and of the nature of philosophy itself are clearly relevant to the second charge.

In addition, however, each of this group of dialogues questions the foundations of philosophy. The *Theaetetus* asks what knowledge is, and offers no clear answer. The *Sophist* asks whether any models of truth, including language and thinking themselves in general, are possible at all[6] and reworks the foundations of the entire preceding philosophical tradition in order to find a positive answer. And the *Statesman* questions the worth of a variety of philosophical methods of inquiry.

Where Socrates' defense speech to the people of Athens in the *Apology* addresses a specifically social questioning of the foundations of philosophy, or a questioning by unrigorous opinion, then, these dialogues present a specifically philosophical questioning of those foundations.[7] I suggest that Plato presents Socrates and philosophy in general—the Stranger is a philosopher, but no particular philosopher—as equally on trial in both of these contexts.[8] And I suggest, as I did in discussing the typical conflicting commitments in Plato's dialogues to both purely philosophical technicality and individual and social context in Chapter 2, section 2.1, that neither context can be understood without sometimes and/or in some respects taking the other into account.

Further, I suggest that Plato, far from rejecting the Athenians' stance out of hand, took their unrigorous kind of questioning seriously as a sometimes legitimate and indispensable requirement for philosophy itself. As I argued above, philosophy is genuine philosophy only to the extent that it questions itself. And only the standpoints that conflict with it allow that questioning. In fact, because rigorous thought is *grounded* in self-questioning, the *nature* of philosophy is sometimes and/or in some respects to be fundamentally on trial. Plato, then, and Socrates, if they were genuine philosophers, sometimes participated on both sides of the trial of Socrates. Perhaps this is one reason Socrates does not speak through almost all of the *Sophist* and *Statesman* but listens to both sides of the debate.

Accordingly, the rigorously understood issue in the actual trial was not simply one of a decision between two standpoints, the philosophical and the antiphilosophical, although it was partly that. It was *also* an issue of the *significance of that kind of* decision. This is a decision, as I discussed in connection with "sometimes always" logic (starting in Idea 1.2), between standpoints that are mutually exclusive to the extent of excluding each other altogether, even as meaningful possibilities. The basic terms of each simply make no sense within the context of the other. Consequently, this kind of decision, if it is rigorous, involves self-canceling or fundamental indecision between fundamentally different loves.

The issue taken unrigorously as one of a simple decision between standpoints is foregrounded in the *Apology,* and the issue taken rigorously as a presentation of the significance of this kind of decision is foregrounded in the other three dialogues. But in accordance with what I argued is the self-canceling and artificial nature of rigorous thought, the decision and indecision are, in the rigorous standpoint, sometimes parts of the same thing. The questioning aim to reach the decision is what allows the indecision. That is, the conflicting social context that provokes this questioning is part of the purely philosophical context. Not only is the philosopher, "Socrates," the "gadfly" that keeps society, "Athens," responsibly awake, as Plato has Socrates say in the *Apology,*[9] but the conventional opinion of society is also the gadfly that keeps philosophy responsibly awake, and so keeps it what it is.

If all of this is true, then the historical Socrates and his historical trial were never *simply* the issue for Plato, or for Socrates. More precisely, they *were* the issue *simply exclusively in their own right* but *also simply exclusively in relation to philosophy* and the truth it seeks. Rigorous thought is what it is by being artificial, tangential and external to itself; it is what gives truth by canceling itself. Accordingly, the historical Socrates, his historical trial, and their pathos *were also and exclusively* the main issue precisely *by virtue of* this kind of focus elsewhere, and vice versa.

The question of the nature of the philosopher may be taken up in the trilogy, then, precisely in the way in which it is not taken up. That is, the nature of philosophy is the fundamental indecision even as to its own nature, even as to whether it is a fundamental indecision, which allows genuinely rigorous seeking of truth. Accordingly, the tangential or indirect way of dealing with it *is* a direct focus on it.

It follows, again, that the "middle" and "late" dialogues are exactly as "Socratic" as the "early" dialogues. *Neither* group simply deals with Socrates, and *by not doing so*, both groups also *do* simply deal with Socrates, and vice versa. Both groups deal with him as a philosopher, after all; and Socrates, as a philosopher, must have dealt with himself in this way.

I now turn to some details of the general structure of the arguments in these dialogues.

4.2. THE *THEAETETUS:* THE PROBLEM OF KNOWLEDGE

In the *Theaetetus,* Theaetetus, on Socrates' request, offers several definitions of knowledge. Socrates is made to show that these definitions make no sense, by drawing out their united meanings. The definitions have in common the idea that knowledge is a homogeneously immediate and direct relation to truth.

The first definition of knowledge—that it is immediate perception or opinion—turns out to imply that every contrasting perception of the same things will be knowledge, and so equivalently true. Socrates attributes this definition to Protagoras and Heraclitus. It follows, however, that the idea of anything specific at all is literally nonsensical: anything will be as much not what it is as what it is.[10] Plato has Socrates apply this definition of knowledge to knowledge of knowledge itself. The definition is self-contradictory here, too, for the same reason: it establishes conflicting perceptions or definitions of knowledge as true.[11] That is, it is self-canceling, and so, as the explicit dimension of the dialogue presents it, it is nonsensical.

The second definition is that knowledge is true opinion. Here the notion of truth that this definition involves is brought out and is shown to make no sense. If "truth" has meaning, then "falsehood" also has meaning. But "falsehood" makes no sense because it describes "what is not," and a description of "what is not" is itself nothing.[12] "Falsehood," and therefore "truth," then, make no sense. This means that any opinion is as "true" as any other, with the consequences of the first definition. It follows implicitly that falsehood and in turn truth are only possible if we can think a relation to "what is not," a relation to nothing. The *Sophist* explicitly argues exactly this. But what creates the problem, what implies that thinking nothing is itself nothing, is conceiving the relation to truth as immediate, simple, and positive. It is therefore that view of the relation to truth that needs to be revised. We need to conceive a nonsimple, nonimmediate, nonpositive relation to truth, involving a relation to its partly *not* being there. That is, we need to conceive of knowledge as involving ignorance or mistakes, and involving them internally *as part of* its successful relation to truth. Otherwise it is not *knowledge* that involves the indirect or partial nonrelation to truth.

The third and final definition is that knowledge is true opinion together with a *logos*, a "rational account" or "speech."[13] Socrates is made to argue that this definition implies that there are basic simple elements without an account, on which the speech or account must be based. Otherwise, for example, there would be an infinite regress of giving accounts of the accounts, such as Socrates describes in a different connection at 200A–B, and knowledge could never start to exist. That is, truth then depends on simple elements with which we have an immediate, positive, direct relation, expressed simply in naming.[14] But as Socrates continues to argue, these simple elements themselves would not be known, since knowledge involves an account, and the simple elements are required not to have an account. But the accounts that give knowledge depend on these unknown elements. Consequently, this definition eliminates the idea of knowledge altogether, and hence of truth that we can meaningfully talk about at all. Again, then, it follows implicitly that if there is to be any truth and so any knowledge at all, a nonsimple, indirect relation to truth must be possible. Knowledge, again, partly involves what does *not* reflect or engage with the truth, something like mistakes and ignorance.

In fact, throughout the dialogue, Plato has Socrates claim to have no knowledge, but to be a midwife who brings others' knowledge to birth and tests it for genuineness.[15] And at the end of the dialogue he is made to say:

> at a later date . . . the ideas with which you'll be pregnant will be better because of this inquiry of ours; and even if you don't get pregnant, you'll be easier to get on with, because you won't make a nuisance of yourself by thinking that you know what you don't know. This self-responsibility [σωφροσύνη, "self-control"] is all my skill is capable of giving, nothing more.[16]

In the process of establishing that mistakes about the topic are being made, a specific ignorance is established in Theaetetus himself as a kind of knowledge, a justified acceptance of and working with the limitations of his positive knowledge. This established ignorance will also play a role as knowledge by helping to improve his later ideas. That is, the dialogue explicitly expresses, in connection with both Socrates and Theaetetus, a mutually contributing internal relation between ignorance and knowledge. In addition, Theaetetus gains his awareness of his own particular limitations by focusing away from them, onto the topic of knowledge in general. That is, the process of the dialogue produces knowledge indirectly, tangentially to its focus. In this way, it exemplifies the kind of indirect or partial nonrelation of knowledge to the truth it knows, that the discussion implicitly shows to be required.

But the dialogue leaves entirely implicit the relation of Socrates' and Theaetetus's respective ignorance to their discussion of the nature of knowledge itself. And it exemplifies the required relation of knowledge to truth in Theaetetus's tangential process without saying so. It even presents a lengthy example of self-cancellation that might allow us to make sense of knowledge as partly a nonrelation to truth, but presents it only insofar as it refutes the first definition, leaving its positive possibilities entirely unmentioned. It is left, then, for the eros and risk of the reader to see the connections of Socrates' concluding statement with the more rigorous insights the dialogue implicitly shows and justifies.

Plato's mode of presentation itself, then, embodies the indirect or partial nonrelation of knowledge to truth that the dialogue implicitly argues.

4.3. THE *SOPHIST:* THE PROBLEM OF REALITY

Where the *Theaetetus* shows that a simple, immediate, positive relation to truth makes no sense from the standpoint of knowledge, or the subjective dimension of truth, the *Sophist* goes on to show the same thing from the standpoint of the truth of reality, or the objective dimension of truth.

As I mentioned above, one expression of Plato's view of Sophists is that they claim to have the kind of direct, unequivocal knowledge that he has Socrates insist is not genuine, because, as Socrates says in the *Apology*, it is "more than human."[17] The *Sophist* sets out to define the Sophist, in order to establish her/his relation to the philosopher and statesman. The Stranger from Elea uses a method of "division." He starts with a very broad genus and divides it into a pair of species (εἴδη: the word usually translated as "Ideas"); then takes one of these as a genus and divides it into two further species; and continues the process until he gets to the desired species, that of the Sophist. That is, he begins with a unity and then focuses on the differences within it. The homogeneity of united meanings that the *Theaetetus* relies on as the standard of sense is replaced here with a coordination of disunited, smaller, varying unities, making room for difference within unity.

Two problems arise. First, as the Stranger divides in different ways, he comes up with several conflicting definitions of the Sophist. That is, even the more flexible coordination of smaller unities does not succeed in being self-consistent. And since the nature of each unity is specified by how it is coordinated with the other unities, these smaller unities themselves are not self-consistent. The Stranger then encompasses all these failed definitions in the genus of "false imitation," the production of false appearances of knowledge,[18] and in doing so, he finds the second problem, one already found in the *Theaetetus*. If the Sophist is a false imitator, someone who presents false appearances of knowledge, we cannot speak or think about him, since falsehood is "what is not," literally nothing. Further, since true speech and thought are also kinds of imitation, they also "are not" what they refer to, so that we cannot speak or think about them either.[19]

Rigorous knowledge sought about knowledge, apparent or real, then, turns out to be self-incompatible, whether it conceives of knowledge in terms of simple self-consistency (unity), as in the *Theaetetus,* or in terms of differences within a self-consistency (unity), as in the *Sophist.*

If we are to make sense of speaking and thinking themselves, then, we must find a way of speaking and thinking "what is not," nothing.[20] That is, precisely in order to make sense of sense itself, of what is self-consistent or one with itself, we must find a way of thinking what simply is not as in some sense what is, thinking what is by definition unthinkable, self-contradictory, *fundamentally* disunited. We must find a way of conceiving nonsensical self-incompatibility, the very problem itself, as part of making sense. Differently put, we need to find a way of conceiving self-contradiction, radical self-externality or self-disunity, as making sense, and what is more, of conceiving it as foundational to internality or "at-oneness" itself.

As the Stranger discusses, the philosopher who first identified that what is thinkable only is, and only is one, was Parmenides. In keeping with the self-canceling nature of self-disparity that I discussed above, this fundamental criticism of what Parmenides showed will also mean, incompatibly, thinking internality or unity as foundational to externality or disunity itself, as Parmenides and his followers did. That the Stranger is from Elea, Parmenides' home, perhaps suggests this balancing consequence.

Similarly, if we are to be able to say or think at all of anything that it is, we must find a way of understanding what is not as something that we can contrast to what is. Without something that contrasts with what is, there is no way to specify what we mean by "what is," to say: "this is what we mean rather than that." As a result, we must understand what is not as something real, something that is.

The Stranger sets out to establish how nothingness, that is, non-self-identity, self-externality, nonimmediateness, or indirection, is included in "what is" itself. I presented his conclusions in Idea 8.1. He argues that "what is not" is really difference, so that it is not entirely contrary to what is, but can blend with it.[21] Something that is can clearly be different from something else, whereas it cannot be what is not.

A new starting point is established, then, in which what is and what is not are combined. This requires a reunderstanding of what is meant by both "what is" and "what is not." The results of drawing out their meanings on the basis of this reunderstanding will also be different. And this allows a reunderstanding of the problem of knowledge about knowledge as it is discussed in the *Theaetetus*.

The problem there was that if things are simply or homogeneously what they are, and the relation to the truth of things that is knowledge is itself also simply or homogeneously what it is, then the idea of knowledge makes no sense. There are incompatible simple relations to the truth of things, including to the truth of knowledge itself, and decision between these relations is literally not conceivable. A "knowledge" is understood as being simply or homogeneously what it is, and as a result, there cannot be a perspective on it that could question or decide about it. Such a perspective on it would have access to it, that is, share it, while not being identical with it, and so would itself be a self-external knowing or awareness. And this is exactly what this view does not allow. Knowledge understood in this way, then, makes no sense: it is both rightly understood in incompatible ways and also only understandable as homogeneously simple. And consequently, since knowledge is knowledge of the truth of things, things themselves also turn out to make no sense, to be simply self-incompatible.

In addition, falsehood and mistakes are impossible, which means knowledge is never gained. Just as Critias understands it in the *Charmides*, knowledge is either entirely and simply there or it is simply and entirely not there.

In the new starting point, by contrast, things are not simply what they are. "What is" is what it is partly by not being other things. And this not simply being what a thing is includes, as one of the things that are, the relation to the truth of things that is knowledge itself.[22] If what is not is part of what is, a relation to truth is possible that does not consist in a homogeneously simple, direct, and immediate presentation of truth. More accurately, since truth itself is not simply what it is, there are times when the homogeneously simple, direct, and immediate relation to truth *is* a heterogeneously or variegatedly tangential, self-canceling nonrelation. And conversely, because the relation or nonrelation to truth is radically self-canceling, this heterogeneity or variegation *also* lies, as I argued above, in this nonrelation's *sometimes (always) or partly (completely) being a simple relation.*

That is, in terms of my own discussion, knowledge is not simply a direct relation to what is known, because, as I discussed in Idea 2, knowledge can intervene in, have effects on, what it knows. Since it is *knowledge* that alters what it knows, it is the *truth* of its object that it knows, which is also what it consequently makes different, so that this truth is then not what it also truly is. But knowledge that is knowledge of *itself,* of knowledge, *immediately* intervenes, has *already* intervened in its own sense and so its very being, as both the *Theaetetus* and the *Sophist* show. Consequently, knowledge that includes knowledge of itself can intervene in and cancel itself, including its own intervention, so as to make itself then a direct and simple relation to what is known. The problem that knowledge alters what it knows, rigorously considered, is also the solution.

A simpler way of thinking about this is that the combination of "is not" and "is" makes for variegated meanings of the same things. (As a result, for example, it is not always simply circular to use knowledge to justify knowledge, because one is not always using the same thing: knowledge is not simply always the same as itself.) On the other hand, "is not" itself is not simply the same as itself either. Consequently, knowledge is still partly or sometimes simply or homogeneously the same as itself. It is still meaningful to talk about it as a specific something. It is only partly or sometimes subject to the refutation of Theaetetus's first definition.

As I discussed above, this heterogeneous or variegated nonrelation is presented in the *Theaetetus* partly as Socrates' knowledge of his own ignorance—his achieved fundamental indecision. It is also presented partly as the self-canceling knowledge-seeking process of refutation that is the practice of that knowledgeable ignorance. And as I discussed in Idea 8.1 in connection with the argument about nonbeing in the *Sophist,* this ongoing self-canceling process, spread out in time and across contexts and so separated from immediate and direct insight, *is also* sometimes and/or in some respects immediate and direct insight, both in the way that its spread-out self-externality makes sense as a grasp of correspondingly self-external things, and also by and as canceling itself into simple, direct immediacy.

The new starting point, then, also legitimates the old one. And more than this, as I mentioned above, the very mistake or problem with the original starting point is itself *part of* the solution, and in a sense *is* the solution. Because the problem concerns knowledge in general, which includes solutions to problems, it is self-referential, self-intervening, in the way I discussed in Idea 2. I argued above that this kind of problem can be resolved by its canceling itself, intervening in its own intervention. Consequently, it is the self-cancellation of the problem, that is, the *problem's* carrying out its *own* logic, that *is* the solution.

Here, the problem was that knowledge, understood as a homogeneously simple relation to truth, is self-contradictory. And in fact, because these dialogues have pursued the problem to the foundations of making sense itself, the problem is that sense itself in general, understood in this homogeneous way, is self-contradictory. As a result, the problem now involves senselessness itself in general, self-contradiction or self-cancellation itself in general.

Now, the solution consists in a shift to a self-contradictory, variegated nonrelation or tangential relation to truth. This tangential relation involves fundamental indecision that cancels itself into decision by focusing, self-contradictorily, elsewhere than its subject matter. As I argued above, what allows the fundamental indecision to be established is the process of refutation by self-contradiction. And that indecision itself, being a holding of incompatible views simultaneously, *is* a self-contradiction. Further, the self-cancellation of rigorous thought, which establishes decision, is itself a matter of the self-contradiction of self-contradiction itself. Like Charmides' and Socrates' paradoxes, the problem is one of self-cancellation, so that the problem is its own solution.[23] The problem directs itself elsewhere than itself, so that it is no longer that problem. Accordingly, the problem of self-contradiction is the heart of the solution of the problem of knowledge in general. And it is so both in the process or method and in the result.

Differently put, knowledge is a digression from what it is knowledge of, a digression that digresses even from itself. Perhaps, as I suggested in Chapter 1, section 1.2, this is why Plato typically places correctives for the mistakes that are made in the dialogues in digressions making up their central parts.[24] In fact, since Socrates invariably takes the discussion off at a tangent in order to address it properly, almost the entirety of each dialogue is a digression.[25] The discussion of nonbeing in the *Sophist* is a digression of this kind. The dialogues then continue as before the digression, but the same statements, given a different starting point by the digression, now mean something different. But further, given a *fundamentally* new starting point, "difference" itself means something different. Accordingly, the same statements mean something different partly or sometimes by meaning the same thing, and vice versa.[26]

For example, the *Theaetetus* contains the argument that Protagoras's understanding of knowledge, rigorously considered, consists in a self-defeating self-contradiction of sense itself. But this kind of self-contradiction also constitutes the successful rigor of philosophy. And the kind of refutation that allows knowledge, and for which Socrates himself is famous even in the world of the dialogues, is characterized in the *Sophist* as one of the Sophist's arts.[27] Further, the fundamental rethinking of knowledge and reality in the *Theaetetus* and the *Sophist* is itself made possible only by the imagined objections of Sophists in both cases. In the *Theaetetus*, Socrates even pretends to speak at length in Protagoras's person. That is, sophistry, *taken exactly in the way it opposes* philosophy, within the context of philosophy functions simply *as* philosophy.

Similarly, the self-defeating eros of the tyrant (that is, the most unrigorous statesperson) and the careless thinking (that characterizes the Sophist and) that, as I argued in Chapter 2, is valid on the basis of that eros are both fundamental to philosophy. As I argued above, careful thinking and rigorously truthful conduct require the standpoint of careless thinking and conduct to allow them to recognize, question, and justify themselves each as a whole. And careless superficiality is involved in rigorous knowledge of and truth to reality, since reality itself is self-cancelingly self-external.[28] That is, these unrigorous things are *internal* to philosophy by and as being external to it. The differences between the philosopher on the one hand and the Sophist and the unrigorous statesperson on the other are therefore genuine differences in which the philosopher is also partly but essentially (in a sense completely) the same as the Sophist and the unrigorous statesperson.

When a dialogue ends, as, for example, I argued the *Charmides* and the *Republic* do, by repeating the inconsistencies with which it began, then, it has both reunderstood them *and* left them exactly as they were. It has both made a difference by demonstrating a particular mistake *and* has undone that difference by putting in question the standpoint of commitment to truth for which it *matters, is meaningful*, that they are a mistake.

The essence of self-contradiction or careless thinking is to say that what is not, is. The most fundamental form of this assertion of nothing is exactly the fundamental indecision, Socrates' rigorously achieved ignorance. The establishment of the possibility of this assertion solves the problem of knowledge. We begin with positive interfering assumptions, and our attempt to eliminate them will also be based on positive—and even partially self-interventive—assumptions, unless we can think nothing, think without thinking anything. (See Chap. 1, sec. 1.1, on explaining things as they are before they are explained, sec. 1.2.2 on the "nothing further to know," and Idea 8.4 on not even needing the concept of "nothing further.") We do this by, for example, the act of simply recognizing both that we have an assumption, and that this recognition is itself based on an assumption. This self-canceling recognition is one of the nothings. It is already the act of *aporia*, fundamental indecision.

I suggest that the addition of this achieved nothing is the difference between the Sophist and the philosopher.[29] If a Sophist says, "I am perhaps being a Sophist here, I am perhaps trying to manipulate you in such and such a way," and takes pains to establish that possibility, then the Sophist is no longer a Sophist but a careful and responsible thinker and agent. The philosopher adds the nothing of fundamental indecision or established ignorance with respect to what s/he is saying.[30] In the same way, Socrates and Charmides resolve their paradoxes by simply identifying them, doing nothing about them, and acting in accordance with that doing nothing. The philosopher gives nothing, literally, and gets nothing, whereas the Sophist claims to give something and so gets, as Plato frequently notes, money and prestige (*doxa*, neatly, is both "opinion" and "reputation") in return.

Now, as I argued above, along with Theaetetus and the Stranger in the *Sophist*, truth in general has some nothing in it already. (In the terms of my discussion, the conditions of truth are self-canceling, or "self-nothing-making.") The nothing I describe here in thinking is therefore itself partly or sometimes a direct descriptive knowledge of what generally "is" there. And because truth in general has some nothing in it, that nothing is part of the conditions of the truths and so of the realities of particular things that are not nothing. The nothing in thinking is, then, also a cognitively known and procedurally acted out knowledge of the conditions of the truths of somethings. Since these conditions, as I argued in Idea 2.3, are part of the truth of the something itself, this nothing in thinking is also part of the descriptive truth of the somethings themselves, and not *simply* of the conditions of their truths. It follows that the philosopher, exactly in giving nothing, gives the foundations and truth of particular somethings.

This is another way of saying that thinking, as Plato understands it, can establish a noninterventive relation to truth, relating to it without adding anything to it.

4.4. THE *STATESMAN:* THE PROBLEM OF METHOD AND CONDUCT

In the *Sophist*, it is not only the results of the discussion, the definitions, that turn out to be inadequate but also the method of division by which the definitions are reached. The various species that are separated from each other by division are not always *simply* separate in the way this kind of division assumes, as in the case of the species of philosopher and Sophist. The Socratic method of refutation by examining self-consistent unity, then, applies to method itself and not only to content. And as a result, the *Sophist* foregrounds the issue of method, so that the act itself of seeking knowledge, which must use *some* method, cannot be simply taken for granted as undistorting.

The *Statesman* builds on the basis of the mixture of being and nonbeing that the *Sophist* establishes (and that the *Theaetetus*'s discussion of knowledge and ignorance implicitly requires), and it makes the issue of method even more prominent than the *Sophist*. In fact, it is a comedy of errors.[31] Where, then, the *Theaetetus* focuses on the problem of knowledge, and the *Sophist* focuses on the problem of reality or being, the *Statesman* focuses on the problem of method in establishing truth, both in knowing truly and, as it will turn out, in *being* true or living truly. That is, it focuses on method in connection with both knowledge and responsible conduct.

The Stranger continues using the method of division that the *Sophist* has already implicitly shown to be inadequate. As a result, he and young Socrates arrive at an inadequate definition of the statesman.[32] In order to correct the definition, the Stranger starts again with a different method: he tells a myth.[33] As he later points out, however, the myth is far longer than is necessary.[34] He then further corrects the initial definition by introducing yet another method, that of using paradigms or examples.[35] Despite this inventive variety of methods, the definition of the statesman with which the dialogue ends has, as I argue below, exactly the flaws of the initial definition that was repeatedly and elaborately corrected. And throughout the dialogue, the Stranger's interlocutor, young Socrates, contrasts thoroughly with his namesake in being entirely unperplexed by a continuing series of inconsistencies and obscurities that the Stranger invariably has to point out to him. (I discuss the comic dimension of these errors in sec. 4.5 and when I return to the context of Socrates' trial in sec. 4.6.)

The myth is told against the implications of the first definition: that the statesman is a kind of herdsman with expert knowledge of how to nurture his particular kind of herd.[36] The myth is about divine herdsmen nurturing the human species in former ages of the cosmos, and it establishes that the statesman we aim to define is not like that. The expertise of a human states-man and so the significance of his contribution cannot be distinguished from that of the other citizens in the way the divine herdsman's can, because his nature and education are similar to that of his fellow citizens.[37] The myth, then, presents something at great length and in great detail in order to make it clear that we should not be concerned with that something.[38] It is pro-ductively self-canceling. I suggest that the overlong clumsiness and self-canceling function of the myth are a miniature paradigm of the carefully mistaken ungainliness and function of the entire dialogue, in each of its parts and as a whole.

With respect to method, the method of paradigms or examples corrects the method of division between species (Ideas) by establishing identities across species (Ideas). The Stranger explains the method as follows:

> the method of example [*paradeigmatos*] . . . operates, does it not, when a fac-tor identical with a factor in a less-known object is rightly believed to exist in some other better-known object in quite another sphere of life? This common factor in each object, when it has been made the basis of a parallel examination of them both, makes it possible for us to achieve a single true judgment about each of them as forming one of a pair.[39]

But this method does more than add the establishing of identities to the establishing of differences. It does both at the same time. These identities are identities of things that are at the same time in "quite another sphere of life."[40] An example *is* a simultaneity of identity and difference, unity and disunity. Sameness and difference, being what something is and not being what something is—"what is" and "what is not"—are combined here.

The *Theaetetus* had a problem with too much sameness, too much homo-geneity of what is: knowledge was understood as homogeneously selfsame and as a direct and immediate relation to the truth of what is. Consequently both knowledge and what is turned out to contradict themselves, that is, to become too different from themselves, to the point of being meaningless. The *Sophist* introduced difference into sameness itself, by allowing it to blend with what it is not. Now, through the structure of examples, the *Statesman* combines difference and sameness in a way that gives equal priority to the (mutually exclusive) terms of each: without eliminating the difference within sameness, it introduces sameness into difference. The difference within sameness, then, is now itself partly characterized by sameness. One possible result is that difference need not necessarily interfere with sameness's simply being sameness. The mutual interference of sameness and difference cancels itself.

In this way the *Statesman* continues to carry out the reunderstanding that shows how the homogeneously selfsame conceptions of the *Theaetetus* are valid: that is, it shows that the (self-canceling) mistakes of the *Theaetetus* are also the truth as they stand. Their mistaken character, the selfsameness that makes them different from truth, cancels itself as a mistake, so that their selfsameness becomes simply a connection with truth, becomes the sameness *of* truth. But it is also *only* their difference from truth, which makes them genuinely *mistakes,* that *can* cancel itself and so result in truth. As I argued above, truth itself is (sometimes) different from itself, is self-external, and so what captures the truth can (sometimes) do so only in also missing it, and allowing that distance from truth to cancel itself. And it does cancel itself simply by virtue of being a distance from truth, whose own truth—that of not being true—catches up with it.

This reunderstanding is carried through into the understanding of method itself. The Stranger introduces the method of using examples in the following way: "It is difficult . . . to demonstrate anything of real importance without the use of examples"; he explains, "I have made a real fool of myself [or "it is very absurd," or "it is very strange": μάλ' ἀτόπως] by choosing this moment to discuss our strange human plight where the winning of knowledge is concerned. . . . Example . . . has been found to require an example."[41] The circularity of requiring knowledge to investigate knowledge, which was demonstrated in the *Theaetetus,* is noted and stressed here again. But the method of example includes difference in its identities. The very examples that show sameness do so by being different from what they are the same as, otherwise they would simply repeat the object they exemplify and so show nothing. They are from "quite another sphere of life." As a result of this rigorously established, revised understanding of sameness, then, circularity in fact does not happen here, not because there are no circles, but because these circles already have gaps in their identity *as* circles. Considered in their truth—and only considered in this rigorous way—they do not *simply* close on themselves. And the Stranger does in fact successfully present an example to explain examples.

The particular example or paradigm the Stranger chooses to explain the statesman is that of weaving. This example illustrates not only the topic of the dialogue, but also its method of combining sameness and difference, division and example itself. They can all be dealt with at once in the same way without circularity, because this "same way" need not be simply or always self-identical. It is an example, or a model (paradigm), or an imitation (resemblance). That is, it is internally or essentially related to what it models, because of their common features, and so can be used to investigate it. But it is also externally related, essentially separate from it, because it is not it, and so can be used to investigate it noncircularly. And it can also be used to investigate other things externally related to what it models and relate them to it without eliminating their differences from each other. The self-canceling relation of sameness and difference, being and nonbeing, that this trilogy of dialogues implicitly and progressively explores, gives a foundation for grasping that and how these internal and external relations (sometimes) operate simultaneously in these ways.

The dimensions of circularity and inadequacy of the arguments in the *Statesman* are well-recognized by commentators on Plato and are often taken to show the ultimate inadequacy of certain kinds of approach to thinking and politics. Mitchell Miller, for example, argues that "we see in retrospect that bifurcation, an initial help in attuning us to kinds, is ultimately a hindrance in concealing forms," and, in bringing us to see that, it "overcomes" itself.[42] And Kenneth Dorter argues that the dialogue's various failures show "the limitations of formal and systematic theorizing"[43] and emphasize, by contrast, the ultimate importance of contextual judgments of value: "The highest science is thus distinguished from the technical sciences by its status as a science of valuation."[44] Differently expressed, the dialogue shows the need to move beyond *techne*, in the sense of articulable know-how, to *sophia*: wisdom, intuitive judgment for the best.

My own suggestion, by contrast, is that the *Statesman*, like Plato's dialogues generally, certainly shows the limitations of formal and technical thought, but that on the *same* grounds it *also* establishes the possibility of the (sometimes) simple truth-bearing validity of that kind of thought, just as it stands. That is, as I argued above, depth and not only superficiality needs to be put in question, and part of wisdom is to leave open the possibility that the very idea of wisdom may be a mistake. Again, the self-canceling relation of sameness and difference, being and nonbeing, gives a foundation for grasping the sense of this self-canceling standpoint.

The Stranger's culminating definition of the statesman is that he is a "weaver" of the state, someone who has real knowledge of how to cooperate with and combine its elements and initiate their actions.[45] But he also argues that all existing statesmen in all existing states are only Sophist-like imitations of this true statesman.[46] In other words, he ends by repeating the initial mistake, which he corrected at such inordinate length, of defining a superhuman statesman rather than a human one.[47]

Unless, that is, one understands knowledge differently, in the way the *Theaetetus* implicitly indicated, as including ignorance and mistakes. That the *Statesman* consists in a series of big mistakes that the ignorant young Socrates does not notice and the Stranger emphasizes foregrounds the role of mistakes and ignorance in reaching the conclusions of the dialogue. If knowledge is understood in this way, then, the real thing would be precisely the human version as the Stranger exhibits it: Sophist-like imitations or models of truth together with the little nothing-added of recognition that they might be Sophist-like imitations. As I argued in Chapter 3, section 3.5, this is also what the *Republic* presents as justice.

Here, as I discuss further below, the reunderstanding of knowledge and truth emerges as also a reunderstanding of human life and conduct.

If one reads an "exoteric" and "esoteric" meaning here—or, a reading simply from the standpoint of opinion and a contrasting rigorous reading— they again turn out to be identical for practical purposes. The esoteric meaning would be that the statesperson's knowledge must be understood to include ignorance. The exoteric meaning is that existing statespeople are ignorant. Either way the statespeople are understood as limited, so that other citizens must also take dialogical responsibility for the state.

As the *Republic* also suggests, then, true statespersonship is something that needs to be practiced as a kind of democratic dialogue among the citizens.

It follows from this discussion that the true statesperson is the sophistic statesperson, the "politician," with a little nothing of self-awareness added. *This* statesperson *is* partly the gap between what is and the fictional or artificial ideal that s/he is not. And since what is *is itself partly this artificial distance from itself,* the rigorous statesperson also *simply* is in partly being this gap. The rigorous statesperson is someone oriented toward truth by fundamental indecision.[48] That is, the true statesperson is also the philosopher, who presents models (or "imitations") while putting them in question, so that the risk-taking *erotes* and truths of her/himself and her/his interlocutors are uninterfered with. And in fact Plato has Socrates claim in the *Gorgias* to be the only practitioner of statesmanship in his time.[49]

The description of the philosopher that results from these comments is that s/he is a little nothing added to the Sophist or sophistical statesperson. This repeats the definition of philosophy in Idea 2.1 as a fundamental indecision together with a definite assumption that is explored.

Again, in the light of this relation between philosophy and being a statesperson or good citizen, then, the self-externality of knowledge turns out to connect the method of establishing truth not only with the negatives of knowledge but also with the knower's social context and conduct. I discussed this connection in Idea 2.3 as part of the conditions of truth, or the truth *about* truth. Method is a matter not only of cognitive knowledge but, as in the *Charmides,* of how one lives and relates to what is external to one. That is, it is partly a matter of truth *to* oneself and others and not only *about* them. This means that it is a matter of relating to oneself and others purely for their own sakes. In other words, it is a matter of what is appropriate to one's nature and that of others: of what is good. Method is partly a matter of responsible conduct. And vice versa, as I argued in discussing the self-externality of virtue (see, for example, Chap. 3, sec. 3.4). The self-externality of knowledge, then, and the self-externality of character and conduct connect each to the other, so that they are different sides of the same coin (or the same side of different coins). As Dorter writes:

> wisdom is not only a matter of intellectual knowledge (i.e., images of reality), but a way of being: at the highest level, what we know and what we are coincide, in precisely the same sense that Aristotle would later argue that the good in particular cases can be known only by a moral person.[50]

Now, to approach the issue of imitation or modeling differently, the *Sophist* notes that language and thinking, the media of philosophy, are themselves a kind of imitation of reality. This is an alternative way of talking about what I am calling descriptive truth. But this imitative description interferes with the truth of its own descriptions, in that it is prevented from being a truthful imitation precisely in being an *imitation or description,* and not the thing itself. That is, it has what I am calling its interventive dimension. Consequently, if one turns this imitation on itself, if, that is, one talks or thinks about language and thinking themselves in general, the kind of paradox emerges that I discussed above. One cannot talk about how language in general, or imitation in general, compares with the independent reality it describes or imitates, because what is meant by reality, like any other meaning, is already within the descriptive imitation.[51] That is, the attempt to question or justify descriptive meaning in general is itself meaningless: it tries to make the words function outside the context that gives them their function. The meaning of this attempt interferes with or intervenes in itself to the extent that it means literally nothing. It is self-canceling.

But performing this meaningless comparison, engaging in this nothing, leaves us *justified* in leaving meaning or imitation in general unquestioned. It leaves us able to examine particular meanings without worrying about the justification of meaning itself. The self-canceling comparison *establishes* that the whole activity of justifying meaning or imitation itself is meaningless, so that any statement or worry we might have about it, itself literally means nothing. The act of raising the issue itself, because it turns out to be meaningless, justifies us in dropping the issue. Here, the very context given by careful thought, of truth-seeking itself, is canceled into meaninglessness and so into noninterfering irrelevance.

Similarly, as I noted above, the myth near the start of the *Statesman* presents something at great length and in great detail in order to make it clear that we should not be concerned with that something at all. And this justifies finding a fresh starting point.

The self-contradiction at the heart of the Sophist Protagoras's view of knowledge, discussed in the *Theaetetus,* is also this kind of self-canceling fundamental paradox.[52] It is not simply false, but instead it is only false if it is true. That is, it makes "falsehood" and "truth" themselves mean what their meanings exclude, and what their meanings *are by excluding.* In other words, it makes them meaningless. Any truth, then, including the truth about meaning itself, is meaningless. And this means that we have said nothing. But this meaninglessness emerges only when we consider the truth about truth itself, truth in general. Consequently this meaninglessness, in turn, allows us to start again, asking questions about particular truths, but now justified in not being concerned with the possibility of truth in general.

I argued above that the drawing out of the united meanings of particular issues to the point of their single universal Idea is a self-canceling activity that returns us capable of fresh and fair or just considering of the many particulars each in its own right again. Similarly, the drawing out of the united meanings of meaning in general, and of the knowledge of knowledge or the truth of truth in general, returns us capable of fresh and fair considering of what is true about particulars in general (that is, about the concept of particulars, about particulars *in general,* rather than about particulars themselves).

(As my various comments on Wittgenstein and ordinary language philosophy may suggest, I would also argue that conceptual analysis, widely favored in contemporary Anglo-American philosophy, is justified exactly because it submits itself to this process of allowing the most general level of thought to cancel itself so that the particulars emerge in a justified way.)

The disappearance into noninterfering irrelevance of the issue of truth-seeking itself applies also to the nothing that I argued, with Plato, that philosophy offers. Even this nothing, too, disappears, and functions only in establishing the tangents to it that, having touched on it and by having touched on it, are directed elsewhere. As I argued in Idea 8.4, it requires us to think not even nothing. The ideas of "nothing" and "meaninglessness," after all, have meanings, and so are canceled themselves. Even that point of touching cancels itself and disappears. It becomes pure empty rhetoric, meaningful only in addressing a mistake. Once the mistake is recognized, the working up of a rigorous answer to it can itself be recognized to be an engagement with a mistake. It is a purely artificial response to a pure artificiality that can now be simply abandoned.

Again, then, the missing dialogue dealing with the definition of the philosopher may not be missing. It may consist in (nothing but) the self-canceling self-questioning of the *Sophist* and *Statesman,* the need for which the *Theaetetus* emphasizes.

Given this role of radical self-cancellation, we can understand metaphysics or theories of reality differently, including epistemologies or theories of knowledge (such as the *Theaetetus* presents) and ontologies or theories of being (such as the *Sophist* presents). We can conceive many incompatible metaphysics that do not interfere with each other, because they are not simply descriptive truths that would permanently compete with each other, but are also essentially (or in a sense completely) self-intervening and self-canceling. As I argued above, once they are canceled, nothing remains—in fact "not even nothing," not even the concept of a consideration—that might affect the concerns with truth of the others. And this process of self-cancellation in fact returns us to the conflicting truth as now rigorously and fully *justified*. Further, any *comparison* of them must *itself* occur partly but essentially as a self-canceling process, since it is also an inquiry into the truth about truth. Now, because they need not interfere with each other and because they also ultimately justify each other, we can also conceive incompatible metaphysics that are each simply true. As a result, since they can be simply true, incompatible, and noninterfering with each other, they are nei-

ther relative nor absolute, or they are both relative and absolute, or sometimes and/or partly one and also sometimes and/or partly the other.

To return to the side of establishing truth that is conduct: in the *Statesman,* the Stranger prominently displays his own capacity for mistakes. I suggest that this is how he puts his (Sophist-like) models of truth in question,
and so protects young Socrates from taking models of truth as *simply* truth,
rather than genuinely orienting himself toward truth by thinking about
these models carefully—that is, by engaging his own truth, eros, and risk.
What is more, in making his mistakes only implicitly, if noticeably to an
attentive listener, the Stranger *also* leaves room for young Socrates to continue being inattentively thoughtless. And further, if young Socrates *were* to
pay attention, the fact that he has to decide for himself and on his own
responsibility that there are so far unnoticed mistakes opens up the further
possibility that he himself might be making an unnoticed mistake in deciding that these *are* mistakes. That is, it opens up the possibility that taking the
mistakes seriously might itself be a mistake. Even in that case, then, the
Stranger would be putting young Socrates in a position to make his own
uninterfered-with decision as to whether the models are in fact simply true,
rather than being questionable.

I suggest that the *Statesman* implicitly pursues the implications for
thought and conduct of the self-canceling self-externality of things, including knowledge and its methods, that was justified in the *Sophist.* This self-
canceling self-externality is what I have called the variegated texture of
truth. Differently put, the *Statesman* emphasizes that careful thinking and
responsible conduct involve not *simply* the achievement of a direct and immediate relation to truth, and so a directly appropriate relation to what it is
the truth of, but the achievement of a relation to truth, and so to the good
of what it is the truth of, which *also* consists in various kinds of nonrelation
to truth: for example, ignorance, deceptive opinion and expertise, and mistakes. These nonrelations to truth are what, for example, allow the interventive dimensions of truth to turn against themselves so that they do not
interfere with its descriptive dimensions. And they are what allow conduct
that engages with the truth of others without interfering unjustly with them
by blindly imposing models of truth. (Another example of the relevance of
these nonrelations to establishing truth: as I mentioned above, in the
Theaetetus and *Sophist* the Sophists' questioning, performed by the philosopher, is what provokes and makes possible the philosopher's developed answers. Theaetetus's, Socrates', and the Stranger's ignorance also play this
fundamental role.) Given this dimension of nonrelation to truth, then, care-

ful thinking and responsible conduct involve what I am calling an *external orientation toward* truth, an orientation that is, however, sometimes or partly *also or even simply a direct relation to truth.*

Differently put again, I suggest that the *Statesman* emphasizes the rigorous self-disparity of both careful thought and responsible conduct, each as a descriptive imitation of truth that, knowing itself to be only an imitation and acting on that knowledge, is not simply an imitation, and—since in this way it attends to what it describes purely in its own right and so for its own sake—is also a just and loving act.

4.5. THE CRANE'S WALK AND PLATO'S DIALOGUES

Before I return to the general context of Socrates' trial that these dialogues give themselves, it will be helpful to make a comment on the relation between Plato's dialogues generally and the crane's walk referred to in the title of this book.

A crane has a large body, thin legs that bend backwards, and very large feet that it has to pick up high to walk. As a result, its walking consists in a series of ungainly movements, some tangential to the overall direction it moves in and some going backward and then overshooting forward. And yet these clumsy movements are always perfectly mutually positioned to produce the most perfect poise.[53] The crane is nature's answer to John Cleese. Similarly, the ignorance and often exaggerated mistakes in the dialogues, in their indirect, nonimmediate relation to insight and truth, *are* sometimes or partly a direct relation to them, and are also the conditions for other direct relations to them. And the dialogues themselves are digressions or artificial fictions whose overshooting of the truth *is* sometimes or partly direct connection with it and also the condition for other direct relations to it. The spirit of the dialogues, in their overall structure and in their detail, then, can be expressed through the example of the crane's walk.

As I argued above, this clumsiness of orientation toward truth also allows the negotiation of different understandings of truth itself, since it can put itself in question to the point of self-cancellation. And I suggest that it does so without simple relativism or simple absolutism. Each understanding cancels itself relative to the other, so that "not even nothing," not even the concept of a consideration, is left: there is nothing there to be relative to. And this cancellation *also* cancels *itself* (or, the position relative to which the other one is canceled is itself also canceled), *also* returning us to the position *before* the cancellation: both (or more) positions are there in relation to each other. Consequently, this negotiation of different understandings both holds each as simply true, without any relativizing consideration of the other's being meaningful, and also does not hold either as simply true, given the other. That is, it involves both an exploration of each understanding of truth *exclusively* and so absolutely in its own terms, and *also* a relativizing indecision with respect to them, an indecision that includes indecision about itself, so that it consequently does not have the last word either, and it involves both these contradictory things at the same time. In this connection it is nice that, when a crane stands still, it can stand equally on one leg (either one) or two.

I also argued above that truth itself, and not only the orientation that gets at it, is variegated in this self-externally self-external way.

I suggest that the *Statesman* in particular focuses especially on presenting or modeling this ungainly-elegant, compatibly self-incompatible character of truth and of careful and responsible thought and life. If this is right, then, rigorously considered, it is a broad and sympathetic comedy.[54]

4.6. THE TRIAL OF PHILOSOPHY, INNOCENCE, AND PRIDEWORTHINESS

I argued at the start of this chapter in section 4.1 that the trilogy deals with Socrates' trial as a particular example of the trial of philosophy in general, and further, that it is the nature of philosophy or of careful thought and conduct to be on trial. In this light, I suggest that the *Statesman,* as the culminating dialogue of this trilogy, is partly a summarizing comment on the trial of philosophy. If one takes it that way, I think, tentatively, that it might say something like the following. Young Socrates, so far apparently untouched by philosophy, and apparently remaining untouched by philosophy, is ignorant, open to discovering that he is ignorant, and so open to correction. Because of this ignorance and his truth to it, he is also innocent of culpable fundamental harm. He knows too little to be held responsible for much. But the philosopher is also ignorant of fundamental issues and open to correction, an ignorance and openness s/he has *achieved* by (externally) and as (internally) the discipline of philosophy. The obvious innocence of young Socrates, then, is a striking image of the philosopher Socrates' innocence of culpable fundamental harm. The philosopher's innocence is achieved as a willingness to be undecided as to whether s/he is innocent, that is, to consider the possibility that s/he is not innocent. I discussed this evaluation of conduct at the metalevel, the level that thinks *about* the level of what is being evaluated, in Ideas 1.2 and 8 (with specific reference to Socrates' trial).

Socrates is not out to mislead or misrepresent—corrupt—but in fact very clearly does the very opposite. He makes room to think about even his own possible guilt, and he does so in the style of the very *presentation* of his innocence. And this style is continuous with the style in which he has led his life generally, the philosophical style of life for which he is tried.

That young Socrates makes an incongruous and comical contrast to the Socrates of whom his name keeps reminding the reader, is, I suggest, exactly appropriate. This contrast is a small paradigm of the elegant, clumsy, perfect poise of truth and the orientation toward truth. And it shows more than innocence. It seems to me that it shows something more profoundly warm and loving toward the human condition, a seeking out of what is worthwhile and nurturing of what is good, not only where it is more easily embraced, where it is grand and proud, but also in its trivialities and shames. Philosophy shows and practices here the grand prideworthiness of at least one kind of silly or ridiculous foolishness. It is prideworthy because this comical, clumsy willingness to make mistakes that turn out to be foolish is, as I argued above, part of the ongoing source of genuine selfhood, knowledge, and responsible accomplishment.[55] In the *Theaetetus,* for example, Plato has Socrates periodically encourage Theaetetus to be willing to make mistakes without shame, with the result that Theaetetus gains both confidence and understanding by the very process of being refuted repeatedly. And perhaps it is significant that the very start of the *Theaetetus* has one person meeting with another whom he has just before failed to find because he was looking in the wrong place.[56] Again, both the *Theaetetus* and *Sophist,* in engaging Socrates' predecessors, show the productive shifts in philosophy itself that can occur precisely by reconsidering what it is to make sense and not to make sense, that is, by reconsidering what it *is* to make mistakes.

And because this foolishness is part of the source of relation to truth and so of acting and being truly, it is part of a sympathy toward truth (or a love of truth), and so more than just, because it is part of the basis of justice. Socrates' *achieved* innocence, then, is more than innocence, because it is also part of the *basis* or *source* of innocence, and so makes it possible to gain innocence where it did not exist before.

Pride, the self-satisfaction we rest and warm ourselves in, is here divided against itself and in this way also extended beyond itself to include shameful or awkward or laughable foolishness.[57] And this self-division shares the self-external, self-canceling structure of truth-seeking, of rigorous thought. This self-canceling self-division is what allows pride to be a *justified simple* self-satisfaction, where the "self" that is satisfied is understood and lived in its "sometimes always" fundamental relations with others and their truths and conflicting standards of what one should esteem, and with what else is more than it. On this self-canceling basis, pride can, rigorously, be simply true or genuine, something we can wholeheartedly have and draw strength from.

Consequently, rigorous pride is the very opposite of unjust self-assertion, of arrogance or hubris. In fact, since it is self-canceling, it is its opposite partly in being identical with it. What is more, the exactly appropriate and fundamental comical incongruity I have been discussing reunderstands the meanings of both pride and shame so that the sheer senselessness, the nonsense, of unjust self-assertion stands out fully by contrast. Truthful pride is based as much on weakness and dimensions of failure as on homogeneous or un-self-canceling self-assertion. Proud or satisfied injustice, proud un-self-canceling refusal to make room for another person or a different perspective, is then something bewilderingly senseless.

Returning to Socrates' representative trial, the members of society are also fundamentally ignorant, and therefore those who are sincere and so open to correction also share the fundamental innocence I am discussing. From the point of view of careful thought, of philosophy, then, both philosophy and the sincere part of society and its opinions are innocent of culpable fundamental harm. This is the tragic dimension of the conflict between philosophy and society, in the ancient Greek sense of tragedy. This conflict produces great harm that cannot be avoided, because it involves what its agents *are,* so that none of them can help it.

But the opinions of society deny such fundamental ignorance. These opinions claim to be knowledge, and understand knowledge to be something homogeneously or simply true and what it is, without being able to have any nothing, any ignorance, in it. That is, from this point of view, neither the philosopher nor the knowledgeable member of society is *also* fundamentally ignorant: the knowledge that either side has cannot be both knowledge *and* questionable. From the point of view of these opinions, then, philosophy is culpably dangerous, because it misleads and interferes with what we simply know should not be interfered with and in doing so it also simply knows what it is doing.

But for exactly the same reasons, the opinions of society are also dangerous. Because the standpoint of opinion insists that philosophy knows what it is doing, it gives philosophy an equivalent claim to be the standpoint that represents what we know should not be interfered with, with the result that social opinion would then be knowingly and dangerously interfering. Philosophy, however, consists precisely in the recognition of that kind of danger in its own activity and the attempt to do something about it. That is, philosophy as attempted careful thought is a practice of attempted justice. But the opinions of society neither recognize the danger on their own side nor try to do anything about it. To express differently this contrast of how knowledge is understood and lived, opinion, unlike genuinely rigorous thought, does not understand mistakes and ignorance as preciously important but assimilates them to shameful foolishness, although it makes mistakes and is often ignorant itself.

Consequently, even on the assumptions of the opinions of society, it turns out that the philosopher is either innocent of culpable fundamental harm, or less guilty of it than the knowledgeable members of society. If responsibility and justice are really the issue rather than insincere covers for something else, then, on the assumptions of the opinions of society themselves, the philosophical life is more just than life lived in accordance with these opinions.[58]

But, again, as I argued above, the standpoint of opinion cannot be held responsible in this way, since this kind of nonhomogeneous thinking does not make sense by its ultimate standards and so cannot be taken to be valid for it. In terms of opinion's own standards for what makes sense, philosophy is simply culpably dangerous. But then, again, from the philosophical standpoint—the standpoint of rigorous, nonhomogeneous, ultimately self-canceling thought—if one grants these rights to the standpoint of opinion, then by *those* rights, by the standards *of that other standpoint*, one also grants that philosophy cannot be held responsible in the terms of opinion either, since philosophy also, equally, has its own limitations of sense-making. Philosophy, that is, holds both mutually exclusive standpoints together, making room for its own rejection by the other standpoint, but by the same standard *also* making room for its own acceptance-and-rejection and rejection *through* acceptance of the other standpoint. I discussed this logic in connection with the *Gorgias* in Chapter 1, section 1.2.6.

In fact, as I argued above, the *purely* philosophical trial of philosophy, however—that is, the standpoint of careful thought and conduct considered exclusively in its own terms without concern for the standpoint of opinion—since it *is* nonhomogeneous, *itself includes and needs* the standpoint of opinion, in that standpoint's role of altogether excluding the sense of the careful standpoint. That is, the philosophical standpoint leaves the *question* of philosophy's innocence as the answer: the ongoing requirement to *start thinking again*, that allows rigorous inquiry and conduct to decide and act by and as their self-cancellation, so that they justly do not interfere with the being of what they engage with. Here philosophy is just, and so innocent, at the metalevel of thought and conduct: it takes its injustice into account and finds essential-rhetorical ways of obviating and/or compensating for it.

The *Statesman,* I suggest, shows the happier innocence, extending even to loving comedy, that the philosophical way would and often does make of what the contribution of opinion occasionally (and *also* rightly) establishes (in both the subjective and objective senses of this word) as an un–self-canceling, simply tragic situation.[59] And it does so, as I argued above that the *Republic* also does, not by eliminating the self-incompatibility of the tragic situation but by recognizing it fully. This recognition allows the self-incompatibility to cancel itself into an incongruous recognition of different genuine commitments, which are in themselves different truths, and which therefore have the same right, if fairness is the issue, to be explored.

And this exploration in turn allows the establishment of where the truth-seeker's own true, simple commitment, and hence simple decision, lies. That is, given a situation involving different understandings of truth, this recognition of tragic self-incompatibility itself produces a simple, self-compatible understanding. This result is the self-incompatibility of this situation taken to its logical conclusion, become incompatible even with itself as self-incompatibility.

The tone or spirit of the *Statesman,* I tentatively propose, shows this odd and fundamental possibility as the working of a delicately poised clumsiness, or a perfect, ungainly poised elegance. It falls over itself in intervening, interfering, in the already constitutional self-interference of its attempt to give answers, and does so in an exact way that allows its failures to succeed. It makes mistakes in making mistakes and in this way successfully avoids making mistakes. And in doing this, it shows that mistakes both are unavoidable and redeem themselves as the necessary path to truth. Its tone or spirit, that is, shows something like the innocent beauty of the crane's walk.

Unsympathetic contempt for fundamentally incompatible views and for culpable foolishness is certainly present in Plato's dialogues. But the truth of love, like truth in general, is variegated, and a fundamental or rigorous or consistent commitment to love must also be willing to learn to love what love excludes. It must be willing, that is, not to include it, but to love it as what it excludes. In other words, it must also be willing to try to love hate and contempt and indifference. And further, since the truth of love, like other truths, is self-divided, hatred and contempt and indifference can be forms of love themselves, as I argued in connection with the *Gorgias* in Chapter 1, section 1.2.6. Truth to the rhetorical context is what makes the difference, and where Plato's characters are destructive, a destruction of their destructiveness is a loving act.

Because this destruction of destructiveness is a loving act in not being loving, it achieves two simultaneous things. First, in *not* being loving, it does not simply deny the legitimacy of the unloving, destructive principle it opposes. And second, in *being* loving in not being loving, from its own standpoint considered on its own, it produces, with respect to its own destructiveness, a self-canceling paradox that disappears. That is, as I argued above in connection with the "not even nothing" that philosophy offers, this destructiveness in the loving position becomes pure empty rhetoric, literally meaningless except as a "self-consuming artifact" in acknowledging the destructiveness in the other standpoint, or in correcting a mistaken view of what the loving standpoint does. Consequently, from this standpoint it is not really destructiveness, and so is *also* true to the principle of the *loving* position considered simply in its own right. On this simultaneous truth to both loving and unloving principles, and to their incompatibility as well, see, again, the discussion in Chapter 1, section 1.2.6.

CONCLUSION

The Unevenly Even Consistency of Truth

1. ARISTOTLE AND PLATO

In his *Posterior Analytics*, Aristotle argues that knowledge is of universals, and therefore cannot be gained through sense perception: "Nor can one *know* [a thing] through sensation. . . . [S]ince demonstrations are universal, and since these [i.e. universals . . .] cannot be sensed, it is evident that we cannot *know* individuals through sensation."[1] Of course, since universals are not sensed, we cannot know *them* through sensation either.

But Aristotle also argues that knowledge begins with a kind of induction from sensation:[2]

a demonstration proceeds from universals, whereas an induction proceeds from particulars. But universals cannot be investigated except through induction . . . and it is impossible to learn by induction without having the power of sensation. For of individuals [there can be only] sensation, and no *knowledge* of them can be acquired; and neither can we demonstrate conclusions from universals without induction, nor can we acquire universals through induction without sensation.[3]

He notes that "from many observations of a fact we might, after the search for the universal, possess a demonstration; for from many individual cases the *universal* [might be made] clear."[4] Although he qualifies this point—it is "not that we would have understood [universally the fact] *by* observation, but that *from* observation we would have gained possession of the universal"[5]—sense perception is nonetheless necessary. The process of gaining knowledge "is impossible . . . without having the power of sensation."

As Aristotle explains, "the immediate primary principles" we need for knowledge[6] arise "from sensation, like a reversal in battle brought about when one man makes a stand, then another, then a third, till a principle [or (military) formation, or ruling order: *arche*] is attained."[7] "Clearly, then, we must come to know the primary [universals] by induction; for it is in this way that [the power of] sensation, too, produces in us the universal."[8] Aristotle calls this capacity for apprehending universals through particulars, "intuition" (*nous*): "Accordingly, . . . intuition would be the principle [or starting point] of scientific knowledge."[9]

For Aristotle, then, knowledge by its nature *depends* on something that its nature equally *excludes* from being something known.[10]

On the other hand, we know sensed particulars only through universals, which in turn we know only through sensed particulars. Knowledge, then, also occurs in a circle.[11] In Aristotle's simile, the difference between knowledge to and from first principles (the principles we know through intuition) is like the "difference . . . in a race-course between the course from the judges to the turning point and the way back."[12]

I suggest that the view of knowledge I am proposing explains how these two incompatible sides of Aristotle's account can make sense together.[13] As I interpreted Socrates' discussion of knowledge in the *Phaedo,* knowledge occurs in two steps (see Idea 8.2.3). The first circularly repeats the meaning of the thing being considered, and the second relates it to different, nonsensically external meanings. And both steps are necessary, since they cancel each other, and in that process their combination both gets to the (self-external) truth of the thing and eliminates the consequent interference of knowledge with that truth. Expressing this more generally, knowledge is a combination of external and internal relations between the knower and the known, and between the foundations of truth and what rests on the foundations. (And here the two kinds of relations themselves are both simply distinct [external to each other] and also confused [internal to each other]). As a result, knowledge is both external and internal (that is, tangential) to what it knows. It cancels itself at the circular point at which it becomes complete and so precipitates, independently of or externally to its interfering self, the truth of the knower, the known, and the process of knowledge itself.

As I argued above, this kind of self-canceling circle more specifically explains how universals and knowledge-founding principles, whose universal character ultimately forms a closed circle that excludes the meanings of being particular, can *also include* those meanings, and not simply despite the circle but also *as and through* it. And it consequently explains how knowledge, by *both* including *and* excluding the meanings of being particular, can both connect with or capture the truths of the particulars given to sensation and not interfere with them.[14]

Both dimensions of Aristotle's account, then, the circularity of explanation *and* its incompatible relation to what is external to knowledge, are necessary for knowledge.

This would harmonize Aristotle's account of knowledge with the view proposed in the *Phaedo*. But Aristotle, of course, rejects the dimension of conceptual redundancy and nonsense that, on my interpretation, makes the *Phaedo*'s proposal succeed. I suggest that the reason Aristotle rejects this dimension is that he does not, as I believe Plato does, put the legitimacy of careful thinking itself seriously in question. And this prevents him from seeing *both* the fundamental problem with thinking, that careful thinking *itself* ultimately *is* circular redundancy and self-intervening nonsense, *and* consequently the solution inherent in the problem, that it cancels itself.

Because Plato, on the other hand, does genuinely question the legitimacy of careful thinking, he is able to develop a foundational account of it. And because this account (like, in fact, the kind that contemporary conceptual analysis offers) is a foundational account of *thinking,* it gives a foundation for meaning, concepts, and sense-making themselves. As Plato has Socrates insist, the most fundamental Idea, the Idea of the Good, is the source of knowledge and truth. More generally, it is beyond, is more fundamental than, any kind of being:[15] that is, it is the foundation of all being and in particular of dimensions of being (or, if one limits the scope of the idea of being, of dimensions of knowledge and truth) such as meanings, concepts, and their relations.

As I argued above, Plato in fact presents a variety of ways of exploring the nature and status of careful thinking and of meaning, and so of the truth of "what is" that thinking engages. One might characterize these ways of exploring as "ontological manners." These manners involve focusing primarily on thinking, meaning, and the truth of being *by focusing on them tangentially:* that is, by focusing elsewhere. As I mentioned in the Introduction to this book, Aristotle was the first to identify the direct focus of thinking on being itself as "first philosophy," which later got the name "metaphysics," the study of being, of the ultimate or true nature of reality. But I argue that this direct focus ultimately interferes with the truth it aims to establish, and so is not the way to succeed as a first, or foundational, philosophy. This approach has the wrong kind of manners.

Another way of showing the necessarily indirect or tangential dimension of talking about foundations emerges from the *Charmides'* and *Republic's* insistence that the primary focus, even for matters of being and knowledge, must be the knowledge of the Good. That is, the primary focus must be ethical, or at least in some way a matter of good and bad value. I suggest that the idea here is not that the consideration of what is best should dictate what we consider true,[16] but that what is true follows from what is best, not as an accommodation of truth to something else, but as part of the *nature* of truth. The *commitment to rigorous thought itself,* and so the very idea and *meaning of rigorous truth* itself, which only exists given the commitment to rigorous thought, presuppose an idea of what is *most worth* doing, what is best—in this case, rigorous thinking.

But if one begins with the idea that ethical or value commitment is the primary issue, then the idea of truth, and hence the idea of being, and even what it means to be "ultimately primary" itself, are not simply the same as they are if one begins with the nature of being as primary. Unlike the issue of being, the issue of valuation involves, for example, questioning the value or worth of that issue itself. Consequently, the priority of value commitment *itself* opens the possibility that it itself is *not* primary, and that issues such as the nature of being are primary instead. That is, since the priority of value commitment can itself justify the priority of the issue of being, it itself can lead to its own exclusion. But in contrast, when the question of the nature of being is primary, value commitment can be understood only as just another kind of being. That is, this priority *simply excludes* possibilities like that of the priority of value commitment as distinct from being.

But a converse dimension of the priority of valuation is that *when* a particular value *is* being pursued, what makes it a value is that it is done simply for its own sake. There is, as I argued in Idea 8.3 and Chapter 1, section 1.2.2, simply "nothing further to know" about it. That is, the priority of value commitment *also excludes* the possibility of alternative priorities which it *nonetheless justifies.*

As I also discussed in other contexts, then, what is ultimately prior, the foundations of being and truth, inherently *includes* the possibility of *wholly mutually exclusive* foundations or ultimate natures. Consequently, in order to focus on the foundations, the ultimate nature, of being and truth, one has to focus simultaneously in directions that wholly exclude each other. That is, at this level, a direct focus on one's object *is* partly a focus away from it, *is* partly tangential.

As I argued as part of this discussion, there is room for more than one entirely mutually exclusive metaphysics of being and/or fundamental thinking and so more than one entirely mutually exclusive hierarchy of priorities. And in some of these, even being itself and/or truth itself need not be primary realities. Further, what is true by the standards of each of these incompatible frameworks is sometimes *absolutely* true: each self-cancelingly but entirely excludes the incompatible meanings, and so truths, of the others. Truth, as I argued above, is unevenly textured.

More particularly, as I also suggested above, there can be more than one mutually exclusive but true interpretation of Plato. For example, Aristotle is quite right to reject Plato's Theory of Ideas on the grounds of redundancy and inconsistency. In order to explore what is, one has to pursue the kind of self-consistent, informative thinking that Aristotle consummately undertakes, otherwise one lands up with what is *simply* nonsense. In fact, even if Plato's standpoint is legitimate, it *itself presupposes* the kind of consistent, informative thinking that justifies Aristotle's rejection of the Theory of Ideas. It is, after all, only pursuing this simply consistent kind of thought *that establishes the need for,* as well as the nature and rigor of, the kind of self-inconsistency that I argue Plato explores. In addition, although I argued above that Plato's kind of thinking provides the self-inconsistent foundation for Aristotle's position, that thinking, as I also argued, is meaningless *within* the positions for which it is the foundation.

Each of these standpoints, then, is sometimes the *only* meaningful one. And sometimes *both* are meaningful, sometimes even *while simultaneously* absolutely excluding each other as entirely *without* meaning. For example, as I noted just above, each can be presupposed by, can be a foundation for, the other, in a way that works only because that foundation is *also* wholly meaningless within the context of the standpoint it founds.

2. THE UNEVENLY EVEN CONSISTENCY OF TRUTH

In general, then, different contexts, among other differences, can involve radically different entire metaphysics or fundamental modes of thinking, and can do so without any of these detracting from the truth of the others at all. And further, as is shown by these incompatible metaphysics' being able to be part of the same focus, or even to presuppose each other, they can also be present together in the *same* context or even be fully relevant to each other without detracting from each other's truths. This can happen even within a single sentence, or even a single term, or a single issue. This describes, for example, the situation when one balances different standpoints on a single issue in order to decide between them. Or it describes the situation when something like forgiveness happens, entirely altering the *kind* of relationship one has with another person. Many of the issues that defined the nature of the previous relationship become entirely irrelevant, even nonexistent, and new defining elements emerge—for example, affection and trust—that simply had no part in the reality of the previous relationship.

Again, conversely, when one recognizes a betrayal, there is a similarly complete transformation as an instant result of the recognition. Here, for example, some defining obligations simply disappear, and some freedoms to neglect the other person's interests emerge *that would not have been among the kinds of things that could be freedoms at all before*, but would instead have been violations even of one's own side of the relationship.

It is in fact a commonplace among some schools of conceptual analysis that the same object can be rightly described in terms of incompatible frameworks of explanation or incompatible concepts exactly *because* these frameworks or concepts are incompatible: they have nothing to do with each other, and so do not really conflict.[17] For example, human beings can be described both as capable of free choice and also as entirely determined by psychological, social, and/or biological causes. Or we can be described both as entirely biological machines and also as having minds. The idea is that each side of these apparently conflicting ways of describing us is a different *kind* of description, doing a different *kind of job* from the other, serving purposes the other simply does not serve, so that each can be true at its own level of description. In that context, this book tries to account for how these mutually irrelevant kinds of concepts can be said to describe *the "same" thing* (see, for example, Idea 1.1). That is, it tries to account for the *mutual relevance* of what are *also* mutually irrelevant concepts. And in doing so, it also allows and takes into account the sense of other, conflicting but also commonplace, intuitions *complementary* to recognizing the mutual irrelevance of various dimensions of things or situations.

For example, as Kant argues, one cannot fit "being moral" within a cost-benefit calculation without making it a subjective matter of one's particular needs, and so no longer a matter of morality at all.[18] But I argued above that, at the most rigorous, a concept or position can have an internal relation to a concept or position that is *also* purely external to it. Consequently, it is conceivable that there are contexts in which one can take utilitarian and practical issues into account without in the least detracting from the purity of the moral issue. And in fact, as I argued above in connection with fundamental "mixture," sometimes one can have that purity *only* by involving it in what is external to it (see Idea 8.1).[19]

For an instance of taking both kinds of issue into account without affecting the purity of the moral issue, generosity is, on the one hand, properly generosity only if it is carried out without being influenced by ideas of benefit or recognition. In fact, a generous act could even be regarded as a privilege for the generous person, who should be grateful for the opportunity to do something good. The recipient's actions, then, are entirely irrelevant to the generous person's actions. They belong to an entirely different concept from the one that corresponds to the generous dimensions of those actions. But on the other hand, if the recipient takes unfair advantage of the generosity, this unfair action nonetheless can and should be taken into account. The recipient's position has its own ethical requirements that the other person is entitled, and ought, to expect to see honored. And because the entirely external relation between different positions and concepts is self-canceling, the other position's ethical requirements *can* be taken into account as relevant to the generous actions. But the recipient's actions are still, though self-cancelingly so, entirely external, irrelevant to those of the generous person. As a result, they can be taken into account in relation to the generous actions *while also* not affecting the purity of those actions *at all*.

Mutually exclusive positions or conceptual domains, then, sometimes can and must be considered simultaneously and in the same respects *both* in relation to each other *and exclusively* each in its own terms, both as relevant to each other *and* as entirely unaffected by each other.

In fact, given the foundational connection of what is external to a position or concept with its sense, with what is internal to it, I suggest that mutually irrelevant concepts or positions can affect each other *most* fundamentally. They can affect each other even to their *being the concepts or positions they are,* and they can do so precisely *because* they have no bearing on each other. So—and this is an instance of being able to have moral purity *only* by taking into account what is external to it—taking unfair advantage of generosity in one position destroys the very meaning or sense of generosity in another. It turns it into support of unethical behavior. And it does so *completely* because it is entirely independent of, has no part in, the concept of generosity, and so makes the generous actions part of something entirely different from what they were. The attitude and actions in the one position, then, *because* of their conceptual independence, their meaninglessness for the other position, make what is happening in that other position an *entirely* different activity.

As a result of considering mutually exclusive positions or concepts simultaneously both in relation to each other and entirely independently, then, both their relations and their own independent meanings sometimes turn out to be different from what they would be *simply* with or *simply* without a relation to the other.

Returning to the example of generosity, one converse connection here between mutually exclusive positions is that *because* appreciation is gratuitous, it can *reestablish* the meaning of generosity. For instance, one can feel *more* good about appreciation for one's having been generous, just because being appreciated has nothing to do with it. And as a result of the unlooked-for appreciation, one can be impressed with dimensions of the nature and worth of generosity in a renewed way: here, for example, that it involves the heartening fact of undeserved good things.[20]

Looking at a different dimension of this discussion, the very idea of ethical "requirements" is, I think, sometimes nonsensical. Ethical actions cannot be imposed: they are genuine only if done of one's own accord (even if *also* unwillingly). Consequently, the idea of requirements is just not part of the same concept as ethical obligation, and as a result, it is nonsense when used to articulate that concept. But this can be a kind of nonsense that helps to establish sense. For example, someone who does not grasp an ethical principle is outside its conceptual boundary, outside its range of meaning. And the idea of requirements, while also outside the concept, is analogous or tangential to it in a way that helps to direct one toward it. The idea of requirements, then, becomes appropriate in part exactly *because* it is outside the concept and so can engage and direct someone who does not grasp the meanings of the concept. But once the ethical concept is grasped, the idea of "requirements" loses its relation to relevant meaning again. Within that context, it no longer exists as an idea related to the conduct and attitudes in question. That is, the idea of requirements leads one to the ethical concept partly by canceling itself into nonsense.

The idea of "should" or "ought," understood as a requirement, then, is only meaningful as a self-canceling term, meaningful in producing or restoring insight into a concept that excludes its meaning.

Another example of relations and interactions between mutually exclusive concepts concerns the nature and possibility of experiencing pride in a prideworthy life.[21] I briefly discussed appropriate pride in Idea 1.2, and the specific prideworthiness of comical, undignified humanity in Chapter 4, section 4.6. Here I want to focus, also briefly, on the importance of the "sometimes always" logic involved in the interactions of mutually exclusive concepts in prideworthiness.

Putting a little differently what I argued in Chapter 4, the practice of what I am calling "ontological manners," of orienting ourselves to truth, requires that we occasionally be honestly weak, confused, at a loss, discomposed, inappropriate, awkward, clumsy, unimpressive, trivial, petty. Because this practice is the result of a very rigorous discipline or exercise of character, these qualities are achievements. And because these accomplishments foster the foundations of human truth and therefore of human being, they are the most important human achievements. Accordingly, they are our most prideworthy accomplishments. It follows that strength, elegance, competence, and brilliance are sometimes deeply shameful. In some contexts they can be self-defeating, destructive, "easy ways out."

The prideworthiness of experiences that we may otherwise find shameful or expressions of inadequacies is all the more true for our having to experience them genuinely as confused, weak, discomposed, awkward, trivial, and so on. We need to live them in the double way that I argued of essential truth. We need to be fully inside these experiences and modes of behavior where, if we were to take pride in them, we would not truly be practicing and undergoing them. And we also need to be at a distance from them, oriented toward them from the outside, where we can and should take pride in them.[22] This kind of "sometimes always straddled" positioning is what I described in the Preface and later as "a delicately poised ungainliness, or a perfect, ungainly poised elegance."

It follows from this discussion of pride that we are sometimes ashamed where we should be proud, and sometimes proud where we should be ashamed, and these in the most important areas of life. More accurately, we are sometimes only ashamed where we should be proud in one way and ashamed or unmoved in another, and we are sometimes only proud where we should be ashamed in one way and proud or unmoved in another.

In fact, even what is prideworthy itself, just by virtue of being prideworthy, can have shameful effects, and vice versa. When Austen's Emma, for example, pictures someone who can "adapt his conversation to the taste of everybody, and has the power as well as the wish of being universally agreeable. . . . just as propriety may require," Mr. Knightley answers, "he will be the most insufferable fellow breathing! What! . . . to . . . make everybody's talents conduce to the display of his own superiority!"[23] And where incompatible sets of principles are relevant, being prideworthy in accordance with one set can shamefully disrespect the other.

Conversely, as I argued above, incompatible principles may be both relevant and entirely external to each other, and then incompatible senses of pride need not conflict. For example, a sense of being uniquely worthwhile or special, and even a sense of superiority involved in that feeling, need not conflict fundamentally with respecting equivalent pride in others. On the contrary, because rigorous pride is partly self-external and self-canceling, it is precisely because one can feel wholehearted, unique pride sometimes and/or in some respects that one can endorse the wholehearted, unique pride of others, with respect to whose experience and concerns one is inadequate. In fact, also because of the self-externality of pride, part of one's own pride, sometimes and/or in some respects, is precisely pride in one's sillinesses and smallnesses as these emerge in the light of others' and the world's contrasting admirable qualities.

If we want to ensure as far as possible that our behavior and attitudes are prideworthy, then, we need to take this self-interfering, interventive dimension into account. That is, we need to operate also at what I called in Idea 1 the metalevel of conduct, conduct dealing with our conduct. And at this level, for example, the ways of maintaining descriptive truth by means of its interventive properties that I described in Idea 2 are all ways of behaving truly to situations, and so are means of trying to be prideworthy.

These include ways of being simply mistaken or clumsy. Like the relation of rigorous thought to thoughtlessness, then, and like the relation of other-sensibility to other-insensibility, this thoughtful way of responding with pride or shame is not simply an opposite to the thoughtless way, but is both opposed or external to it and also entirely of it.[24]

If these are insights, I suggest that Plato's writings work everywhere with them and insights like them. His writings are a wealth of exquisitely delicate clumsinesses, showing the firmly hesitant, perfectly poised ungainliness with which truth and reality are, sometimes always, at odds with themselves and, sometimes always, at odds even with this being at odds. I have tried to show in this book that recognizing and actively living in keeping with this kind of unevenly even consistency of truth are also deeply relevant to our own relation to truth, and to our own lives and social concerns.

Notes

Preface

1. One variety of this is camp. Perhaps this is the bottom of camp.

Introduction

1. For variations of the view that the dialogues are designed to guide the reader's own thinking, see, e.g., Angelo Corlett, "Interpreting Plato's Dialogues," *Classical Quarterly* 47.2 (1997): 423–437, who gives a helpful overview of the literature on both these and an opposed view; Hans-Georg Gadamer, *Dialogue and Dialectic: Eight Hermeneutical Studies on Plato,* trans. P. Christopher Smith (New Haven, Conn.: Yale University Press, 1980); Jacob Klein, introductory remarks, *A Commentary on Plato's* Meno (Chicago: University of Chicago Press, 1965), esp. 9; Berel Lang, *The Anatomy of Philosophical Style* (Cambridge, Mass.: Basil Blackwell, 1990), 15; Mitchell H. Miller, Jr., "Introduction," in *Plato's* Parmenides: *The Conversion of the Soul* (Princeton, N.J.: Princeton University Press; University Park: Pennsylvania State University Press, 1991 [1986]); Kenneth M. Sayre, *Plato's Literary Garden: How to Read a Platonic Dialogue* (Notre Dame, Ind.: University of Notre Dame Press, 1995).

2. I. M. Crombie, *An Examination of Plato's Doctrines,* 2 vols. (London: Routledge & Kegan Paul, 1962), 1:14–23, gives a helpful discussion of the difficulties of interpretation resulting from Plato's use of dialogue form.

3. Plato spells this out himself by putting the following words into Socrates' mouth in the *Phaedrus:* the speechmaker "must analyse . . . the nature of soul, and discover what type of speech is suitable for each type of soul. Finally, he must arrange and organize his speech accordingly, addressing a simple speech to a simple soul, but to those which are more complex something of greater complexity which embraces the whole range of tones"; *Phaedrus,* in Plato, *Phaedrus and Letters VII and VIII,* trans. W. Hamilton (Harmondsworth, U.K.: Penguin, 1973), 277B–C. Unless otherwise indicated, I use this translation throughout. Socrates is earlier made to specify that the art of rhetoric is a matter not only of "words . . . spoken in a court of law or before some other public body" but also those spoken "in private conversation" (261A). His statements about speeches would therefore apply also to dialogues, with respect to both the words passing between the characters in the dialogue and the words of the dialogue as intended for specific kinds or situations of readers.

It is true that Plato himself does not make these statements but says them through the mouth of one of his characters. But they are thoughts presented cogently in this dialogue, and as Plato also has Socrates say in this same dialogue, criticizing Phaedrus, "truth is not enough for you; you think it matters who the speaker is and where he comes from" (275C). I return to this principle of attending to the truth despite the speaker in another section of the book.

4. Plato, *Phaedrus*, 278B–E.

5. Plato, *Letter VII*, trans. L. A. Post, in *Plato: The Collected Dialogues*, ed. Edith Hamilton and Huntington Cairns (Princeton, N.J.: Princeton University Press, 1961), 341B–342A. Unless otherwise indicated, I use this translation throughout.

6. See Klein, *Commentary*, 3; Eric Voegelin, *Plato* (Baton Rouge: Louisiana State University Press, 1966 [1957]), 10–11; Martha C. Nussbaum, *The Fragility of Goodness: Luck and Ethics in Greek Tragedy and Philosophy* (New York: Cambridge University Press, 1986), 12: "epic and tragic poets were widely assumed to be the central ethical thinkers and teachers of Greece; nobody thought of their work as less serious, less aimed at truth, than the speculative prose treatises of historians and philosophers." For a detailed discussion of the relations between Plato's dialogues and both the comic and tragic poetry with which he was familiar, see Jill Gordon, *Turning toward Philosophy: Literary Device and Dramatic Structure in Plato's Dialogues* (University Park: Pennsylvania State University Press, 1999), chap. 3.

7. See Crombie, *Examination*, 1:20–21: "entertainment" is one "of the elements which I take to be commonly present in the dialogues. . . . This takes two forms, firstly simple comedy, whether broad or sophisticated, and secondly intellectual teasing."

The classical Greeks have been widely thought since the start of the modern period to have embodied the most perfect form of Western human culture, in which art, religion, and social and personal life all harmonized, whether serenely or in impressive and productive tension, to make a life lived at its fullest and best. For example, Shelley, preface to "Hellas: A Lyrical Drama," in *The Poetical Works of Shelley*, ed. N. F. Ford (Boston, Mass.: Houghton Mifflin, 1975), 319: "The human form and the human mind attained to a perfection in Greece, which has impressed its image on those faultless productions whose very fragments are the despair of modern art." This view goes with a depreciation, if not a deprecation, of modern ignobility. In particular, the modern enjoyment of mere trivial entertainment (like the novel, seen to be a decadent art form, as in the Hellenistic period following the "decline" of classical Greek culture), detached from and replacing the sacred and politically effective dimensions of life, is contrasted with the immediate social and sacred importance of classical Greek art.

I believe this view of the classical separation of the sacred and the trivial is a little simple. I think it is possibly true that art for the classical Greeks was not just entertainment as we think of entertainment. But I think it is also true that entertainment for them was in many respects as trivial as it is for us. A quick glance at Aristophanes' comedies will support this statement. And as Marcel Gutwirth explains, "laughter is rigorously incompatible with awe. . . . The ease, in fact, with which Homeric religion slides in and out of a sense of the gods' divinity marks it as possessed of a free-dom from awe we can no longer fully understand. Laughter is not out of place on Mount Olympus . . . and we mere mortals join in"; Marcel Gutwirth, *Laughing Matter: An Essay on the Comic* (Ithaca, N.Y.: Cornell University Press, 1993), 17–18. The difference between the classical Greeks and us, perhaps, is that they were big or noble enough to accept what is sacred and socially and politically significant about what is purely and simply trivial. Perhaps it is we who impoverish entertain-ment by regarding triviality as not good enough for the human condition, rather than the Greeks who gave life its due by not settling for "mere" entertainment. Perhaps they gave life its due by settling for just that, and perhaps we need to get off our high horses and learn from the classical imperfection of the classical Greeks.

8. Corlett, "Interpreting," for example, defends a variant of this view.

9. Diogenes Laertius, for example, reports that Plato burned his poetry on meeting Socrates; Diogenes Laertius, *Lives of Eminent Philosophers,* 2 vols., trans. R. D. Hicks, Loeb Classical Library (Cambridge, Mass.: Harvard University Press, 1972), 1:281.

10. Drew Hyland, *The Virtue of Philosophy: An Interpretation of Plato's* Charmides (Athens, Ohio: Ohio University Press, 1981), 91. Charles Griswold also argues that "the philosopher is compelled to question not just this or that doctrine but also why anyone should be persuaded by the metaphilosophical view that philosophy as such is possible." Even more, "Socrates cannot 'justify' or 'demonstrate' his own activity except by coming across . . . someone who is *not* already persuaded by its possibility and worth"; Charles L. Griswold, Jr., "Plato's Metaphilosophy: Why Plato Wrote Dialogues," in *Platonic Writings, Platonic Readings,* ed. Charles L. Griswold, Jr. (New York: Routledge; University Park: Pennsylvania State University Press, 2002 [1988]), 156–157. Similarly, Debra Nails notes that what she calls Plato's "method-ological double open-endedness" demands "that the dialectical method itself—its assumptions, its procedures, and its results—remain subject to radical challenge"; Debra Nails, *Agora, Academy, and the Conduct of Philosophy* (Dordrecht, Netherlands: Kluwer Academic, 1995), 226. See also Charles Altieri, "Plato's Masterplot: Ideal-ization, Contradiction, and the Transformation of Rhetorical Ethos," in *Intimate Conflict: Contradiction in Literary and Philosophical Discourse,* ed. Brian G. Caraher (Albany: State University of New York Press, 1992), 51: "Plato's task" in the *Gorgias* "is to refute" the antiphilosophical Callicles "without relying on the authority of philosophy."

11. For a thorough history of interpretive approaches to Plato, see E. N. Tiger-stedt, *Interpreting Plato* (Uppsala, Sweden: Almqvist & Wiksell, 1977). For an illumi-nating overview, different from mine, of modern approaches, see Francisco J. Gonzalez, *Dialectic and Dialogue: Plato's Practice of Philosophical Inquiry* (Evanston, Ill.: Northwestern University Press, 1998), 1–6.

12. A few examples of a very extensive literature: Francis M. Cornford, *Before and after Socrates* (Cambridge, U.K.: Cambridge University Press, 1932); W. D. Ross, *Plato's Theory of Ideas* (Oxford: Clarendon Press, 1951); J. E. Raven, *Plato's Thought in the Making* (Cambridge, U.K.: Cambridge University Press, 1965).

13. Plato, *Sophist*, trans. F. M. Cornford, in *Plato: The Collected Dialogues,* ed. Edith Hamilton and Huntington Cairns (Princeton, N.J.: Princeton University Press, 1961), 243C. Unless otherwise noted, I use this translation throughout.

14. Shelley, for example, also found it true:

The One remains, the many change and pass;
Heaven's light forever shines, Earth's shadows fly;
Life, like a dome of many-colored glass,
Stains the white radiance of Eternity.

Percy Bysshe Shelley, "Adonais: An Elegy on the Death of John Keats," in *Poetical Works,* 316.

15. Aristotle, *Aristotle's* Posterior Analytics, trans. Hippocrates G. Apostle (Grinnell, Iowa: Peripatetic Press, 1981), i.22.83a33–34. Unless otherwise noted, I use this translation throughout. Nussbaum comments on the word translated here by "meaningless sound" that "*Teretismata* are meaningless sounds you make when you are singing to yourself; we might render them as 'dum-de-dum-dums'"; Nussbaum, *Fragility,* 257.

16. "If, now, the good itself is to be different from what it is to be good, and 'animal itself' from what it is to be an animal, and being itself from what it is to be, then there will be other primary beings and natures and ideas beyond those recognized; and if 'what it is to be' belongs to primary beings, those others will be the prior primary beings. Similarly, if the being of ideas and the meaning of ideas are disconnected from one another, there will be no knowledge of the former, and the latter will not be. . . . It is necessary, accordingly, for the good to be one with what it is to be good . . . and so in the case of all things that . . . are primary and in themselves. For it is enough if beings have this trait, even if there are no ideas; or rather, perhaps, even if there are ideas." Aristotle, *Metaphysics,* trans. R. Hope (New York: Columbia University Press; Ann Arbor: University of Michigan Press, 1960 [1952]), vii.6.1031a26–1031b16. Unless otherwise noted, I use this translation throughout. And, "Now, since it is equally impossible to exclude the good from first principles and to include it among them in the manner of these men, it is clear that there is something wrong in the way principles and the most primary beings have been conceived" (Aristotle, *Metaphysics,* xiv.5.1092a8–15).

17. See Aristotle, *Metaphysics,* iv.1, on the science of "being as being" (1003a17), and i.2, on the various ways in which knowledge of being in this sense is the most important knowledge.

18. See, e.g., Joseph Owens, *The Doctrine of Being in the Aristotelian Metaphysics: A Study in the Greek Background of Mediaeval Thought,* 3rd ed. (Toronto: Pontifical Institute of Mediaeval Studies, 1978), 73–74.

19. Plato, *Republic,* 2 vols., trans. Paul Shorey, Loeb Classical Library (Cambridge, Mass.: Harvard University Press, 1935), 2:505A: "μέγιστον μάθημα."

20. Plato, *Republic,* 2:509B: "ἐπέκεινα τῆς οὐσίας."

21. See Klein, *Commentary,* 3–4; Gonzalez, *Dialectic,* 3–6. For helpful contemporary collections, see Charles L. Griswold, Jr., ed., *Platonic Writings, Platonic Readings*

(New York: Routledge; University Park: Pennsylvania State University Press, 2002 [1988]); James C. Klagge and Nicholas D. Smith, eds., *Methods of Interpreting Plato and His Dialogues* (New York: Oxford University Press, 1992); Gerald A. Press, ed., *Plato's Dialogues: New Studies and Interpretations* (Lanham, Md.: Rowman & Littlefield, 1993). For the ancient beginnings of this tradition, see, e.g., Julia Annas, "Plato the Skeptic," in Klagge and Smith, *Methods*.

22. "[T]he Good . . . is not simply a different *being,* but precisely the *oneness* of all beings . . . that within which *different* things are *at one.* . . . Socrates, recognizing the ultimate powerlessness of *logos* [approximately, speech or language] to convey this One . . . remains silent; for, as far as the greatest matter is concerned, Plato thinks that 'it can never be just said' "; Eva Brann, "The Music of the *Republic,*" in *Four Essays on Plato's* Republic, double issue of *St. John's Review* 39.1–2 (1989–1990): 70–71 (Annapolis, Md.: St. John's College, 1990), my insertion. And "the Good has everywhere prepared places for the soul to know" (74). Brann argues on the basis of the *Republic* that the One, as a source that runs through all the Ideas, "ought not to be called" an Idea (83). John Sallis writes: "To say that the good confers truth means: the good confers, makes possible, that kind of showing in which something can show itself as one"; and "the good is 'beyond being.' To be beyond being means: to be beyond (outside of) all showing in which something would show itself as one. Hence, Socrates is saying that it belongs to the good not to show itself as one; the one does not show itself as one. This means, in turn, that the good always shows itself *as it is not* (since it is one—even *the* one). *The good shows itself only through images*"; John Sallis, *Being and Logos: The Way of Platonic Dialogue,* 2nd ed. (Atlantic Highlands, N.J.: Humanities Press, 1986), 409, 412. And Robert Williamson: "The *agathon*[Good]-One is the exemplary source of all communities . . . of relata without being itself essentially related to anything else"; Robert B. Williamson, "*Eidos* and *Agathon* in Plato's *Republic,*" in *Four Essays on Plato's* Republic, 121, my insertion.

23. Jane Austen, *Pride and Prejudice* (Harmondsworth, U.K.: Penguin, 1972), 51.

24. Plato, *Republic,* 1:382A–B.

25. Jane Austen, *Emma* (Harmondsworth, U.K.: Penguin, 1966), 39–40.

26. Judith Butler, for example, writes, "The cultural matrix through which gender identity has become intelligible requires that certain kinds of 'identities' cannot 'exist.' . . . Indeed, precisely because certain kinds of 'gender identities' fail to conform to those norms of cultural intelligibility, they appear only as developmental failures or logical impossibilities from within that domain." Judith Butler, *Gender Trouble: Feminism and the Subversion of Identity* (New York: Routledge, 1990), 17. Rosalind Coward and John Ellis, in the course of a neo-Marxist account of political ideology, write that such ideology is "effective precisely for the reason that it appears as 'natural,' 'the way things are.' " And "it is not perceived as a limitation," but "has succeeded when it has produced the 'natural attitude,' when for example the existing relations of power are . . . perceived precisely as the way things are, ought to be and will be." In fact, they argue, "what is produced in ideology is the very basis of the [human] subject's activity, . . . and the coherency of that subject." This coher-

ency, since it is constructed by ideology, is that of socially acceptable forms of being a subject or a person, and these are then also perceived as natural, as the only way they can be. Rosalind Coward and John Ellis, *Language and Materialism: Developments in Semiology and the Theory of the Subject* (London: Routledge and Kegan Paul, 1977), 67–68, my insertion.

27. In a different way, Donald Davidson also argues that an account of mistakes cannot simply eliminate them, whether by explaining them away or by entirely rejecting them as "just mistakes": "The underlying paradox of irrationality, from which no theory can entirely escape, is this: if we explain it too well, we turn it into a concealed form of rationality; while if we assign incoherence too glibly, we merely compromise our ability to diagnose irrationality by withdrawing the background of rationality needed to justify any diagnosis at all"; Donald Davidson, "Paradoxes of Irrationality," in *Philosophical Essays on Freud,* ed. Richard Wollheim and James Hopkins (New York: Cambridge University Press, 1982), 303. More simply, Bernard Williams comments that, "As more than one philosopher has remarked, illusion is itself part of reality"; Bernard Williams, *Shame and Necessity* (Berkeley: University of California Press, 1993), 11.

28. Thomas Nagel, *The View from Nowhere* (New York: Oxford University Press, 1986), 4, 7–8. See also Nagel, "What Is It Like to Be a Bat?," in *Mortal Questions* (New York: Cambridge University Press, 1979).

29. In the very different context of arguing that relativism need not be self-refuting or paradoxical, Steven Hales makes a case for the sense of similar kinds of distinction, so that we can and need to specify, for example, "truths" that are "merely relative (and not also absolutely true)"; Steven D. Hales, "A Consistent Relativism," *Mind* 106.421 (1997):38.

30. Other-insensibility is a more profound problem than "prejudice" in the contemporary sense of "unreasonable discrimination." Such discrimination is at least sensible of (recognizes or registers) the other consciousness, so that there is in fact mutual engagement and the bare reality itself of the other is acknowledged. I think Austen's sense of "prejudice" is closer to what I am calling "other-insensible"—it refers to assumptions or preconceptions ("prejudgments") as much as to feelings and attitudes.

I should emphasize that none of this is to say that the reality of the other as the person who is *sensible* of others her/himself sees it is automatically the truth, nor that recognizing the reality of another is automatically not itself insensibility. It is to say, rather, that the insensible consciousness recognizes only the *possibility* of one view of the issue, and to that extent the perception of the *mere possibility* of two views is comparatively not other-insensible. The recognizing person could happen (on some occasion or constitutionally) also to recognize only the possibility of one view, in this case the view of the other person, and in that case is also other-insensible. Austen writes of Mrs. Dashwood reacting to ungenerous conduct, "in *her* mind there was a sense of honour so keen, a generosity so romantic, that any offence of the kind, by whomsoever given or received, was to her a source of immoveable disgust"; Jane Austen, *Sense and Sensibility* (Harmondsworth, U.K.: Penguin, 1969),

41. As Austen suggests, what is needed to live fairly is also sense, and not only sensibility.

31. On this issue, see, e.g., Jacques Derrida, "White Mythology: Metaphor in the Text of Philosophy," in *Margins of Philosophy,* trans. A. Bass (Chicago: University of Chicago Press, 1982), 207–272.

32. See, e.g., on Plato's relation to comedy and tragedy, Edward G. Ballard, *Socratic Ignorance: An Essay on Platonic Self-Knowledge* (The Hague, Netherlands: Martinus Nijhoff, 1965), 31, 34.

33. G. C. Field, *Plato and His Contemporaries: A Study in Fourth-Century Life and Thought* (London: Methuen & Co, 1930), 51.

34. Plato, *Charmides,* trans. Donald Watt, in *Early Socratic Dialogues,* ed. T. J. Saunders (Harmondsworth, U.K.: Penguin, 1987), 166C–E. Unless otherwise noted, I use this translation throughout.

35. Aristotle, *Nicomachean Ethics,* trans. W. D. Ross, in *The Basic Works of Aristotle,* ed. Richard McKeon (New York: Random House, 1941), i.6.1096a12–16.

36. See, e.g., Terry Penner, "Socrates and the Early Dialogues," in *The Cambridge Companion to Plato,* ed. Richard Kraut (New York: Cambridge University Press, 1992), 124.

37. For an influential defense of the "periods" view, and in particular of the difference between Socratic and Platonic dialogues, see Gregory Vlastos, *Socrates: Ironist and Moral Philosopher* (Ithaca, N.Y.: Cornell University Press, 1991). For challenges to the distinction between Socratic and Platonic dialogues, see, e.g., Gonzalez, *Dialectic,* 275 n. 2, which also gives helpful references to the recent literature; and Charles H. Kahn, "Did Plato Write Socratic Dialogues?" in *Essays on the Philosophy of Socrates,* ed. Hugh H. Benson (New York: Oxford University Press, 1992 [1981]), e.g., 47: "I . . . doubt the historicity of the dialogues . . . as reports of philosophical conversations in the fifth century. The dialogues belong to Plato and to the fourth century."

38. See, e.g., Nails, *Agora,* pt. II.

39. Ibid., 55. Ruby Blondell, similarly, notes "the findings of modern scholarship showing that chronological claims based on the putative development of Plato's style and/or the content of the dialogues are untenable"; Ruby Blondell, *The Play of Character in Plato's Dialogues* (New York: Cambridge University Press, 2002), 11.

Part I: Introductory

1. See especially Jacob Klein, *A Commentary on Plato's* Meno (Chicago: University of Chicago Press, 1965). This kind of reading reaches a consummation, I think, in Anne Freire Ashbaugh's beautiful *Plato's Theory of Explanation: A Study of the Cosmological Account in the* Timaeus (Albany: State University of New York Press, 1988).

But, with respect to my choice of example, see Stanley Rosen, *Plato's* Statesman: *The Web of Politics* (New Haven, Conn.: Yale University Press, 1995), who mentions "the path-breaking work of Leo Strauss (itself anticipated by

Heidegger . . .)" in connection with "the substantive importance of the dramatic structure of the [*Statesman*]," and "a spreading tendency to accept Strauss' thesis without giving him credit for it" (192, 193, my insertion, 194).

2. Hans-Georg Gadamer, *Plato's Dialectical Ethics: Phenomenological Interpretations Relating to the* Philebus, trans. R. M. Wallace (New Haven, Conn.: Yale University Press, 1991), xxv.

3. For a contemporary account sympathetic to the idea and kind of approach that I think is to be found more comprehensively in Plato, see Susan Sontag's essay "Against Interpretation," especially if read together with her "Notes on 'Camp.'" Both essays are in Susan Sontag, *Against Interpretation and Other Essays* (New York: Doubleday, 1966).

4. So, for example, Fichte writes, "From anywhere whatsoever—from somewhere invisible to you and to all mortal eyes—a spark reaches you. You are . . . led into your own most secret depths, without knowing how you got there." "Concerning the Difference between the Spirit and the Letter within Philosophy," in *Fichte: Early Philosophical Writings,* trans. D. Breazeale (Ithaca, N.Y.: Cornell University Press, 1988), 195. See also Martin Heidegger, *Early Greek Thinking: The Dawn of Western Philosophy,* trans. D. F. Krell and F. A. Capuzzi (San Francisco: Harper & Row, 1975, 1984), 55: "To search for influences and dependencies among thinkers is to misunderstand thinking. Every thinker is dependent—upon the address of Being."

5. Plato, *Phaedrus,* 275C–D.

6. For example, "you have often heard me say before . . . that I am subject to a divine or supernatural experience, . . . a sort of voice which comes to me, and . . . always dissuades me from what I am proposing to do." Plato, *Apology,* trans. H. Tredennick, in *Collected Dialogues,* 31C–D. Unless otherwise noted, this translation will be used throughout. See also *Phaedrus,* 242B–C.

7. Plato's *Ion,* for example, is devoted to questions about the truthfulness of divine inspiration. Plato, *Ion,* trans. Lane Cooper, in *Collected Dialogues.*

8. George Plochmann, for example, writes, "Plato uses . . . no single ladder of methods, but instead an enormously complicated checker-board of features, based upon leading terms in each dialectic, their number, the direction of their application, the kinds of opposition to which each term is subject, the use and kinds of causes sought, the purposes held in view, the varying degrees of flexibility, precision, and comprehensiveness of each method." "Socrates, the Stranger from Elea, and Some Others," *Classical Philology* 49.4 (1954): 229–230.

With respect to metaphysics in general, R. G. Collingwood writes of the "logical relation . . . between the presuppositions" whose "constellation" makes up a metaphysics, that "it need not be a relation of such a kind that a person supposing any one of them is logically committed to supposing all or indeed any of the others. Metaphysicians have often thought it was; but that is because they thought of metaphysics as a kind of quasi-mathematics, and did not realize that it was a kind of history." In fact Collingwood argues that the relation between the suppositions of a metaphysics not only "need not be of this kind; but actually it cannot be," and, he continues, "It follows that the literary form of a treatise in which a metaphysician sets out to enumerate and discuss the absolute presuppositions of thought . . . cannot be the form of a continuous argument . . . It must be the form of a *catalogue raisonné*, as in the fourth book of Aristotle's *Metaphysics* or in the *Quaestiones* of a medieval metaphysician." That is, it must be partly just a list, in whatever arrangement is convenient. *An Essay on Metaphysics* (Oxford: Clarendon Press, 1940), 66–68. And Wittgenstein writes, for example, "Mere description is so difficult because one believes that one needs to fill out the facts in order to understand them. It is as if one saw a screen with scattered color-patches, and said: the way they are here, they are unintelligible; they only make sense when one completes them into a shape.— Whereas I want to say: Here *is* the whole. (If you complete it, you falsify it.)" *Remarks on the Philosophy of Psychology*, 2 vols., trans. G. E. M. Anscombe, ed. G. E. M. Anscombe and G. H. von Wright (Chicago: University of Chicago Press, 1980), 1:52e.

9. Plato, *Statesman,* trans. J. B. Skemp, in *Plato: The Collected Dialogues,* ed. Edith Hamilton and Huntington Cairns (Princeton, N.J.: Princeton University Press, 1961), 278C, my emphasis. Unless otherwise indicated, I use this translation throughout.

10. Plato, *Parmenides,* trans. F. M. Cornford, in *Collected Dialogues,* 130C–E. Unless otherwise noted, I use this translation throughout.

Idea 1

1. Berel Lang, ed., *The Anatomy of Philosophical Style* (Cambridge, Mass.: Basil Blackwell, 1990), 159–167, touches on this idea in a provocative discussion of the distinction between fiction and reality. He also asks, "The distinction between fiction and nonfiction. . . . Is *that* distinction fiction or nonfiction?" (169).

2. This argument embraces and holds for an understanding of "fairness" both in terms of its effects (that is, in a consequentialist or instrumentalist way) and in terms of simply doing the right thing because it is right (that is, in a deontological way). The conflict between nature and artifice also emerges in a deontological account because of the role here of truth to oneself: one ought not to lie (pretend to be other than one is) *and* one ought not to be unfairly prejudiced. And of course there are effects of suppressing the truth about oneself, like unfair resentment, that are also simply bad from a deontological viewpoint.

Plato's own ethics is very largely based on achieving happiness (that is, it is eudaimonistic), as was typical of his society and age. While I have included a comment about effects on the person's happiness, it is really rather part of a consequentialist argument and also of an argument from principle. Nonetheless, the eudaimonist view is really a restricted form of consequentialism, so the consequentialist arguments should hold for Plato's view too. I try to show later in the book, however, that eudaimonism does not exhaust Plato's ethical insights.

3. Donald Davidson, for example, notes, about a person who "forms a positive or negative judgment of some of his own desires, and . . . acts to change these

desires," that "From the point of view of the changed desire, there is no reason for the change—the reason comes from an independent source, and is based on further, and partly contrary, considerations. The agent has reasons for changing his own habits and character, but these reasons come from a domain of values necessarily extrinsic to the contents of the views or values to undergo change"; Donald Davidson, "Paradoxes of Irrationality," in *Philosophical Essays on Freud,* ed. Richard Wollheim and James Hopkins (New York: Cambridge University Press, 1982), 305.

4. Hyland argues that "we are always oriented out of ourselves toward that which we are not but which we wish to become or possess. Adequate reflection on what we are leads us beyond ourselves to that which we, as mediators, bind together, namely the world of our experience and the source of intelligibility of that world. . . . In this sense, then, Sartre's famous dictum 'we are what we are not and are not what we are' has a Platonic counterpart"; Drew Hyland, *The Virtue of Philosophy: An Interpretation of Plato's* Charmides (Athens, Ohio: Ohio University Press, 1981), 66. And Günter Figal notes, analogously, that for Plato, "action and understanding must not be closed off from each other. . . . Yet both are forms of life in themselves, each with its own different experiences of freedom. If it is to be otherwise, then the actual end of action must become the point of reference for understanding, and by breaking free from its place in action, it first establishes action's freedom. A life which is thoroughly consistent with freedom must be able to be at home elsewhere and at the same time remain itself"; Günter Figal, "The Idea and Mixture of the Good," trans. Michael McGettigan and Cara Gendel Ryan, in *Retracing the Platonic Text,* ed. John Russon and John Sallis (Evanston, Ill.: Northwestern University Press, 2000), 94–95.

Collingwood notes, more generally, that "a thinking mind is never 'simply' anything: it is its own activities of thought, and it is not these 'simply' (which, if it means anything, means 'immediately'), for thought is not mere immediate experience but always reflection or self-knowledge, the knowledge of oneself as living in these activities." Robin George Collingwood, *The Idea of History,* rev. ed. by Jan van der Dussen (New York: Oxford University Press, 1994), 297. Jacqueline Rose nicely expresses the nature of the kind of conflict I am discussing here in connection with this identity that is not simply the same as itself, although she does so on a different basis, in a feminist critique of Freud's analysis of "Dora": "Dora's bodily symptoms . . . are the expression of a masculine identification, through which identification alone access to the maternal and feminine body is possible. . . . Thus access to the (maternal) body is only possible now through a masculine identification, which access *then threatens the very category of identification itself,* that is, Dora as subject"; Jacqueline Rose, "Dora: Fragment of an Analysis," in *In Dora's Case: Freud—Hysteria—Feminism,* ed. Charles Bernheimer and Claire Kahane (New York: Columbia University Press. 1985), 137, my emphasis. In other words, if what it is to be one's self is to be female, and one achieves that self through identifying with—becoming the same as—a male, then to be one's self is to be the same as what one's self excludes.

5. In fact, for Plato "really to be is to be 'its own self according to itself: αὐτὸ
καθ αὐτό.' The ultimate mark of true being lies therefore in 'selfhood.' . . . [When]
we ask ourselves what it would mean, for any one of us, to 'become another
one' . . . the question does not make sense. *I cannot become another,* for the very
simple reason that, so long as I can say *I,* I am not yet another, whereas, as soon as
the other is there, there appears on the scene a second *I* which is wholly unrelated
to me." Etienne Gilson, *Being and Some Philosophers,* 2nd ed. (Toronto: Pontifical
Institute of Mediaeval Studies, 1952), 10–11, my insertion. In keeping with the
longer tradition of Plato interpretation, Gilson understands the consequence of this
to be that "for all that which is . . . the abolition of its self-identity amounts to its
pure and simple annihilation" (11).

6. See the end of note 5 above.

7. Since the status of the ideas of "falsehood," "difference," and "artificiality,"
for example, needs to remain undecided while thinking about the truth of a particular case, it would be more accurate to write "falsehood"/falsehood, "difference"/
difference, and "artificiality"/artificiality.

8. Karl Jaspers also argues that it is necessary for thinking at its deepest and most
comprehensive to accept the contradiction of conceiving more than one absolute
position. He describes our existence as coming to stand "before its final limits: that
there are many truths in the sense of existential absolutes"; Karl Jaspers, *Reason and
Existenz: Five Lectures,* trans. William Earle (Milwaukee, Wis.: Marquette University Press, 1997), 100. He elaborates, "Through reason I catch sight of something
which is only communicable in the form of contradiction and paradox. Here a
rational a-logic arises, a true reason which reaches its goal through the shattering of
the logic of the understanding" (112). Nelson Goodman argues for an analogous
paradox of incompatible "right versions" of the world (for his use of the term "paradox," see note 21 to Idea 2 below), although he does not see it as involving contradiction. (He argues that each version is simply a different world from the others. As
a result there is no common world in which to compare them, and therefore no
conflict between them.) In discussing different versions of the world, he points out
that, "If I ask about the world, you can offer to tell me how it is under one or more
frames of reference; but if I insist that you tell me how it is apart from all frames,
what can you say? We are confined to ways of describing whatever is described."
As a result we have "contrasting right versions not all reducible to one." Nelson
Goodman, *Ways of Worldmaking* (Indianapolis, Ind.: Hackett, 1978), 2–3, 5. See also
Maurice Merleau-Ponty, *Signs,* trans. Richard C. McCleary (Evanston, Ill.: Northwestern University Press, 1964), on even individual *things,* within one and the same
world: "each thing claiming an absolute presence which is not compossible with
the absolute presence of the other things, and which they nevertheless have all
together by virtue of a configurational meaning which is in no way indicated by its
'theoretical meaning'" (181).

9. Goodman suggests that "one might say that there is only one world but this
holds for each of the many worlds. . . . [T]he equivocation is stark—yet perhaps
negotiable." He advocates "a policy common in daily life and impressively endorsed

by modern science: namely, judicious vacillation. . . . We are monists, pluralists, or nihilists . . . as befits the context." Nelson Goodman, "Notes on the Well-Made World," *Partisan Review* 51 (1984):276–288, 278. And in *Ways of Worldmaking* he notes, "While I stress the multiplicity of right world-versions, I by no means insist that there are many worlds—or indeed any; for . . . the question whether two versions are of the same world has as many good answers as there are good interpretations of the words 'versions of the same world.' The monist can always contend that two versions need only be right to be accounted versions of the same world. The pluralist can always reply by asking what the world is like apart from all versions" (96). See also Bernard Williams, who argues in the context of ethics (to very different conclusions from my own) that "Even if there is no way in which divergent ethical beliefs can be brought to converge by independent inquiry or rational argument, this fact will not imply relativism. Each outlook may still be making claims it intends to apply to the whole world, not just to that part of it which is its 'own' world"; Bernard Williams, *Ethics and the Limits of Philosophy* (Cambridge, Mass.: Harvard University Press, 1985), 159.

Clearly this idea of a "sometimes always" logic is relevant to pluralist ideas of truth and so also to a political pluralism. In pluralist political philosophy, Ernesto Laclau and Chantal Mouffe, for example, take a step potentially in the direction of this kind of logic. They recognize different and conflicting "social logics," that cannot "be embraced and explained by a single discourse," but instead form "a polyphony of voices, each of which constructs its own irreducible discursive identity"; Ernesto Laclau and Chantal Mouffe, *Hegemony and Socialist Strategy: Towards a Radical Democratic Politics,* trans. W. Moore and P. Cammack (London: Verso, 1985), 183, 191. As I understand them, however, they stop short of pursuing the implication that each also irreducibly constructs the identity of *all the others* within its own terms too. Its own logic is a *logic,* and so must govern the sense it makes of everything and not just of its own identity. And if it conflicts with other logics, it must make sense of other "voices" and of other logics themselves in ways that conflict with and exclude how they make sense of themselves. This consequence brings us to the logic of "sometimes a thing is exclusively this and sometimes the same thing is exclusively that." Laclau and Mouffe certainly also stop short of recognizing that, by the very principle that conflicting logics are possible, there may be logics that rightly reject the idea of differing social logics, that is of pluralism itself: "this point is decisive: there is no radical and plural democracy without renouncing the discourse of the universal and its implicit assumption of a privileged point of access to 'the truth' "; ibid., 191–192. Mouffe's later work is no different in these respects. For example, "conflict and division are inherent to politics and . . . there is no place where reconciliation could be definitively achieved as the full actualization of the unity of 'the people' "; Chantal Mouffe, *The Democratic Paradox* (London: Verso, 2000), 15–16. See, similarly, James Tully, *Strange Multiplicity: Constitutionalism in an Age of Diversity* (Cambridge, U.K.: Cambridge University Press, 1995), e.g., "The aspectival character of [just political] constitutions is not grasped by a comprehensive representation, but by participation in a practical dialogue where limited and complementary stories are exchanged. . . . There is not one . . . narrative that gives the partnership its unity, but a diversity of criss-crossing and contested narratives" (183, my insertion). This kind of rejection of "grand narratives" is a commonplace in postmodern literature. But as David Simpson comments, "What, we might wonder, is the grand narrative behind the compulsive appeal of little stories?" David Simpson, *The Academic Postmodern and the Rule of Literature: A Report on Half-Knowledge* (Chicago: University of Chicago Press, 1995), 29. See also Alain Badiou, *Manifesto for Philosophy*, ed. and trans. Norman Madarasz (Albany, N.Y.: State University of New York Press, 1999), e.g., "The announcement of the 'End of the Grand Narratives' is as immodest as the Grand Narrative itself, the certainty of the 'end of metaphysics' proceeds within the metaphysical element of certainty. . . . The end of the End of History is cut from the same cloth as this End" (30–31).

Leo Strauss makes the point that "Historicism assumes that . . . the thought of all epochs is equally 'true,' because every philosophy is essentially the expression of its time. . . . But classical philosophy, which claimed to teach *the* truth, and not merely the truth of classical Greece, cannot be understood on the basis of this assumption"; Leo Strauss, "On a New Interpretation of Plato's Political Philosophy," *Social Research* 13 (1946):326–367, 330–331. Less happily for me, Strauss says in the same paper that "One can imagine a man writing a book on the political problem of our time in the guise of a book on Plato's political philosophy. . . . it would be a very bad book if regarded as an interpretation of Plato" (364). There is very good reason to think that he is right.

Like Laclau and Mouffe, again, Jean-Luc Nancy, *The Inoperative Community*, trans. Peter Connor, Lisa Garbus, Michael Holland, and Simona Sawhney (Minneapolis: University of Minnesota Press, 1991), argues for a "regime" of experience or "exposure" that "does not live under the regime of contradiction," not even "the contradiction of contradiction and of noncontradiction" (87–89), and notes that "[t]he two regimes do not exclude one another (they do not form a contradiction)" (89); but he still insists that the regime of exposure excludes the kind of "universality and . . . totality" (87) that the regime of contradiction produces, that the regime of exposure "plays" without "ever forming into the substance or higher power of a Whole" (76). We "understand only that there is no common understanding of community" (69). Nancy shares the theme of these two coexisting regimes, and also the insufficient paradox, with Maurice Blanchot. See Maurice Blanchot, *The Unavowable Community*, trans. Pierre Joris (Barrytown, N.Y.: Station Hill Press, 1988), which is in part a response to Nancy's *Inoperative Community*; and, for example, Blanchot, *The Writing of the Disaster*, trans. Ann Smock (Lincoln: University of Nebraska Press, 1986). In *Writing*, Blanchot argues that "there must *always* be at least two languages, or two requirements: one dialectical, the other not; . . . the other . . . cut off from both being and from not-being" (20, my emphasis). And he calls for a writing that is, for example, "[d]etached from everything, including detachment" (12), that articulates "the disaster" that "ruins everything, all the while leaving everything intact" (1). But, again, this is "always" the case, and this writing never "provides us . . . with anything to which we could entrust ourselves, not with anything like an answer that would satisfy us" (16–17). It may seem peculiar to those who are familiar with Blanchot's work to accuse him of insufficient paradox. But there it is.

William Corlett, *Community without Unity: A Politics of Derridian Extravagance* (Durham, N.C.: Duke University Press, 1989), takes a further step, arguing that while the fixed, exclusive standpoints of "our individual and collective lives as we know them are in principle incomplete" and "require a supplement" that "would completely undermine" the sense they make, these considerations themselves are similarly incomplete and so are undermined before they can do the damage, are "themselves always already postponed" (162). (See also Blanchot, *Writing*, 36, on "the disaster": "it is not there—the disaster. It has already diverted the word 'be,' realizing itself to such a degree that it has not begun. A rose blossoming into a bud.") But Corlett also insists that these exclusive standpoints therefore only "provide provisional order" (183), that "nothing 'adds up' and never did" (161), and that "[e]verything definitive is necessarily postponed" (236 n. 30). But then, which he does not say or explore, these statements themselves—that every fixed and exclusive standpoint is only provisional and incompletely definitive—must also be only provisional and incompletely definitive.

There are political pluralists who challenge the rejection of universal truths and overall or "total" understandings. But these seem to argue either for global standpoints that escape pluralism altogether ("always always" views), or, like Corlett, for a global standpoint that is always only provisional (another version of "always sometimes"). William Connolly, for example, is clear about the permanent commitment of his own version of pluralism to a particular and comprehensive standpoint: e.g., "Pluralists think it is extremely important, for instance, *how* people of diverse faiths hold and express their faiths in public space. And we seek to limit the power of those who would invest their own creed with unquestioned territorial hegemony. . . . *Expansive pluralism supports the dissemination of general virtues across diverse faiths*"; William Connolly, *Pluralism* (Durham, N.C.: Duke University Press, 2005), 48, Connolly's emphasis. See also Charles E. Larmore, *Patterns of Moral Complexity* (New York: Cambridge University Press, 1987), who argues that recognition of the need for all citizen groups of a state to live together peacefully is rationally neutral and common to all rational parties (chaps. 3–5); Peter Murphy, "Postmodern Perspectives and Justice," *Thesis Eleven* 30 (1991):117–132, e.g., "Freedom is the common measure of all the discourses of modernity" (127). For the always-provisional totality, see also, e.g., Peter McLaren, *Critical Pedagogy and Predatory Culture: Oppositional Politics in a Postmodern Era* (New York: Routledge, 1995), esp. 215–223.

10. Alasdair MacIntyre gives a different argument for the same point, that mutually exclusive systems of concepts can be said to discuss the *same* thing even though they construe it in incompatible ways (and so they can *be* incompatible, rather than simply dealing with entirely unrelated things). Discussing confrontation between communities with incomparable or incommensurable systems of concepts, he writes, "Each community, using its own criteria of *sameness* and *difference*, recognizes

that it is one and the same subject matter about which they are advancing their claim; incommensurability and incompatibility are not incompatible." Alasdair C. MacIntyre, "Relativism, Power, and Philosophy," in *Relativism: Interpretation and Confrontation,* ed. Michael Krausz (Notre Dame, Ind.: University of Notre Dame Press, 1989), 190.

11. Jane Austen again: "'I do not attempt to deny,' said she, 'that I think very highly of him—that I greatly esteem, that I like him.' Marianne here burst forth with indignation—'Esteem him! Like him! Cold-hearted Elinor! Oh! worse than cold-hearted! Ashamed of being otherwise. . . .' Elinor could not help laughing. '. . . I am by no means assured of his regard for me. There are moments when the extent of it seems doubtful; and till his sentiments are fully known, you cannot wonder at my wishing to avoid any encouragement of my own partiality, by believing or calling it more than it is. There are moments when the extent of it seems doubtful; and till his sentiments are fully known, you cannot wonder at my wishing to avoid any encouragement of my own partiality, by believing or calling it more than it is'"; Jane Austen, *Sense and Sensibility* (Harmondsworth, U.K.: Penguin, 1969), 55.

12. Maurice Merleau-Ponty, *The Primacy of Perception,* trans. James M. Edie, et al. (Evanston, Ill.: Northwestern University Press, 1964), 19.

13. Plato, *Sophist,* trans. F. M. Cornford, in *Plato: The Collected Dialogues,* ed. Edith Hamilton and Huntington Cairns (Princeton, N.J.: Princeton University Press, 1961), 252D–E. Unless otherwise noted, I use this translation throughout.

14. Nicholas Rescher points out, similarly, that "we can assess . . . validity/cogency/plausibility only from a cognitive-value orientation that is bound to be doctrinally committed in a way that prejudices the issue for any given appraiser"; Nicholas Rescher, *The Strife of Systems: An Essay on the Grounds and Implications of Philosophical Diversity* (Pittsburgh, Pa.: University of Pittsburgh Press, 1985), 145. Thomas Kuhn famously argues the impossibility of comparing standpoints whose ways of interpreting basic aspects of reality are different, standpoints he describes as incommensurable paradigms; Thomas Kuhn, *The Structure of Scientific Revolutions,* 2nd ed. (Chicago: University of Chicago Press, 1970). For related arguments, see, e.g., Paul Feyerabend, *Against Method,* 3rd ed. (London: Verso, 1993), chap. 16; Alasdair C. MacIntyre, *Whose Justice? Which Rationality?* (Notre Dame, Ind.: University of Notre Dame Press, 1988); Willard Van Orman Quine, "Ontological Relativity," in *Ontological Relativity and Other Essays* (New York: Columbia University Press, 1969), 26–68; Liz Stanley and Sue Wise, *Breaking Out Again: Feminist Ontology and Epistemology* (London: Routledge, 1993), chap. 5; Charles Taylor, *Philosophical Papers, Vol. 2: Philosophy and the Human Sciences* (Cambridge, U.K.: Cambridge University Press, 1985), esp. chaps. 3–5.

There is an extensive literature of disagreement as to whether the idea of incommensurability between frameworks is valid or even intelligible. In arguing for the sense of conflicting absolutes or of "sometimes" logic—or, more accurately, "sometimes always" logic—I will be wholeheartedly supporting and drawing on both sides of this debate. I shall therefore not enter into the debate in its current form, but instead draw on each side of the literature as it becomes appropriate to my discussion. For some good samples of this literature, see Martin Hollis and Steven Lukes, eds., *Rationality and Relativism* (Cambridge, Mass.: MIT Press, 1982); Michael Krausz, ed., *Relativism: Interpretation and Confrontation* (Notre Dame, Ind.: University of Notre Dame Press, 1989); Bryan R. Wilson, ed., *Rationality* (Oxford: Basil Blackwell, 1970).

For a particularly influential argument that the idea of incommensurability fails to make sense at all, see Donald Davidson, "On the Very Idea of a Conceptual Scheme," in *Inquiries into Truth and Interpretation* (Oxford: Clarendon Press, 1984), 183–198. I discuss Davidson's argument in Jeremy Barris, "The Problem of Comparing Different Cultural or Theoretical Frameworks: Davidson, Rorty, and the Nature of Truth," *Method and Theory in the Study of Religion* 18.2 (2006):124–143. Davidson argues, roughly, that we would not be able to make sense *at all* of a framework or language incommensurable with our own, not even as a framework or language. This is part of what is involved in its being incommensurable with ours. As a result, the "very idea" of a framework involving radically different meanings from ours is incoherent. And equally, without even the idea of a framework that is not ours, there is no sense to the idea of *ours* as a framework either, nothing for it to contrast with. The very idea *of this kind of framework* or "conceptual scheme" is incoherent, and not just the idea of *other* frameworks. As Davidson concludes, if its *very idea* is incoherent, it makes no sense, for example, to assert *or* to deny that it exists. But it seems to me that once we eliminate the intelligibility of both the alternatives of an old and a new language, we have also eliminated the contrast that might make sense of the idea of *neither* of those alternatives. As a result, we also eliminate the intelligibility of the result that Davidson draws from this argument: it becomes incoherent to say that the idea of a conceptual scheme radically different from others is incoherent. Hilary Putnam also makes this point in connection with Richard Rorty's related argument about the idea of reality as completely independent of the framework offered by our language or concepts: "if we agree that it is *unintelligible* to say, 'We sometimes succeed in comparing our language and thought with reality as it is in itself,' then we should realize that it is also unintelligible to say, 'It is *impossible* to stand outside and compare our thought and the world.' . . . [I]n this case to say that it is impossible to do '*p*' . . . involves a '*p*' which is unintelligible"; Hilary Putnam, *Words and Life,* ed. James Conant (Cambridge, Mass.: Harvard University Press, 1994), 299. See also Peter Winch, who notes against a similar argument by Alasdair MacIntyre that "his argument . . . does not in fact show that our *own* standards of rationality occupy a peculiarly central position. The appearance to the contrary is an optical illusion engendered by the fact that MacIntyre's case has been advanced in the English language and in the context of 20th Century European culture. But a formally similar argument could be advanced in *any* language containing concepts playing a similar role in that language to those of 'intelligibility' and 'rationality' in ours"; Peter Winch, "Understanding a Primitive Society," *American Philosophical Quarterly* 1.4 (1964):307–324, 318. This essay and MacIntyre's are reprinted in Wilson, *Rationality.* Putnam, again, makes this point as well, specifically in response to Davidson's "radical interpretation": "if one recognizes that the radical interpreter himself may have more than one 'home' conceptual scheme, and that 'translation practice' may be governed by more than one set of constraints, then one sees that conceptual relativity does not disappear when we inquire into the 'meanings' of the various conceptual alternatives: it simply reproduces itself at a metalinguistic level!" Hilary Putnam, *Realism with a Human Face,* ed. James Conant (Cambridge, Mass.: Harvard University Press, 1990), 104.

Later, MacIntyre also came to defend the intelligibility of incommensurability, arguing that we can learn a second, incomparable language, with its own, different standards for truth, just as we learned the first one: "Just as a child does not learn its first language by matching sentences with sentences, since it initially possesses no set of sentences of its own, so an adult who has in this way become a child again does not either"; MacIntyre, *Whose Justice?* 374.

15. Plato, *Sophist,* 238D–E.

16. Ibid., 235D–241C, 259A–260B.

17. Ibid., 260A.

18. Socrates listens silently almost throughout the *Sophist.* Perhaps his role is partly to draw attention to the nature of the thinking that is exhibited by the other participants as they think about and therefore focus on particular subjects, in contrast with the immediate content of their thinking as it deals with those subjects. On the meaningful character of silence here and elsewhere in the dialogues, see, e.g., Mitchell H. Miller, Jr., *The Philosopher in Plato's* Statesman (The Hague, Netherlands: Martinus Nijhoff, 1980), xi.

Idea 2

1. Terence H. Irwin, *Plato's Ethics* (New York: Oxford University Press, 1995), 19, my insertion. See also Richard Robinson, *Plato's Earlier Dialectic* (Oxford: Oxford University Press, 1953), 15.

2. Hugh H. Benson, *Socratic Wisdom: The Model of Knowledge in Plato's Early Dialogues* (New York: Oxford University Press, 2000), 211. See also Drew Hyland, *The Virtue of Philosophy: An Interpretation of Plato's* Charmides (Athens, Ohio: Ohio University Press, 1981), 92: "because, for Socrates, knowledge is at least in part a mode of being, the mere formulation, however correct, will not by itself qualify as knowledge."

3. The idea that knowledge, or a statement of truth, can and sometimes does interfere with itself is now, in one form or another, a commonplace in natural science (Heisenberg's uncertainty principle), logic (Russell's paradox, Gödel's theorem and its "undecidability"), rhetorical studies, argumentation theory, sociology of knowledge, and various branches of philosophy. Michael Williams, for example, discusses "the capacity of epistemological reflection to destroy . . . one's erstwhile knowledge," because it changes the relevant context of inquiry. One consequence is that some of our knowledge "is necessarily tacit, in that any attempt to make it explicit will undermine it. . . . [C]ertain propositions cannot be made the object of

explicit knowledge claims," for then "they will fail." Michael Williams, *Unnatural Doubts: Epistemological Realism and the Basis of Scepticism* (Princeton, N.J.: Princeton University Press, 1996), 352, 355. For some everyday examples of necessarily tacit knowledge, see note 35 below. On the general theme of statements of truth interfering with themselves, see, for more examples, Derek Attridge, *Peculiar Language: Literature as Difference from the Renaissance to James Joyce* (Ithaca, N.Y.: Cornell University Press, 1988), e.g., 121; Tony Bennett, *Formalism and Marxism* (New York: Routledge, 1979), esp. chap. 8; John Dewey, *Logic: The Theory of Inquiry* (New York: Henry Holt and Co., 1938), e.g., "declarative propositions . . . are means . . . of effecting . . . controlled transformation of subject-matter" (160); and, more specifically, the "propositions formed during the course of deliberation . . . exercise a determining influence upon the very subject-matter they are about" (178); Michel Foucault, *Power/Knowledge: Selected Interviews and Other Writings 1972–1977*, ed. Colin Gordon (New York: Pantheon, 1980), e.g., "Truth isn't outside power, or lacking in power. . . . Truth is a thing of this world: . . . it induces regular effects of power" (131); Steven Mailloux, *Rhetorical Power* (Ithaca, N.Y.: Cornell University Press, 1989), whose notes in the first chapter also give a helpful introduction to some of the relevant literature; Nancy Tuana, ed., *Feminism and Science* (Bloomington: Indiana University Press, 1989).

4. Explaining why he introduces the idea of potentiality, in opposition to doctrines that state that something is simply what it is and as it is, Aristotle adds, "if what has been deprived of a power is incapacitated, then whatever has not yet come into being cannot possibly come into being. . . . Consequently, these doctrines take away all possibility of change and of coming into being." He insists that in contrast, "something may be capable of being without actually being, and capable of not being, yet be"; Aristotle, *Metaphysics,* ix.3.1047a10–25.

5. In discussing the principle of noncontradiction, Aristotle argues, "if there is such a thing as 'being a man' . . . it has one meaning; namely, to define the being of something. And to signify its being means that its being is not something else. But if 'being a man' means 'being nonman' or 'not being a man,' then a man's being will be something else. Hence they must argue that there cannot be such a definition of the being of anything, but that all attributes are accidental [i.e., nonessential]. . . . But if all statements merely predicate accidents, then there will be no first point of reference"; Aristotle, *Metaphysics,* iv.4.1007a20–1007b1.

6. Plato, *Theaetetus,* trans. R. Waterfield (Harmondsworth, U.K.: Penguin, 1987), 152A–E. Unless otherwise noted, I use this translation throughout.

7. Aristotle's view of essence is something of a combination of both of these senses. His forms, which constitute the essences of things, do not change and are necessarily what they are. But on the other hand, what the forms are is discovered through the (changeable) physical senses. Against what he understands Plato to say, Aristotle argues that one needs to look to sensible things first, rather than beginning with principles of thought that are independent of what happens to turn up in experience. What one can meaningfully say the forms necessarily are, therefore, depends on what one happens to find in experience.

I argue in some of the notes in Idea 6 that Aristotle's combination of these two senses of essence fails because it does not explain how they *can* go together without undermining each other. To obviate this mutual canceling, they need either to be properly coordinated or to be maintained in their full distinctness—or, as I argue Plato does, both.

In addition, Aristotle aims to account for change, and introduces the concept of potentiality mentioned in note 4 to this Idea for that purpose. But because his forms are unchanging and so without potentiality, they retain the first sense of essence without any modification by the second. Accordingly, he can say only that they are instantaneously created or destroyed without undergoing change. That is, he fails to offer an account of change precisely at the most fundamental level of his thinking about the nature of the truth of changing things. As Etienne Gilson writes, for Aristotelian metaphysics, "the world has always been just what it is." Individuals may be "subject to change, but they do not count," since being is defined only by the actuality of forms; Etienne Gilson, *Being and Some Philosophers*, 2nd ed. (Toronto: Pontifical Institute of Mediaeval Studies, 1952), 59–60.

Part of the problem with invoking Aristotle in talking about the prejudiced person is that in his thinking, essences do not belong to individuals, but to species. Individuals are what they are as individuals only because what Aristotle calls matter is compounded with the form to differentiate one individual from another. And matter has no essence, is not anything, since form, as distinguished from matter, is what makes something what it is. Accordingly, individuals have no essence as individuals. As I said above, however, I think his thinking fails precisely in the area of essence; and it is precisely the necessity of accounting for concrete individuality, and for the role of the senses—which begin with individuals—that forces such a "concept" as matter on him. Gilson again: "Individuals, [Aristotle] says, are such in virtue of their matter. . . . But the matter of a being . . . of itself, has no being. However we look at it, there is something wrong in a doctrine in which the supremely real [concrete individual substance] is such through that which exhibits an almost complete lack of reality"; Gilson, *Being and Some Philosophers*, 48, my insertions.

8. This problem has surfaced in gay/lesbian/queer and feminist studies, both being areas that obviously call for a questioning of the categories of "nature" and "essence." The trends here have for the most part been either an "essentialism," which deals in immutable essences, or a "constructionism," which theorizes an opposing social and historical construction of identities. A kind of thinking has gradually been developing that undertakes the very difficult task of questioning this cleavage without dismissing what has been learned from it. Diana Fuss, for example, argues that constructionism and essentialism in fact depend on each other; Diana Fuss, *Essentially Speaking: Feminism, Nature and Difference* (New York: Routledge, 1989), xii. For related arguments, see also Judith Butler, *Gender Trouble: Feminism and the Subversion of Identity* (New York: Routledge, 1990). Gregory Bredbeck points out that "over the course of the Renaissance we can see that 'sodomy' itself appears as a *construction,* an epistemological category that rebounds, mutates, fades, brightens, etc. It is clearly not essential; it is constructed. And yet we can also see

that *at any point in time,* what is *constructed* has an *essential force.* . . . What over time changes can, in the present tense, *be.* This formulation . . . asks that we in many ways reassess what we mean by the terms 'construction' and 'essence'"; Gregory Bredbeck, *Sodomy and Interpretation: Marlowe to Milton* (Ithaca, N.Y.: Cornell University Press, 1991), 237–238. He gives this nice clarification of the essentialist side: "After all, we seldom walk into a bar on a Saturday night and say to our friends, 'I really hope I find a hot *false unity* tonight'" (236). Eve Kosofsky Sedgwick offers a more detailed account of this point. She begins her *Epistemology of the Closet* with the assumption that there is no way to decide legitimately in advance between contrasting construals of the ultimate reality of human events (an assumption the present book tries to justify more elaborately). She draws the conclusion that I try centrally to endorse: "While there are certainly rhetorical and political grounds on which it may make sense to choose at a given moment between articulating, for instance, essentialist and constructivist (or minoritizing and universalizing) accounts of gay identity, there are, with equal certainty, rhetorical and political grounds for underwriting continuously the legitimacy of both accounts. And beyond these, there are crucial reasons of respect"; Eve Kosofsky Sedgwick, *The Epistemology of the Closet* (Berkeley: University of California Press, 1990), 27.

In a different context from sexual studies, and in connection with the identity of societies, Peter Burke writes, "Cultural historians used to assume that the outward forms of culture 'expressed' or 'reflected' some deeper inward reality. Nowadays this assumption is often criticized as too reductionist or determinist and the metaphor currently favored is not 'reflection' but 'construction.' The reaction was salutary but it may have gone too far, in the sense of encouraging us to forget the constraints on collective creativity. . . . Some attempts at construction are successful, others fail"; Peter Burke, *The Art of Conversation* (Ithaca, N.Y.: Cornell University Press, 1993), 68–69.

9. Consequently, the particular assumption that allows the truth about ourselves to be revealed is not simply separate from the fundamental indecision that allows the truth of the subject matter to be revealed. In fact, the definite assumption and the basic indecision are themselves in important respects, or sometimes, aspects of the same thing. I discuss this dimension of it further in Idea 5.

10. I discuss the dimension of risk further in Idea 7.

11. Frederick Keener writes, "the use of a trope by a metaphysician . . . is not rhetorical but epistemological. . . . he employs the trope to think. The metaphysics *is* a synecdoche"; Frederick Keener, *The Chain of Becoming* (New York: Columbia University Press, 1983), 204. It will become clear that I argue rather that metaphysics is epistemological *by being* rhetorical: it engages truth by being disengaged from truth, for example by being undecided about it.

12. For a variety of attempts to show the relation between dimensions of "literature" and the central concerns of philosophy, see Berel Lang, ed., *Philosophical Style: An Anthology about the Reading and Writing of Philosophy* (Chicago: Nelson-Hall, 1980). See also Jacques Derrida, "White Mythology: Metaphor in the Text of Phi-

losophy," in *Margins of Philosophy*, trans. A. Bass (Chicago: University of Chicago Press, 1982).

13. Eve Kosofsky Sedgwick, *Between Men: English Literature and Male Homosocial Desire* (New York: Columbia University Press, 1985), takes something like what is described in the above paragraph superbly into account. Introducing her own critique of ideology, for example, she writes, "It is . . . important that the sutures of contradiction in these ideological narratives become most visible under the disassembling eye of an alternative narrative, ideological as that narrative may itself be. In addition, the diachronic opening-out of contradictions within the status quo, even when the project of that diachronic recasting is to conceal those very contradictions, can have just the opposite effect of making them newly visible, offering a new leverage for critique. For these reasons, distinguishing between the construction and the critique of ideological narrative is not always even a theoretical possibility" (15).

14. Plato, *Meno*, trans. W. K. C. Guthrie, in *Collected Dialogues*, 84C. Unless otherwise noted, I use this translation throughout. Similarly, Elizabeth in *Pride and Prejudice*: " 'How despicably have I acted!' she cried.—'I, who have prided myself on my discernment! . . . vanity . . . has been my folly. . . . I have courted prepossession and ignorance, and driven reason away. . . . Till this moment, I never knew myself!' " Jane Austen, *Pride and Prejudice* (Harmondsworth, U.K.: Penguin, 1972), 233–237.

15. In this connection I note that Plato's and Socrates' predecessors, who are usually thought of as philosophers of nature in contrast with moral and social philosophers, seem to me not to have made this distinction and so not to fall on any side of it. If this is correct, then we need not see Plato and Socrates as turning away from their predecessors' concerns to moral and political philosophy, as their thought is usually understood (with strong support from Plato's presentations of Socrates' history in the *Apology* and the *Phaedo*, and from Aristotle, e.g., *Metaphysics*, i.6.987b1–4). Cornford, for example, writes, "philosophy had to give up, for the moment, the search after material substance in external Nature, and turn its eyes inwards to the nature of the human soul. This was the revolution accomplished by Socrates"; Francis M. Cornford, *Before and after Socrates* (Cambridge, U.K.: Cambridge University Press, 1932), 28. Instead, I suggest, we have to see them as introducing a distinction between kinds of philosophy that may well have kept them in perfect continuity with their predecessors' thinking on humanity *and* nature while also allowing newly distinct lines of focus in certain respects.

16. Some of the ancient Sophists argued this in one way or another. See, e.g., W. K. C. Guthrie, *The Sophists* (New York: Cambridge University Press, 1971 [1969]), 201–202: "It was these sceptics whom Aristotle criticized for making every statement true and false, or true statements impossible, and they included Protagoras and Gorgias" (202).

17. Plato, *Theaetetus*, trans. M. J. Levett, rev. M. Burnyeat (Indianapolis: Hackett, 1992), 171A. Berel Lang identifies this kind of paradox in a variety of connections and discusses some of its implications: Lang, *Philosophical Style*, 168–169 and then

throughout. And see Steven Seidman, "Identity and Politics in a 'Postmodern' Gay Culture: Some Historical and Conceptual Notes," in *Fear of a Queer Planet: Queer Politics and Social Theory*, ed. Michael Warner (Minneapolis: University of Minnesota Press, 1993), 128: "If categories of same-sex intimacies are marked by the sociocultural context of their origin, is not the same true of our categories of analysis?"

18. There is a burgeoning literature on the inescapability of this and other logical paradoxes. R. M. Sainsbury, for example, concludes that "our use of 'true' is governed by certain principles, and there is no *a priori* guarantee that these principles permit [for example] a noncontradictory stipulation of a disjoint predicate"; R. M. Sainsbury, *Paradoxes*, 2nd ed. (Cambridge, U.K.: Cambridge University Press, 1995), 144, my insertion. And Manuel Bremer, *An Introduction to Paraconsistent Logics* (Frankfurt am Main: Peter Lang, 2005), esp. chap. 2, discusses the formal admissibility of true contradictions. See also Graham Priest, *An Introduction to Non-Classical Logic* (Cambridge, U.K.: Cambridge University Press, 2001); and Priest, *Beyond the Limits of Thought* (Oxford: Oxford University Press, 2002). In *Beyond the Limits*, Priest argues that "the limits of thought are boundaries which cannot be crossed, but yet which are crossed"; these limits are "the subject, or locus, of true contradictions" (3).

For criticisms of various contemporary evasions of or attempts to solve these and related problems of the self-interference of knowledge or truth statements, see Christopher Norris, *The Contest of Faculties: Philosophy and Theory after Deconstruction* (New York: Methuen, 1985); Talbot J. Taylor, *Mutual Misunderstanding: Scepticism and the Theorizing of Language and Interpretation* (Durham, N.C.: Duke University Press, 1992).

19. Samuel Weber, *Institution and Interpretation* (Minneapolis: University of Minnesota Press, 1987), discusses the political implications of this issue. He offers this quote from Derrida: "What happens when acts or performances (discourse or writing, analysis or description, etc.) form part of the objects they designate? When they can give themselves as examples of that of which they speak or write? There is certainly no gain in self-reflexive transparency, on the contrary. An accounting is no longer possible, an account can no longer be rendered, nor a simple report or *compte rendu* given. And the borders of the whole are neither closed nor open. Their trait is divided" (140, Weber's translation). Weber gives the reference as Jacques Derrida, *La Carte Postale* (Paris: Flammarion, 1980), 417. And in a different context, Jonathan Goldberg writes of "the unassimilable nature of sodomy," which, since knowledge already involves certain attitudes toward it in advance, acts for knowledge as "an origin that is a divided and doubled one"; Jonathan Goldberg, "Sodomy in the New World: Anthropologies Old and New," in *Fear of a Queer Planet*, 9.

20. The idea that a line of thought can operate so as to cancel itself completely, and so bring its subject matter to light without distorting it by the effects of putting it into the context of being a subject of thought (that the observer need not "interfere with the observed," as happens in quantum physics) is defended for his own skeptical purposes by Sextus Empiricus in the second century CE: "Just as . . . fire

after consuming the fuel destroys also itself, and like as purgatives after driving the fluids out of the body expel themselves as well, so too the argument . . . can cancel itself also. And again, just as it is not impossible for the man who ascends to a high place to overturn the ladder with his foot after the ascent, so also it is not unlikely that the Sceptic after he has arrived at the demonstration of his thesis by means of the argument . . . as it were a step ladder, should then abolish this very argument"; Sextus Empiricus, *Against the Logicians*, 2:480–481, quoted in Priest, *Beyond the Limits*, 47. Wittgenstein also insists on the possibility of this kind of radically self-canceling thought, famously using the same ladder analogy: "My propositions serve as elucidations in the following way: anyone who understands me eventually recognizes them as nonsensical, when he has used them—as steps—to climb up beyond them. (He must, so to speak, throw away the ladder after he has climbed up it.) He must transcend these propositions, and then he will see the world aright." Ludwig Wittgenstein, *Tractatus Logico-Philosophicus*, trans. D. F. Pears and B. F. McGuinness (London: Routledge & Kegan Paul, 1961), 74, prop. 6.54.

This idea is also related to Stanley Fish's idea of "self-consuming artifacts." Fish writes, for example, that the reader of Plato's *Phaedrus* should realize at a certain point that "a new standard . . . has been introduced, one that invalidates the very basis on which the discussion, and his reading experience, had hitherto been proceeding. At that moment, this early section of the dialogue will have achieved its true purpose, which is, paradoxically, to bring the reader to the point where he is no longer interested in the issues it treats. . . . Thus . . . this space of prose and argument will have been the vehicle of its own abandonment." And, "as a result of passing through [the dialogue's words], the reader is altered to such an extent that if he were to go back they would mean quite differently. The value of such words lies not in their truth content . . . but in their effect. . . . As objects themselves they do not survive the moment of speech"; Stanley E. Fish, *Self-Consuming Artifacts: The Experience of Seventeenth-Century Literature* (Berkeley and Los Angeles: University of California Press, 1972), 10, 14, my insertion. Similarly, Michel de Certeau argues for an "art of speaking" which is really an "art . . . of operating." Commenting on the example of Foucault, he writes that "he makes what he says appear evident to the public he has in view, he disturbs the fields into which he moves . . . , creating a new disposition of the whole. But with this . . . 'description' this art tricks its other [the previous and genuinely descriptive understanding of the 'disposition of the whole'] and modifies its law without replacing it by a different one. It does not have its own discourse. It does not say itself. It is the practice of nowhere"; Michel de Certeau, *The Practice of Everyday Life*, trans. Steven Rendall (Berkeley: University of California Press, 1984), 79–80, my insertion. Neither Fish nor de Certeau, however, is concerned with the kind of undecidability I mention in the text above as to whether the line of thought is canceled or not. As I discuss below, my own focus is on cases where, expressing this undecidability differently, the cancellation is so fundamental that it even cancels itself, restoring the possibility of the original, uncanceled meaning *as well as* maintaining its complete cancellation. This is an instance of the "sometimes always" logic I began to discuss in Idea 1.2.

See also William James's argument (which he makes, however, in order to show that we can have perceptions uncontaminated by concepts, and so is mainly on a very different tack from my own) that, "the concept 'reality,' which we restore to immediate perception, is . . . only a kind of practical relation . . . which reasoning had temporarily interfered with, but which, when the reasoning was neutralized by still further reasoning, reverted to its original seat as if nothing had happened. That concepts can neutralize other concepts is one of their great practical functions. This answers also the charge that it is self-contradictory to use concepts to undermine the credit of conception in general. The best way to show that a knife will not cut is to try to cut with it. Rationalism itself it is that has so fatally undermined conception, by finding that, when worked beyond a certain point, it only piles up dialectic contradictions"; William James, *Some Problems of Philosophy: A Beginning of an Intro-duction to Philosophy* (Lincoln: University of Nebraska Press, 1996), 111–112.

With respect to the dimension of undecidability (or, with respect to whether the cancellation is so fundamental as to cancel even itself): "If . . . there is no reason to believe that anything matters, then that does not matter either, and we can approach our absurd lives with irony instead of despair"; Thomas Nagel, "The Absurd," in *Mortal Questions* (New York: Cambridge University Press, 1979), 23.

21. Hume comments, with analogous implications, that "A true sceptic will be diffident of his philosophical doubts, as well as of his philosophical conviction." David Hume, *A Treatise of Human Nature* (New York: Oxford University Press, 2000), I.4.7.14. And in a different context (but without aiming to legitimate contra-diction, as I do), Goodman writes, "Getting the facts straight is easy enough so long as we bear in mind that the facts are paradoxical"; Nelson Goodman and Catherine Z. Elgin, *Reconceptions in Philosophy and Other Arts and Sciences* (Indianapolis, Ind.: Hackett, 1988), 100.

22. Mitchell Miller, although he understands the nature of truth in Plato very differently from the way I do, notes this deceptive logic by which a fundamental problem, rigorously thought through, reverses into its own solution, precisely in connection with Plato's Ideas or forms: "That the form is, in its essential being, related to itself alone implies that it has no essential relatedness to things. . . . Strik-ingly, just this nonrelatedness permits the form to stand as a true foundation for things. . . . [O]nly if the form is essentially independent from its participants, can these be essentially dependent upon it. Furthermore, since form does not stand to its participant things as to commensurate others, there is nothing to keep it apart from them; since they are not terms in a real relation, the separation that such a relation implies does not apply. . . . [I]t is only *because* the form is 'in and of itself' that it *can* be 'in our domain'"; Mitchell Miller, *Plato's* Parmenides: *The Conversion of the Soul* (Princeton, N.J.: Princeton University Press; University Park: Pennsylva-nia State University Press, 1991 [1986]), 63–64. The Ideas are *so* different from ordinary things that even what it means to be different is different for them. Accord-ingly, *their* kind of difference does not exclude what, in the thinking appropriate to ordinary things, is considered to be sameness.

23. Gadamer, following Helmholtz, argues that there is a "tact which functions in the human sciences" as "a mode of knowing and a mode of being," and that shares "something essential" with the tact of "manners and customs"; Hans-Georg Gadamer, *Truth and Method,* 2nd ed., trans. Joel Weinsheimer and Donald G. Marshall (New York: Continuum, 1989), 16. See also de Certeau, *Practice,* 72–73, on Kant's view of aesthetic judgment as "a 'middle term' . . . between theory and praxis," and so an "art of thinking" that involves what Kant "calls . . . a 'logical tact' ": "this art also designates that which, in scientific work itself, does not depend on the (necessary) application of rules or models and so remains in the final analysis, as Freud also says, 'a matter of tact.' "

One can experience a dimension of this foundational relation to truth already at the social level, in the form of the subtle delight in and gratitude for life and existence themselves, or of the opposite of these feelings, that the consistent exercise or omission of this kind of tact can catalyze. (As Austen writes of one of her characters, "she was sometimes worried down by officious condolence to rate good-breeding as more indispensable to comfort than good-nature"; Jane Austen, *Sense and Sensibility* [Harmondsworth, U.K.: Penguin, 1969], 224.) These feelings involve a judgment about, a relation to, the truth of reality itself, that is, to truth as a whole. And here it is tact or tactlessness that evokes this relation to and enables this judgment about the nature of truth itself.

24. For an excellent account of the importance of indirect rhetorical maneuvers in Plato's dialogues generally, to allow truth to be communicated in non-self-defeating ways, see Mitchell H. Miller, Jr. *The Philosopher in Plato's* Statesman (The Hague, Netherlands: Martinus Nijhoff, 1980), xii–xvi.

25. As identified and translated by Woodruff, one of the translators of Plato, *Symposium,* trans. Alexander Nehamas and Paul Woodruff (Indianapolis, Ind.: Hackett, 1989), 3, n. 2. He identifies the proverb as Eupolis, fr. 289. Unless otherwise noted, I use this translation throughout.

26. Plato, *Symposium,* 174A–C, my insertions.

27. Agamemnon has just declared for the necessity of avoiding quarreling among his allies, and is making the sacrifice in preparation for fighting a battle in which Menelaus, who is his brother, will assist him. Furthermore, the war is being fought on Menelaus's behalf, since it is his wife Helen who was stolen by the Trojan Paris. Menelaus clearly has a stake in the proceedings. In Homer's words, "Of his own accord came Menelaos of the great war-cry/who knew well in his own mind the cares of his brother"; Homer, *Iliad,* trans. Richmond Lattimore (Chicago: University of Chicago Press, 1951), 87 (ii, 11. 408–409).

28. Plato, *Symposium,* 174C–D.

29. J. L. Austin, for example, writes, "descriptions, which are said to be true or false, . . . are selective and uttered for a purpose. It is essential to realize that 'true' and 'false,' like 'free' and 'unfree,' do not stand for anything simple at all; but only for a general dimension of being a right or proper thing to say as opposed to a wrong thing, in these circumstances, to this audience, for these purposes and with these intentions"; J. L. Austin, *How to Do Things with Words* (Cambridge, Mass.: Harvard

University Press, 1962), 144. Similarly, F. C. S. Schiller argues that "it is far from evident that truth and falsity have nothing to do with anything but judgments or propositions. . . . The impetus given to inquiry by desires and wishes can hardly be pronounced entirely irrelevant to a logic that concerns itself with actual knowing. And only the narrowest Formalism can sever judgments wholly from the trains of thought in which they occur and the questions which they are meant to answer, and treat them in abstraction as self-dependent entities. . . . [W]e find that truth and falsity are incidents in cognitive inquiry; and this is far too much of a whole to make it desirable, or even possible, to restrict the predicates 'true' and 'false' to a single portion of it. A logic that observes the facts of actual knowing may fairly be required to envisage cognitive process as a whole, and to consider 'truth' as its *success* and 'falsity' as its *failure*"; F. C. S. Schiller, *Logic for Use: An Introduction to the Voluntarist Theory of Knowledge* (New York: Harcourt, Brace and Company, 1930), 117. Bernard Williams makes the related point (in the course of an argument very different from and possibly opposed to my own) that while we should not "confuse truth-conditions or content with the conditions of appropriate assertion," still, "the point or pointlessness of making a given assertion to a given person in a given situation can help someone in picking up the content of that assertion. For some purposes, such as the theory of deductive inference, the content of assertions can be treated in abstraction from their appropriateness, but basically there is no understanding of the one without the other"; Bernard Williams, *Truth and Truthfulness: An Essay in Genealogy* (Princeton, N.J.: Princeton University Press, 2002), 48.

Paolo Freire, similarly, notes that "Within the word we find two dimensions, reflection and action, in such radical interaction that if one is sacrificed—even in part—the other immediately suffers. There is no true word that is not at the same time a praxis. Thus, to speak a true word is to transform the world. . . . When a word is deprived of its dimension of action, reflection automatically suffers as well; and the word is changed into idle chatter, into *verbalism,* into an alienated and alienating 'blah.' It becomes an empty word, one which cannot denounce the world, for denunciation is impossible without a commitment to transform"; Paolo Freire, *Pedagogy of the Oppressed,* trans. Myra Bergman Ramos (New York: Seabury Press, 1968), 75–76.

30. "I . . . doubt the historicity of the dialogues . . . as reports of philosophical conversations in the fifth century. The dialogues belong to Plato and to the fourth century"; Charles H. Kahn, "Did Plato Write Socratic Dialogues?" in *Essays on the Philosophy of Socrates,* ed. Hugh H. Benson (New York: Oxford University Press, 1992 [1981]), 47.

31. The initial setting of the *Symposium,* narrated by Apollodorus, focuses on issues of social decorum, specifically the competing statuses of philosophical and more usual lifestyles: "my greatest pleasure comes from philosophical conversation. . . . All other talk, especially the talk of rich businessmen like you, bores me to tears, and I'm sorry for you and your friends because you think your affairs are important when really they're totally trivial. Perhaps, in your turn, you think I'm a failure, and, believe me, I think that what you think is true. . . . Of

course, my dear friend, it's perfectly obvious why I have these views about us all: it's simply because I'm a maniac, and I'm raving!" Plato, *Symposium*, 173C–E.

32. Plato, if he really is the author of the *Laws,* gives symposia or drinking parties an important place there, too, while also allowing for their possible triviality. The first two books of the *Laws* are largely taken up with an argument about the importance of symposia in the formation of good citizens. Plato has the Athenian say that "the genuinely correct way to regulate drinking can hardly be explained adequately and clearly except in the context of a correct theory of culture; and it is impossible to explain this without considering the whole subject of education." A little later he says that "it may well be thought that this is a triviality on which a great deal too much has been said, but equally it may turn out that the topic really does deserve this extended discussion"; Plato, *The Laws,* trans. T. J. Saunders (Harmondsworth, U.K.: Penguin, 1970), 642A, 645C. Unless otherwise noted, I use this translation throughout. The argument takes symposia as a crucial model and training ground for peaceful interaction, as opposed to war, including civil war (640B).

33. Plato, *Symposium*, 173B. Although it is Aristodemus who is in love with Socrates here, rather than the other way round, he is described in the same passage in terms that evoke Socrates: "a real runt of a man, who always went barefoot" (173B). And near the end of the dialogue, Socrates is indirectly identified with love, in that his beloved, Alcibiades, is prompted to give a speech on him instead of on love (214D–222C).

34. If this discussion of the truth of truth, taking into account dimensions other than its immediate descriptive validity considered in isolation, has a relation to Nietzsche's focus on the value of truth (which asks what a range of the effects of truth are, its costs and benefits), then it indicates that that focus (1) does not fall simply outside the issue of truth itself, and (2) can turn out to support traditional senses of truth in just the way they stand in the tradition. It follows from my thesis in this book, of course, that Nietzsche was not the first to take this question seriously, despite some contemporary claims of the radicality of Nietzsche's "critique of the value of truth." Part of my aim is to clarify the logic by which truth can be questioned truthfully, that is, why this circle is not simply circular.

35. The eighteenth-century rhetorician George Campbell writes, "the assault of him who ridicules is, from its very nature, covert and oblique. What we profess to contemn, we scorn to confute." The act of directly expressing that something is beneath one's notice shows that it is not, and so performatively contradicts the truth it claims. But one can successfully express it indirectly. Similarly, "If the fact be notorious, it will not only be superfluous in the speaker to attempt to prove it, but it will be pernicious to his design. The reason is plain. By proving he supposeth it questionable, and by supposing actually renders it so to his audience: he brings them from viewing it in the stronger light of certainty, to view it in the weaker light of probability: in lieu of sunshine he gives them twilight"; George Campbell, in James L. Golden and Edward P. J. Corbett, eds., *The Rhetoric of Blair, Campbell, and Whately* (Carbondale: Southern Illinois University Press, 1990), 164, 213. See also the reference to Michael Williams, *Unnatural Doubts,* in note 3 above.

Idea 3

1. This was Quintilian's definition, in the first century CE (so well after Plato's time). As George Kennedy notes, not irrelevantly to the themes I am developing, in *"bene dicendi scientia,* 'a knowledge of speaking well' . . . *bene* . . . does imply both artistic excellence and moral goodness"; George Kennedy, *Classical Rhetoric and Its Christian and Secular Tradition from Ancient to Modern Times* (Chapel Hill: University of North Carolina Press, 1980), 101.

2. For a history of the changing relations of rhetoric, logic, and dialectic as labels, see Richard McKeon, *Rhetoric: Essays in Invention and Discovery,* ed. M. Backman (Woodbridge, U.K.: Ox Bow Press, 1987).

3. There is an extensive, comparatively recent literature of attempts to show that what have traditionally been understood to be truth-independent rhetorical features of argumentation, such as context and audience, are relevant to (for example) its purely logical validity. Charles Willard, *A Theory of Argumentation* (Tuscaloosa: University of Alabama Press, 1989), 15, for instance, writes, "arguments are happenings whose nature is altered by abstraction from context." James Hikins argues that "because rhetoric is . . . anchored in reality, humans are assured at least minimally objective criteria with which to compose discourse, evaluate rhetorical praxis, and generate theory"; James Hikins, "Realism and Its Implications for Rhetorical Theory," in *Rhetoric and Philosophy,* ed. Richard A. Cherwitz (Hillsdale, N.J.: Lawrence Erlbaum, 1990), 67. For a critique of these attempts, see Jeremy Barris, "The Foundation in Truth of Rhetoric and Formal Logic," *Philosophy and Rhetoric* 29.4 (1996):314–328. See also Richard A. Cherwitz and James W. Hikins, *Communication and Knowledge: An Investigation in Rhetorical Epistemology* (Columbia: University of South Carolina Press, 1986); Henry W. Johnstone, Jr., *Validity and Rhetoric in Philosophical Argument: An Outlook in Transition* (University Park, Pa.: Dialogue Press of Man and World, 1978); Chaim Perelman, *The New Rhetoric and the Humanities: Essays on Rhetoric and Its Applications* (Dordrecht, Netherlands: D. Riedel, 1979), 50.

Derrida specifically addresses the issue of presentation. Introducing his own text, he writes, "These texts are assembled otherwise; it is not my intention here to *present* them. The question astir here, precisely, is that of presentation. . . . the book form alone can no longer settle . . . the case of those writing processes which, in *practically* questioning that form, must also dismantle it. . . . the question would already be caught up in a whole system of presuppositions . . . for example, here, that of the signifier's *simple* exteriority to 'its' concept"; Jacques Derrida, *Dissemination,* trans. Barbara Johnson (Chicago: University of Chicago Press, 1981), 3.

4. See the quotes from the *Phaedrus* given near the start of the introduction to the book. And Aristotle in the *Rhetoric:* "The use of persuasive speech is to lead to decisions. (When we know a thing, and have decided about it, there is no further use in speaking about it.) This is so even if one is addressing a single person and urging him to do or not to do something . . . : the single person is as much your 'judge' as if he were one of many. . . . Nor does it matter whether we are arguing against an actual opponent or against a mere proposition; in the latter case we still

have to use speech and overthrow the opposing arguments, and we attack these as we should attack an actual opponent"; Aristotle, *The* Rhetoric *and the* Poetics *of Aristotle,* trans. W. R. Roberts [*Rhetoric*] and I. Bywater (New York: Modern Library of Random House, 1984 [1954]), ii.18.1391b7–17.

5. Allen Scult, for example, points out that argumentation has the requirement: "risk yourself"; Allen Scult, "Perelman's Universal Audience: One Perspective," in *The New Rhetoric of Chaim Perelman: Statement and Response,* ed. Ray D. Dearin (Lanham, Md.: University Press of America, 1989), 160. More elaborately, Johnstone argues that "genuine argument . . . can occur only when the respondent is himself interested in the outcome of the argument; that is, where the respondent takes a risk." Consequently "philosophy makes clear the structure of the risks faced by a person who argues or listens to argument. . . . It tells the self who it is and where it stands. Thus philosophy may be said to serve the emerging self by contributing to its morale. Philosophical arguments, then, have a morale function rather than an information function. If we expect general agreement regarding their conclusions, we simply do not understand them correctly"; Johnstone, *Validity and Rhetoric,* 109, 113.

6. Hans-Georg Gadamer, *Plato's Dialectical Ethics: Phenomenological Interpretations Relating to the* Philebus, trans. R. M. Wallace (New Haven, Conn.: Yale University Press, 1991), 65.

7. Rescher argues (in the fuller version of the passage I quoted in note 14 to Idea 1 above) that "Protagoras was only partly right. Each side of a philosophical dispute can defend its pro-or-con position with equal rigor and vigor. But certainly not with equal *validity*—since we can assess this matter of validity/cogency/plausibility only from a cognitive-value orientation that is bound to be doctrinally committed in a way that prejudices the issue for any given appraiser"; Nicholas Rescher, *The Strife of Systems: An Essay on the Grounds and Implications of Philosophical Diversity* (Pittsburgh: University of Pittsburgh Press, 1985), 145.

8. Berel Lang argues that if "knowledge . . . compels action . . . one property of an idea . . . will be its implication for writing or practice," so that if "the very structure of an idea, its status *as* an idea, is linked to the form of its articulation . . . then to weigh ideas and their representations in terms of the way in which they engage their audience is not at all arbitrary"; Berel Lang, *Philosophical Style: An Anthology about the Reading and Writing of Philosophy* (Chicago: Nelson-Hall, 1980), 77. And Jill Gordon argues of Plato in particular that "what to modern eyes and ears are literary elements of Plato's texts, are the very vehicles necessary for his philosophy. These qualities of his texts are not embellishments, or finery, or even mere artistry"; Jill Gordon, *Turning toward Philosophy: Literary Device and Dramatic Structure in Plato's Dialogues* (University Park: Pennsylvania State University Press, 1999), 12. My own argument is that the literary elements in Plato (and generally) are necessary to establishing truth precisely *in their being* mere finery. In any event, given this relation of truth and rhetoric, research into formal elements of rhetoric and style becomes relevant to purely philosophical concerns, such as the philosophy of knowledge.

9. See, e.g., Steven Mailloux, *Rhetorical Power* (Ithaca, N.Y.: Cornell University Press, 1989), 17; and Derek Attridge, *Peculiar Language: Literature as Difference from the Renaissance to James Joyce* (Ithaca, N.Y.: Cornell University Press, 1988), 122. This conclusion is often argued to result from deconstruction (Attridge is a particularly sophisticated example), but I believe this entirely misses the point of what Derrida introduced and developed under that name. For Derrida, opposites like logic and rhetoric presuppose each other in ways that also maintain them as opposites. The result is that the meanings of *both* become *undecidable*, not that one is reduced to the other. In other words, we no longer know what we mean (or we recognize that we never knew what we meant) when we use those terms. This, of course, does not authorize decisions about them or their mutual relations.

10. Ludwig Edelstein argues that for Plato, "Nothing in this world . . . exists without its opposite (*Phaedo*, 60B). . . . It is impossible to strive for the one without accepting the other. In the same way, seriousness would defeat its own purpose if it were not willing to admit playfulness. . . . Is it not difficult to say whether men, the ingenuous puppets of the gods, were contrived as playthings of theirs, or rather for some serious purposes (*Laws*, I, 644C)? . . . Thus the terms seriousness and playfulness are imbued with the peculiar ambiguity of Platonic irony"; Ludwig Edelstein, "The Function of the Myth in Plato's Philosophy," *Journal of the History of Ideas* 10.4 (1949):463–481, 470.

Idea 4

1. F. C. S. Schiller writes, in a more general context, "the characteristic features in our intelligence are . . . *processes*. . . . Experience is . . . nearly always a reaction upon the given. One of the most . . . important of these reactions is the assumption, which we make almost continuously, that what we experience *means* something. This assumption is the taking up of an *attitude* towards our experience which is an addition to the mere experiencing." That is, our awareness is already a doing something, in itself, even before it is applied. F. C. S. Schiller, *Formal Logic: A Scientific and Social Problem* (London: Macmillan, 1912), 89–90.

2. Plato, *Laches*, trans. B. Jowett, in *Plato: The Collected Dialogues*, ed. Edith Hamilton and Huntington Cairns (Princeton, N.J.: Princeton University Press, 1961), 193E. Unless otherwise noted, I use this translation throughout.

3. Plato, *Meno*, trans. W. K. C. Guthrie, in *Collected Dialogues*, 80D. Unless otherwise noted, I use this translation throughout.

4. "Socrates explicitly makes the point that his argument shows that a mind must at all times, whether before or after birth, *have already* learnt everything that it can come to understand; therefore there never was a moment at which the learning occurred"; I. M. Crombie, *Plato: The Midwife's Apprentice* (New York: Barnes & Noble, 1964), 36.

5. Plato, *Meno*, 81A–B.

6. "So I soon made up my mind about the poets too. I decided that it was not wisdom that enabled them to write their poetry, but a kind of instinct or inspiration,

such as you find in seers and prophets who deliver all their sublime messages without knowing in the least what they mean"; Plato, *Apology*, trans. H. Tredennick, in *Collected Dialogues*, 22B–C. Unless otherwise noted, I use this translation throughout.

7. See, e.g., Hans-Georg Gadamer, *The Idea of the Good in Platonic-Aristotelian Philosophy*, trans. P. Christopher Smith (New Haven, Conn.: Yale University Press, 1986), 34, although in a different context: "Our task . . . is to raise this mythical unity . . . to the level of conceptual thinking."

8. Gadamer comments on this passage of the *Meno:* "the mythical horizons within which Plato places this certainty—and not without ironic ceremoniousness—serve essentially only to display and explicate the capacity of the human mind to place things in question"; Gadamer, *Idea of the Good,* 54.

9. Plato, *Meno,* 81D–E.

10. Gordon argues that the *Meno* as a whole consistently emphasizes the importance of Meno's character for learning, that is, for establishing truth; Jill Gordon, *Turning toward Philosophy: Literary Device and Dramatic Structure in Plato's Dialogues* (University Park: Pennsylvania State University Press, 1999), chap. 4.

11. Plato, *Meno,* 86B–C.

12. Jacob Klein, *A Commentary on Plato's* Meno (Chicago: University of Chicago Press, 1965), 96–97. See also Gadamer, *Idea of the Good,* 53–54: "The only thing accepted is the practical certainty that we are better off holding firmly to the belief that one can indeed seek the truth."

13. Klein, *Commentary,* 96.

14. Plato, *Phaedrus,* in *Phaedrus and Letters VII and VIII,* trans. W. Hamilton (Harmondsworth, U.K.: Penguin, 1973), 275C.

15. Gregory Vlastos, "The Socratic Elenchus," in *Socratic Studies* (New York: Cambridge University Press, 1993).

16. Hence, "Sokrates examines not just . . . beliefs, but . . . the personality, way of life, and social roles that condition those beliefs and are in turn conditioned by them"; Ruby Blondell, *The Play of Character in Plato's Dialogues* (New York: Cambridge University Press, 2002), 113. And Drew Hyland writes, "In the case of human virtues such as *sophrosyne* ['temperance' or 'self-control']," what we are trying to understand "is we ourselves as we act. . . . *Being sophron* is therefore the most primordial mode of 'knowing' *sophrosyne,* and is the condition for any subsequent and therefore founded 'knowledge,' such as articulated definition or even *episteme* ['science']." This knowledge is "a way of being or living"; Drew Hyland, *The Virtue of Philosophy: An Interpretation of Plato's* Charmides (Athens, Ohio: Ohio University Press, 1981), 139, my insertions.

Winch argues, following Wittgenstein, that our ways of making sense involve "systems of *action* rather than of ideas," people "responding systematically in action to real situations." Consequently, we can "see *Genesis* and *On the Origin of Species* as the outcome of different kinds of search" and, therefore, "the respective objects of those searches as equally diverse." But as for what the relation between the claims of these books specifically is, "there is no universally valid, definitive answer. It's a question individuals have to answer for themselves by considering what significance religious worship and scientific investigation have in their lives; and by meditating on whether, and if so how, they can live with both of them." Winch points out that this Wittgensteinian line of thought "forges a link between contemporary philosophy and the tradition exemplified by Socrates' response to the Delphic injunction: 'Know thyself' "; Peter Winch, *Trying to Make Sense* (New York: Basil Blackwell, 1987), 133, 137, 138.

I quoted in the introduction to the book Nagel's more general comment on this topic: "the subjectivity of consciousness is an irreducible feature of reality—without which we couldn't do physics or anything else—and it must occupy as fundamental a place in any credible world view as matter, energy, space, time, and numbers"; Thomas Nagel, *The View from Nowhere* (New York: Oxford University Press, 1986), 7–8. William James makes the further, more specific argument that "the philosopher himself" must be "taken up into the universe which he is accounting for. . . . Our philosophies swell the current of being, add their character to it. They are part of all that we have met, of all that makes us be. . . . Our thoughts determine our acts, and our acts redetermine the previous nature of the world"; William James, *A Pluralistic Universe,* in *William James: Writings 1902–1910,* ed. Bruce Kuklick (New York: Library of America, 1987), 774. Dewey notes, similarly, that "complete determination would not hold of existences as an *environment.* For Nature is an environment only as it is involved in interaction with an organism, or self"; John Dewey, *Logic: The Theory of Inquiry* (New York: Henry Holt and Co., 1938), 106. And F. C. S. Schiller argues that "the objective world remains relative to a subject in the background, however much he strives to efface himself. There is no thought without a thinker, no observation without an observer, not even a dream without a dreamer, and no object without a subject"; F. C. S. Schiller, *Logic for Use: An Introduction to the Voluntarist Theory of Knowledge* (New York: Harcourt, Brace, 1930), 374. Further, "metaphysics . . . has the duty of making its synthesis all-inclusive. Now personality is a fact, and a fact of the utmost importance. For it pervades all knowing, and affects the results of knowing very subtly. . . . Even, therefore, if we regard its influence as dangerous (as it may be), it is important that it should be recognised." In fact, not only has "metaphysics . . . to include the personal *data* in its total synthesis, but it has to draw the principles on which its syntheses proceed, the skeleton which holds together every metaphysical system, from the personality of individual metaphysicians" (453). As Schiller explains in *Formal Logic,* "What does, in fact, generate and hold together any actual inference is the personality of the man who draws it in a particular context, and the nature of his intelligence, interests, purposes, and ends; its value is determined partly by its relevance to these, partly by the social impression it makes on others whose thinking is similarly personal" (221). Again, Bernard Williams argues that, while "the demand for truthfulness and the rejection of truth can go together . . . in pursuing truthfulness, what are you supposedly being true to? . . . Truthfulness implies a respect for the truth"; Bernard Williams, *Truth and Truthfulness: An Essay in Genealogy* (Princeton, N.J.: Princeton University Press, 2002), 2, 11. And he cautions that "This is not an abstract difficulty or just a paradox. It has consequences for real politics, and it signals a danger that our intellectual activities . . . may tear themselves to pieces" (2). Gilson, discussing Kierkegaard, writes about subjective knowledge (for example the knowledge of being in love, or of ethical and religious matters) that "the truth of subjective knowledge . . . lies in its very subjectivity. It does not aim to know . . . that that with which it establishes relations is true: in subjective knowledge the relationship itself *is* the truth, which means that the subject itself *is* the truth. In short . . . in it truth is one with existence and existence with truth"; Etienne Gilson, *Being and Some Philosophers,* 2nd ed. (Toronto: Pontifical Institute of Mediaeval Studies, 1952), 149. See also C. I. Lewis, who argues that "This reality which everybody knows . . . is a whole in which mind and what is given to mind already meet and are interwoven. . . . This experience of *reality* exists only because the mind of man takes attitudes and makes interpretations"; C. I. Lewis, *Mind and the World Order: Outline of a Theory of Knowledge* (New York: Dover Publications, 1929), 29–30.

17. Plato, *Gorgias,* trans. W. D. Woodhead, in *Collected Dialogues,* 472B–C. Unless otherwise indicated, I use this translation throughout.

18. Plato, *Protagoras,* trans. W. K. C. Guthrie, in *Collected Dialogues,* 331C. Unless otherwise noted, I use this translation throughout.

19. Plato, *Phaedrus,* 230A–B.

20. It follows from this argument that Heidegger's thinking, because it obviates subject-object dualism (among other dualisms), eliminates categories that allow us to grasp all sorts of aspects of truth and its establishment. His thinking is therefore inadequate to deal with the problem of truth in general. More fundamentally, what allows this particular inadequacy is that Heidegger does not see the dimension of simple externality or triviality as having any fundamental significance. Hegel shares both this view and the resulting inadequacy, although he does go a long way toward giving simple externality a fundamental place. For an example of this inclusion on Hegel's part, "contact between these actualities appears therefore as an empty externality; the actuality of the one in the other is *only* possibility, contingency. . . . But this *contingency* is rather absolute necessity; it is the *essence* of those free, inherently necessary actualities. . . . The *simplicity* of their being and their self-support is absolute negativity; . . . it is the *freedom* of their reflectionless . . . immediacy"; G. W. F. Hegel, *Science of Logic,* trans. A. V. Miller (Atlantic Highlands, N.J.: Humanities Press International, 1969), 553. I discuss Hegel further in note 2 to Idea 6.

Heidegger's method consists in finding what must be thought in order to understand the possibility of humanly experienced phenomena. In this way he moves from phenomenology, the investigation of what appearances are, to the question of being, the investigation of what that which is is (including appearance in what is), and beyond (a beyond that accounts for the possibility of appearance and what is). He therefore claims that his findings are at a level before such ideas as "subject" and "object" even arise, since these ideas are given their *possibility* only at that level. These ideas are refuted in advance, by being shown to be inadequate before they arise. Their level is more "trivial." But his starting point, which comes *after* such ideas have already arisen, determines the character of this deeper level. We need not begin by finding the possibility only of appearances. If, on the one hand, we start as Heidegger does by saying that we *must* start exclusively with appearance, because everything is in fact presented to us as appearance, we say this before reaching the deeper level that allows Heidegger to refute the alternatives. That is, we have already settled for a theory that is as "superficial" or "trivial" and therefore as questionable as subject-object dualism, and we have allowed the entire investigation to be guided by it down to its deepest levels. But if, on the other hand, we grant that we can question the idea of starting with appearance (actually, with what is in fact only a particular construal of appearance, at that), we can investigate impersonal logics and structures and contrivances and investigate them on the assumption that they are not fundamentally appearances. We could think, with the Stoics, for example, that these logics are impersonally in the nature of things and that we are given access to them by a rationality that is in fact independent of our human constitutions. Our experience of appearances then belongs to a different, more trivial order of being from our rational thought. The possibility of rationality is then independent of appearance and not to be found by beginning with appearance. And rationality can then judge our more trivial experience of appearance by its own external and impersonal laws. One can certainly refute this kind of theory by adopting a different starting point, as Heidegger and Hegel do: a different starting point for their *method* of answering questions. This theory is then required to constrain itself to an alien method, an alien sequence and direction of thought. But as I argue in this note, this choice of starting point is in fact arbitrary, and the alien constraint on the theory is therefore unjustified.

Part of my own project is to try to investigate both appearances and impersonal logics, and sometimes one thing as both, on the basis of the kind of indecision between two fundamental construals that I discuss. In this way, I argue that one can take into rigorous and responsible account the truth that one's starting points are *fundamental as well as trivial, external and arbitrary*. And that the *possibility* of fundamental thought *depends on* this kind of triviality, and must be understood and practiced accordingly.

It also follows from my argument, however, that Heidegger's account will sometimes be fully valid and mine invalid. In this light, perhaps what Heidegger's thought is (sometimes always) missing is a dimension of trivial rhetoric, necessary to articulate and negotiate this kind of occasionally nonsensical situation. Then the question is what status one gives to trivial rhetoric. No doubt this is a question of delicate, and perhaps trivial, sensibility. Certainly the answer will differ depending on where one stands as who one is.

21. For a contrasting view of Aristotle's idea of knowledge, see Terence H. Irwin, *Aristotle's First Principles* (New York: Oxford University Press, 1988). Irwin argues that Aristotle does not rely most ultimately on demonstration but on what Irwin calls "strong dialectic," i.e., an argument that shows that a plausible belief is also "quite fundamental, and could not be given up without serious loss." For instance, "the assumption that there is such a thing as being qua being is a presupposition of any scientific study of an objective world at all" (176–177).

Nussbaum, among others, argues that for Aristotle the grasp of primary principles in demonstration is not knowledge at all, but *understanding* of what we, as the human beings we are, speaking our particular language, cannot help but think; Martha C. Nussbaum, *The Fragility of Goodness: Luck and Ethics in Greek Tragedy and Philosophy* (New York: Cambridge University Press, 1986), 250–258. But if there can be the kind of conflict in our basic understandings for which I am arguing, then the comments in the text below apply to this kind of grasp as well as to knowledge.

22. For example, "in relation to the ultimate bases of the principles used in the several sciences. . . . it is impossible to discuss them at all from the principles proper to the particular science in hand, seeing that the principles are the *prius* of everything else: . . . this task belongs properly . . . to dialectic: for dialectic is a process of criticism wherein lies the path to the principles of all inquiries"; Aristotle, *Topics*, trans. W. A. Pickard-Cambridge, in *The Basic Works of Aristotle*, ed. Richard McKeon (New York: Random House, 1941), i.2.101a34–101b4. Alternatively, the "immediate primary principles" of demonstration are known through repeated "sensation, like a reversal in battle brought about when one man makes a stand, then another, then a third, till a principle [or, in this case, a military formation] is attained"; Aristotle, *Aristotle's Posterior Analytics*, trans. Hippocrates G. Apostle (Grinnell, Iowa: Peripatetic Press, 1981), ii.19.99b20–100a14, my insertion.

23. Irwin, *Aristotle's First Principles*, 141.

24. Donald Davidson and Richard Rorty offer related arguments against relativism in different ways from each other and in the service of very different conclusions from my own, and mainly couched in terms of being within conceptual frameworks rather than being inside a viewpoint. I discuss these arguments and defend my own view against them, in Jeremy Barris, "The Problem of Comparing Different Cultural or Theoretical Frameworks: Davidson, Rorty, and the Nature of Truth," *Method and Theory in the Study of Religion* 18.2 (2006):124–143.

25. For references to some of the discussions of this kind of "incommensurability" of positions, see note 14 to Idea 1.

26. In this case we begin with conflicting construals (of the truth about the "same" thing), whereas there we began with the truth of the thing, which produces the conflicting construals (of its "sameness").

27. For the necessity of this kind of dialogue in the political context, see, e.g., James Tully, *Strange Multiplicity: Constitutionalism in an Age of Diversity* (Cambridge, U.K.: Cambridge University Press, 1995): e.g., approaching a culturally different group "in the right spirit does not consist in recognising it as something already familiar to us and in terms drawn from our own traditions and forms of thought. . . . Rather, recognition involves acknowledging it in its own terms and traditions." The participants in the dialogue should not be either "silenced or . . . recognised and constrained to speak within the institutions and traditions of interpretation" of only one participant (23, 24).

28. In the *Gorgias*, Socrates is presented as being at considerable pains to note not only the difference in claims between his interlocutors and himself but also the difference in the very criteria for meaningful discussion and demonstration. (That is,

the difference in the *approach* to thinking itself in the first place.) For example, "Now here is one form of refutation accepted by you and by many others, but there is also another according to my opinion. Let us compare them, then, and consider whether there is any difference between them"; Plato, *Gorgias*, 472C. Socrates' form of refutation depends on convincing the single interlocutor (as I quoted above in the text), while his interlocutor Polus's depends on producing "many reputable witnesses" (471E). Each view reconstitutes the claims of the other, basing them on its own criteria for truth. For Socrates, "a man may be the victim of false witness on the part of many people of repute" (472A), while for Polus, "views that nobody would accept" are "already refuted" (473E).

Crombie suggests in connection with the *Republic* that the reason "Socrates is allowed to reduce [Thrasymachus] to silence by a series of inconclusive arguments which often seem to depend on verbal equivocations" is that "Socrates and Thrasymachus are not allowed to make genuine contact with other because we are meant to see that neither understands the other's presuppositions. . . . It is only when it is advanced against Thrasymachus that [Socrates'] argument becomes sophistical. . . . neither understands the meaning which is to be put upon such expressions as 'virtue' or 'folly' in the other's mouth"; I. M. Crombie, *An Examination of Plato's Doctrines,* 2 vols. (London: Routledge & Kegan Paul, 1962), 83–84, my insertions.

Idea 5

1. Plato, *Sophist*, trans. F. M. Cornford, in *Plato: The Collected Dialogues,* ed. Edith Hamilton and Huntington Cairns (Princeton, N.J.: Princeton University Press, 1961), 252D–E. Unless otherwise noted, I use this translation throughout.

2. Plato, *Sophist*, 253D–E, my insertions. Kenneth Dorter describes this as "one of the most puzzling passages to be found anywhere in Plato," and discusses a variety of conflicting interpretations; Kenneth Dorter, *Form and Good in Plato's Eleatic Dialogues: The* Parmenides, Theaetetus, Sophist, *and* Statesman (Berkeley: University of California Press, 1994), 152–154.

3. Plato, *Republic,* trans. P. Shorey, in *Collected Dialogues,* 557C–E. Unless otherwise noted, I use this translation throughout.

4. "In Plato we find unmixed all the pure types of Greek prose in their classic individuality, and often incongruously juxtaposed: the logical, the physical, the mimical, the panegyrical, . . . the mythical . . . the dithyrambical"; Friedrich Schlegel, *Philosophical Fragments,* trans. P. Firchow (Minneapolis: University of Minnesota Press, 1991), 39.

5. Plato, *Phaedrus,* in *Phaedrus and Letters VII and VIII,* trans. W. Hamilton (Harmondsworth, U.K.: Penguin, 1973), 277C. Unless otherwise indicated, I use this translation throughout.

6. Hyland argues, "Because phenomena, Forms, and the knowing soul are different, speech about each, if it is to be an accurate reflection of that difference, must be heterogeneous. . . . Plato's diverse writing style is founded in this most fundamental philosophic conviction about the heterogeneity of the whole and of speech

about the whole"; Drew Hyland, *The Virtue of Philosophy: An Interpretation of Plato's Charmides* (Athens, Ohio: Ohio University Press, 1981), 141.

Another image of variegation and unevenness, this time attributed to the true world, is given in the *Phaedo*: "'Well, my dear boy,' said Socrates, 'the real earth, viewed from above, is supposed to look like one of these balls made of twelve pieces of skin, variegated [ποικίλη] and marked out in different colors. . . . Even these very hollows in the earth, full of water and air, assume a kind of color as they gleam amid the different hues around them, so that there appears to be one continuous surface of varied colors'"; Plato, *Phaedo, in The Last Days of Socrates,* trans. H. Tredennick (Harmondsworth, U.K.: Penguin, 1969), 110C–D. Unless otherwise stated, I use this translation throughout.

7. Sallis argues that the *Republic* is a comedy, at times uproariously so when it proceeds with an apparent blithe obliviousness of the body and the necessities the body involves. See, e.g., John Sallis, *Being and Logos: The Way of Platonic Dialogue,* 2nd ed. (Atlantic Highlands, N.J.: Humanities Press, 1986), 451.

And Miller argues that Plato presents the young Socrates in the *Parmenides* as replacing Zeno as Parmenides' true heir, and that the mature Socrates of the *Republic* is the consummated result of that beginning. Since Zeno is well-known for his method of refuting assumptions by pursuing them to their logical absurd conclusions, these claims fit well with the present suggestions about the *Republic.* See Mitchell H. Miller, Jr., *Plato's* Parmenides: *The Conversion of the Soul* (Princeton, N.J.: Princeton University Press; University Park: Pennsylvania State University Press, 1991 [1986]), chap. 1.

8. Plato's "sentiments were democratic in that there is nothing but superior knowledge which gives a man the right to superior political status; and he does not hold that such status carries with it the right to wealth or privilege, nor that those who are well-born are particularly likely to be gifted with superior knowledge. The democracy which he found it impossible to work in was not democracy as we know it"; I. M. Crombie, *Plato: The Midwife's Apprentice* (New York: Barnes & Noble, 1964), 172.

9. Linda Hutcheon argues, but without bringing self-cancellation into the picture, that irony generally does balance both the literal and the ironic meanings: "ironic meaning is *simultaneously* double (or multiple), and . . . therefore you don't actually have to reject a 'literal' meaning in order to get at what is usually called the 'ironic' or 'real' meaning of the utterance"; Linda Hutcheon, *Irony's Edge: The Theory and Politics of Irony* (New York: Routledge, 1995), 60. And Gregory Vlastos argues of Socrates' irony in particular that "what is said both is and isn't what is meant: its surface content is meant to be true in one sense, false in another"; Gregory Vlastos, *Socrates: Ironist and Moral Philosopher* (Ithaca, N.Y.: Cornell University Press, 1991), 31. Gordon comments, "Socratic irony is . . . inherently unstable; there is no 'resting place' for meaning when one is dealing with an ironist. Irony remains ironic, resonating among various meanings. If we erase the ambiguity or incongruity . . . to understand the irony simply, we erase the irony"; Jill Gordon, *Turning toward Philosophy: Literary Device and Dramatic Structure in Plato's Dialogues* (University

Park: Pennsylvania State University Press, 1999), 129. My own argument is that the self-canceling dimension of Socratic irony *also* allows simple meanings.

10. Hutcheon argues that "it is not the two 'poles' [of meaning] themselves that are important; it is the idea of a kind of rapid . . . hermeneutic *movement between* them . . . a playing together of two or more semantic notes to produce . . . a third— the actual ironic—meaning"; Hutcheon, *Irony's Edge*, 60, my insertion. I argue, by contrast, that both the third, "moving" meaning and the individual meanings are important, though each also excludes the importance of the other.

11. The *Republic* is often considered to be a Platonic rather than Socratic work, since it contains the "metaphysical" (dealing with the nature of reality) theory of Ideas rather than exclusively moral, practical issues investigated exclusively by refutational questioning. See, e.g., Vlastos, *Socrates.* But on the present argument it would rather be typically Socratic. It leaves us only with refuted positions and questionable refutations, and some clues and food for thought. As a result it does not present a theory of justice, but works to catalyze the hearers' or readers' own decisions in their own concrete, practical circumstances. But in any event, as I discuss at the end of Idea 6, the theory of Ideas itself need not be incompatible with a Socratic presentation. (For some comments on the distinction made between Platonic and Socratic thought generally, see the end of the general Introduction.)

12. Here is another nice example of this kind of irony from *Pride and Prejudice.* Jane has been deeply hurt by being jilted, and while she is trying very hard to make the best of it, her mother continually rubs salt into the wound by lamenting the situation. Her father has a different approach:

> "So, Lizzy, . . . your sister is crossed in love I find. I congratulate her. . . . It is something to think of, and gives her a sort of distinction among her companions. When is your turn to come? You will hardly bear to be long outdone by Jane. Now is your time. Here are officers enough at Meryton to disappoint all the young ladies in the country. Let Wickham be *your* man. He is a pleasant fellow, and would jilt you creditably."
>
> "Thank you, Sir, but a less agreeable man would satisfy me. We must not all expect Jane's good fortune."
>
> "True," said Mr Bennet, "but it is a comfort to think that, whatever of that kind may befal you, you have an affectionate mother who will always make the most of it."

Jane Austen, *Pride and Prejudice* (Harmondsworth, U.K.: Penguin, 1972), 176.

Another writer who typically exemplifies this self-ironizing kind of irony is Noel Coward. His particular brand of sentimentality often depends on being caught up in the sentimental view while also separately and simultaneously having an outside perspective on it, for example in being delighted by a clever way of phrasing it or in an awareness of its beauty or value beyond itself, perhaps as seen from a spectator's point of view. And his satire often involves being wholly absorbed in the satirized viewpoint, while also and separately including sharp satirical observations *from* that viewpoint. Which viewpoint is then being satirized—the initial object of his satire, or the view that satirizes a view capable of sharp satire?

13. Plato, *Gorgias*, trans. W. D. Woodhead, in *Collected Dialogues,* 472C. Unless otherwise indicated, I use this translation throughout. See Idea 4, note 28, on the *Gorgias*.

14. See Plato, *Apology*, trans. H. Tredennick, in *Collected Dialogues,* 21D, 23A. Unless otherwise indicated, I use this translation throughout.

15. Ibid., 28E.

16. Ibid., 19E.

17. Ibid., 20E.

18. See ibid., 33A: "those whom some people maliciously call my pupils"; and also 23A: "various malicious suggestions, including the description of me as a professor of wisdom." "Professor of wisdom" translates "σοφὸς,", which was already a derogatory term in contemporary common usage.

19. Ibid., 33A–B.

20. Plato, *Charmides*, 165B–C.

21. Plato, *Apology*, 29D–30B.

22. Plato, *Protagoras*, 314A–B.

23. Plato, *Symposium*, 202A–204C.

24. See, e.g., Plato, *Phaedrus,* 230A.

25. See Idea 2, note 9, and the corresponding text.

26. Plato, *Meno,* 84A–D.

27. Socrates introduces the idea of the soul's knowledge before birth as one he "heard from men and women who understand the truths of religion," and from "poets who are divinely inspired"; Plato, *Meno,* 81A–B. The *Gorgias*, the *Phaedo*, and the *Republic*, for example, end with myths, and the central part of the *Phaedrus* is a myth. Socrates' report of Diotima's teachings in the *Symposium* is presumably a fiction, too.

28. Plato, *Theaetetus*, 201D–E.

29. Charles Griswold argues, relatedly, that "the rhetorical, dramatic, or mimetic dimension of Plato's dialogues may serve as a partial response" to the problem of "a true mediation between philosophy and its critics." For "the prephilosophical is not already a construction of the philosopher, and so provides a common starting point for philosophy as well as its critics, thus eliminating one basis for accusing the philosopher of begging the question." The "starting point" is then "opinion; it gives us an *already intelligible,* but nonmethodological, 'beginning' for our philosophizing. Thus, for Plato, opinion is not a starting point that can ever be left behind"; Charles L. Griswold, Jr., "Plato's Metaphilosophy: Why Plato Wrote Dialogues," in *Platonic Writings, Platonic Readings,* ed. Charles L. Griswold, Jr. (New York: Routledge; University Park: Pennsylvania State University Press, 2002 [1988]), 165. Peter Levine makes what I think is a similar point about the *Protagoras:* "In Plato's . . . *Protagoras,* the quintessential philosopher . . . clashes with the ideal humanist. . . . Apparently, Plato realized that it is difficult to discuss the conflict between philosophy and humanism impartially, for if we use deductive arguments, they often favor moral

philosophy, but if we use narratives and 'thick' descriptions, they generally support humanism." Rather than "approach the issue with the methods of just one side in the quarrel . . . he worked out a . . . stylistic synthesis, the Socratic dialogue, which incorporates elements of logical argument while simultaneously presenting *characters* whose methods and values can be judged morally." He points out earlier in the same book that "In a dialogue . . . each protagonist can exemplify a different mode of reasoning—for there is nothing awkward about one participant offering a deductive argument, and then an opponent telling a relevant story. Meanwhile, the author of the dialogue can show . . . us something about the higher-order question: namely, which style of argument is better"; Peter Levine, *Living without Philosophy: On Narrative, Rhetoric, and Morality* (New York: State University of New York Press, 1998), 83, 8. I quoted Charles Altieri in note 10 to the general Introduction as, I think also similarly, arguing that "Plato's task" in the *Gorgias* "is to refute" the antiphilosophical Callicles "without relying on the authority of philosophy"; Charles Altieri, "Plato's Masterplot: Idealization, Contradiction, and the Transformation of Rhetorical Ethos," in *Intimate Conflict: Contradiction in Literary and Philosophical Discourse,* ed. Brian G. Caraher (Albany: State University of New York Press, 1992), 51.

Gilles Deleuze goes further: "it is a question of someone . . . not managing to know what everybody knows. . . . Not an individual endowed with good will and a natural capacity for thought, but an individual full of ill will who does not manage to think, either naturally or conceptually. Only such an individual is without presuppositions. . . . At the risk of playing the idiot, do so in the Russian manner: that of an underground man who . . . lacks the compass with which to make a circle"; Gilles Deleuze, *Difference and Repetition,* trans. Paul Patton (New York: Columbia University Press, 1994), 130. With respect to the need for complete thoughtlessness and incomprehension, my own view coincides with Deleuze's.

30. Plato, *Timaeus,* trans. B. Jowett, in *Collected Dialogues,* 71E–72B. Unless otherwise indicated, I use this translation throughout.

Idea 6

1. Ortega writes, though on very different grounds and motives from my own, that for philosophy "our most habitual and plausible beliefs, those which constitute the assumptions, the native soil on which we live, remain in suspension. In this sense philosophy is anti-natural, and . . . paradoxical to its very root. The '*doxa*' is opinion which is daily and spontaneous; even more, it is 'natural' opinion. Philosophy sees itself obliged to give this up, to go above or below it in search of another opinion, another *doxa* which is firmer than that which is spontaneous. This, then, is the *para-doxa.*" José Ortega y Gasset, *What Is Philosophy?,* trans. M. Adams (New York: W. W. Norton, 1960), 132–133.

2. See the reference to Fish's "self-consuming artifacts" in note 20 to Idea 2. Hegel also makes this point about productive self-cancellation, very strongly, in arguing that concepts that fix their meanings are only vanishing and self-canceling moments of the true concept: "Understanding . . . as separating and remaining fixed

in its separations . . . *equally* . . . must transcend these its *separating* determinations and straightway *connect* them. . . . The rising above those determinations which attains to an insight into their conflict is the great negative step towards the true Notion of reason. . . . The contradiction is precisely the rising of reason above the limitations of the understanding and the resolving of them"; G. W. F. Hegel, *Science of Logic*, trans. A. V. Miller (Atlantic Highlands, N.J.: Humanities Press International, 1969), 45–46. As moments, these concepts are also self-preserving: they are stable as the movement of vanishing that contributes to the larger concept. This true concept, in turn, is the stability that is the permanent flux and self-contradiction of these moments. For example, "Ground emerges merely as an illusory being that immediately vanishes; accordingly this emergence is the tautological movement of the fact to itself, and its mediation by conditions and ground is the vanishing of both. The emergence into Existence is therefore immediate in such a manner that it is mediated only by the vanishing of mediation"; ibid., 477. Consequently, as the term "moments" suggests, Hegel tries to establish the truth of something like a "sometimes" logic, my own concern here, a logic in which what is said truly is nonetheless also at another "moment" not true. It seems to me, however, that Hegel does not properly think through the cancellation of this true concept of "moments" itself. It is true that this true concept *already means* something that cancels and preserves itself. But then it must also mean something that does not do that. Differently put, the "sometimes" *itself* must only be "sometimes." And Hegel seems to me to have neglected this dimension of it. (Alternatively, he consciously limits this dimension by an idea of the completion of history and hence a final, once-for-all form of the appearance of truth. But it seems to me that the very justification of this idea of completion itself depends on the limitation, the final fixing, of the true concept that Hegel bases on that idea. He cannot, then, appeal to the completion of history for this purpose.) Consequently in his system lucidity and coherence win out as permanent (not "sometimes") acquisitions of fully true thought, and only one perspective on truth, the one that includes all the perspectives on truth, is always the one that is most fully true. "The absolute Idea alone is *being,* imperishable *life, self-knowing truth,* and is *all truth.* It is the sole subject matter and content of philosophy. . . . it has various shapes, and the business of philosophy is to cognize it in these. . . . Philosophy embraces those shapes of real and ideal finitude as well as of infinitude and holiness, and comprehends them and itself"; ibid., 824. This result, I think, does not follow from his own thought, given its neglected (sometimes *simply* self-external) dimension, and, considered independently of his thought, simply is not the case. In a manner of speaking, it is sometimes the case.

I am arguing for a kind of thinking, I believe after Plato, in which only some insights can be truly captured by an expression such as Hegel's system. But to grasp the truth of other insights, one needs to abandon the idea that one can grasp truth in general in a single internally or organically connected statement or series of statements, even if this statement or series is Hegel's speculative proposition or syllogism. Some of these other insights require a collocation of mutually irrelevant statements, or a combination of such a collocation and one or another kind of organically related series of statements, whether speculative or of the kind Hegel rejects. There are presumably indefinitely many kinds of combination and hence of relations between these two broad kinds of statement, and presumably indefinitely many cases where the combination of both kinds is not necessary.

3. Plato, *Sophist*, trans. F. M. Cornford, in *Plato: The Collected Dialogues,* ed. Edith Hamilton and Huntington Cairns (Princeton, N.J.: Princeton University Press, 1961), 235D–241C, 259A–260B.

4. This is one of Aristotle's most basic insights: there is a difference between what comes first in being most intelligible absolutely or in itself, and what comes first in being most intelligible for us who are inquiring into it. The former is the truer "first," as it gives the truth that the inquirer seeks through her/his "first": "For we do not think that we know a thing until we are acquainted with its primary conditions or first principles. . . . The natural way of doing this is to start from the things which are more knowable and obvious to us and proceed towards those which are clearer and more knowable by nature; for the same things are not 'knowable relatively to us' and 'knowable' without qualification"; Aristotle, *Physics,* trans. R. P. Hardie and R. K. Gaye, in *The Basic Works of Aristotle,* ed. Richard McKeon (New York: Random House, 1941), i.1.184a11–18.

5. As Wittgenstein notes, for example, "In giving explanations [of language] I already have to use language full-blown. . . . Philosophy may in no way interfere with the actual use of language; it can in the end only describe it. . . . It leaves everything as it is." Ludwig Wittgenstein, *Philosophical Investigations,* trans. G. E. M. Anscombe (Malden, Mass.: Blackwell, 1958), 49e, my insertion. And Husserl argues, analogously, that, "That which is . . . given is, in perception, experienced as 'the thing itself,' in immediate presence, or, in memory, remembered as the thing itself. . . . Every mediate cognition belonging to this sphere—broadly speaking, every manner of induction—has the sense of an induction of something intuitable, something possibly perceivable as the thing itself or rememberable as having-been-perceived, etc. All conceivable verification leads back to these modes of self-evidence [or givenness] because the 'thing itself' . . . lies in these intuitions themselves as that which is actually, intersubjectively experienceable and verifiable and is not a substruction of thought; whereas such a substruction, insofar as it makes a claim to truth, can have actual truth only by being related back to such self-evidences." Edmund Husserl, *The Crisis of European Sciences and Transcendental Phenomenology: An Introduction to Phenomenological Philosophy,* trans. David Carr (Evanston, Ill.: Northwestern University Press, 1970), 127–128, my insertion.

For a superb Wittgensteinian expansion of this point with respect to explanation of human and social phenomena, see Peter Winch, *The Idea of a Social Science and Its Relation to Philosophy* (London: Routledge & Kegan Paul, 1958). See also A. R. Louch, *Explanation and Human Action* (Oxford: Basil Blackwell, 1966); R. S. Peters, *The Concept of Motivation* (London: Routledge & Kegan Paul, 1958), e.g., 13.

6. To avoid confusion here, given my recent reference to Aristotle, it is true that for Aristotle, explanation of "what" something is is incomplete, and requires a more ultimate explanation of "why": "men do not think they know a thing till

they have grasped the 'why' of it (which is to grasp its primary cause)"; Aristotle, *Physics*, ii.3.194b18–20. But for Aristotle, a complete explanation requires all four kinds of cause when they exist, including the formal cause (and a relevant formal cause always exists): "we think that we *know* a thing when we know its cause, and . . . the causes are four"; Aristotle, *Aristotle's Posterior Analytics*, trans. Hippocrates G. Apostle (Grinnell, Iowa: Peripatetic Press, 1981), ii.11.94a20–21, translator's emphasis, intended to mark the translation of a specific Greek word). Now the formal cause answers the question "what" the thing is. "What" it is, therefore, is part of the ultimate "why."

7. Wittgenstein: "Your questions [about words] refer to words; so I have to talk about words. . . . One might think: if philosophy speaks of the use of the word 'philosophy' there must be a second-order philosophy. But it is not so: it is, rather, like the case of orthography, which deals with the word 'orthography' among others without then being second-order"; Ludwig Wittgenstein, *Philosophical Investigations*, 49e, my insertion. For Derrida, see note 19 to Idea 2 and note 3 to Idea 3.

8. See, e.g., the references in note 5 above.

9. See, e.g., the references in note 5 above, and Maurice Merleau-Ponty, *The Primacy of Perception*, trans. James M. Edie, et al. (Evanston, Ill.: Northwestern University Press, 1964), 52, 92.

10. Presumably this is involved in Wittgenstein's insistence in the *Tractatus* that logical propositions, that is, propositions about the nature of reality, can only *show* their own truth and cannot *say* it in an additional step. He argues that this additional step would be meaningless. A proposition about the nature of reality cannot directly express its relation with reality, since it itself is the ultimate means of expressing the reality it relates to ("ultimate" because it expresses the very *nature* of reality): in directly expressing its relation to reality, through itself, it would simply be repeating itself. That is, it would be meaningless because its meaning is redundant while trying to add something. (As in the case of Aristotle's criticism of Plato's Ideas, too, although Aristotle might not have expressed the outcome in terms of meaninglessness.) But his attention to what such propositions show is an attention to what the meaningless addition indirectly achieves or tries to mark. In fact his conclusion (which I quoted above in connection with the possibility of fully self-canceling thought) is that, "My propositions serve as elucidations in the following way: anyone who understands me eventually recognizes them as nonsensical, when he has used them—as steps—to climb up beyond them"; Ludwig Wittgenstein, *Tractatus Logico-Philosophicus*, trans. D. F. Pears and B. F. McGuinness (London: Routledge & Kegan Paul, 1961), 8–10, prop. 2.1–2.182, 74, prop. 6.54.

11. For example, "I did not get my picture of the world by satisfying myself of its correctness. . . . No: it is the inherited background against which I distinguish between true and false. . . . The propositions describing this world-picture might be part of a kind of mythology. . . . It might be imagined that some propositions, of the form of empirical propositions, were hardened and functioned as channels for such propositions as were not hardened but fluid; and that this relation altered with time, in that fluid propositions hardened, and hard ones became fluid. . . . But if

someone were to say, 'So logic too is an empirical science' he would be wrong. Yet this is right: the same proposition may get treated at one time as something to test by experience, at another as a rule of testing." Ludwig Wittgenstein, *On Certainty*, trans. Denis Paul and G. E. M. Anscombe, ed. G. E. M. Anscombe and G. H. von Wright (New York: Harper & Row, 1969), 15e.

12. See note 22 to Idea 2 for Miller's very helpful suggestion on this point in connection with Plato's Ideas.

13. Eric Toms writes, "in explaining the unity of a class by means of an abstract common property [or, equivalently, universal], this property has to be separated from each of its instances, and before the original explanation can be made effective we have first to explain how each instance can be one with its property, in the face of its separation from it." As a result, "there must be a more fundamental kind of differentiation than that of classification by properties, but . . . it is to be found in an unorthodox logic, not in types or different meanings of to 'be.'" By an "unorthodox logic," Toms means one that does not uphold "the standard laws of thought (Identity, Non-Contradiction, and Excluded Middle)." Eric Toms, *Being, Negation and Logic* (Oxford: Basil Blackwell, 1962), 22, 1, my insertion.

Peter Abelard, among many other Scholastic philosophers, raises both problems mentioned in the text and sharpens the second by pointing out that the *entirety* of "the community of the universal . . . as Boethius says, must be in *each* individual, and it is in this point that the universal is distinguished from the type of community which is common by its parts, as for example a field of which the different parts belong to different men." He notes earlier in the same work "that the universal is common, Boethius says, in such a way that the same universal is at the same time entirely in the different things of which it constitutes the substance." Arthur Hyman and James J. Walsh, eds., "The Glosses of Peter Abailard on Porphyry," in *Philosophy in the Middle Ages,* 2nd ed. (Indianapolis, Ind.: Hackett, 1973), 176, 173, my emphasis.

Plato formulates the same point as a question in the *Parmenides.* I give Miller's translation, since, as Miller advises, Cornford's replaces the question with a negative assertion. As Miller points out, this replacement conceals the probability that Plato wanted his readers to work out that the answer should be "yes" (Parmenides' interlocutor, young Aristotle, answers "no," but Plato gives strong indications that Aristotle is unreliable; accordingly, his answers are likely to signal that the points at which he speaks are important places for the reader to think twice): Parmenides: "Tell me then, can [Oneness], being one, be in many places at the same time as a whole? Reflect on this"; 144C, Mitchell H., Miller Jr., *Plato's* Parmenides: *The Conversion of the Soul* (Princeton, N.J.: Princeton University Press; University Park: Pennsylvania State University Press, 1991 [1986]), 97.

14. Stephen Toulmin makes a distinction between "force" and "criterion" (e.g., of meaning) that obviates the kind of conclusions I am drawing here. While, for example, "it may . . . seem that the terms of commendation and condemnation in which we . . . express our judgements of value have as many meanings as there are different sorts of thing to evaluate . . . it has to be recognised that the *force* of com-

mending something as 'good' or condemning it as 'bad' remains the same . . . even though the criteria for judging or assessing the merits of different kinds are very variable." Consequently, "the differences between all the varied uses of the words" need not "amount to differences in meaning. . . . As we shift from one use to another, the criteria may change while the force remains the same: whether or no we decide to *call* this a change of meaning will be a matter of comparative indifference." Stephen Toulmin, *The Uses of Argument* (Cambridge, U.K.: Cambridge University Press, 1958), 33–35. Though I cannot do justice to his very thorough argument here, the problem seems to me simply to shift to the idea of "force," which we now have to understand as the same though in radically different contexts.

15. Ortega notes that while "truth is *that which is*" (rather than, say, the property of a statement or proposition: I give his argument below), the "appearance of a thing is not the thing itself," so that when we consider things "in terms of their non-mediate appearance, they happen not to coincide with themselves, they are not equal to what they genuinely are, to what they are in their truth." As a result, "Behind the light I see, there is . . . the true light, which I do not see. And the truth of my judgment about it will not amount just to the coincidence [of my judgment] with the light, or simply with the thing, but with the truth of the light, or the light in its truth." If truth is "that which is," then, it follows that the truth of the "thing," insofar as it as well as its truth "are," both is *and* is not what the thing is (or, in my language in the text, the thing's truth both departs from and redundantly repeats the thing's nature, or truth). Differently put, the thing does not coincide with itself *in itself* as well as in its "non-mediate appearance," and so its truth does not coincide with itself either, and this means that its truth is both the same as and different from its (the truth's) self. I doubt that Ortega wanted to go to this particular conclusion, but it seems to follow from the argument anyway.

Ortega prefaces this line of thought by arguing that "One of the most radical and enduring errors committed in philosophy has been to suppose that the truth is originarily an attribute of judgment, of thinking." For, for example, "if someone were to inquire into the nature of the truth of a judgment, the reply would be forthcoming to the effect that it is a character it possesses whenever what we think therein about a thing corresponds to what the thing in question is. The truth is thus transferred from the judgment to the being of the thing. . . . Truth is *that which is*"; José Ortega y Gasset, *What Is Knowledge?,* ed. and trans. Jorge García-Gómez (New York: State University of New York Press, 2002), 91, translator's insertion.

16. Scholastic philosophers struggled with Aristotle's view of universals, for example (at least as this view was understood from the time of Porphyry's commentary in the third century CE; Ernest A. Moody, *The Logic of William of Ockham* [New York: Russell & Russell, 1935], 15–18), partly because it seemed to leave out of account precisely the concrete individuals that it was supposed to account for. For Aristotle (even in his own right), while concrete individuals are the basis of reality, there is no scientific knowledge of them, since what makes individuals what they are is the form (species) common to all things of the same kind. For example,

"though one senses"—the act with which knowledge begins—"an individual, [the power of] sensation is of the universal—e.g., of man, not of the man Callias"; Aristotle, *Posterior Analytics,* ii.19.100a17–100b1, translator's insertion. For Duns Scotus, in contrast to Aristotle, the ultimate knowable reality is the individual thing. William of Ockham extended Duns Scotus's departure from Aristotle in this respect. He clarified the importance of the distinction between the terms of thinking and language in their own right and those terms as referring to their subject matter. That is, he clarified the sense in which thinking and language are, in my phrase, artificial constructs that do not necessarily reflect realities. "In the words of Ockham, logic deals principally with those concepts and intentions 'fabricated by the mind, not outside of itself as artificial things are fabricated, but within itself'" (though this fabrication requires pregiven natural realities); Moody, *Logic of William of Ockham,* 34. As a result, Ockham was able to extend Scotus's shift of focus to dismiss the reality of forms altogether in relating thought to truth, on the grounds that to speak of forms as real within the mind is to misunderstand the nature of thought in its separateness from reality. Forms in this context, then, like universals, are artificial constructs. And precisely *because* Ockham identified language and thought in their separateness from reality, he was able to argue that the realities that the universals of thought signify are in turn entirely independent of them and of their universal character: that is, that they can be individual realities; ibid., 52. Forms as realities are entirely redundant in this account, and in fact would make this account impossible. If they were real, rather than merely signs that signify beyond themselves, then what we would know in knowing them would not be able to refer beyond them to individuals that do not share their universal nature. (In fact this treatment of universals as mere abstractions was a self-conscious return to Aristotle in his own right, against Porphyry's interpretation; ibid., 7–11. Ockham followed Aristotle in understanding universals to be *true of* individual things, but of these things "signified . . . in abstraction from this or that . . . accidental . . . circumstance"; ibid., 33. It is these abstract universals that we genuinely know, but what they signify is nonetheless concrete individual realities. The relation to Aristotle of Ockham's elimination of forms in knowledge is, however, I believe, more ambiguous. In any event, however we understand the mutual relations of these views, what they show about the problems of relating the universal to the truth of the individual remains.) Ockham's argument, then, applies to Aristotle's forms, at least in part, the kind of criticism of redundancy and falsehood with which Aristotle dismissed the theory of Ideas. My argument implies that Plato anticipated Ockham in this insight, but that he nonetheless *also* saw a place for real universals, in the "artificiality" of thought itself and of the "natural" individual thing. Aristotle, however, did not fully appreciate the nonsensical nature of rigorous universal thought, and consequently, I believe, was unable adequately to think the concrete individual as he aimed to do. For Ockham's focus on thinking and language in their own right, and his application of this focus, see the selections in Hyman and Walsh, eds., *Philosophy in the Middle Ages,* 653–700. For Scotus on the ultimate knowable reality of a thing, see the selections from *The Oxford Commentary* in the same volume, 361. For a detailed account of these developments and the literature on them, see, e.g., Sebastian J. Day, *Intuitive Cognition: A Key to the Significance of the Later Scholastics* (St. Bonaventure, N.Y.: Franciscan Institute, 1947); Moody, *Logic of William of Ockham*; Katherine H. Tachau, *Vision and Certitude in the Age of Ockham: Optics, Epistemology and the Foundation of Semantics 1250–1345* (Boston: Brill Academic, 1988).

17. Plato, *Theaetetus*, in *Theaetetus, Sophist*, trans. H. N. Fowler, Loeb Classical Library (Cambridge, Mass.: Harvard University Press, 1921), 146C–147B.

18. Socrates prefaces his answer to Theaetetus's "What do you mean by that" with "Nothing [οὐδέν], perhaps; but I will tell you what I think I mean." And in the course of his explanation, he asks, "Or is there nothing [οὐδὲν] in what I say?" Plato presents Socrates as at least uncertain about the existence of universals, at least in this case. But it fits nicely with the general framework I am presenting that he might mean exactly what he says. The universals or Ideas (whether the Ideas are universals or not) may in fact be literally nothing, nonsensical notions. To add to this possible interpretation, Socrates asks Theaetetus twice here to "define that to which each form ['form' is not present in the Greek] of knowledge belongs" with a question like, "when you say 'carpentry' . . . do you mean anything else than the art of making wooden furnishings?" and each time Theaetetus answers, "Nothing else [οὐδέν]"; Plato, *Theaetetus*, 146D–E, my insertion. But the universals may *also* be worth pursuing, as Socrates suggests by proceeding to do so. And consequently Socrates may *also* be being ironic in saying "nothing, perhaps," and in a way that in turn also ironizes itself, since his ironic statement might itself be saying nothing. The process of coming to knowledge is *itself* ironic, ironizes itself, in the way I argued in Idea 5.

If this is true, my interpretation includes the interpretations that see Socrates as being simply ironic here. But it is important to note that this inclusion modifies them fundamentally, putting the simple irony in a context that changes its significance. It rejects them as they are prior to the inclusion. If they are to be justified, and as I argued in Idea 4, they must be, their justification must occur in their own terms and as a rejection of the present interpretation.

19. Ortega, for whom life is the fundamental metaphysical reality, writes, "I believe that all life, and consequently the life of history, is made up of simple moments, each of them relatively undetermined in respect of the previous one, so that in it reality hesitates, walks up and down, and is uncertain whether to decide for one or other of various possibilities. It is this metaphysical hesitancy which gives to everything living its unmistakable character of tremulous vibration." José Ortega y Gasset, *The Revolt of the Masses*, trans. anon. (New York: W. W. Norton, 1960 [1932]), 78. And Dewey makes the argument, helpful here, that "indeterminate situations . . . are disturbed, troubled, ambiguous, confused, full of conflicting tendencies, obscure, etc. It is the *situation* that has these traits. *We* are doubtful because the situation is inherently doubtful. . . . The notion that in actual existence everything is completely determinate has been rendered questionable by the progress of physical science itself. Even if it had not been, complete determination would not hold of existences as an *environment*. For nature is an environment only as it is involved

in interaction with an organism, or self"; John Dewey, *Logic: The Theory of Inquiry* (New York: Henry Holt, 1938), 105–106. See also Peirce, who argues that what a true proposition describes occurs in reality, and since there are true vague propositions, vagueness occurs in reality. Vagueness is another way of referring to possibility, and "a state of things has the Modality of the possible . . . only in case the contradictory state of things is likewise possible." We may think "of the variety in the universe as vaguely analogous to the indecision of a person," and this "act of hypostatic abstraction . . . in itself is no violation of logic, however it may lend itself to a dress of superstition"; Charles Sanders Peirce, "Issues of Pragmaticism," in *Charles S. Peirce: Selected Writings*, ed. Philip P. Wiener (New York: Dover Publications, 1958), 215–218.

20. Perhaps this will serve as an example of an indeterminacy about the truth of what is being said in the description corresponding to an indeterminacy about what the truth is in the reality: "[His] joyful consent . . . formed just such a contrast with his early opinion on the subject . . . as time is for ever producing between the plans and decisions of mortals, for their own instruction, and their neighbours' entertainment." Jane Austen, *Mansfield Park* (Harmondsworth, U.K.: Penguin, 1966), 455, my insertion. If "time is for ever producing" a contrast between decisions, and this contrast instructs us, then presumably we will come to be instructed, that is, given the truth, differently about this outcome too.

21. Plato, *Republic*, trans. P. Shorey, in *Collected Dialogues*, 340E–347A.

22. Analogously, Nietzsche points out in *The Birth of Tragedy* that the purely chaotic Dionysian principle and the purely ordered Apollonian principle are only aspects of each other and make no sense considered on their own; Friedrich Nietzsche, *The Birth of Tragedy and the Genealogy of Morals,* trans. F. Golffing (New York: Doubleday, 1956), e.g., 33: "they mutually require one another." In the present perspective, they are purely artificial.

The problematic nature of matter in Aristotle also makes sense in this perspective. For Aristotle, the form of a thing, which is common to all things of that kind or species, is what makes that thing what it is. But Aristotle distinguishes his thought from Plato's by insisting that in almost all cases the thing also needs matter to be what it is. The common form requires matter to fulfill its function, to be what *it* is. But matter cannot be conceived at all unless it is already thought as formed by some form, since form is precisely what makes something what it is, what makes it a specific being that can therefore be conceived. Consequently form, in being dependent on matter to be what it is, is dependent on itself, and it is very unclear just what matter contributes here. In the present perspective, the extremes of pure form and pure matter, or form and matter distinguished from each other and so each considered on its own, are purely artificial and only have the meaning of (productive) self-cancellation.

If matter could be thought on its own, as medieval philosophers tried to do, it would, as some of them noted, be even more universal than form, since it is common to all different species differentiated by different forms. But at that point of its universality, it disappears as meaningful, since it is common to absolutely everything and therefore is absolutely nothing in particular, nothing specifiable or identifiable. Bodily form, if it could be thought on its own—again as some medieval philosophers tried to do—would be even more particular than Aristotle's matter, since it is what transforms matter from something entirely nonspecific into being capable of being "this thing" at all. But at that point of its individuality, it disappears as meaningful, since it is only form by being common to all things of the same kind. This is why Aristotle insists that there can be no real knowledge of any particular thing taken as only this particular thing.

These self-cancellations of Aristotle's thought into meaninglessness are the characteristics of artificiality that I argue. These fundamental problems of Aristotle's thought therefore illustrate my thesis, as well as being supported by it as not being simply problems but also elements of genuinely rigorous solutions in his thought.

23. Hegel, for example, argues that this is the case. The truth of the thing is not given adequately, for Hegel, by the simple and immediate presence or description of the thing. This truth needs to be arrived at and supported by reasons, by the method or process or history of the thought about the thing, so that it is a mediated truth. But this mediated truth, precisely because it has presented reasons and not only the thing on its own, has moved away from the thing, has presented what is partly not the thing, and has thereby negated the thing in presenting it. Consequently this negation in turn needs to be negated, to be moved away from, back to the thing. But the very fact that this process is necessary to reach the truth of the thing demonstrates that the move away from the thing must itself in fact be part of the truth of the thing as it is. The movement back to the thing must therefore preserve the movement away from it, its negation. The thing is then seen not to be something on its own at all, but to be what it is only as an element of a greater whole that includes what is not the thing. The nature or being of the thing is to be in itself also something other than itself. This is the thesis, antithesis, synthesis movement, or the movement of the negation of the negation. See, however, my criticism of Hegel in note 2 to this Idea.

24. Plato, *Phaedo*, in *The Last Days of Socrates*, trans. H. Tredennick (Harmondsworth, U.K.: Penguin, 1969), 100E.

25. To consider the relation of the Ideas to the sensible more superficially—and, for the reasons given in this Idea, equally importantly: Plato inscribes the Ideas in remarkably, wonderfully sensuous and sensual language and contexts, offering this as their texture. Accordingly, their impact is that of both pure intelligibility and pure sensuality. There seems to be no reason to privilege the one over the other, except in specific contexts or in specific kinds or phases of investigations. One could appeal to the understanding of priorities in philosophy in the history of philosophy, but Plato's works precede and to some extent found that history, which must therefore to some extent take its cues from them in making sense of them. The obvious message, rather, seems to be that conceptuality and sensuousness must sometimes be thought together. And that they must be thought together in such a way that the extreme of one *is* also the extreme of the other, while each *also* remains itself, indifferently to the other.

One merit of this reading is that it registers the information given by outstanding features of Plato's meaning and mode of presentation, and reads that information, at least initially, exactly as it stands.

There are contemporary attempts to think in this way about conceptuality and sensuousness. John Sallis, for example, takes Heidegger's thought to the point of a rigorous and beautiful variant of this kind of thinking. Playing on the double meaning of "sense"—both "meaning" and "physical sense"—he writes, "If one could still speak of a horizon from which Being would be understood, if—granting all the slippage to which such a way of speaking would now be exposed—one could thus extend the Heideggerian question, it would be necessary to speak of that horizon as extended, as broken, interrupted, and yet as gathering—in a perhaps still unheard-of sense—existentially determined meaning and an irreducibly sensible shining, twisting them together while, with the other hand, untwisting them, contorting and distorting the senses of Being. Then it could be said that Being is to an extent sensible, in every sense of this word, which yet would no longer be either sense or word"; John Sallis, *Echoes: After Heidegger* (Indianapolis: Indiana University Press, 1990), 96.

Idea 7

1. W. V. O. Quine famously undermined distinctions like that between a priori and a posteriori truth, with the result that a priori truth becomes, in a sense, a variant of a posteriori truth. See, e.g., Willard Van Orman Quine, "Two Dogmas of Empiricism," in *From a Logical Point of View: Nine Logico-Philosophical Essays,* 2nd ed. (Cambridge, Mass.: Harvard University Press, 1961). And Saul Kripke has shaken up the distinctions between these terms, arguing that "necessary *a posteriori* truths, and probably contingent *a priori* truths, both exist," where "necessary" and "*a priori*" have been understood by modern philosophers (that is, at least since Kant) to be interchangeable. Saul Kripke, *Naming and Necessity* (Cambridge, Mass.: Harvard University Press, 1980), 38. For the historical comment, see James F. Ross and Todd Bates, "Duns Scotus on Natural Theology," in *The Cambridge Companion to Duns Scotus,* ed. Thomas Williams (New York: Cambridge University Press, 2003), 230 n. 43: "The mistake that a necessary truth cannot be known a posteriori was only widespread after Kant and till the mid-twentieth century. Now everyone knows two things that Scotus knew: that a necessary truth is implied by everything, that what is true no matter what, is entailed and often can be known from what is true contingently, and also, some necessary truths are known from some things that are contingently false." Kant himself also rethought some dimensions of these distinctions, though without unsettling them in these ways, by arguing for synthetic a priori principles: that is, principles true only of objects of experience, and found directly on the basis of knowledge of them, but nonetheless a priori since they precede objects of experience as what makes their reality possible. See, e.g., Immanuel Kant, *Prolegomena to Any Future Metaphysics,* trans. L. W. Beck (New York: Bobbs-Merrill, 1950), 56 (308–309). This contrasts, for example, with Aristotle's under-

standing of universals that directly depend on sense knowledge of concrete objects to be grasped, as therefore abstractions entirely dependent on the reality of the concrete objects, and so simply a posteriori.

2. Plato, *Symposium*, trans. Alexander Nehamas and Paul Woodruff (Indianapolis, Ind.: Hackett, 1989), 219B–C.

3. See note 5 to Idea 3 for some references on establishing truth as risking oneself.

4. "I've not yet succeeded in obeying the Delphic injunction to 'know myself,' and it seems to me absurd to consider problems about other beings while I am still in ignorance about my own nature. So I . . . make myself . . . the object of my investigations"; Plato, *Phaedrus*, in *Phaedrus and Letters VII and VIII*, trans. W. Hamilton (Harmondsworth, U.K.: Penguin, 1973), 230A–B.

5. For an argument that, for example, "Wittgenstein's conceptual analyses can in fact be regarded as a kind of foundation of conservatism," see J. C. Nyíri, "Wittgenstein's Later Work in Relation to Conservatism," in *Wittgenstein and His Times,* ed. Brian McGuinness (Chicago: University of Chicago Press, 1982), 61. But as Alice Crary notes, there are commentators who "argue that . . . to the extent that Wittgenstein shows that changes in our way of life are unconstrained by responsibility to our critical concepts [since our concepts depend on our way of life, not vice versa, so that it is ultimately independent of them] he enables us to make sense of social changes which go beyond the realm of possibilities imaginable from within those ways of life"; Alice Crary, "Wittgenstein's Philosophy in Relation to Political Thought," in *The New Wittgenstein,* ed. Alice Crary and Rupert Read (New York: Routledge, 2000), 118, my insertion. Crary's own thesis is that "both positions in the debate draw on a misinterpretation of his view of meaning and that both are therefore unable to illuminate ways in which his philosophy can inform political thought" (118), which I think is right.

6. By way of concrete analogy: in *Mansfield Park,* Maria exclaims, "I really cannot undertake to harangue all the rest upon a subject of this kind.—*There* would be the greatest indecorum I think." And Edmund replies, "No—let your conduct be the only harangue. . . . All who can distinguish, will understand your motive"; Jane Austen, *Mansfield Park* (Harmondsworth, U.K.: Penguin, 1966), 164. A direct presentation of the truth can be presumptuous and rude, so that the act of presenting it undermines its effect, making it appear falsely grounded. And as I argued above, because (the truth about) a truth is internally connected to its presentation and the outcome of its presentation, there is something right here about the appearance of falsehood. In addition, if it is in fact presumptuous, it is false to the speaker's position and so false in yet another way internally related to the situation in which it functions. Sometimes the right way to present truth is to present the truth at a distance from, external to, itself, so that it can be identified only via an inference. In this way it is presented without internal falsehood, and in addition, whoever acts on it acts not arbitrarily but on a truth, because it has been established for him/her, in her/his own risk of thinking and deciding.

Idea 8

1. Gadamer comments on Plato's *Philebus* that, "human life, just as all other being, belongs to the mixed genus. . . . Everything that exists has reality only in its concrete determinacy. And that means precisely that it is set in, and surrounded by, the unlimitedly variable—genesis. . . . Any deed, to the extent that it is decision, always includes a component of uncertainty"; Hans-Georg Gadamer, *The Idea of the Good in Platonic-Aristotelian Philosophy*, trans. P. Christopher Smith (New Haven, Conn.: Yale University Press, 1986), 122.

2. While Gadamer does not understand mixture as being self-external in this way, I believe that his own interpretation of Plato requires him to do so: "True reality, or 'being,' is one but nevertheless in all the many things. And that means that it is separated from itself 'which, however, seems to be the most impossible thing of all' (*Philebus, *15b)"; Gadamer, *Idea of the Good*, 118. If the mixture is itself a genus of *reality* (see note 1 above), then surely it itself must also be separated from itself, too, since it is a part of the reality to which it applies. In that case, the concrete determinacy of the mixture is not the last basis for reality.

3. Plato, *Sophist*, trans. F. M. Cornford, in *Plato: The Collected Dialogues,* ed. Edith Hamilton and Huntington Cairns (Princeton, N.J.: Princeton University Press, 1961), 252D–E.

4. Ibid., 235D–241C, 259A–260B.

5. The problem is complicated in that the Stranger suggests in the dialogue (the validity of this suggestion is ultimately unclear: it is found inadequate, and then the theory that finds it inadequate is in turn found inadequate in a different connection; ibid., 249C–250D) that what is real is what is "so constituted as to possess any sort of power either to affect anything else or to be affected, in however small a degree, by the most insignificant agent, though it be only once"; ibid., 247D–E. Though Plato does not draw this inference, this means that falsehoods, which have effects, are real despite being based on what is not, so that it is tricky to distinguish them in an essential way from truths. This is a form of the discussion of the natural and the artificial in Idea 1.

6. Ibid., 257C–258B.

7. Ibid., 258C.

8. Ibid., 256A, translator's insertion.

9. Ibid., 258B.

10. Ibid., 258E.

11. Plato, *Crito,* trans. Hugh Tredennick, in *Collected Dialogues*, 49D. Unless otherwise noted, I use this translation throughout.

12. Plato, *Phaedo*, in *The Last Days of Socrates*, trans. H. Tredennick (Harmondsworth, U.K.: Penguin, 1969), 101E.

13. Ibid., 91B–C.

14. Plato, *Sophist*, 260A.

15. Gadamer gives a very helpful explanation of the indeterminate dyad and its unnamed presence in the dialogues; Hans-Georg Gadamer, *Dialogue and Dialectic:*

Eight Hermeneutical Studies on Plato, trans. P. Christopher Smith (New Haven, Conn.: Yale University Press, 1980), 124–155. While he also argues that the indefinite dyad is cofoundational with the One, he differs from my account in seeing the dyad's indeterminacy as homogeneously affecting all knowledge, where I argue for a "sometimes" reality of basic categories, or alternatively of basic realities, like this one. See my criticism of Gadamer's standpoint in note 2 above.

    16. Plato, *Phaedo,* 89D, my insertion.

    17. Ibid., 89E–90A.

    18. Ibid., 89D.

    19. Ibid., 67E.

    20. "[I]n the case of Plato's 'demonstration' of immortality we are dealing with a mere stage in a dialogical exposition, whose deeper concern is not immortality at all but rather that which constitutes the actual being of the soul—not in regard to its possible mortality or immortality but to its ever vigilant understanding of itself and of reality"; ibid., 29. And Brann notes "several clues that . . . the ascetic depiction of philosophy as the practice of death and hatred of the body, is perhaps more caricature than characterization"; Eva Brann, Peter Kalkavage, and Eric Salem, Introduction to *Plato's* Phaedo, trans. Eva Brann, Peter Kalkavage, and Eric Salem (Newburyport, Mass.: Focus, 1998), 4.

    21. Phaedo himself, that is, the narrator of most of the dialogue, may also be talking to Pythagoreans in reporting the discussion with Socrates in the jail. Klein points out that Phlius, where Phaedo's narration of the dialogue is set, contained a Pythagorean brotherhood; Jacob Klein, *Lectures and Essays,* ed. R. B. Williamson and E. Zuckerman (Annapolis, Md.: St. John's College Press, 1985), 379.

    22. Or if Phaedo was not one of Socrates' circle, he was at least very familiar with Socrates, who, for example, Phaedo says, "never missed a chance to tease me about my hair"; Plato, *Phaedo,* 89B. According to Diogenes Laertius, while Phaedo was a slave, "he would . . . contrive to join Socrates' circle," and Socrates was responsible for his being ransomed, after which "he studied philosophy as became a free man"; Diogenes Laertius, *Lives of Eminent Philosophers,* 2 vols., trans. R. D. Hicks, Loeb Classical Library (Cambridge, Mass.: Harvard University Press, 1972), 1:233.

    23. Holger Thesleff defends the idea of the "pedimental" principle of composition in some of Plato's dialogues, "an arrangement of things so as to put the most important or intrinsically interesting ones in the centre"; Holger Thesleff, "Looking for Clues: An Interpretation of Some Literary Aspects of Plato's 'Two-Level' Model," in *Plato's Dialogues: New Studies and Interpretations,* ed. Gerald A. Press (Lanham, Md.: Rowman & Littlefield, 1993), 19 n. 4.

    24. Plato, *Phaedo,* 89B, my insertions.

    25. "This affectionate gesture is alone sufficient to dispel any notion that Socrates is simply a hater of bodily things"; Brann, et al., Introduction to *Plato's* Phaedo, 11. Here is one way in which the reading of Plato as simply developing a theory of Ideas deals with this passage: "An interval before the resumption of close argument is welcome . . . and the artistry of Plato fills the interval in a most satisfying way . . .

partly by the incident of Socrates stroking Phaedo's hair—an incident combining raillery and pathos, evoking both a smile and a tear. By this time . . . Plato's readers are braced for a vigorous warning against intellectual defeatism"; Reginald Hackforth, *Plato's* Phaedo (Cambridge, U.K.: Cambridge University Press, 1972 [1955]), 109–110. This seems clearly right, even granting the view I have suggested. But why should it not be the *whole* truth of that passage, rightly excluding my own view? It does show how what is important for one approach to understanding, what orients which aspects it selects as evidence for what, and how it weighs what it selects, can be comparatively trivial for another approach or orientation of understanding. A thorough interpretation, then, needs to go with an interpretation of interpretation itself.

26. Plato, *Phaedo*, 90B.

27. Ibid., 89C.

28. "The remarkable drama that takes place between Socrates and Phaedo, so carefully placed at the center of the dialogue, suggests that the hatred of argument is more terrible than the fear of death"; Brann, et al., Introduction to *Plato's* Phaedo, 12.

29. Mixtures, as opposed to Pythagorean purity, are also emphasized in other ways in the dialogue. The first thing Phaedo talks about in beginning to report the events in prison is his "extraordinary" feeling, "an absolutely incomprehensible emotion, a sort of curious blend of pleasure and pain combined. . . . All of us who were there were affected in much the same way, between laughing and crying"; Plato, *Phaedo*, 58E–59A. And the second thing Socrates is made to say (after having his weeping wife, Xanthippe, taken home), the chains having been removed from his leg, is "What a queer thing it is, my friends, this sensation which is popularly called pleasure! It is remarkable how closely it is connected with its conventional opposite, pain. . . . I am sure that if Aesop had thought of it he would have made up a fable about them"; ibid., 60B–C. Phaedo mentions mixture in connection with emotions, which Socrates will later argue, I suggest for the benefit of the Pythagoreans, are distractions from the purity of knowledge and therefore belong to the body rather than the soul. And Socrates mentions mixture in connection with physical sensations, that is, with the body itself.

Klein draws attention to the lengthy references to the myth of Theseus at the start of the dialogue, and suggests that Socrates is given the role of Theseus, while the Minotaur he has to kill, in threading his way through the labyrinth of arguments, is the fear of death; Klein, *Lectures*, 375–378. But as I noted above, Socrates tells us, at the only point at which he is speaking philosophically to one of his own circle rather than to Pythagoreans, that the greatest misfortune is dislike of argument. The dialogue seems to say perfectly clearly, then, that the Minotaur that is most important to confront is not the fear of death but the dislike of argument. This, in turn, suggests that the entire discussion of the immortality of the soul and therefore of the reality and purity of the Ideas misses the main point, does not address the fundamental philosophical issues, as far as Plato's Socrates is concerned.

Yet another reason for thinking that Socrates does not mean what he says for most of this dialogue lies in the reference to Aesop's fables. Socrates had apparently been adapting Aesop's fables (in fact he offers an imaginary one here about the mixture of pleasure and pain), and one of the Pythagoreans asks why he has been doing so when he "had never done anything of the kind before"; Plato, *Phaedo*, 60C–D. But in fact the reverse is the case: Plato typically presents Socrates as engaging in all kinds of adaptations of fictions. Something basic is clearly already being missed at the start of the *Phaedo*. Or, an indication of pure artificiality, of a basic nothing ("what is not" the truth), is clearly being presented as we are introduced to the dialogue. Klein, for example, argues that the entire Phaedo is invented by Plato, and that it is in its entirety a Platonic myth; Klein, *Lectures*, 378.

I suggest that it is certainly fiction, but perhaps more like a sour-grapes story. There is perhaps a hint that the Pythagoreans, for whose philosophy of eternal and pure reality Socrates argues, aim to despise bodily life because they recognize that they cannot have it forever. The recognition of mortality, at least as an issue to think about, is important, and at least to that extent, Pythagorean thought is worthwhile. But I suggest that for Plato, the reaction of rejecting life altogether is perhaps not philosophically good enough. And I suggest that, correspondingly, Socrates is made to present the theory of eternal and pure Ideas as being worthwhile, but perhaps not good enough.

Klein argues that Phaedo plays the role of Ariadne, who gave Theseus the thread that allowed him to find his way out of the labyrinth; ibid., *Lectures,* 377. I suggest that the thread he offers Socrates is that of the notion of mixture, as against the Pythagorean presupposition of the validity of purity that Socrates has been exploring. He and Socrates both mention mixture in their initial statements in the narration of the prison dialogue: these two characters are linked in this way from the start. Phaedo then offers this thread again in the central passage in which Socrates digresses from the main argument to present the real issue, the dislike of argument, and Phaedo's contribution there is described by Socrates as itself a digression. But in this way, as also a digression, it is formally linked with Socrates' own most important contribution.

30. Plato, *Phaedo*, 90B.

31. Ibid., 61D.

32. Ibid., 63B.

33. Ibid., 69D–E.

34. "Socrates will not profess knowledge where he is conscious of his own ignorance. That being so, he can hardly have held that attitude to life expressed in the *Phaedo* account of the 'true philosophers'"; Hackforth, *Plato's* Phaedo, 15–16.

35. Plato, *Phaedo*, 91A-C, my insertion.

36. Ibid., 90C–D.

37. In the myth about the variegated true world near the end of the *Phaedo,* Socrates is made to include a short piece of reasoning. In this way the form of the myth is mixed, just as the form of the dialogue as a whole is rendered mixed by the inclusion of the myth. Given the above comments about ungainly poise, the clash of the

form of this piece of reasoning with its story-like context, together with the content of the reasoning, are perhaps significant. Its content is that the earth, being "spherical and in the middle of the heavens," needs nothing to support it. For "any body in equilibrium, if it is set in the middle of a uniform medium, will have no tendency to sink or rise in any direction more than another, and having equal impulses will remain suspended"; Plato, *Phaedo*, 108E–109A. Analogously, given the ungainly poise I have discussed, this "sometimes" balance of ways of making sense, there is, again, no necessary infinite regress in explanatory thinking. One can come to recognize the "nothing further" that needs to be thought to make sense of a thing or a state of affairs, the boundaries of relevant sense.

As Wittgenstein notes, though it is difficult, one can "begin at the beginning. And not . . . try to go further back"; Ludwig Wittgenstein, *On Certainty*, trans. Denis Paul and G. E. M. Anscombe, ed. G. E. M. Anscombe and G. H. von Wright (New York: Harper & Row, 1969), 62e. For "somewhere I must begin with not-doubting; and that is not, so to speak, hasty but excusable: it is part of judging"; ibid., 22e. For example, "It's no good saying 'Perhaps we are wrong' when, if *no* evidence is trustworthy, trust is excluded in the case of the present evidence" (including evidence that suggests we might be wrong); ibid., 39e.

38. Plato, *Phaedo*, 92C–D.

39. Ibid., 95E.

40. Ibid., 98B–99C.

41. Ibid., 97B, my insertion.

42. Ibid., 99D–100A, my insertion.

43. Similarly, in the *Protagoras:* "When you buy food and drink . . . before you receive it into your body . . . you can . . . take the advice of an expert as to what you should eat and drink . . . and how much . . . and when . . . But knowledge cannot be taken away in a parcel. When you have paid for it you must receive it straight into the soul. You go away having learned it and are benefited or harmed accordingly. So I suggest we give this matter some thought"; Plato, *Protagoras*, trans. W. K. C. Guthrie, in *Collected Dialogues*, 314A–B.

44. Plato, *Phaedo*, 100A.

45. Hugh H. Benson, ed., *Socratic Wisdom: The Model of Knowledge in Plato's Early Dialogues* (New York: Oxford University Press, 2000), 109.

46. Vlastos also argues that Plato is aiming at a kind of combination of the two kinds of explanation: "a *physical* law that has *logical* necessity. Since Plato claims that the snow of our experience is cold because the Form, Snow, entails the Form, Cold, and since all forms . . . sustain only immutable relations between each other, he is implying that the laws of nature, could we but know them, would have the same necessity as do the truths of arithmetic and logic"; Gregory Vlastos, "Reasons and Causes in the *Phaedo*," in *Platonic Studies* (Princeton, N.J.: Princeton University Press, 1981), 105. And he notes some modern philosophers with similar views; ibid., 106. While I have no objection to the idea of logically necessary physical laws, however, this is not the kind of combination I am suggesting. On the contrary, I am arguing for a self-canceling relation between the two kinds of explanation, that pre-

serves their mutual exclusiveness (although it may *also* allow or account for the kind of combination Vlastos suggests).

47. Plato, *Phaedo*, 100E.

48. Vlastos, "Reasons and Causes," 100, my insertion. See also I. M. Crombie, *Plato: The Midwife's Apprentice* (New York: Barnes & Noble, 1964), 19: Socrates "seems to imply" that the theories he criticizes here "were guilty of what we might almost call category-confusions, or at any rate inattention to differences of logical level."

49. Plato, *Sophist*, 253D, my insertion.

50. Plato, *Phaedo*, 102A.

51. Ibid., 64A–B.

52. Ibid., 64B–C.

53. See the quote from *Mansfield Park* and my comment on it in note 6 to Idea 7.

54. Plato, *Phaedo*, 105B–C.

55. Plato, *Sophist*, 255A–260B.

56. Ibid., 246A–B.

57. Ibid., 249C–D.

58. One way in which the simple theory of Ideas interpretation of Plato deals with this: "It seems clear, though the question has been much debated, that the idealists' theory represents Plato's own theory of Forms . . . which he now wishes to modify." The editor's note gives references "for arguments against the view that Plato is modifying the substance of the theory of Forms"; R. S. Bluck, *Plato's Sophist*, ed. G. C. Neal (Manchester, U.K.: Manchester University Press, 1975), 94. And see Kenneth Dorter, *Form and Good in Plato's Eleatic Dialogues: The* Parmenides, Theaetetus, Sophist, *and* Statesman (Berkeley: University of California Press, 1994), 146–150, for a discussion of some arguments that this passage does not compromise the purity of the Ideas. My own view, of course, is that for Plato, the theory of Ideas is already, for example, "sometimes" entirely false, and "sometimes" entirely true just as it stands. But, with respect to the traditional reading: again, why should *it* not be entirely true just as it stands?

59. Plato, *Timaeus*, trans. B. Jowett, in *Collected Dialogues*, 52B–C, translator's insertions.

60. Ibid., 52B–C.

61. It also fits other strands of my discussion that the whole description of the construction of the cosmos is prefaced by Timaeus's insistence that in speaking about things whose nature is to change, "we ought to accept the tale which is probable and inquire no further." Socrates has already anticipated "a perfect and splendid feast of reason." But it is a tale, an image (εἰκὼς λόγος) that he is given, and he accepts it without surprise: "the prelude is charming and is already accepted by us"; ibid., 27B–29D. (As Sallis notes, "Like the images of which it speaks, such discourse would be removed from the truth itself, set at a distance from it"; John Sallis, *Chorology: On Beginning in Plato's* Timaeus [Bloomington: Indiana University Press, 1999], 55.) Again, fiction is not alien to the reasoned thinking Plato presents us.

Ashbaugh, however, warns, "Whatever else it is, the Timaean cosmology is not, strictly speaking, poetry"; Anne Freire Ashbaugh, *Plato's Theory of Explanation: A Study of the Cosmological Account in the* Timaeus (Albany: State University of New York Press, 1988), 14. That is, this kind of tale gives genuine explanations. But Ashbaugh's warning depends on thinking of poetry as not giving genuine explanations, which in turn may depend on reading Plato as simply opposing poetry to philosophy and so rejecting it.

62. Albert Levi writes, " 'My propositions,' says Wittgenstein [*Tractatus,* 74, prop. 6.54], 'are elucidatory in this way: he who understands me finally recognizes them as senseless, when he has climbed out through them, on them, over them. (He must so to speak throw away the ladder, after he has climbed up on it.) He must surmount these propositions; then he sees the world rightly.' One can imagine the aged Plato reading over the Dialogues of his youth and attempting to put himself back into the Socratic atmosphere to sum up the intention of their therapy; he could have chosen no better words than these." And, "[s]ince argument lives in language, linguistic 'understanding,' the 'significance' of terms, the 'meaning' of propositions become increasingly relevant, and dialectic turns to discourse itself as its domain. This is, of course, the meaning of the rhetorical and Sophistic revolution of the fifth century—into whose whirlpool Socrates himself descends. . . . It is precisely within this tradition of the adjustment of interpretive contexts that Wittgenstein can describe the program of the *Philosophical Investigations*"; Albert Levi, "Wittgenstein as Dialectician," in *Ludwig Wittgenstein: The Man and His Philosophy,* ed. K. T. Fann (New York: Dell, 1967 [1964]), 372, 379, my insertion.

Karl-Otto Apel argues that Wittgenstein's view that there are multiple "language games" (in Levi's terms, "interpretive contexts"), each with its own rules for sense, presupposes a universal language game "by which . . . communication with all language games . . . is possible without getting dependent on the different, and eventually incommensurable" particular language games. If there is no independent universal language game, any discussion of language games can only be given its meanings by a particular language game and therefore will necessarily distort the meanings of all the others it tries to discuss. As a result, without his realizing it, Wittgenstein's thinking presupposes a "paradigm or ideal norm for judging all other language games," or a "transcendental a priori" standpoint; Karl-Otto Apel, *Selected Essays, Volume One: Towards a Transcendental Semiotics,* ed. Eduardo Mendieta (Atlantic Highlands, N.J.: Humanities Press, 1994), 103–104. Apel endorses and offers a way of making sense of this "universal" standpoint in terms of an "ideal (indefinite) communication community" (103). My own proposal, by contrast, is that Wittgenstein recognizes this problem of the language in which he discusses language, and already responds to it by showing why and how his own language games, in whose terms he discusses the others, both function and cancel themselves into nonsense. I agree, then, that Wittgenstein's philosophy involves a transcendental a priori standpoint, but I believe that Wittgenstein explicitly argues for it in his work and that he understands the nature of the transcendental (as something like productively self-canceling nonsense) very differently from the way Apel understands it. Also, for all the reasons I have given for a "sometimes always" logic in connection with social and political pluralism (see, e.g., notes 9 and 14 to Idea 1), I do not believe that Apel's universal, ideal community's viewpoint can itself be meaningful in only one way. If I am right, then different interpretive contexts can legitimately understand the universal, ideal viewpoint itself differently, and as a result, that viewpoint cannot succeed in being the legitimate adjudicator between them.

63. Plato, *Phaedo*, 97B–D.

64. Plato, *Republic,* 2 vols., trans. Paul Shorey, Loeb Classical Library (Cambridge, Mass.: Harvard University Press, 1935), 1:433A–B.

65. I believe that the connection between goodness and truth, and the self-canceling nature of the Ideas, answers arguments like Vlastos's distinguishing the Socratic from the properly Platonic dialogues; see note 11 to Idea 5, and Gregory Vlastos, *Socrates: Ironist and Moral Philosopher* (Ithaca, N.Y.: Cornell University Press, 1991). The theory of Ideas adds literally nothing to the "nonmetaphysical" and concrete practical concerns of "Socrates." In fact, as I argue, it is an extremely elaborate and rigorous demonstration that nothing *needs* to be added.

Speaking of goodness and truth in connection with this kind of self-cancellation, Wittgenstein (see note 62 and the text) argues in the *Tractatus* both that: "the propositions of logic say nothing," so that "[l]ogic is transcendental" (Ludwig Wittgenstein, *Tractatus Logico-Philosophicus*, trans. D. F. Pears and B. F. McGuinness [London: Routledge & Kegan Paul, 1961], 59, prop. 6.11, 65, prop. 6.13), and that "[i]t is clear that ethics cannot be put into words. Ethics is transcendental" (ibid., 71, prop. 6.421). For "[t]he sense of the world must lie outside the world. . . . If there is any value that does have value, it must lie outside the whole sphere of what happens and is the case. For all that happens and is the case is accidental. What makes it non-accidental cannot lie *within* the world, since if it did it would itself be accidental"; ibid., 71, prop. 6.41. And it turns out that these too, his own propositions, cannot be said, are nonsense that "we must pass over in silence"; ibid., 74, prop. 7.

66. Plato, *Phaedo*, 97E.

67. As Wittgenstein insists, again, "anyone who understands me eventually recognizes [my propositions] as nonsensical, when he has used them—as steps—to climb up beyond them. . . . He must transcend these propositions, and then he will see the world aright. What we cannot speak about we must pass over in silence"; ibid., 74, props. 6.54, 7. And see the comments from and on the *Tractatus* in note 62.

Part II: Chapter 1

1. In contrast with conceptual analysis, the once-dominant and still influential "logical construction" does not follow this principle. "Constructional theory constructs an object by seeking an infallible . . . indicator for it. . . . This . . . does not . . . achieve what we generally require of a definition in the sense of a conceptual definition. As such it would have to indicate the essential characteristics of a con-

cept, but these are frequently not contained in the indicator." Unlike a conceptual definition or translation, which is required to "leave invariant . . . the sense of the statements," or their "intuitive meaning," a constructional definition or translation only "requires that the translated statements have the same logical value as the original ones," that is, that they are true or false whenever the original statements are true or false. Rudolf Carnap, *The Logical Structure of the World and Pseudoproblems in Philosophy,* trans. R. A. George (Berkeley and Los Angeles: University of California Press, 1967), 83–85. For an extremely thorough and influential argument that one can, rather, ultimately only account for a concept at least partly in terms of its ordinary or informal contexts, see Wilfrid Sellars, "Empiricism and the Philosophy of Mind," in *Science, Perception and Reality* (Atascadero, Calif.: Ridgeview, 1991 [1956]).

2. I quoted in the Introduction, note 27, Davidson's related comment on accounting for error in subjectivity: "The underlying paradox of irrationality, from which no theory can entirely escape, is this: if we explain it too well, we turn it into a concealed form of rationality; while if we assign incoherence too glibly, we merely compromise our ability to diagnose irrationality by withdrawing the background of rationality needed to justify any diagnosis at all"; Donald Davidson, "Paradoxes of Irrationality," in *Philosophical Essays on Freud,* ed. Richard Wollheim and James Hopkins (New York: Cambridge University Press, 1982), 303. See the quote from Bernard Williams in that note, too.

In this connection, Deleuze writes, "Among the most extraordinary pages in Plato, demonstrating the anti-Platonism at the heart of Platonism, are those which suggest that the different, the dissimilar, the unequal . . . may well be not merely defects which affect copies . . . but rather models [that is, Ideas, ultimate reality] themselves, terrifying models of the *pseudos* [lie, falsehood] in which unfolds the power of the false"; Gilles Deleuze, *Difference and Repetition,* trans. Paul Patton (New York: Columbia University Press, 1994), 128, my insertions. Deleuze explores the value of this deep being of untruth, this untruth that is part of being itself, and that provides "the means of challenging *both* the notion of the copy *and* that of the model" (128). He does not, however, see it as self-canceling in the sense for which I am arguing. See, e.g., Gilles Deleuze, *The Logic of Sense,* trans. Mark Lester with Charles Stivale (New York: Columbia University Press, 1990), 81, where he develops the idea that "sense is the object of fundamental paradoxes which repeat the figures of nonsense." It is true, for Deleuze, that "the gift of sense occurs only when the conditions of signification are also being determined. The terms of the series . . . will subsequently be submitted to these conditions, in a tertiary organization which will relate them to . . . [nonparadoxical] good sense, common sense" (my insertion). But, apart from the "subsequent" nature of this relation to nonparadox, it "is necessarily affected . . . by an extreme and persistent fragility." This perspective also contributes to making his reading of Plato very different from mine: so, for example, in Plato "this hypothesis [of the deep being of untruth] is quickly put aside, silenced and banished"; Deleuze, *Difference,* 128, my insertion.

3. Plato, *Sophist*, trans. F. M. Cornford in *Plato: The Collected Dialogues,* ed. Edith Hamilton and Huntington Cairns (Princeton, N.J.: Princeton University Press, 1961), 236D–241C.

4. "That thing about which we ask 'What is it?' is there, in one sense or another it has being; otherwise it would never occur to us to ask about it. But it follows that we are not content that it exists and is there. . . . Obviously because what it is, as it is, is not sufficient in itself"; José Ortega y Gasset, *What Is Philosophy?* trans. M. Adams (New York: W. W. Norton, 1960), 82.

5. Crombie, for example, refers to "the bad arguments which are quite often to be met with in the dialogues"; I. M. Crombie, *Plato: The Midwife's Apprentice* (New York: Barnes & Noble, 1964), 6. See also the references in note 1 to the Introduction.

6. Plato, *Republic*, 2 vols., trans. Paul Shorey, Loeb Classical Library (Cambridge, Mass.: Harvard University Press 1935), 2:543C.

7. Ibid., 2:505A–509B.

8. Plato has Socrates distinguish between truth and being in this passage. I argued in Idea 6.2 that the same considerations apply to both as far as the bases of rigorous thought are concerned, and that Plato makes the same point in a variety of different ways. Socrates is using terms in ways familiar to his audience here, so this distinction in this passage need not conflict with my assimilation of the terms.

9. "That Plato uses only the word *idea,* and never *eidos,* for the *agathon* [good] . . . indicates that the idea of the good has a character all its own"; Hans-Georg Gadamer, *Idea of the Good in Platonic-Aristotelian Philosophy,* trans. P. Christopher Smith (New Haven, Conn.: Yale University Press, 1986), 27, my insertion.

10. Kant, for example, identifies a similar thoughtless unification of concepts in the method of "pure reason" predominant in his time. In what he calls this "dogmatic [or, from the Greek root, "opinion-like"] procedure," which does not question the scope of its validity, "perhaps the greatest part" consists in "analysis" which is "nothing but . . . elucidation of what has already been thought in our concepts, though in a confused manner"; Immanuel Kant, *Critique of Pure Reason,* trans. N. K. Smith (New York: St Martin's Press, 1929), A:5–6; B:9, my insertion. As a result "reason is so far misled as surreptitiously to introduce, without itself being aware of so doing, assertions of an entirely different order, in which it attaches to given concepts others completely foreign to them"; ibid., A:6; B:10. This thoughtless unity of concepts, again, hides real, mutually distinct unities of concepts.

Kant's response is to demarcate the limits of conceptual analysis, partly by showing that each object of which we can have a concept needs to be understood in two senses, one that we can know and another that we can think but not know; ibid., B:xxvii–xxviii. This is the famous distinction between the thing as appearance and the thing in itself. And while our knowledge of what we can know is genuine knowledge, it also depends ultimately and entirely on what we can only think without knowing (B:xx–xxi), which is the ultimate, the only unconditioned reality. For Kant, as I argue for Plato, the truth of the world is therefore unified, but this unity occurs also *as* a fundamental disparity *within* itself, between two incomparable senses of each object. And, like Plato, Kant begins by emphasizing and working with the simple unity of reason, in order to show the validity of dogmatic science as well as of a nondogmatic or critical metaphysics.

11. Plato, *Sophist*, 249C–D, 255A–260B.

12. With respect to the Ideas as tangents, Hyland argues that "one of the decisive lessons of the *aporia* dialogues, both early and late, is that we go about the effort to understand our world incorrectly when we try directly to define the *source* of its intelligibility.... Platonic philosophy ... has its *archè*, or origin, in a critical dimension of human incompleteness, our lack of wisdom or the ability to account for the whole. But ... we see that [the] world *can* be intelligible due to the presence of the *archè* of its intelligibility—the Ideas. This means that we could give a logos [account] of our experience by the oblique reference to the Ideas present in any such account"; Drew Hyland, *The Virtue of Philosophy: An Interpretation of Plato's* Charmides (Athens, Ohio: Ohio University Press, 1981), 66–67, my insertions.

13. Plato, *Republic*, 2:506B–E.

14. Sallis, among others, argues this, though to different effect. See the citations in note 22 to the introduction.

15. Like Kant in this respect (see note 10 above). In fact, in the *Critique of Judgment*, Kant argues for a version of what I am presenting as the ultimately necessary self-canceling or self-emptying orientation entirely away from the object of the inquiry, and toward the truth of truth in general. He argues that our ability to judge nature's purposiveness is the bridge between, on the one hand, the domain of things in themselves, to which we have access only through morality and the freedom that morality presupposes, and on the other hand, the domain of appearances, which we can know theoretically rather than only morally. But it is "the aesthetic judgment ... that prompts this concept of purposiveness" and "makes that concept ... suitable for mediating the connection of the domain of the concept of nature with that of the concept of freedom"; Immanuel Kant, *Critique of Judgment*, trans. W. S. Pluhar (Indianapolis, Ind.: Hackett, 1987), 37–38 (197). Now, aesthetic judgment, which these descriptions make the linchpin of the whole system, cannot share the objectivity of theoretical knowledge. If it did, it would just *be* theoretical knowledge, and so could not be a bridge between it and something else. But it must still be a priori and universal, otherwise, again, it could not be an ultimate bridge between the basic kinds of knowledge. Kant's solution is that aesthetic judgment is nothing but the feeling of all of one's subjective cognitive powers, those that know morally and those that know theoretically, balancing harmoniously with each other, and not conceptualizing or imagining or reasoning about any particular object. "The mental state in this presentation must be a feeling, accompanying the given presentation, of a free play of the presentational powers directed to cognition in general"; ibid., 62 (217). In this way the judgment is a priori. And since we all share the same types of cognitive powers, whatever object ("presentation") can prompt these powers to harmonize in one of us must necessarily do so universally in all of us: "this subjective relation suitable for cognition in general must hold just as much for everyone"; ibid., 62 (218). But for Kant, the structure of one's subjective powers

is the structure of knowable reality. So in fact, in feeling the harmony of one's subjective powers doing nothing but harmonize with one another, one is feeling the structure of knowable reality in general and as a whole. In other words, one grasps reality as a whole when and only when one turns entirely away from the content of that reality and focuses only on the structure of knowledge itself, as it is when it is empty of any reference to its objects. It is knowledge focusing exclusively on itself: when "the pure power of judgment" makes "*aesthetic* judgments . . . it is, subjectively, object to itself as well as law to itself"; ibid., 153 (288). In fact, this linchpin of the domains of knowledge is so empty of reference to a subject matter that it is not even knowledge: "the presentation communicate[s] itself not as a thought but as the inner feeling of a purposive state of mind"; ibid., 162 (296), my insertion.

16. M. W. Isenberg comments on "the constant shifting of [Plato's] terms" that "The important thing is that the reader go through in his own soul and mind the dialectical treatment of a problem. The solution of a problem apart from this dialectical experience is valueless. Consequently, fixed terms, as such, can only be a hindrance and an unwise shortcut to correct knowledge. Once the shifting 'structure' of the Platonic dialectic is grasped, the terms themselves take on a meaning appropriate to the context"; M. W. Isenberg, "Plato's *Sophist* and the Five Stages of Knowing," *Classical Philology* 46.4 (1951):209 n. 4, my insertion.

17. Plato, *Symposium*, trans. Alexander Nehamas and Paul Woodruff (Indianapolis, Ind.: Hackett, 1989), 211B.

18. Because of this "ladder," the *Symposium* is most often read as teaching us simply to move beyond the particular, limited beauties that, in contrast, I am arguing it teaches us how to appreciate. For a detailed argument that other parts of the *Symposium* show the value of loving particular, limited beauties in particular contexts, see Martha C. Nussbaum, *The Fragility of Goodness: Luck and Ethics in Greek Tragedy and Philosophy* (New York: Cambridge University Press, 1986), chap. 7. Again unlike my own view, however, Nussbaum also argues that the dialogue wholly opposes this kind of love to the love the "ladder" discusses. See also, Jean-Luc Nancy, *The Inoperative Community*, trans. Peter Connor, Lisa Garbus, Michael Holland, and Simona Sawhney (Minneapolis: University of Minnesota Press, 1991), 85: "All the different kinds of loves are welcomed in the *Symposium;* there is discussion, but there is no exclusion." Here, although in Nancy's view this is atypical for Plato, Plato's "thinking . . . broaches its own limit . . . ; it effaces itself before the love (or in the love?) that it recognizes as its truth."

19. Both Aristotle and Kant recognize this conceptual difference even while, in different ways, trying to abolish it. In both cases, while the subjective/objective distinction is abolished by the terms they arrive at, which solve the problem of knowledge, it is replaced by another conceptual difference. Aristotle argues that we can know the forms of things, given that forms are defined, but then we cannot have knowledge of individual instances of matter, which is indefinite and so inaccessible to knowledge. More fundamentally, we can know forms because they are by nature "knowledge-like," being nothing but intelligible or, alternatively, perceptible, definition itself. If I may extrapolate from his argument: while forms are "knowl-

edge-like," matter lacks definition; but definition is in turn a defining feature of knowledge, and so matter cannot be related to knowledge. Forms exist both, or neither, "subjectively" and "objectively," but they are conceptually distinct from matter, and so another conceptual difference emerges. (I should note that this is exactly the kind of interpretation of Aristotle that Ockham denied, arguing instead that, with respect to knowledge, the forms exist *only* as mental or logical entities; see note 16 to Idea 6. But then, irrespective of the results for knowledge, the distinction between subjective and objective is simply retained.) Kant argues that we can know only what can relate to the "subjective" categories that make knowledge what it is for us knowers, so that we cannot know things in themselves, but only things as they appear to us. The objectivity of things as they appear to us is then *given* by the "subjective" categories, and so is not distinct from those categories. But then things in themselves are conceptually distinct from things for us.

I argued above, however, that both "forms" and "categories," like all the elements of rigorous thought, have the peculiarity of existing as self-canceling. Consequently, while it is true that we are limited to what can relate to something like "forms" or "categories," this limitation itself, being self-canceling, *is* the means of relating to what is conceptually distinct from and so beyond it.

Hegel and Heidegger see the distinction between the concepts of "subjective" and "objective" as an inadequate starting point, precisely because it leads necessarily to the impossibility of relating parts of reality that nonetheless need to be related. They begin instead with the connection of what these distinct concepts are supposed to refer to, a connection seen as the more fundamental source from which the concepts are derived. But in Hegel's case, this connection is thought as "contradiction," and in Heidegger's, as something like "fundamentally conflicted difference." Heidegger identifies in Heraclitus, for example, what he stresses in a variety of ways in his own thought: "If we take the basic meaning of *logos* [Heraclitus's term for the ultimate nature of things] as gathering and togetherness, we must note the following: Gathering . . . maintains in a common bond the conflicting and that which tends apart. It does not let them fall into haphazard dispersion"; Martin Heidegger, *An Introduction to Metaphysics,* trans. R. Manheim (New Haven, Conn.: Yale University Press, 1959), 134, my insertion. It can be seen immediately that in both cases this only displaces the problem without affecting its nature. As I argued above, however, this kind of fundamental contradiction or difference is so fundamental as to contradict or cancel itself also, in this way reinstating the acceptability of the distinctions it also refutes.

20. This might be a good place to point out that Nietzsche, in arguing in *The Birth of Tragedy and the Genealogy of Morals,* trans. F. Golffing (New York: Doubleday, 1956) that there is dreadful nothingness behind Greek tragedy, and that Socrates diminished tragic insight by denying this nothingness, misses the *comic* nothingness ("comic" in the sense of what gives delight, and even a happy ending) *combined* with the tragic nothingness in Plato. The *Symposium,* for example, ends with Socrates' arguing against Agathon, a tragic poet, and Aristophanes, a comic poet, that the same person can write both tragic and comic poetry; Plato, *Symposium,* 223D.

21. For example, "'I regard you [Protagoras] as a man of wide experience, deep learning, and original thought'"; Plato, *Protagoras*, trans. W. K. C. Guthrie, in *Plato: The Collected Dialogues*, ed. Edith Hamilton and Huntington Cairns (Princeton, N.J.: Princeton University Press, 1961), 320B, my insertion. And "'our friend Prodicus [the butt of a lot of Socrates' jokes] . . . I have a notion that his branch of wisdom is an old and god-given one'"; ibid., 340E, my insertion. Again, for instance, "I was filled with admiration for the man [Cephalus] by these words"; Plato, *Republic*, 1:329D, my insertion. The drunken Alcibiades makes a nice contrast in the *Symposium:* "'O Erixymachus, best possible son to the best possible, the most temperate father: Hi!'"; Plato, *Symposium*, 214B.

22. Plato, *Sophist,* in *Theaetetus, Sophist,* trans. H. N. Fowler, Loeb Classical Library (Cambridge, Mass.: Harvard University Press, 1921), 231B–C, my transliteration.

23. Plato, *Symposium*, 219C.

24. Ibid., 212C–222C.

25. Plato, *Republic*, 1:382A–B.

26. See, for instance, Denise Riley, *Am I That Name? Feminism and the Category of "Women" in History* (Minneapolis: University of Minnesota Press, 1988), 3–4: "Feminism has intermittently been as vexed with the urgency of disengaging from the category 'women' as it has with laying claim to it."

27. See, e.g., Judith Butler, "Imitation and Gender Insubordination," in *Inside/Out: Lesbian Theories, Gay Theories,* ed. Diana Fuss (New York: Routledge, 1991), 13: "To write or speak *as a lesbian* . . . is . . . to come out or write in the name of an identity which, once produced, sometimes functions as a politically efficacious phantasm."

28. Sontag makes this comment on sensibility in her "Notes on 'Camp'": "Most people think of sensibility or taste as the realm of purely subjective preferences, those mysterious attractions, mainly sensual, that have not been brought under the sovereignty of reason." But "taste governs every free—as opposed to rote—human response. Nothing is more decisive. There is taste in people, visual taste, taste in emotion—and there is taste in acts, taste in morality. Intelligence, as well, is really a kind of taste: taste in ideas. Taste has no system and no proofs. But there is something like a logic of taste: the consistent sensibility that underlies and gives rise to a certain taste. A sensibility is almost, but not quite, ineffable." She adds in a footnote that "One may capture the ideas (intellectual history) and the behavior (social history) of an epoch without ever touching upon the sensibility or taste that informed those ideas, that behavior"; Susan Sontag, "Notes on 'Camp,'" in *Against Interpretation and Other Essays* (New York: Doubleday, 1966), 276.

29. Though Irwin, for example, argues that Plato and Socrates each understand this point differently. For instance, "Plato believes, contrary to Socrates, that purely cognitive training is insufficient for knowledge, but he may nonetheless believe that once we have knowledge, supported by the right non-cognitive training, we thereby also have the rest of virtue"; Terence H. Irwin, *Plato's Ethics* (New York: Oxford University Press, 1995), 237.

30. "But is there any reason why we should nourish our own commitment to a system of moral principles? Self-interest, certainly as ordinarily construed, cannot do it, for, while it can lead us to . . . the actions which morality enjoins, it does so only as a means of gaining rewards and avoiding penalties, and has no tendency to take us to . . . the impersonal point of view. The only frame of mind which can provide *direct* support for moral commitment is what Josiah Royce called Loyalty, and what Christians call Love (Charity)"; Wilfrid Sellars, "Science and Ethics," in *Philosophical Perspectives: Metaphysics and Epistemology* (Atascadero, Calif.: Ridgeview, 1967), 231.

31. "Urbanity is wit of harmonious universality, and that is the beginning and the end of historical philosophy, and Plato's most sublime music"; Friedrich Schlegel, *Philosophical Fragments*, trans. P. Firchow (Minneapolis: University of Minnesota Press, 1991), 91. It is not unlikely that this evaluation of a "good participant" was shared by Plato's culture. The cultures of the city-states and historical periods of ancient Greece differed widely from each other, but some themes were fairly common. To take one widely representative quote from Theognis, writing in Megara about a century before Plato: "The wise at a party sees no gaffes; /For him, they never happened. While he dines /He jokes and puts his serious self aside; / Matching his mood to everyone he meets"; Theognis, *Elegies,* in *Hesiod and Theognis,* trans. D. Wender (Harmondsworth, U.K.: Penguin, 1973), 11.309–312. See also Charles O. Lloyd, *Sophistication and Refinement in Greek Literature from Homer to Aristophanes,* Diss., Indiana University, 1976.

32. Plato, *Phaedrus*, in *Phaedrus and Letters VII and VIII,* trans. W. Hamilton (Harmondsworth, U.K.: Penguin, 1973), 249C–E.

33. Plato, *Republic*, 1:474C–476B.

34. Ibid., 2:572D–579E.

35. "The existential differences between the speakers are . . . more precisely defined by the variants of Eros"; Eric Voegelin, *Plato* (Baton Rouge: Louisiana State University Press, 1966 [1957]), 28.

36. Plato, *Gorgias*, trans. W. D. Woodhead, in *Collected Dialogues,* 481D.

37. Ibid., 513C.

38. See Altieri's comment on the *Gorgias* in note 29 to Idea 5, and Crombie's comment on Socrates and Thrasymachus in the *Republic* in note 28 to Idea 4.

39. See note 28 to Idea 4.

40. Plato, *Gorgias*, 472B–C.

41. Ibid., 471E.

42. Ibid., 472C.

43. Seth Benardete suggests that "the moral fervor of the *Gorgias* is an atmospheric effect of how Gorgias, Polus and Callicles understand what Socrates is saying"; Seth Benardete, *The Rhetoric of Morality and Philosophy: Plato's* Gorgias *and* Phaedrus (Chicago: University of Chicago Press, 1991), 1.

44. Voegelin, *Plato,* 37.

45. Plato, *Gorgias*, e.g., 507C.

46. Plato, *Apology*, trans. H. Tredennick, in *Collected Dialogues,* 42A.

47. In fact Socrates introduces the discussion of friendship by describing himself as looking "on the acquisition of friends, with all a lover's passion" [τῶν φίλων κτῆσιν πάνυ ἐρωτικῶς]; Plato, *Lysis,* trans. J. Wright, in *Collected Dialogues,* 211E.

48. Ibid., 218C–220B. I have reconstructed part of the argument. After presenting the potential perpetual regress of other things for the sake of which we love something ("But is he not again a friend to that thing for the sake of some other thing to which he is a friend"), it actually reads, "Can we possibly help, then, being weary of going on in this manner, and is it not necessary that we advance at once to a beginning, which will not again refer us to friend upon friend, but arrive at that . . . for the sake of which we say we are friends to all the rest?"; ibid., 219C–D.

49. Jane Austen, *Sense and Sensibility* (Harmondsworth, U.K.: Penguin, 1969), 67.

50. Because the fundamental practice is relating to things for their own sake (see the argument from the *Lysis* just above in the text and in note 48), Plato's ethics is not accurately described, as the major tradition has it, as instrumental or teleological, goal-oriented. (For this traditional description, see, e.g., Irwin, *Plato's Ethics,* 72–77.) The problem is to understand the "Good" as a *self-canceling* goal. This ethics can then be seen to be, like Kant's, deontological, doing things simply because they ought to be done. But it also gives the practical means of achieving this deontological orientation. What often prevents us from doing things simply because they ought to be done is a concern with things not for their own sakes but as means to a goal different from them. That is, what often stands in the way of a deontological attitude and practice is teleological attitude and practice. Plato's ethics allow us to overcome teleological attitudes and practices, when they are there, by recognizing them and allowing their rigorous self-cancellation. As a result, we then know we are doing the thing for its own sake and have also established the attitude or orientation that allows us to do so. Because it is the self-cancellation of teleological attitudes and practices that then precipitates the deontological ones, Plato's ethics reconciles both kinds of ethics, without detracting from their sharp difference.

51. "[L]aughter is called upon to disrupt an order, briefly and reversibly, in the interest of a more viable continuation of that order"; Marcel Gutwirth, *Laughing Matter: An Essay on the Comic* (Ithaca, N.Y.: Cornell University Press, 1993), 44.

52. Plato, *Republic,* 2:612A.

53. C. S. Peirce seems to have a closely related understanding of the relation between truth and error. (Although he opposes a different dimension of the standpoint I argue for here, in that he sees truth as a property of propositions and not of reality. Even there, however, he makes room for a sense of "truth" as "not an affection of a sign, but of things as things. Such truth is called *transcendental truth*"; C. S. Peirce, "Truth and Falsity and Error," in *Collected Papers of Charles Sanders Peirce,* vol. 5, ed. Charles Hartshorne and Paul Weiss [Cambridge, Mass.: Harvard University Press, 1935], 572.) He writes that "Truth is that concordance of an abstract statement with the ideal limit towards which endless investigation would tend to bring scientific belief, which concordance the abstract statement may possess by virtue of the confession of its inaccuracy and one-sidedness, and this confession

is an essential ingredient of truth" (565). That is, honesty about the possibility of one's being mistaken is *essential* to truth, it is *that by virtue of which* we have truth. It is not, for example, just a confession that frees one to recognize and recover from mistakes and then afterwards continue with the proper business of finding truth, but a permanent *ingredient* of truth *itself,* and so something *necessary* to it.

Schelling writes, about "the incomprehensible basis of reality in things," that "Out of this which is unreasonable, reason in the true sense is born. Without this preceding gloom, creation would have no reality; darkness is its necessary heritage." And he argues that neither darkness nor the light of reason would exist if they were not in some way anticipated in the ultimate source of reality. F. W. J. Schelling, *Philosophical Inquiries into the Nature of Human Freedom,* trans. J. Gutmann (La Salle, Ill.: Open Court, 1936), 34, 88. While "unreasonable" here need not include what actually conflicts with reason, like error, the context in Schelling's discussion of evil makes it clear that he is concerned with a conflictual type of opposition between the "two principles" of "light and darkness." He argues similarly, in that connection, that "nothing is given us for the explanation of evil except the two principles in God" (51), and comments, for example, on the "dark foundation which must, to be sure, also be the foundation of knowledge" (95).

In contrast with my own view of variously combined internal and external connections, he understands the relation of the source of reality (the "groundless") to these oppositions to be "a relation of total indifference, it is neutral toward both." As a result, the terms of the oppositions do not apply to the source. Nonetheless, "*without* indifference, that is, *without* the groundless, there would be no twofoldness of the principles" (88). If the dualism is not based on an indifference, it would be based on an opposition, and opposites are really opposite sides of one common thing (88): they must, for example, have some common point in order to bear on it in opposite ways. Unlike Hegel and Heidegger, then, Schelling sees trivial, purely external relation—pure indifference—as fundamentally important. But in contrast with my own view, and perhaps to his credit, he does not understand it as *also* external to *itself* and so (sometimes) canceling itself. There is no "sometimes always" logic here, no indifference to another principle that can also cancel itself in favor of the other principle's indifference to it. And once the rigorously external relation has played its foundational role, it does not enter into the texture of truth in general. For example, "God as spirit is the absolute identity of both principles . . . because . . . both are *subjected* to his personality" (90); and, despite the "dark foundation . . . of knowledge . . . only reason [which, for Schelling, involves light and clarity] can bring forth what is contained in these depths . . . we actually trust only vigorous reason" (95–96, my insertion).

Jean-Luc Nancy does think this kind of externality in the context of experience in general, but still does not see it as also sometimes thoroughly canceling itself. For example, "the articulation from which community is formed . . . is only a juncture . . . : what takes place where different pieces touch each other without fusing together." But they touch "without ever forming into" an "organic whole," the kind of "whole" that can "close in around the singularities to elevate them to its power"; Nancy, *Inoperative Community,* 75–76. See my brief comment on Nancy in note 9 to Idea 1.

On error, see also Martin Heidegger, "On the Essence of Truth," trans. J. Sallis, in *Basic Writings,* ed. D. F. Krell (New York: Harper & Row, 1977), 136: "the open site for and ground of *error*" is "errancy," which "is the essential counter-essence to the primordial essence of truth. . . . [A]s leading astray, errancy at the same time contributes to . . . the possibility that, by experiencing errancy itself and by not mistaking the mystery of Da-sein, he *not* let himself be led astray."

54. Plato, *Seventh Letter,* 341B–342A.

55. Plato, *Protagoras,* 328E. Similarly, in the *Symposium,* " 'allow me to ask Agathon a few little questions' "; Plato, *Symposium,* 199B.

Chapter 2

1. For discussions of the importance of the dialogue form for Plato's philosophy, see, e.g., I. M. Crombie, *An Examination of Plato's Doctrines,* 2 vols. (London: Routledge & Kegan Paul, 1962), 1:14–23; Hans-Georg Gadamer, *Dialogue and Dialectic: Eight Hermeneutical Studies on Plato,* trans. P. Christopher Smith (New Haven, Conn.: Yale University Press, 1980); Francisco J. Gonzalez, *Dialectic and Dialogue: Plato's Practice of Philosophical Inquiry* (Evanston, Ill.: Northwestern University Press, 1998); Jill Gordon, *Turning toward Philosophy: Literary Device and Dramatic Structure in Plato's Dialogues* (University Park: Pennsylvania State University Press, 1999); Jacob Klein, *A Commentary on Plato's Meno* (Chicago: University of Chicago Press, 1965), introductory remarks; Mitchell H. Miller, Jr., "Introduction," in *The Philosopher in Plato's Statesman* (The Hague, Netherlands: Martinus Nijhoff, 1980); Miller, "Introduction," in *Plato's Parmenides: The Conversion of the Soul.* Princeton, N.J.: Princeton University Press; University Park: Pennsylvania State University Press, 1991 [1986]; George K. Plochmann, "Socrates, the Stranger from Elea, and Some Others," *Classical Philology* 49.4 (1954):223–231; Eric Voegelin, *Plato* (Baton Rouge: Louisiana State University Press, 1966 [1957]), e.g., 10–14.

2. Plato, *Charmides,* trans. Donald Watt, in *Early Socratic Dialogues,* ed. T. J. Saunders (Harmondsworth, U.K.: Penguin, 1987), 153A.

3. Ibid., 153A.

4. Ibid., 155A.

5. See, e.g., Andrew R. Burn, *The Pelican History of Greece* (Harmondsworth, U.K.: Penguin, 1965), 302. On Charmides, see Debra Nails, *The People of Plato: A Prosopography of Plato and Other Socratics* (Indianapolis, Ind.: Hackett, 2002), 92: "it is . . . a common mistake in the literature" to take "Charmides for a member of the Thirty." I am indebted to one of Fordham University Press's anonymous readers for this corrective reference.

6. Plato, *Charmides,* 153B–C.

7. Ibid., 154B–C.

8. Ibid., 154D–E.

9. Altieri makes a related point about Callicles in the *Gorgias:* "He is not a skeptic. He simply subscribes to a hierarchy of values in which 'truth' is not a very sig-

nificant factor so long as one knows what one wants to do"; Charles Altieri, "Plato's Masterplot: Idealization, Contradiction, and the Transformation of Rhetorical Ethos," in *Intimate Conflict: Contradiction in Literary and Philosophical Discourse,* ed. Brian G. Caraher (Albany: State University of New York Press, 1992), 52.

10. Plato, *Charmides,* 155D.

11. Ibid., 155B–C.

12. Ibid., 156C–D.

13. Ibid., 155D.

14. Ibid., 156D.

15. Ibid., 156A.

16. Ibid., 158C.

17. Ibid., 158C–D.

18. Plato, *Apology,* trans. H. Tredennick, in *Plato: The Collected Dialogues,* ed. Edith Hamilton and Huntington Cairns (Princeton, N.J.: Princeton University Press, 1961), 20E–23B.

19. Plato, *Charmides,* 153B.

20. Plato, *Apology,* 21B.

21. John Sallis, *Being and Logos: The Way of Platonic Dialogue,* 2nd ed. (Atlantic Highlands, N.J.: Humanities Press, 1986), 46–49.

22. Plato, *Apology,* 23B.

23. Plato, *Charmides,* 158D–E.

24. See Martha C. Nussbaum, *The Fragility of Goodness: Luck and Ethics in Greek Tragedy and Philosophy* (New York: Cambridge University Press, 1986), in which she explores the relation of "the thorough intermingling of what is ours and what belongs to the world, . . . of making and being made, . . . present . . . in any human life" to "the beliefs that sustain human ethical practices" (2).

25. Plato, *Charmides,* 158E–159A.

26. Ibid., 159B.

27. Ibid., 160E.

28. Ibid., 161B.

29. Ibid., 159B–160D.

30. Ibid., 162B–E.

31. Ibid., 163E.

32. Ibid., 163C.

33. Ibid., 164B–C.

34. Ibid., 164C–D

35. Ibid., 165B.

36. Ibid., 165B–C.

37. This was one of Crombie's correctives to "the text-book doctrine that for Plato the sphere of knowledge is forms or *a priori* truths, and the sphere of belief is matters of empirical fact": with respect to "knowing and not knowing . . . Plato was convinced of the obvious truth that there is a spectrum of intermediate conditions in between these two extremes"; I. M. Crombie, *Plato: The Midwife's Apprentice* (New York: Barnes & Noble, 1964), 97, 98.

38. Plato, *Charmides*, 166C.
39. Ibid., 166C.
40. Ibid., 166C.
41. Ibid., 166C–D.
42. Ibid., 166D–E.
43. Ibid., 167C–D.
44. Ibid., 172B.
45. Ibid., 166E.
46. Ibid., 169C–D.
47. Ibid., 163B–C.
48. Ibid., 164D–165B.
49. See, e.g., Nagel's comments quoted in the Introduction, e.g.: "the subjectivity of consciousness is an irreducible feature of reality . . . and it must occupy as fundamental a place in any credible world view as matter, energy, space, time, and numbers"; Thomas Nagel, *The View from Nowhere* (New York: Oxford University Press, 1986), 7–8.
50. Plato, *Charmides*, 170B–C.
51. Ibid., 171C.
52. Ibid., 173A, my insertions.
53. Ibid., 174B–C.
54. Ibid., 175A.
55. Ibid., 175D–E.
56. Ibid., 175E.
57. Ibid., 175E–176A.
58. Ibid., 176A, my insertions.
59. Ibid., 176A–B.
60. Ibid., 176B–C.
61. Ibid., 176C.
62. Ibid., 176C.
63. Ibid., 176C–D.

Chapter 3

1. E.g., "it is . . . a book of moral philosophy. (It starts from the question, 'What is justice?.' . . .) . . . [T]he real question in it is, as Plato says, how to live best. . . . [T]he question, What is the best life? Is to him inseparable from the question, What is the best order or organization of human society?" Richard Lewis Nettleship, *Lectures on the Republic of Plato* (New York: St. Martin's Press, 1968), 4–5.
2. Plato, *Republic*, 2 vols., trans. Paul Shorey, Loeb Classical Library (Cambridge, Mass.: Harvard University Press 1935), 335B–D.
3. Ibid., 335D–335E.
4. Ibid., 334C.
5. Ibid., 339E–340B.
6. See Plato, *Theaetetus,* trans. M. J. Levett and rev. M. Burnyeat (Indianapolis, Ind.: Hackett, 1992), 171A–B, 183A–C. Kant writes of "the undeniable, and in the

dogmatic [unself-questioning] procedure of reason also unavoidable, contradictions of reason with itself"; Immanuel Kant, *Critique of Pure Reason,* trans. N. K. Smith (New York: St. Martin's Press, 1929), B:24, my insertion.

7. Plato, *Republic,* 327C.

8. Ibid., e.g., 338A–D.

9. Ibid., 339D–E.

10. Ibid., 340C–341B.

11. Ibid., 341C–342E.

12. Ibid., 351B–E.

13. Ibid., 351E–352A.

14. Ibid., 352B.

15. Ibid., 353E.

16. Ibid., 357A–367E.

17. Ibid., 366E.

18. Ibid., 369C.

19. Ibid., 368E–369A.

20. See Robert B. Williamson, "*Eidos* and *Agathon* in Plato's *Republic,*" in *Four Essays on Plato's* Republic, double issue of *St. John's Review* 39.1–2 (1989–1990), Annapolis, Md.: St. John's College, 1990, 109; John Sallis, *Being and Logos: The Way of Platonic Dialogue,* 2nd ed. (Atlantic Highlands, N.J.: Humanities Press, 1986), 364.

21. Plato, *Republic,* 369B–C.

22. Ibid., 372A–D.

23. Ibid., 375C.

24. Ibid., 412C.

25. Ibid., 427E–433B.

26. This was Charmides' third and Critias's first definition of self-control in the *Charmides.*

27. Plato, *Republic,* 433B.

28. Ibid., 440E–441C.

29. Ibid., 443D.

30. Ibid., 444B–445B.

31. Ibid., 445B.

32. Ibid., 449A–B.

33. See also Allan Bloom, ed., *The Republic of Plato,* 2nd ed. (New York: Basic Books, 1968), 379, 457 n. 1.

34. Plato, *Republic,* 543C.

35. Ibid., 473C–D.

36. And see Eva Brann, "The Music of the *Republic,*" in *Four Essays on Plato's* Republic, double issue of *St. John's Review* 39.1–2 (1989–1990), Annapolis, Md.: St. John's College, 1990, 13–14: "no such city *can* come to be now or later, *by the design and intent of the argument itself.* These word constructions are not 'constitutions,' . . . they are instead contrivances for a different purpose, and intended to reveal themselves as such."

37. Plato, *Republic,* 432B–D, my insertion.

38. Ibid., 435C–D.

39. See the related, if rather different, comments by Sallis, *Being and Logos,* 333. I think Sallis's reading is compatible with my main point about the inconsistency of the account of the city-state.

40. Plato, *Republic,* 376A–B.

41. E.g., ibid., 374D–E.

42. Ibid., 434E–435A.

43. Ibid., 416D–417B.

44. Ibid., 423E–424A, 457D.

45. Ibid., 451D–457C.

46. Ibid., 479E.

47. Ibid., 479A.

48. Ibid., 479B–C.

49. Ibid., 484B–D.

50. Ibid., 505A.

51. Ibid., 505A.

52. Ibid., 506C.

53. Ibid., 507A.

54. Ibid., 509C.

55. Ibid., 474C–476B.

56. Ibid., 475B.

57. Ibid., 340C–E.

58. Plato, *Charmides,* trans. Donald Watt, in *Early Socratic Dialogues,* ed. T. J. Saunders (Harmondsworth, U.K.: Penguin, 1987), 163D.

59. On this and the inadequacy Socrates indicates of the earlier division of the soul into three "parts," see Brann, "Music," 40–44; Sallis, *Being and Logos,* 371, 381.

60. As I noted above, at the start of the dialogue Polemarchus playfully threatens to use force to get Socrates to stay with him, and Socrates playfully counters by insisting on the use of persuasion. Sallis suggests that a phrase that Socrates uses at the end of this initial encounter—"well, if it is so resolved . . . that's how we must act" (Plato, *Republic,* 328B)—is "an imitation of the way in which the outcome of voting was proclaimed in the assembly. . . . the outcome of this episode has been the forming of a little community . . . now ratified by the vote"; Sallis, *Being and Logos,* 322.

61. Plato, *Republic,* 518D. And see Hans-Georg Gadamer, *The Idea of the Good in Platonic-Aristotelian Philosophy,* trans. P. Christopher Smith (New Haven, Conn.: Yale University Press, 1986), 69 n.: "the true sophrosyne [self-control, temperance] is already introduced in book 4 (*Republic,* 431Eff.) as arete [virtue] common to all" (my insertions).

62. This "liar's paradox," often identified with Epimenides the Cretan (probably about the sixth or fifth centuries BCE), became a crucially important problem for logic, in Bertrand Russell's work, at the beginning of the last century, and has remained so.

63. Plato, *Republic,* 546A–547A.

64. Ibid., 565D–580A.

65. Ibid., 572E–575D. "Plato's term for this deepest lust which casts a glow of evil over the life of passions, is Eros"; Eric Voegelin, *Plato* (Baton Rouge: Louisiana State University Press, 1966 [1957]), 126.

66. Plato, *Republic*, 573B.

67. Ibid., 573D.

68. "In the two Erotes of Socrates and Callicles [in the *Gorgias*] is implied the . . . development of the *Republic* with its distinction of the good and the evil Eros"; Voegelin, *Plato*, 29, my insertion.

69. Plato, *Republic*, 521C–524D.

70. "Surely one must read the whole book [the *Republic*] as one grand dialectical myth. On one occasion Plato himself virtually says that dialectic is its principle. (See 497e: '*tounantion e nun*' [the opposite of what is now].) . . . Here, reading dialectic-ally means relating these utopian demands in each instance to their opposite, in order to find, somewhere in between, what is really meant—that is, in order to recognize what the circumstances are, and how they could be made better"; Gadamer, *Idea of the Good*, 70–71, first insertion mine, second insertion translator's. And Sallis, though with a different result in mind, says: "the upward way [the movement towards the Idea of the Good in the *Republic*] belongs inextricably together with a downward way [the degeneration of the city-state]"; Sallis, *Being and Logos*, 534, my insertions.

71. Plato, *Republic*, 369B–C.

72. The Athenian in the *Laws* (which may not be Plato's work, and even if it is, may arguably express a change in Plato's views from those of the *Republic*) is made to propose saying to tragic poets visiting his imagined state that "we're tragedians ourselves," although most likely ones who express different sentiments from theirs; Plato, *The Laws*, trans. T. J. Saunders (Harmondsworth, U.K.: Penguin, 1970), 817B–D. The Athenian is also made to say, a little earlier, that "to honour a man with hymns and panegyrics during his lifetime is to invite trouble: we must wait until he has come to the end of the course after running the race of life successfully"; Plato, *Laws*, 801E–802A. This seems to evoke the end of Sophocles' tragedy *King Oedipus:* "none can be called happy until that day when he carries / His happiness down to the grave in peace"; Sophocles, *King Oedipus*, in *The Theban Plays*, trans. E. F. Watling (Harmondsworth, U.K.: Penguin, 1947), 68 (11.1529–1530).

73. Edward G. Ballard, *Socratic Ignorance: An Essay on Platonic Self-Knowledge* (The Hague, Netherlands: Martinus Nijhoff, 1965), 159.

74. Plato, *Republic*, 612A.

75. Ibid., 595B.

76. Ibid., 596E.

77. Ibid., 395C–396A.

78. Ibid., 450D.

79. Ibid., 451A–B.

80. Ibid., 607D.

81. Ibid., 330D–331D.

82. "[T]hough starting from the same facts and arriving at similar conclusions, he [the philosopher] has in the interval gone through a process of thinking, and the truth he holds is reasoned truth. What seems at first sight the same truth, and may be put in the same words that anybody else would use, is yet a very different truth to the philosopher, containing a great deal that is not present to the minds of most men"; Nettleship, *Lectures,* 3–4, my insertion. My point, though, is that the process of rigorous thinking is essentially self-canceling, so that the difference is not *simply,* or not always, a difference.

83. José Ortega y Gasset, *What Is Philosophy?* trans. M. Adams (New York: W. W. Norton, 1960), 238–239.

84. Ibid., 239.

85. Plato, *Lysis,* 218C–220B.

86. Plato, *Phaedrus,* 249D–E.

87. Ibid., 248B–250D.

88. Plato, *Republic,* 475E.

89. Ibid., 592A–B, my insertion.

90. Ibid., 592B.

91. "*idea tou agathou* (idea of the good) implies not so much the 'view of the good' as a 'looking to the good'"; Gadamer, *Idea of the Good,* 28.

92. Plato, *Republic,* 343A.

93. Ibid., 344C.

94. Suggestively, the *Laches,* whose topic is the definition of courage, links knowledge with courage and then ends with a general admission of ignorance. The dialogue pursues the argument that courage is a kind of knowledge at some length (194C–199E), and at the end Socrates, on being asked to teach his friends' children about courage, answers, "as we are all in the same perplexity [*aporiai*], why should one of us be preferred to another? I certainly think that no one should, and . . . every one of us should seek out the best teacher whom he can find, first for ourselves who are greatly in need of one, and then for the youths. . . . But I cannot advise that we remain as we are"; Plato, *Laches,* trans. B. Jowett, in *Plato: The Collected Dialogues,* ed. Edith Hamilton and Huntington Cairns (Princeton, N.J.: Princeton University Press, 1961), 200E–201A. Laches testifies to Socrates' courage in battle at the start of the dialogue, and is in turn described as an estimable witness (181A–B). Socrates, then, is courageous, ignorant of what courage is, and insistent that the condition of ignorance is an inadequacy. Given the argument that courage is a kind of knowledge, this suggests that courage involves inadequacy.

95. Plato, *Protagoras,* trans. W. K. C. Guthrie, in *Collected Dialogues,* 350C.

96. See the discussion of the ladder to the Idea of Beauty in the *Symposium* in Chapter 1, section 1.2.4.

97. "[P]articipation in the order [of justice] is by imitation and likening"; Brann, "Music," 69, my insertion. I mentioned above (note 72) that in the *Laws,* Plato has the Athenian imagine saying to tragic poets on behalf of his proposed city-state that "we're tragedians ourselves"; he continues, "our entire state has been constructed so as to be a 'representation' of the finest and noblest life. . . . So we are poets . . .

and . . . artists and actors in the finest drama, which true law alone has the natural power to 'produce' to perfection"; Plato, *Laws*, 817B.

98. In a passage in the *Protagoras* that I quoted above, Socrates is made to warn a friend, who is enthusiastic about learning from the sophist Protagoras, that "knowledge cannot be taken away in a parcel," so that its goodness or badness cannot be tested before one takes it into oneself. "When you have paid for it you must receive it straight into the soul. You go away having learned it and are benefited or harmed accordingly. So I suggest we give this matter some thought, not only by ourselves"; Plato, *Protagoras*, 314A–B. And he then cancels even this advice (this piece of knowledge) in a beautifully deadpan way: "we can bring others into our consultations also. . . . There is Hippias . . . and Prodicus . . . and many other wise men" (314B–C). Hippias and Prodicus, who will wisely help us, are Sophists like Protagoras, so that their advice, like Protagoras's teaching, will presumably itself go directly and untested into the soul. The dialogue also shows them to be even less unequivocally trustworthy than Protagoras.

99. "The dialogue, unlike a poetic imitation [or image, or model], does not try to hide its flaws . . . because, rather than attempting to take the place of the original, it wants to draw our vision beyond itself. . . . [T]he philosopher in using imitation works against it rather than with it. He recognizes that it is not a proper medium for the expression of the truth he seeks. Yet as long as this recognition exists, as long as the imitation does not hide its flaws, a philosophical use of imitation remains possible. . . . The philosopher is a bad poet, but for precisely this reason he makes better use of poetry than does any poet"; Francisco J. Gonzalez, *Dialectic and Dialogue: Plato's Practice of Philosophical Inquiry* (Evanston, Ill.: Northwestern University Press, 1998), 145, my insertion. Gonzalez's illuminating interpretation of Plato has many points of contact with my own, but is very different in at least two ways. First, it simply excludes the possibility of models that are *not* flawed but are simply descriptively true (in his terminology, it excludes the possibility of ultimately adequate "propositional" knowledge, in contrast with the "non-propositional" knowledge that the flawed images, terms and propositions point to beyond themselves; e.g., ibid., 7–9, 244). Second, Gonzalez does not think of Plato as putting the legitimacy of rigorous thought itself in question. As a result, I would argue, the "non-propositional" truth that thinking might make manifest (rather than directly state) is *just as* ultimately unjustified, just as based on an only *assumed* legitimacy of careful thought, as he argues that directly stated propositional truth is in assuming propositions are suited to expressing ultimate truth (7). On my own interpretation, Plato provides a way of *fully* justifying *both*.

On Plato's presenting models that also put themselves in question, see also Gadamer, *Dialogue and Dialectic*, 70: "Plato is not concerned with vivid and forceful accounts but with . . . the maieutic power of these discussions (*Theaetetus*, 149Cff.), with the movement of philosophizing that redevelops in every repetition. Precisely because of the seriousness of his purpose, Plato gives his mimesis [imitation] the levity of a jocular play. Insofar as his dialogues are to portray philosophizing in order to compel us to philosophize, they shroud all of what they say in the ambiguous twilight of irony" (my insertion)—though I argue that this irony is not *simply* an "ambiguous twilight." And see Brann, "Music," 33–36, e.g., "The *Republic* itself, however, has that form which is exactly designed to provide at once the most complete poetic responsibility, the greatest mimetic force, and the most worthwhile imitation. For the narrator, Socrates himself, is always present and responsible, and he keeps himself before us with the ever-recurring phrases 'he said' and 'I said.' . . . (We see here . . . one reason why Hesiod, who . . . warns the reader that his source, the Muses, will sometimes lie . . . is . . . more acceptable to Socrates [*Republic*, 546E1, 607C8]). . . . [T]he *Republic* as a whole . . . is Plato's imitation of Socrates, an imitation that will prove its authenticity by serving the double function of commenting on the original while representing it"; Brann, "Music," 33–34.

More generally, Drucilla Cornell, following Derrida, argues that justice needs to be "conceived as aporia," as involving "an inherent and ultimately irresolvable paradox. Justice so conceived resists its own collapse into . . . the definition by any system of the good embodied in the *nomos*." This acknowledgment or "exposure" of the necessarily exercised but always doubtful character of just decisions "protects justice from being encompassed by whatever convention described as the good of the community," and so "is in and of itself ethical"; Drucilla Cornell, *The Philosophy of the Limit* (New York: Routledge, 1992), 118. But like Corlett, Laclau and Mouffe (see Idea 1, note 9), and Nancy (see Idea 1, note 9, and Chapter 1, note 53), who also draw on Derrida, she does not see this aporia as (sometimes) thoroughly self-canceling.

I should add that I believe that this very widespread way of working with Derrida's thought is mistaken, whether or not it accurately reflects Derrida's self-understanding; and I am also inclined to think that Derrida himself at least sometimes pursues his thought in ways more consistent with what I am calling "sometimes always" logic. Derrida's deconstructive work, for example, does not result in particular conclusions, but brings us to the point where we can understand that and why we no longer know what we are saying: he shows that the meanings of our words include what they only function by excluding, by differentiating themselves from. The problem is then to reconsider the foundations of meaning or sense itself in the relevant context, rather than to proceed on the basis of the deconstruction's nonexistent "conclusions." This is clearly a Socratic/Platonic, and also Wittgensteinian, procedure. See, e.g., Ludwig Wittgenstein, *Philosophical Investigations*, trans. G. E. M. Anscombe (Malden, Mass.: Blackwell, 1958), no. 182: "what we need to understand in order to resolve philosophical paradoxes" is the "role" of words where "the game with these words, their employment in the linguistic intercourse that is carried on by their means, is more involved—the role of these words in our language other—than we are tempted to think."

100. Collingwood, for example, points out that, "Neither the rule of a family over its own children nor the rule of a body politic over its own subjects can dispense with the use of deceit. . . . ; deceit on the part of rulers if it is for the good of the ruled . . . is not only justified; it is, whatever sentimentalists may say, a duty"; Robin George Collingwood, *The New Leviathan, or Man, Society, Civilization, and*

Barbarism (New York: Thomas Y. Crowell, 1971), 204. It should be clear by now that any disagreement between us on this issue is not about the need for deception, but about the nature of truth, and so about the relation of deception to truth in the relevant kinds of context, its status as being simply deception.

101. Sallis argues that what "marks" the "decisive transition" from the domain of opinion to that of philosophy is "that images be recognized as images despite the fact that the originals themselves are not visible"; Sallis, *Being and Logos,* 391. He is not restricting images to artful presentations here, however, but referring to all appearances.

Chapter 4

1. The term "statesman" is sexist. But Plato *was* what we would understand as sexist, and since he is a focus of this book, I would rather show that reality than alter it. As it happens, I think that showing the reality is a better intervention in this context, since alteration would also disguise the problem.

2. See Jacob Klein, *Plato's Trilogy* (Chicago: University of Chicago Press, 1977), 3–5; John Sallis, *Being and Logos: The Way of Platonic Dialogue,* 2nd ed. (Atlantic Highlands, N.J.: Humanities Press, 1986), 457.

3. Plato, *Apology,* trans. H. Tredennick, in *Plato: The Collected Dialogues,* ed. Edith Hamilton and Huntington Cairns (Princeton, N.J.: Princeton University Press, 1961), 24B.

4. Ibid., 19B–20C.

5. Ibid., 23D, 26D.

6. Plato, *Sophist,* trans. F. M. Cornford, in *Plato: The Collected Dialogues,* ed. Edith Hamilton and Huntington Cairns (Princeton, N.J.: Princeton University Press, 1961), e.g., 260A–B.

7. See, e.g., Mitchell H. Miller, Jr., *The Philosopher in Plato's* Statesman (The Hague, Netherlands: Martinus Nijhoff, 1980), 1–3, who argues that the trilogy is "a distinctively philosophical version of Socrates' trial," (2).

8. Cp. Klein, *Plato's Trilogy,* 5: "In the *Statesman,* Old Socrates says (258A4–6) . . . that Young Socrates should now . . . answer to the Stranger, and 'to me, well, at a later time.' Does this mean that Old Socrates envisages a conversation with Young Socrates about the 'philosopher' [Socrates had asked the Stranger at the start of the *Sophist* whether the philosopher, the Sophist, and the statesman were the same or different, but Plato did not write a dialogue called the "philosopher"], as some scholars have understood this remark? Is it not, rather, a playful removal of this possibility, especially if we consider Socrates' awareness of the impending trial? It may even not be wrong to assert that the trial of Socrates, the Philosopher, replaces the dialogue about the 'philosopher' " (my insertion).

9. Plato, *Apology,* 30E–31A.

10. Plato, *Theaetetus,* trans. R. Waterfield (Harmondsworth, U.K.: Penguin, 1987), 183A–B.

11. Ibid., 171A–B.

12. Ibid., 187D–89B.

13. Ibid., 201C–D.

14. Ibid., 200A–B.

15. E.g., ibid., 157C–D.

16. Ibid., 210B–C, my insertion.

17. Plato, *Apology,* 20E.

18. Plato, *Sophist,* 232A–236C.

19. Ibid., 235C–236C, 259A–260B.

20. Ibid., 259A–260B.

21. Ibid., 258B–259B.

22. Cp. Sallis, *Being and Logos,* 522–523: "for most men . . . images and appearance are necessary for *episteme* [knowledge]" (my insertion).

23. The Stranger from Elea is caught in a similar paradox at the start of the *Sophist.* If he agrees to answer Socrates' question, he must speak at great length, an inappropriate imposition for a stranger and guest: he would be unmannerly. But if he refuses to answer, he would also be unmannerly, a guest refusing to do a favor. Like Charmides, he resolves the problem by first speaking *about* it, accepting it in its unresolved form, rather than trying to resolve it directly in its own terms; Plato, *Sophist,* 217D–218A.

24. "Digressions, in Plato, are never fortuitous or aimless"; David Lachterman, "What Is 'The Good' of Plato's *Republic?*" in *Four Essays on Plato's* Republic, double issue of *St. John's Review* 39.1–2 (1989–1990), Annapolis, Md.: St. John's College, 1990, 141.

25. The *Gorgias,* as an extreme example, even begins with Socrates arriving late for Gorgias's presentation, so that Socrates' opening question has no relation, other than a possible accidental one, to the content of the preceding discussion.

26. The shift in standpoint and meanings stands out in high relief by contrast with the unrevised standpoint and meanings when characters enter the dialogue without having been present up to and including the shift. In the *Meno,* for example, Anytus enters late (Plato, *Meno,* trans. W. K. C. Guthrie, in *Plato: The Collected Dialogues,* 90A), and in the *Symposium* Alcibiades does; Plato, *Symposium,* trans. Alexander Nehamas and Paul Woodruff (Indianapolis, Ind.: Hackett, 1989), 212C–E. In each case they accuse Socrates of something he has already shown to be true, but in such a way that it means the reverse of what they now take it to mean, and ironically means the reverse by *also* meaning the same thing. Anytus accuses Socrates of being "too ready to run people down" (Plato, *Meno,* 94E). Socrates has already insisted that he does run people down, in that he shows them to be ignorant, but that ignorance is a good thing, valuable and respectworthy. And he also means by ignorance exactly what Anytus might take it to be. Alcibiades accuses Socrates of arrogantly disdaining his physical beauty; Plato, *Symposium,* 219C. Socrates has already insisted that physical beauty is not important, but in my interpretation, he does so because its real importance can only be appreciated by looking elsewhere. This "elsewhere" is certainly as far away from Alcibiades as his vanity might object to, but it also gives as much status to physical beauty as Alcibiades might want.

27. Plato, *Sophist*, 231B.

28. In keeping at least with my view that the self-externality of both knowledge and reality connects them, Louise Karon writes, "the mind is engaged in *the real, because paradoxically *the real* lies in search of itself*"; Louise Karon, "Presence in *The New Rhetoric,*" in *The New Rhetoric of Chaim Perelman: Statement and Response,* ed. Ray D. Dearin (Lanham, Md.: University Press of America, 1989), 176–177.

29. Scult, for example, argues that "The rhetor must be able to aim at truth, knowing he will never reach it. . . . This cannot be accomplished by a series of definitive rules of invention. It can only be done by use of a metaphor *that defines nothing* for the rhetor, but acts upon him in such a way as to make of his inventional process the rational core of the rhetorical relationship. It is in that relationship that 'truth' resides. . . . This relationship grows out of the metaphor [Chaim Perelman's] of universal audience"; Allen Scult, "Perelman's Universal Audience: One Perspective," in *The New Rhetoric of Chaim Perelman,* 156, my emphasis, my insertion.

30. Sallis, though his account has little or no connection with mine, writes of the Stranger's summing-up in the *Sophist* that "when he proceeds to ironic imitation practiced by men who are aware of their ignorance and . . . to those . . . who give short speeches in private . . . we realize to what extent the description remains . . . more nearly a description of Socrates than of the Sophist"; Sallis, *Being and Logos,* 532.

31. Klein also comments on what he sees as the comic errors in the *Statesman;* Klein, *Plato's Trilogy,* 158, 171–172. See also Miller, *Philosopher,* 28–32, who discusses the role of various more explicit jokes in the argument of the dialogue; Stanley Rosen, *Plato's* Statesman: *The Web of Politics* (New Haven, Conn.: Yale University Press, 1995), 36.

32. Plato, *Statesman,* trans. J. B. Skemp, in *Plato: The Collected Dialogues,* ed. Edith Hamilton and Huntington Cairns (Princeton, N.J.: Princeton University Press, 1961), 267C–268D.

33. Ibid., 268D–274E.

34. Ibid., 286B.

35. Ibid., 277D.

36. Ibid., 258B, 267A–C.

37. Ibid., 275B–C.

38. I owe this insight to my former student Michael Adkins.

39. Plato, *Statesman,* 278C, my insertion.

40. See Rosen, *Plato's* Statesman, 93: "a model is the conception of the sameness of two distinct instances," and the surrounding discussion.

41. Plato, *Statesman,* 277D, my insertion.

42. Miller, *Philosopher,* 79.

43. Kenneth Dorter, *Form and Good in Plato's Eleatic Dialogues: The* Parmenides, Theaetetus, Sophist, *and* Statesman (Berkeley: University of California Press, 1994), 224.

44. Ibid., 220.

45. Plato, *Statesman,* 304A–305E.

46. Ibid., 303B–C.

47. "[T]he dialogue has in fact come full circle back to the opening steps of the first diaeresis [division]"; Dorter, *Form and Good*, 223, my insertion. Miller, however, argues that this is not simply a return to the initial mistake, but that the statesman is now transformed by being understood as part of the community, even though he also transcends it in certain respects; Miller, *Philosopher*, 94–95.

48. F. R. Ankersmit, *Aesthetic Politics: Political Philosophy beyond Fact and Value* (Stanford, Calif.: Stanford University Press, 1996), makes a related point with respect to representative democracy. Drawing on a combination of Machiavelli's political thought and Arthur Danto's aesthetic theory, Ankersmit argues that "political reality only comes into being after and due to representation. . . . According to Danto . . . 'something is "real" ' when it satisfies a representation of itself, just as something only becomes a 'bearer of a name' when it is named by a name" (47). But "[w]e can only talk about representation when there is a difference—and *not* an identity—between the representative and the person represented" (46). And there is "an intrinsic relationship" between both artistic and political representation and "debates that are in principle undecidable" (23). These divisions within both representation and belief do not only affect the relations between large social institutions, but also the relation of "the *individual* voter . . . to him- or herself" (363). As a result, "neither prince nor citizen is completely 'at home' with himself; there always is in him something that is alien to himself" (120). Here "the political domain no longer has . . . the unity we always find in the metaphysical tradition, but is essentially a *broken* world" (119). Ankersmit argues that we should "see in this gap" between the represented and the representation and within ourselves "both the origin of all legitimate political power and the only guarantee for the possibility of an effective democratic control of the exercise of legitimate power. . . . Only this relation can ensure that in democracy the tensions, frictions, and oppositions can be created that will illuminate and make visible the kind of political problems that we will have to address" (347). If we do not acknowledge and live in keeping with this gap, we only conceal our inevitable uncertainties, differences, and conflicts behind a "deceitful . . . unity and harmony" (347), and so let the problems they cause develop unchecked. Ankersmit gives the Danto reference as A. C. Danto, "Artworks and Real Things," in *Aesthetics Today*, ed. M. Philipson and P. J. Gudel (New York: New American Library, 1980), 323.

49. Plato, *Gorgias*, trans. W. D. Woodhead, in *Collected Dialogues*, 522D.

50. Dorter, *Form and Good*, 219.

51. Socrates makes a related point in the *Cratylus*: e.g., "if we are correct in our view, the only way of learning and discovering things is either to discover names for ourselves or to learn them from others. . . . But if things are only to be known through names, how can we suppose that the givers of names had knowledge . . . before there were names at all, and therefore before they could have known them?" Plato, *Cratylus*, trans. Benjamin Jowett, in *Collected Dialogues*, 438A–B.

52. A passage from Merleau-Ponty I quoted in Idea 1.2: "the accusation of contradiction is not decisive, *if the acknowledged contradiction appears as the very condition of*

consciousness. It is in this sense that Plato and Kant, to mention only them, accepted the contradiction of which Zeno and Hume wanted no part." But see my criticism there of Merleau-Ponty's continuation.

53. My brother, Kenneth Barris, pointed out something like this to me in a park in Durban, South Africa, when I was a teenager. He admired, in his phrase, whose sense was enigmatic to me, the crane's "articulation in space."

54. "Precisely because of the seriousness of his purpose, Plato gives his mimesis [imitation] the levity of a jocular play. . . . His dialogues are nothing more than playful allusions which say something only to him who finds meanings beyond what is expressly stated in them and allows these meanings to take effect within him"; Hans-Georg Gadamer, *Dialogue and Dialectic: Eight Hermeneutical Studies on Plato*, trans. P. Christopher Smith (New Haven, Conn.: Yale University Press, 1980), 70–71, my insertion. As I argued above, though, I believe that the dialogues are, but not *simply*, "nothing more than playful allusions."

55. Gutwirth argues that "the comic as the . . . exercise of the faculty of turning the tables on what we value, . . . the capacity to let go of that control [the control knowledge gives] for a spell, time and again . . . , testifies to a saving elasticity that shores up mastery in the act of mocking it. The animal that laughs may yet escape entrapment in its own achievement"; Marcel Gutwirth, *Laughing Matter: An Essay on the Comic* (Ithaca, N.Y.: Cornell University Press, 1993), 130, my insertion. And nicely in keeping with my discussion of the trilogy, Gutwirth also quotes Joachim Ritter: "What plays itself out and is caught up in laughter is the secret connection of nothingness with being. It plays itself out . . . in such a way that it is shown to inhere in the order which at one and the same time excludes it" (114–115). Gutwirth gives the reference as "Über das Lachen," 10. *Blätter für Deutsche Philosophie* 14 (1940/41):1–21.

56. Plato, *Theaetetus*, 142A.

57. I do not believe that implicit meanings embedded in language are inevitably relevant, nor even that it is necessarily or even usually right to say that they are really present in language as it is used. But for what it is worth, at the beginning of the *Sophist*, Socrates asks if the newly arrived Stranger is not a god, since "Homer tells us that gods attend upon the goings of men of mercy and justice, and . . . to mark the orderly or lawless doings of mankind. Your companion may be one of those higher powers, who intends to observe and expose our weakness in philosophical discourse, like a very spirit of refutation"; Plato, *Sophist*, 216A–B. The phrase "mercy and justice" translates αἰδοῦς δικαίας, which is variously translated also as, more literally, "just shame" (by Seth Benardete in Plato, *Plato's Sophist*, trans. Seth Benardete [1984; Chicago: University of Chicago Press, 1986], and "due reverence" (by Fowler in Plato, *Theaetetus, Sophist,* trans. H. N. Fowler [Loeb Classical Library. Cambridge, Mass.: Harvard University Press, 1921]). At the start of the dialogue, then, Socrates raises the issue of whether his and his companions' conduct is acceptable, and in expressing what is acceptable in this context, he puts the word "just" together with a word that literally means "shame." As I mentioned, one legitimate translation of this "just shame" is "due reverence," that is, due humility

in the face of what is beyond human decision, like the sanctity of laws while they stand, or, perhaps, the fact that human beings have limitations and weaknesses.

58. "The nonphilosopher with power is finally the best justification for philosophy, a common state of affairs that only philosophy is strange enough and idealistic enough to be able to explain"; Charles Altieri, "Plato's Masterplot: Idealization, Contradiction, and the Transformation of Rhetorical Ethos," in *Intimate Conflict: Contradiction in Literary and Philosophical Discourse,* ed. Brian G. Caraher (Albany: State University of New York Press, 1992), 68.

59. As I quoted above, "the admission of self-ignorance forestalls exorbitant claims. Thus it prevents the initiation of tragedy and places one in the way of moving through the foreseen and controlled catastrophes of comedy"; Edward G. Ballard, *Socratic Ignorance: An Essay on Platonic Self-Knowledge* (The Hague, Netherlands: Martinus Nijhoff, 1965), 159.

Conclusion

1. Aristotle, *Aristotle's Posterior Analytics,* trans. Hippocrates G. Apostle (Grinnell, Iowa: Peripatetic Press, 1981), i.31.87b29–36, translator's insertions and emphases here and in all quotes from this text below, unless otherwise specified. These emphases are usually intended to indicate translations of specific Greek words.

2. This is not induction in the modern sense of collecting sensory observations and then finding a general law that describes their relations to each other, but a kind of insight into the nature of the observed thing, through the sense perception of it. "*Epagoge*" is literally "leading beyond": the sensations lead us beyond themselves. In contemporary terms, observation is "theory-laden": the observed things are already meaningful for the observer in a variety of ways, are already part of a system of relations to other things and of relations among their own properties and possibilities. See, e.g., Hans-Georg Gadamer, *Truth and Method,* 2nd ed., trans. J. Weinsheimer and D. G. Marshall (New York: Continuum, 1989), 350–353, e.g., for Aristotle, "the birth of experience" is "an event . . . in which everything is coordinated," although "in a way that is ultimately incomprehensible"; ibid., 352; Martha C. Nussbaum, *The Fragility of Goodness: Luck and Ethics in Greek Tragedy and Philosophy* (New York: Cambridge University Press, 1986), 244–258, esp. 250–258.

3. Aristotle, *Posterior Analytics,* i.18.81a41–81b10.

4. Ibid., i.31.88a3–5.

5. Ibid., i.31.88a13–14.

6. Ibid., ii.19.99b20–21.

7. Ibid., ii.19.100a12–13, my insertion.

8. Ibid., ii.19.100b5–7.

9. Ibid., ii.19.100b15–16.

10. On interpretations of Aristotle like Gadamer's and Nussbaum's (see notes 2 above and 11 below), there is no sharp break between sensation and knowledge of universals. For a detailed discussion of this continuity specifically in connection with

the *Posterior Analytics*, see, e.g., James H. Lesher, "The Meaning of NOYΣ in the Posterior Analytics," *Phronesis* 18 (1973):44–68, e.g., 53: "some connection holds universally in the simple act of perception itself." In fact, I myself insist below on the dimension of continuity—really, of circularity—between these two poles of knowledge. But the reasons Aristotle gives for regarding these two poles as *also* sharply distinct remain.

11. As Nussbaum argues, "To have *nous,* or insight, concerning first principles is to come to see the fundamental role that principles we have been using all along play in the structure of a science. . . . We move from . . . the grasp that [already] goes with use to the ability to give accounts"; Nussbaum, *Fragility,* 251, my insertion. Nicely in keeping with my own account of knowledge and explanation, Nussbaum adds, "The appearances, then, can go all the way down."

12. Aristotle, *Nicomachean Ethics,* trans. W. D. Ross, in *The Basic Works of Aristotle,* ed. Richard McKeon (New York: Random House, 1941), i.4.1095a30–1095b1. Perhaps significantly, "intuition," or *nous,* the term for the kind of insight with which knowledge starts, is also Aristotle's term for the most developed kind of knowledge.

13. Without also glossing over their incompatibility, as I think the attempts to show their continuity typically do (see the references in notes 2, 10, and 11 above).

14. For a more detailed account, see Idea 6.2 and 6.3.

15. If there is anything to my interpretation, then, Plato did not, as Heidegger argued, get caught up in taking the nature of Being and of truth themselves for granted, so that he could not question them themselves or, more accurately, let their inherent mysteriousness or questionableness emerge. See, e.g., Martin Heidegger, "Plato's Doctrine of Truth," trans. T. Sheehan, in *Pathmarks,* ed. W. McNeill (New York: Cambridge University Press, 1998), e.g., 176, where Heidegger remarks on "the unspoken event" in Plato's thought "whereby ἰδέα [Idea] gains dominance over ἀλήθεια [truth]," so that "The essence of truth gives up its fundamental trait"; Heidegger, "Plato's Doctrine," my insertions. On my reading this "event" was not simply unspoken but, on the contrary, was designed both to be reflected on and to be considered in relation to conflicting "events." Further, Plato presents a way of taking into account precisely that we inescapably take some things for granted. Hence the relevance of self-cancellation as a structural feature of thought. Heidegger is right, then, that there are unspoken, taken-for-granted dimensions in Plato's thought, but he misses the dimension of Plato that—much like Heidegger's own thought—responds to and works with the *fact that there are* such dimensions, with the necessary limitation or finitude of human thought. As a result, Heidegger, like Aristotle in a different respect, on my reading, fails to recognize that Plato is not simply displaying a blind spot, but instead—again like Heidegger himself—justifies and explores this blindness's *relation to truth.* In fact, as I argued above, Plato goes further than Heidegger in this respect: he argues for what is *simply, absolutely right* about blindly taking some things for granted. Plato, then, has not failed to see what Heidegger sees, but instead offers a different kind of response to it.

16. Or, as Nietzsche argued, that what we consider the most noble should dictate what we consider true (which, for Nietzsche, is still only what we *consider* true). See, e.g., "Our thoughts should grow out of our values with the same necessity as the fruit out of the trees"; Friedrich Nietzsche, *The Genealogy of Morals,* in *The Birth of Tragedy and the Genealogy of Morals,* trans. F. Golffing (New York: Doubleday, 1956), 150. See also, e.g., "to speak of spirit and the good as Plato did [in terms of absolute, eternal Ideas] meant standing truth on her head and denying *perspective* itself, the basic condition of all life"; Nietzsche, *Beyond Good and Evil: Prelude to a Philosophy of the Future,* trans. R. J. Hollingdale (Harmondsworth, U.K.: Penguin, 1972), 14, my insertion; "The exoteric and the esoteric . . . differ . . . in that . . . the exoteric . . . sees things from below—but the esoteric [the "higher type of man"] sees them *from above!*"; ibid., 43, my insertion.

17. See, for a paradigmatic example, Gilbert Ryle, *Dilemmas* (Cambridge, U.K.: Cambridge University Press, 1960).

18. So, for example, "a basic subjective feeling of pleasure or displeasure" determines "what we require in order to be satisfied with our condition. But just because this . . . ground of determination [motive] can be known by the subject only empirically, it is impossible to regard this demand for happiness as a law, since the latter must contain exactly the same determining ground for the will of all rational beings and in all cases." Immanuel Kant, *Critique of Practical Reason,* trans. L. W. Beck (New York: Macmillan, 1993), 24 [25], translator's insertion.

19. On this point in connection with the relation between Kant's and Plato's ethics, see Chapter 1, note 50.

20. Yet another kind of connection here between mutually exclusive positions is that, on the one hand, generosity is only genuinely generosity when it is carried out without regard to its feeling good. This means that generosity *exists only* when one acts without a sense of the relevance of feeling good about it. But, on the other hand, one *can* legitimately feel good about being generous, because of the privilege of participating in something good that it is. And in fact, one *should* feel good about it, otherwise one is being unappreciative of the gift of a privilege. This happy experience of goodness, then, again, legitimately requires simultaneously taking one's generosity into account and leaving it entirely out of account.

21. The issue of pride appears explicitly in Plato's dialogues, although it is not discussed in its own right. In the *Phaedrus,* for example, Plato has Socrates mention his concern to establish whether he is monstrously "puffed up with pride"; Plato, *Phaedrus,* in *Phaedrus and Letters VII and VIII,* trans. W. Hamilton (Harmondsworth, U.K.: Penguin, 1973), 230A–B. And in the *Symposium,* as I quoted in Idea 7, Plato presents Alcibiades as accusing Socrates of "amazing arrogance and pride" for not sleeping with him despite his beauty; Plato, *Symposium,* trans. Alexander Nehamas and Paul Woodruff (Indianapolis, Ind.: Hackett, 1989), 219C. For a discussion of the central importance of shame in Plato's approach to truth, see Jill Gordon, *Turning toward Philosophy: Literary Device and Dramatic Structure in Plato's Dialogues* (University Park: Pennsylvania State University Press, 1999), 22–28.

22. Schlegel writes that "Socratic irony is the only involuntary and yet completely deliberate dissimulation. . . . In this sort of irony, everything should be playful and serious, guilelessly open and deeply hidden. It originates . . . in the conjunction of a perfectly instinctive and a perfectly conscious philosophy"; Friedrich Schlegel, *Philosophical Fragments*, trans. P. Firchow (Minneapolis: University of Minnesota Press, 1991), 13.

23. Jane Austen, *Emma* (Harmondsworth, U.K.: Penguin, 1966), 167.

24. "Elinor agreed to it all, for she did not think he deserved the compliment of rational opposition"; Jane Austen, *Sense and Sensibility* (Harmondsworth, U.K.: Penguin, 1969), 255.

Bibliography

Altieri, Charles. "Plato's Masterplot: Idealization, Contradiction, and the Transformation of Rhetorical Ethos." In *Intimate Conflict: Contradiction in Literary and Philosophical Discourse,* edited by Brian G. Caraher. Albany: State University of New York Press, 1992.

Ankersmit, F. R. *Aesthetic Politics: Political Philosophy beyond Fact and Value.* Stanford, Calif.: Stanford University Press, 1996.

Annas, Julia. "Plato the Skeptic." In *Methods of Interpreting Plato and His Dialogues,* edited by James C. Klagge and Nicholas D. Smith. New York: Oxford University Press, 1992.

Apel, Karl-Otto. *Selected Essays, Volume One: Towards a Transcendental Semiotics.* Edited by Eduardo Mendieta. Atlantic Highlands, N.J.: Humanities Press, 1994.

Aristotle. *Aristotle's Posterior Analytics.* Translated by Hippocrates G. Apostle. Grinnell, Iowa: Peripatetic Press, 1981.

———. *The Basic Works of Aristotle.* Edited by Richard McKeon. New York: Random House, 1941.

———. *Metaphysics.* Translated by R. Hope. New York: Columbia University Press; Ann Arbor: University of Michigan Press, 1960 [1952].

———. *Nicomachean Ethics.* Translated by W. D. Ross. In *The Basic Works of Aristotle,* edited by Richard McKeon. New York: Random House, 1941.

———. *Physics.* Translated by R. P. Hardie and R. K. Gaye. In *The Basic Works of Aristotle,* edited by Richard McKeon. New York: Random House, 1941.

———. *The* Rhetoric *and the* Poetics *of Aristotle.* Translated by W. R. Roberts and I. Bywater. New York: Modern Library of Random House, 1984 [1954].

———. *Topics.* Translated by W. A. Pickard-Cambridge. In *The Basic Works of Aristotle,* edited by Richard McKeon. New York: Random House, 1941.

Ashbaugh, Anne Freire. *Plato's Theory of Explanation: A Study of the Cosmological Account in the* Timaeus. Albany: State University of New York Press, 1988.

Attridge, Derek. *Peculiar Language: Literature as Difference from the Renaissance to James Joyce.* Ithaca, N.Y.: Cornell University Press, 1988.

Austen, Jane. *Emma.* Harmondsworth, U.K.: Penguin, 1966.

———. *Mansfield Park.* Harmondsworth, U.K.: Penguin, 1966.

———. *Pride and Prejudice.* Harmondsworth, U.K.: Penguin, 1972.

———. *Sense and Sensibility.* Harmondsworth, U.K.: Penguin, 1969.

Austin, John L. *How to Do Things with Words.* Cambridge, Mass.: Harvard University Press, 1962.

Badiou, Alain. *Manifesto for Philosophy.* Edited and translated by Norman Madarasz. Albany, N.Y.: State University of New York Press, 1999.

Ballard, Edward G. *Socratic Ignorance: An Essay on Platonic Self-Knowledge.* The Hague, Netherlands: Martinus Nijhoff, 1965.

Barris, Jeremy. "The Foundation in Truth of Rhetoric and Formal Logic." *Philosophy and Rhetoric* 29.4 (1996):314–328.

———. "The Problem of Comparing Different Cultural or Theoretical Frameworks: Davidson, Rorty, and the Nature of Truth." *Method and Theory in the Study of Religion* 18.2 (2006):124–143.

Benardete, Seth. *The Rhetoric of Morality and Philosophy: Plato's* Gorgias *and* Phaedrus. Chicago: University of Chicago Press, 1991.

Bennett, Tony. *Formalism and Marxism.* New York: Routledge, 1979.

Benson, Hugh H., ed. *Essays on the Philosophy of Socrates.* New York: Oxford University Press, 1992.

———. *Socratic Wisdom: The Model of Knowledge in Plato's Early Dialogues.* New York: Oxford University Press, 2000.

Bernheimer, Charles, and Claire Kahane, eds. *In Dora's Case: Freud—Hysteria—Feminism.* New York: Columbia University Press, 1985.

Blanchot, Maurice. *The Unavowable Community.* Translated by Pierre Joris. Barrytown, N.Y.: Station Hill Press, 1988.

———. *The Writing of the Disaster.* Translated by Ann Smock. Lincoln: University of Nebraska Press, 1986.

Blondell, Ruby. *The Play of Character in Plato's Dialogues.* New York: Cambridge University Press, 2002.

Bloom, Allan, ed. *The Republic of Plato.* 2nd ed. New York: Basic Books, 1968.

Bluck, R. S. *Plato's* Sophist. Edited by G. C. Neal. Manchester, U.K.: Manchester University Press, 1975.

Brann, Eva. "The Music of the *Republic.*" In *Four Essays on Plato's* Republic. Double issue of *St. John's Review* 39.1–2 (1989–1990). Annapolis, Md.: St. John's College, 1990.

Brann, Eva, Peter Kalkavage, and Eric Salem. "Introduction." In *Plato's* Phaedo, translated by Eva Brann, Peter Kalkavage, and Eric Salem. Newburyport, Mass.: Focus, 1998.

Bredbeck, Gregory W. *Sodomy and Interpretation: Marlowe to Milton.* Ithaca, N.Y.: Cornell University Press, 1991.

Bremer, Manuel. *An Introduction to Paraconsistent Logics.* Frankfurt am Main: Peter Lang, 2005.

Burke, Peter. *The Art of Conversation.* Ithaca, N.Y.: Cornell University Press, 1993.

Burn, Andrew R. *The Pelican History of Greece.* Harmondsworth, U.K.: Penguin, 1965.

Butler, Judith. *Gender Trouble: Feminism and the Subversion of Identity.* New York: Routledge, 1990.

———. "Imitation and Gender Insubordination." In *Inside/Out: Lesbian Theories, Gay Theories,* edited by Diana Fuss. New York: Routledge, 1991.

Caraher, Brian G., ed. *Intimate Conflict: Contradiction in Literary and Philosophical Discourse.* Albany: State University of New York Press, 1992.

Carnap, Rudolf. *The Logical Structure of the World and Pseudoproblems in Philosophy.* Translated by R. A. George. Berkeley and Los Angeles: University of California Press, 1967.

Cherwitz, Richard A., ed. *Rhetoric and Philosophy.* Hillsdale, N.J.: Lawrence Erlbaum, 1990.

Cherwitz, Richard A., and James W. Hikins. *Communication and Knowledge: An Investigation in Rhetorical Epistemology.* Columbia: University of South Carolina Press, 1986.

Collingwood, Robin George. *An Essay on Metaphysics.* Oxford: Clarendon Press, 1940.

———. *The Idea of History.* Revised edition by Jan van der Dussen. New York: Oxford University Press, 1994.

———. *The New Leviathan, or Man, Society, Civilization, and Barbarism.* New York: Thomas Y. Crowell, 1971.

Connolly, William E. *Pluralism.* Durham, N.C.: Duke University Press, 2005.

Corlett, Angelo. "Interpreting Plato's Dialogues." *Classical Quarterly* 47.2 (1997):423–437.

Corlett, William. *Community without Unity: A Politics of Derridian Extravagance.* Durham, N.C.: Duke University Press, 1989.

Cornell, Drucilla. *The Philosophy of the Limit.* New York: Routledge, 1992.

Cornford, Francis M. *Before and after Socrates.* Cambridge, U.K.: Cambridge University Press, 1932.

Coward, Rosalind, and John Ellis. *Language and Materialism: Developments in Semiology and the Theory of the Subject.* London: Routledge and Kegan Paul, 1977.

Crary, Alice. "Wittgenstein's Philosophy in Relation to Political Thought." In *The New Wittgenstein,* edited by Alice Crary and Rupert Read. New York: Routledge, 2000.

Crary, Alice, and Rupert Read, eds. *The New Wittgenstein.* New York: Routledge, 2000.

Crombie, I. M. *An Examination of Plato's Doctrines.* 2 vols. London: Routledge & Kegan Paul, 1962.

———. *Plato: The Midwife's Apprentice.* New York: Barnes & Noble, 1964.

Danto, A. C. "Artworks and Real Things." In *Aesthetics Today,* edited by M. Philipson and P. J. Gudel. New York: New American Library, 1980.

Davidson, Donald. *Inquiries into Truth and Interpretation.* Oxford: Clarendon Press, 1984.

———. "On the Very Idea of a Conceptual Scheme." In *Inquiries into Truth and Interpretation.* Oxford: Clarendon Press, 1984.

———. "Paradoxes of Irrationality." In *Philosophical Essays on Freud,* edited by Richard Wollheim and James Hopkins. New York: Cambridge University Press, 1982.

Day, Sebastian J. *Intuitive Cognition: A Key to the Significance of the Later Scholastics.* St. Bonaventure, N.Y.: Franciscan Institute, 1947.

Dearin, Ray D., ed. *The New Rhetoric of Chaim Perelman: Statement and Response.* Lanham, Md.: University Press of America, 1989.

de Certeau, Michel. *The Practice of Everyday Life.* Translated by Steven Rendall. Berkeley: University of California Press, 1984.

Deleuze, Gilles. *Difference and Repetition.* Translated by Paul Patton. New York: Columbia University Press, 1994.

———. *The Logic of Sense.* Translated by Mark Lester with Charles Stivale. New York: Columbia University Press, 1990.

Derrida, Jacques. *Dissemination.* Translated by Barbara Johnson. Chicago: University of Chicago Press, 1981.

———. *Margins of Philosophy.* Translated by A. Bass. Chicago: University of Chicago Press, 1982.

———. "White Mythology: Metaphor in the Text of Philosophy." In *Margins of Philosophy,* translated by A. Bass. Chicago: University of Chicago Press, 1982.

Dewey, John. *Logic: The Theory of Inquiry.* New York: Henry Holt, 1938.

Dorter, Kenneth. *Form and Good in Plato's Eleatic Dialogues: The* Parmenides, Theaetetus, Sophist, *and* Statesman. Berkeley: University of California Press, 1994.

Edelstein, Ludwig. "The Function of the Myth in Plato's Philosophy." *Journal of the History of Ideas* 10.4 (1949):463–481.

Fann, K. T., ed. *Ludwig Wittgenstein: The Man and His Philosophy.* New York: Dell, 1967.

Feyerabend, Paul. *Against Method.* 3rd ed. London: Verso, 1993.

Fichte, J. G. "Concerning the Difference between the Spirit and the Letter within Philosophy." In *Fichte: Early Philosophical Writings,* translated by D. Breazeale. Ithaca, N.Y.: Cornell University Press, 1988.

———. *Fichte: Early Philosophical Writings.* Translated by D. Breazeale. Ithaca, N.Y.: Cornell University Press, 1988.

Field, G. C. *Plato and His Contemporaries: A Study in Fourth-Century Life and Thought.* London: Methuen, 1930.

Figal, Günter. "The Idea and Mixture of the Good." Translated by Michael McGettigan and Cara Gendel Ryan. In *Retracing the Platonic Text,* edited by John Russon and John Sallis. Evanston, Ill.: Northwestern University Press, 2000.

Fish, Stanley E. *Self-Consuming Artifacts: The Experience of Seventeenth-Century Literature.* Berkeley and Los Angeles: University of California Press, 1972.

Foucault, Michel. *Power/Knowledge: Selected Interviews and Other Writings 1972–1977.* Edited by Colin Gordon. New York: Pantheon, 1980.

Freire, Paulo. *Pedagogy of the Oppressed.* Translated by Myra Bergman Ramos. New York: Seabury Press, 1968.

Fuss, Diana. *Essentially Speaking: Feminism, Nature and Difference.* New York: Routledge, 1989.

———, ed. *Inside/Out: Lesbian Theories, Gay Theories.* New York: Routledge, 1991.

Gadamer, Hans-Georg. *Dialogue and Dialectic: Eight Hermeneutical Studies on Plato.* Translated by P. Christopher Smith. New Haven, Conn.: Yale University Press, 1980.

———. *The Idea of the Good in Platonic-Aristotelian Philosophy.* Translated by P. Christopher Smith. New Haven, Conn.: Yale University Press, 1986.

———. *Plato's Dialectical Ethics: Phenomenological Interpretations Relating to the* Philebus. Translated by R. M. Wallace. New Haven, Conn.: Yale University Press, 1991.

———. *Truth and Method.* 2nd ed. Translated by J. Weinsheimer and D. G. Marshall. New York: Continuum, 1989.

Gilson, Etienne. *Being and Some Philosophers.* 2nd ed. Toronto: Pontifical Institute of Mediaeval Studies, 1952.

Goldberg, Jonathan. "Sodomy in the New World: Anthropologies Old and New." In *Fear of a Queer Planet: Queer Politics and Social Theory,* edited by Michael Warner. Minneapolis: University of Minnesota Press, 1993.

Golden, James L., and Edward P. J. Corbett, eds. *The Rhetoric of Blair, Campbell, and Whately.* Carbondale: Southern Illinois University Press, 1990.

Gonzalez, Francisco J. *Dialectic and Dialogue: Plato's Practice of Philosophical Inquiry.* Evanston, Ill.: Northwestern University Press, 1998.

Goodman, Nelson. "Notes on the Well-Made World." *Partisan Review* 51 (1984):276–288.

———. *Ways of Worldmaking.* Indianapolis, Ind.: Hackett, 1978.

Goodman, Nelson, and Catherine Z. Elgin. *Reconceptions in Philosophy and Other Arts and Sciences.* Indianapolis, Ind.: Hackett, 1988.

Gordon, Jill. *Turning toward Philosophy: Literary Device and Dramatic Structure in Plato's Dialogues.* University Park: Pennsylvania State University Press, 1999.

Griswold, Charles L., Jr., ed. *Platonic Writings, Platonic Readings.* New York: Routledge; University Park: Pennsylvania State University Press, 2002 [1988].

———. "Plato's Metaphilosophy: Why Plato Wrote Dialogues." In *Platonic Writings, Platonic Readings,* edited by Charles L. Griswold, Jr. New York: Routledge; University Park: Pennsylvania State University Press, 2002 [1988].

Guthrie, W. K. C. *The Sophists.* New York: Cambridge University Press, 1971 [1969].

Gutwirth, Marcel. *Laughing Matter: An Essay on the Comic.* Ithaca, N.Y.: Cornell University Press, 1993.

Hackforth, Reginald. *Plato's* Phaedo. Cambridge, U.K.: Cambridge University Press, 1972 [1955].

Hales, Steven D. "A Consistent Relativism." *Mind* 106.421 (1997):33–52.

Hegel, G. W. F. *Science of Logic.* Translated by A. V. Miller. Atlantic Highlands, N.J.: Humanities Press International, 1969.

Heidegger, Martin. *Basic Writings.* Edited by D. F. Krell. New York: Harper & Row, 1977.

———. *Early Greek Thinking: The Dawn of Western Philosophy.* Translated by D. F. Krell and F. A. Capuzzi. San Francisco: Harper & Row, 1984 [1975].

———. *An Introduction to Metaphysics*. Translated by R. Manheim. New Haven, Conn.: Yale University Press, 1959.

———. "On the Essence of Truth." Translated by J. Sallis. In *Basic Writings*, edited by D. F. Krell. New York: Harper & Row, 1977.

———. *Pathmarks*. Edited by W. McNeill. New York: Cambridge University Press, 1998.

———. "Plato's Doctrine of Truth." Translated by T. Sheehan. In *Pathmarks*, edited by W. McNeill. New York: Cambridge University Press, 1998.

Hikins, James W. "Realism and Its Implications for Rhetorical Theory." In *Rhetoric and Philosophy*, edited by Richard A. Cherwitz. Hillsdale, N.J.: Lawrence Erlbaum, 1990.

Hollis, Martin, and Steven Lukes, eds. *Rationality and Relativism*. Cambridge, Mass.: MIT Press, 1982.

Homer. *Iliad*. Translated by Richmond Lattimore. Chicago: University of Chicago Press, 1951.

Hume, David. *A Treatise of Human Nature*. New York: Oxford University Press, 2000.

Husserl, Edmund. *The Crisis of European Sciences and Transcendental Phenomenology: An Introduction to Phenomenological Philosophy*. Translated by David Carr. Evanston, Ill.: Northwestern University Press, 1970.

Hutcheon, Linda. *Irony's Edge: The Theory and Politics of Irony*. New York: Routledge, 1995.

Hyland, Drew. *The Virtue of Philosophy: An Interpretation of Plato's* Charmides. Athens, Ohio: Ohio University Press, 1981.

Hyman, Arthur, and James J. Walsh, eds. *Philosophy in the Middle Ages*. 2nd ed. Indianapolis, Ind.: Hackett, 1973.

Irwin, Terence H. *Aristotle's First Principles*. New York: Oxford University Press, 1988.

———. *Plato's Ethics*. New York: Oxford University Press, 1995.

Isenberg, M. W. "Plato's *Sophist* and the Five Stages of Knowing." *Classical Philology* 46.4 (1951):201–211.

James, William. *A Pluralistic Universe*. In *William James: Writings 1902–1910*, edited by Bruce Kuklick. New York: Library of America, 1987.

———. *Some Problems of Philosophy: A Beginning of an Introduction to Philosophy*. Lincoln: University of Nebraska Press, 1996.

Jaspers, Karl. *Reason and Existenz: Five Lectures*. Translated by William Earle. Milwaukee, Wis.: Marquette University Press, 1997.

Johnstone, Henry W., Jr. *Validity and Rhetoric in Philosophical Argument: An Outlook in Transition*. University Park, Pa.: Dialogue Press of Man and World, 1978.

Kahn, Charles H. "Did Plato Write Socratic Dialogues?" In *Essays on the Philosophy of Socrates*, edited by Hugh H. Benson. New York: Oxford University Press, 1992 [1981].

Kant, Immanuel. *Critique of Judgment*. Translated by W. S. Pluhar. Indianapolis, Ind.: Hackett, 1987.

————. *Critique of Practical Reason*. Translated by L. W. Beck. New York: Macmillan, 1993.

————. *Critique of Pure Reason*. Translated by N. K. Smith. New York: St. Martin's Press, 1929.

————. *Prolegomena to any Future Metaphysics*. Translated by L. W. Beck. New York: Bobbs-Merrill, 1950.

Karon, Louise A. "Presence in *The New Rhetoric*." In *The New Rhetoric of Chaim Perelman: Statement and Response,* edited by Ray D. Dearin. Lanham, Md.: University Press of America, 1989.

Keener, Frederick M. *The Chain of Becoming*. New York: Columbia University Press, 1983.

Kennedy, George A. *Classical Rhetoric and Its Christian and Secular Tradition from Ancient to Modern Times*. Chapel Hill: University of North Carolina Press, 1980.

Klagge, James C., and Nicholas D. Smith, eds. *Methods of Interpreting Plato and His Dialogues*. New York: Oxford University Press, 1992.

Klein, Jacob. *A Commentary on Plato's* Meno. Chicago: University of Chicago Press, 1965.

————. *Lectures and Essays*. Edited by R. B. Williamson and E. Zuckerman. Annapolis, Md.: St. John's College Press, 1985.

————. *Plato's Trilogy*. Chicago: University of Chicago Press, 1977.

Krausz, Michael, ed. *Relativism: Interpretation and Confrontation*. Notre Dame, Ind.: University of Notre Dame Press, 1989.

Kraut, Richard, ed. *The Cambridge Companion to Plato*. New York: Cambridge University Press, 1992.

Kripke, Saul. *Naming and Necessity*. Cambridge, Mass.: Harvard University Press, 1980.

Kuhn, Thomas S. *The Structure of Scientific Revolutions*. 2nd ed. Chicago: University of Chicago Press, 1970.

Lachterman, David. "What Is 'The Good' of Plato's *Republic?*" In *Four Essays on Plato's* Republic. Double issue of *St. John's Review* 39.1–2 (1989–1990). Annapolis, Md.: St. John's College, 1990.

Laclau, Ernesto, and Chantal Mouffe. *Hegemony and Socialist Strategy: Towards a Radical Democratic Politics*. Translated by W. Moore and P. Cammack. London: Verso, 1985.

Laertius, Diogenes. *Lives of Eminent Philosophers*. 2 vols. Translated by R. D. Hicks. Loeb Classical Library. Cambridge, Mass.: Harvard University Press, 1972.

Lang, Berel. *Philosophical Style: An Anthology about the Reading and Writing of Philosophy*. Chicago: Nelson-Hall, 1980.

————, ed. *The Anatomy of Philosophical Style*. Cambridge, Mass.: Basil Blackwell, 1990.

Larmore, Charles E. *Patterns of Moral Complexity*. New York: Cambridge University Press, 1987.

LePore, Ernest, ed. *Truth and Interpretation: Perspectives on the Philosophy of Donald Davidson*. Cambridge, Mass.: Basil Blackwell, 1986.

Lesher, James H. "The Meaning of ΝΟΥΣ in the *Posterior Analytics.*" *Phronesis* 18 (1973):44–68.

Levi, Albert W. "Wittgenstein as Dialectician." In *Ludwig Wittgenstein: The Man and His Philosophy,* edited by K. T. Fann. 1964. New York: Dell, 1967.

Levine, Peter. *Living without Philosophy: On Narrative, Rhetoric, and Morality.* New York: State University of New York Press, 1998.

Lewis, Clarence Irving. *Mind and the World Order: Outline of a Theory of Knowledge.* New York: Dover, 1929.

Lloyd, Charles O. "Sophistication and Refinement in Greek Literature from Homer to Aristophanes." Diss., Indiana University, 1976.

Louch, A. R. *Explanation and Human Action.* Oxford: Basil Blackwell, 1966.

MacIntyre, Alasdair C. "Relativism, Power, and Philosophy." In *Relativism: Interpretation and Confrontation,* edited by Michael Krausz. Notre Dame, Ind.: University of Notre Dame Press, 1989.

———. *Whose Justice? Which Rationality?* Notre Dame, Ind.: University of Notre Dame Press, 1988.

Mailloux, Steven. *Rhetorical Power.* Ithaca, N.Y.: Cornell University Press, 1989.

McGuinness, Brian, ed. *Wittgenstein and His Times.* Chicago: University of Chicago Press, 1982.

McKeon, Richard. *Rhetoric: Essays in Invention and Discovery.* Edited by M. Backman. Woodbridge, U.K.: Ox Bow Press, 1987.

McLaren, Peter. *Critical Pedagogy and Predatory Culture: Oppositional Politics in a Postmodern Era.* New York: Routledge, 1995.

Merleau-Ponty, Maurice. *The Primacy of Perception.* Translated by James M. Edie, et al. Evanston, Ill.: Northwestern University Press, 1964.

———. *Signs.* Translated by Richard C. McCleary. Evanston, Ill.: Northwestern University Press, 1964.

Miller, Mitchell H., Jr. *The Philosopher in Plato's* Statesman. The Hague, Netherlands: Martinus Nijhoff, 1980.

———. *Plato's* Parmenides: *The Conversion of the Soul.* Princeton, N.J.: Princeton University Press; University Park: Pennsylvania State University Press, 1991 [1986].

Moody, Ernest A. *The Logic of William of Ockham.* New York: Russell & Russell, 1935.

Mouffe, Chantal. *The Democratic Paradox.* London: Verso, 2000.

Murphy, Peter. "Postmodern Perspectives and Justice." *Thesis Eleven* 30 (1991):117–132.

Nagel, Thomas. "The Absurd." In *Mortal Questions.* New York: Cambridge University Press, 1979.

———. *Mortal Questions.* New York: Cambridge University Press, 1979.

———. *The View from Nowhere.* New York: Oxford University Press, 1986.

———. "What Is It Like to Be a Bat?" In *Mortal Questions.* New York: Cambridge University Press, 1979.

Nails, Debra. *Agora, Academy, and the Conduct of Philosophy.* Dordrecht, Netherlands: Kluwer Academic, 1995.

———. *The People of Plato: A Prosopography of Plato and Other Socratics.* Indianapolis, Ind.: Hackett, 2002.

Nancy, Jean-Luc. *The Inoperative Community.* Translated by Peter Connor, Lisa Garbus, Michael Holland, and Simona Sawhney. Minneapolis: University of Minnesota Press, 1991.

Nettleship, Richard Lewis. *Lectures on the Republic of Plato.* New York: St. Martin's Press, 1968.

Nietzsche, Friedrich. *Beyond Good and Evil: Prelude to a Philosophy of the Future.* Translated by R. J. Hollingdale. Harmondsworth, U.K.: Penguin, 1972.

———. *The Birth of Tragedy and the Genealogy of Morals.* Translated by F. Golffing. New York: Doubleday, 1956.

Norris, Christopher. *The Contest of Faculties: Philosophy and Theory after Deconstruction.* New York: Methuen, 1985.

Nussbaum, Martha C. *The Fragility of Goodness: Luck and Ethics in Greek Tragedy and Philosophy.* New York: Cambridge University Press, 1986.

Nyíri, J. C. "Wittgenstein's Later Work in Relation to Conservatism." In *Wittgenstein and His Times,* edited by Brian McGuinness. Chicago: University of Chicago Press, 1982.

Ortega y Gasset, José. *The Revolt of the Masses.* Translated by Anon. New York: W. W. Norton, 1960 [1932].

———. *What Is Knowledge?* Edited and translated by Jorge García-Gómez. New York: State University of New York Press, 2002.

———. *What Is Philosophy?* Translated by M. Adams. New York: W. W. Norton, 1960.

Owens, Joseph. *The Doctrine of Being in the Aristotelian Metaphysics: A Study in the Greek Background of Mediaeval Thought.* 3rd ed. Toronto: Pontifical Institute of Mediaeval Studies, 1978.

Peirce, Charles Sanders. *Collected Papers of Charles Sanders Peirce.* Vol. 5. Edited by Charles Hartshorne and Paul Weiss. Cambridge, Mass.: Harvard University Press, 1935.

———. "Issues of Pragmaticism." In *Charles S. Peirce: Selected Writings.* Edited by Philip P. Wiener. New York: Dover, 1958.

———. "Truth and Falsity and Error." In *Collected Papers of Charles Sanders Peirce,* vol. 5, edited by Charles Hartshorne and Paul Weiss, 565–573. Cambridge, Mass.: Harvard University Press, 1935.

Penner, Terry. "Socrates and the Early Dialogues." In *The Cambridge Companion to Plato,* edited by Richard Kraut. New York: Cambridge University Press, 1992.

Perelman, Chaim. *The New Rhetoric and the Humanities: Essays on Rhetoric and Its Applications.* Dordrecht, Netherlands: D. Riedel, 1979.

Peters, R. S. *The Concept of Motivation.* London: Routledge & Kegan Paul, 1958.

Philipson. M., and P. J. Gudel, eds. *Aesthetics Today.* New York: New American Library, 1980.

Plato. *Apology.* Translated by H. Tredennick. In *Plato: The Collected Dialogues,* edited by Edith Hamilton and Huntington Cairns. Princeton, N.J.: Princeton University Press, 1961.

———. *Charmides.* Translated by Donald Watt. In *Early Socratic Dialogues,* edited by T. J. Saunders. Harmondsworth, U.K.: Penguin, 1987.

———. *Cratylus.* Translated by Benjamin Jowett. In *Plato: The Collected Dialogues,* edited by Edith Hamilton and Huntington Cairns. Princeton, N.J.: Princeton University Press, 1961.

———. *Crito.* Translated by Hugh Tredennick. In *Plato: The Collected Dialogues,* edited by Edith Hamilton and Huntington Cairns. Princeton, N.J.: Princeton University Press, 1961.

———. *Early Socratic Dialogues.* Edited by T. J. Saunders. Harmondsworth, U.K.: Penguin, 1987.

———. *Gorgias.* Translated by W. D. Woodhead. In *Plato: The Collected Dialogues,* edited by Edith Hamilton and Huntington Cairns. Princeton, N.J.: Princeton University Press, 1961.

———. *Ion.* Translated by Lane Cooper. In *Plato: The Collected Dialogues,* edited by Edith Hamilton and Huntington Cairns. Princeton, N.J.: Princeton University Press, 1961.

———. *Laches.* Translated by B. Jowett. In *Plato: The Collected Dialogues,* edited by Edith Hamilton and Huntington Cairns. Princeton, N.J.: Princeton University Press, 1961.

———. *The Last Days of Socrates.* Translated by H. Tredennick. Harmondsworth, U.K.: Penguin, 1969.

———. *The Laws.* Translated by T. J. Saunders. Harmondsworth, U.K.: Penguin, 1970.

———. *Letter VII.* Translated by L. A. Post. In *Plato: The Collected Dialogues,* edited by Edith Hamilton and Huntington Cairns. Princeton, N.J.: Princeton University Press, 1961.

———. *Lysis.* Translated by J. Wright. In *Plato: The Collected Dialogues,* edited by Edith Hamilton and Huntington Cairns. Princeton, N.J.: Princeton University Press, 1961.

———. *Meno.* Translated by W. K. C. Guthrie. In *Plato: The Collected Dialogues,* edited by Edith Hamilton and Huntington Cairns. Princeton, N.J.: Princeton University Press, 1961.

———. *Parmenides.* Translated by F. M. Cornford. In *Plato: The Collected Dialogues,* edited by Edith Hamilton and Huntington Cairns. Princeton, N.J.: Princeton University Press, 1961.

———. *Phaedo.* In *The Last Days of Socrates,* translated by H. Tredennick. Harmondsworth, U.K.: Penguin, 1969.

———. *Phaedrus and Letters VII and VIII.* Translated by W. Hamilton. Harmondsworth, U.K.: Penguin, 1973.

———. *Philebus.* Translated by R. Hackforth. In *Plato: The Collected Dialogues,* edited by Edith Hamilton and Huntington Cairns. Princeton, N.J.: Princeton University Press, 1961.

———. *Plato's Sophist.* Translated by Seth Benardete. Chicago: University of Chicago Press, 1986 [1984].

———. *Plato: The Collected Dialogues.* Edited by Edith Hamilton and Huntington Cairns. Princeton, N.J.: Princeton University Press, 1961.

———. *Protagoras.* Translated by W. K. C. Guthrie. In *Plato: The Collected Dialogues,* edited by Edith Hamilton and Huntington Cairns. Princeton, N.J.: Princeton University Press, 1961.

———. *Republic.* 2 vols. Translated by Paul Shorey. Loeb Classical Library. Cambridge, Mass.: Harvard University Press 1935.

———. *Republic.* Translated by Paul Shorey. In *Plato: The Collected Dialogues,* edited by Edith Hamilton and Huntington Cairns. Princeton, N.J.: Princeton University Press, 1961.

———. *Sophist.* Translated by F. M. Cornford. In *Plato: The Collected Dialogues,* edited by Edith Hamilton and Huntington Cairns. Princeton, N.J.: Princeton University Press, 1961.

———. *Statesman.* Translated by J. B. Skemp. In *Plato: The Collected Dialogues,* edited by Edith Hamilton and Huntington Cairns. Princeton, N.J.: Princeton University Press, 1961.

———. *Symposium.* Translated by Alexander Nehamas and Paul Woodruff. Indianapolis, Ind.: Hackett, 1989.

———. *Timaeus.* Translated by B. Jowett. In *Plato: The Collected Dialogues,* edited by Edith Hamilton and Huntington Cairns. Princeton, N.J.: Princeton University Press, 1961.

———. *Theaetetus.* Translated by M. J. Levett and revision by M. Burnyeat. Indianapolis, Ind.: Hackett, 1992.

———. *Theaetetus.* Translated by R. Waterfield. Harmondsworth, U.K.: Penguin, 1987.

———. *Theaetetus, Sophist.* Translated by H. N. Fowler. Loeb Classical Library. Cambridge, Mass.: Harvard University Press, 1921.

Plochmann, George K. "Socrates, the Stranger from Elea, and Some Others." *Classical Philology* 49.4 (1954):223–231.

Press, Gerald A., ed. *Plato's Dialogues: New Studies and Interpretations.* Lanham, Md.: Rowman & Littlefield, 1993.

Priest, Graham. *Beyond the Limits of Thought.* Oxford: Oxford University Press, 2002.

———. *An Introduction to Non-Classical Logic.* Cambridge, U.K.: Cambridge University Press, 2001.

Putnam, Hilary. *Realism with a Human Face.* Edited by James Conant. Cambridge, Mass.: Harvard University Press, 1990.

———. *Words and Life.* Edited by James Conant. Cambridge, Mass.: Harvard University Press, 1994.

Quine, Willard Van Orman. *From a Logical Point of View: Nine Logico-Philosophical Essays.* 2nd ed. Cambridge, Mass.: Harvard University Press, 1961.

———. "Ontological Relativity." In *Ontological Relativity and Other Essays.* New York: Columbia University Press, 1969.

———. *Ontological Relativity and Other Essays.* New York: Columbia University Press, 1969.

———. "Two Dogmas of Empiricism." In *From a Logical Point of View: Nine Logico-Philosophical Essays.* 2nd ed. Cambridge, Mass.: Harvard University Press, 1961.

Raven, J. E. *Plato's Thought in the Making.* Cambridge, U.K.: Cambridge University Press, 1965.

Rescher, Nicholas. *The Strife of Systems: An Essay on the Grounds and Implications of Philosophical Diversity.* Pittsburgh: University of Pittsburgh Press, 1985.

Riley, Denise. *Am I That Name? Feminism and the Category of "Women" in History.* Minneapolis: University of Minnesota Press, 1988.

Ritter, Joachim. "Über das Lachen." *Blätter für Deutsche Philosophie* 14 (1940–1941):1–21.

Robinson, Richard. *Plato's Earlier Dialectic.* Oxford: Oxford University Press, 1953.

Rose, Jacqueline. "Dora: Fragment of an Analysis." In *In Dora's Case: Freud—Hysteria—Feminism,* edited by Charles Bernheimer and Claire Kahane. New York: Columbia University Press, 1985.

Rosen, Stanley. *Plato's Statesman: The Web of Politics.* New Haven, Conn.: Yale University Press, 1995.

Ross James F., and Todd Bates. "Duns Scotus on Natural Theology." In *The Cambridge Companion to Duns Scotus,* edited by Thomas Williams. New York: Cambridge University Press, 2003.

Ross, W. D. *Plato's Theory of Ideas.* Oxford: Clarendon Press, 1951.

Russon, John, and John Sallis, eds. *Retracing the Platonic Text.* Evanston, Ill.: Northwestern University Press, 2000.

Ryle, Gilbert. *Dilemmas.* Cambridge, U.K.: Cambridge University Press, 1960.

Sainsbury, R. M. *Paradoxes.* 2nd ed. Cambridge, U.K.: Cambridge University Press, 1995.

Sallis, John. *Being and Logos: The Way of Platonic Dialogue.* 2nd ed. Atlantic Highlands, N.J.: Humanities Press, 1986.

———. *Chorology: On Beginning in Plato's Timaeus.* Bloomington: Indiana University Press, 1999.

———. *Echoes: After Heidegger.* Indianapolis: Indiana University Press, 1990.

Sayre, Kenneth M. *Plato's Literary Garden: How to Read a Platonic Dialogue.* Notre Dame, Ind.: University of Notre Dame Press, 1995.

Schelling, F. W. J. *Philosophical Inquiries into the Nature of Human Freedom.* Translated by J. Gutmann. La Salle, Ill.: Open Court, 1936.

Schiller, F. C. S. *Formal Logic: A Scientific and Social Problem.* London: Macmillan, 1912.

———. *Logic for Use: An Introduction to the Voluntarist Theory of Knowledge.* New York: Harcourt, Brace, 1930.

Schlegel, Friedrich. *Philosophical Fragments.* Translated by P. Firchow. Minneapolis: University of Minnesota Press, 1991.

Scult, Allen. "Perelman's Universal Audience: One Perspective." In *The New Rhetoric of Chaim Perelman: Statement and Response,* edited by Ray D. Dearin. Lanham, Md.: University Press of America, 1989.

Sedgwick, Eve Kosofsky. *Between Men: English Literature and Male Homosocial Desire.* New York: Columbia University Press, 1985.

———. *The Epistemology of the Closet.* Berkeley: University of California Press, 1990.

Seidman, Steven. "Identity and Politics in a 'Postmodern' Gay Culture: Some Historical and Conceptual Notes." In *Fear of a Queer Planet: Queer Politics and Social Theory,* edited by Michael Warner. Minneapolis: University of Minnesota Press, 1993.

Sellars, Wilfrid. "Empiricism and the Philosophy of Mind." In *Science, Perception and Reality.* Atascadero, Calif.: Ridgeview, 1991 [1956].

———. *Philosophical Perspectives: Metaphysics and Epistemology.* Atascadero, Calif.: Ridgeview, 1967.

———. "Science and Ethics." In *Philosophical Perspectives: Metaphysics and Epistemology.* Atascadero, Calif.: Ridgeview, 1967.

———. *Science, Perception and Reality.* Atascadero, Calif.: Ridgeview, 1991 [1956].

Shelley, Percy Bysshe. "Adonais: An Elegy on the Death of John Keats." In *The Poetical Works of Shelley,* edited by N. F. Ford. Boston, Mass.: Houghton Mifflin, 1975.

———. "Hellas: A Lyrical Drama." In *The Poetical Works of Shelley,* edited by N. F. Ford. Boston, Mass.: Houghton Mifflin, 1975.

———. *The Poetical Works of Shelley.* Edited by N. F. Ford. Boston, Mass.: Houghton Mifflin, 1975.

Simpson, David. *The Academic Postmodern and the Rule of Literature: A Report on Half-Knowledge.* Chicago: University of Chicago Press, 1995.

Sontag, Susan. *Against Interpretation and Other Essays.* New York: Doubleday, 1966.

———. "Notes on 'Camp.'" In *Against Interpretation and Other Essays.* New York: Doubleday, 1966.

Sophocles. *The Theban Plays.* Translated by E. F. Watling. Harmondsworth, U.K.: Penguin, 1947.

Stanley, Liz, and Sue Wise. *Breaking Out Again: Feminist Ontology and Epistemology.* London: Routledge, 1993.

Strauss, Leo. "On a New Interpretation of Plato's Political Philosophy." *Social Research* 13 (1946):326–367.

Tachau, Katherine H. *Vision and Certitude in the Age of Ockham: Optics, Epistemology and the Foundation of Semantics 1250–1345.* Boston: Brill Academic, 1988.

Taylor, Charles. *Philosophical Papers, Vol. 2: Philosophy and the Human Sciences.* Cambridge, U.K.: Cambridge University Press, 1985.

Taylor, Talbot J. *Mutual Misunderstanding: Scepticism and the Theorizing of Language and Interpretation.* Durham, N.C.: Duke University Press, 1992.

Theognis. *Elegies.* In *Hesiod and Theognis,* Translated by D. Wender. Harmondsworth, U.K.: Penguin, 1973.

Thesleff, Holger. "Looking for Clues: An Interpretation of Some Literary Aspects of Plato's 'Two-Level' Model." In *Plato's Dialogues: New Studies and Interpretations,* edited by Gerald A. Press. Lanham, Md.: Rowman & Littlefield, 1993.

Tigerstedt, E. N. *Interpreting Plato.* Uppsala, Sweden: Almqvist & Wiksell, 1977.

Toms, Eric. *Being, Negation and Logic.* Oxford: Basil Blackwell, 1962.

Toulmin, Stephen. *The Uses of Argument.* Cambridge, U.K.: Cambridge University Press, 1958.

Tuana, Nancy, ed. *Feminism and Science.* Bloomington: Indiana University Press, 1989.

Tully, James. *Strange Multiplicity: Constitutionalism in an Age of Diversity.* Cambridge, U.K.: Cambridge University Press, 1995.

Vlastos, Gregory. *Platonic Studies.* Princeton, N.J.: Princeton University Press, 1981.

———. "Reasons and Causes in the *Phaedo.*" In *Platonic Studies.* Princeton, N.J.: Princeton University Press, 1981.

———. *Socrates: Ironist and Moral Philosopher.* Ithaca, N.Y.: Cornell University Press, 1991.

———. "The Socratic Elenchus." In *Socratic Studies.* New York: Cambridge University Press, 1993.

———. *Socratic Studies.* New York: Cambridge University Press, 1993.

Voegelin, Eric. *Plato.* Baton Rouge: Louisiana State University Press, 1966 [1957].

Warner, Michael, ed. *Fear of a Queer Planet: Queer Politics and Social Theory.* Minneapolis: University of Minnesota Press, 1993.

Weber, Samuel. *Institution and Interpretation.* Minneapolis: University of Minnesota Press, 1987.

Wender, D., trans. *Hesiod and Theognis.* Harmondsworth, U.K.: Penguin, 1973.

Wiener, Philip P., ed. *Charles S. Peirce: Selected Writings.* New York: Dover, 1958.

Willard, Charles A. *A Theory of Argumentation.* Tuscaloosa: University of Alabama Press, 1989.

Williams, Bernard. *Ethics and the Limits of Philosophy.* Cambridge, Mass.: Harvard University Press, 1985.

———. *Shame and Necessity.* Berkeley: University of California Press, 1993.

———. *Truth and Truthfulness: An Essay in Genealogy.* Princeton, N.J.: Princeton University Press, 2002.

Williams, Michael. *Unnatural Doubts: Epistemological Realism and the Basis of Scepticism.* Princeton, N.J.: Princeton University Press, 1996.

Williams, Thomas, ed. *The Cambridge Companion to Duns Scotus.* New York: Cambridge University Press, 2003.

Williamson, Robert B. "*Eidos* and *Agathon* in Plato's *Republic.*" In *Four Essays on Plato's Republic.* Double issue of *St. John's Review* 39.1–2 (1989–1990). Annapolis, Md.: St. John's College, 1990.

Wilson, Bryan R., ed. *Rationality.* Oxford: Basil Blackwell, 1970.

Winch, Peter. *The Idea of a Social Science and Its Relation to Philosophy.* London: Routledge & Kegan Paul, 1958.

———. *Trying to Make Sense.* New York: Basil Blackwell, 1987.

————. "Understanding a Primitive Society." *American Philosophical Quarterly* 1.4 (1964):307–324.

Wittgenstein, Ludwig. *The Blue and Brown Books.* New York: Harper & Row, 1960.

————. *Culture and Value.* Translated by Peter Winch, edited by G. H. von Wright and Heikki Nyman. Chicago: University of Chicago Press, 1980.

————. *On Certainty.* Translated by Denis Paul and G. E. M. Anscombe, edited by G. E. M. Anscombe and G. H. von Wright. New York: Harper & Row, 1969.

————. *Philosophical Investigations.* Translated by G. E. M. Anscombe. Malden, Mass.: Blackwell, 1958.

————. *Remarks on the Philosophy of Psychology.* 2 vols. Translated by G. E. M. Anscombe, edited by G. E. M. Anscombe and G. H. von Wright. Chicago: University of Chicago Press, 1980.

————. *Tractatus Logico-Philosophicus.* Translated by D. F. Pears and B. F. McGuinness. London: Routledge & Kegan Paul, 1961.

Wollheim, Richard, and James Hopkins, eds. *Philosophical Essays on Freud.* New York: Cambridge University Press, 1982.

Index

Abelard, Peter, 290*n*13
absolute(s), 255*n*8, 257*n*8, 261*n*14; versus relativism, 32, 55, 228, 230; truths, 188, 201, 239
Adeimantus, 181, 183, 185
Adkins, Michael, 328*n*38
advantage of stronger, justice as, 180
afterlife, *Republic* on, 198–99
Agamemnon, 46–47, 271*n*27
Alcibiades, 131
alienation, 139
Altieri, Charles, 286*n*29, 315*n*9, 329*n*58
Anaxagoras, 107, 112
Ankersmit, F. R., 327*n*48
Apel, Karl-Otto, 304*n*62
Apology, 73–74, 91, 152–53, 209
aporia: Delphic oracle and, 153; and Idea of the Good, 125; and letting-be, 129; and orientation toward truth, 76–77; *Republic* and, 194; *Sophist* and, 130. *See also* fundamental indecision
appearance, and reality, 14, 179; justice and, 196
appreciation, 242–43
approach in thinking: in *Phaedo,* 106–12; sometimes always logic and, 99; term, 41
a priori truth, 90, 93
Aristodemus, 49
Aristophanes, 130
Aristotle: on being, 250*n*17; on causes, 289*n*6; on dialectic, 64, 281*n*22; on essence, 264*n*7; on firsts, 288*n*4; Gadamer on, 329*n*2; on matter, 294*n*22,

309*n*19; on noncontradiction, 264*n*5; and Plato, 236–40; on potentiality, 264*n*4; on rhetoric, 274*n*4; on theory of Ideas, 7–8, 16–17, 39, 250*n*16; on universals, 83, 291*n*16
artificiality: and nature, 26–36; particulars and, 86–87; and reality, 82–86; of rigorous thought, 79–82; and theory of Ideas, 87–89
Ashbaugh, Anne Freire, 253*n*1, 304*n*61
Athens, versus just city-state, 185
Austen, Jane: *Emma,* 12, 244; *Mansfield Park,* 294*n*20, 297*n*6; *Pride and Prejudice,* 10–11, 267*n*14, 284*n*12; *Sense and Sensibility,* 51–52, 139, 252*n*30, 261*n*11, 271*n*23, 332*n*24
Austin, J. L., 271*n*29
auxiliaries, in *Republic,* 182

Badiou, Alain, 259*n*9
balancing views, 31–32, 66–67, 73
Ballard, Edward G., 197, 329*n*59
Barris, Kenneth, 328*n*53
beauty, *Charmides* on, 149
becoming, 29
being, 8; Aristotle on, 250*n*17; as doing, 58; of knower, 59–65; nature and artificiality and, 26–36; simple, 127–31. *See also* essence
Benardete, Seth, 312*n*43
Benson, Hugh, 37, 107
Blanchot, Maurice, 259*n*9
Blondell, Ruby, 253*n*39, 277*n*16
bodily life, 299*n*25, 301*n*29; and Ideas, 124; in *Phaedo,* 101–2

349